MW01554047

HOW TO PLAY

CHORDAL BEBOP LINES

FOR GUITAR

"A guide for developing a linear chordal vocabulary for improvisation. Written with the styles of Wes Montgomery, Cal Collins, and Barney Kessel in mind!"

VOLUME 1

JIM BASTIAN

LAYOUT BY JOHN ALEXANDER

COASTAL PUBLISHING

How To Play

CHORDAL BEBOP LINES

For Guitar
VOLUME I

Jim Bastian

Layout by John Alexander

 SpeakPeace Press

Educational Resources Division

All rights reserved. No part of this book may be reproduced or copied in any manner whatsoever without written permission.

Copyright 2017 by
SpeakPeace Press and Jim Bastian
Original Copyright Registration 2005; Library of Congress,
U.S. Copyright Office, Washington, D.C.

Printed in the United States of America

Table of Contents

Introduction   3

Part I - *Chord Forms and Chord Scales*

- **Glossary of Common Chord Voicings**   5
  Exercises in Chromatic and Scalar Movement
- Inversions of Gmaj7   8
- Inversions of G7   10
- Inversions of Gmi7   11
- Inversions of Gmi7b5   12
- Inversions of Gdim7   13
- Inversions of G7b5   14
- Introduction on Chord Scales   15
- Major Chord Scales   16
- Harmonic Minor, Natural Minor, and Dorian Chord Scales   20
- Mixolydian and Blues Chord Scales   21
- Quartal Harmony *Chord Scales in Fourths*   22

Part II: *Chordal Phrases*

- Introduction on the Patterns   24
- Patterns around the Dominant 7   26
- Patterns around the Minor   43
- Patterns around the Major   59
- Conclusion *Suggested Practicing*   80

In the last 50 years of jazz history there have been a number of guitar players that have shown an interest in harmonizing improvised melodic lines (playing long lines of chords which have an improvised melody as the highest sounding voice). Barney Kessel, Cal Collins, Django Reinhardt, and Wes Montgomery are a few of the more famous guitarists who masterfully use this device. Among these it was Wes Montgomery who really brought the technique into the spotlight, improvising chorus after chorus entirely of chordal passages…..with not one single-note line mixed in. Wes significantly advanced this craft, showing us that it is possible to play bebop lines, shout chorus lines, melodic phrases, and blues licks, all harmonized in three to five voices in a pianistic style.

Throughout much of jazz history the piano has lead the way in the evolution of harmony. More recently a large number of method books for guitarists have emerged, many of which deal with the topic of chords and harmony. However, I have found that many of these book deal with chord forms, comping, and chord-melody playing, but do not provide a vocabulary for the kind of harmonized soloing that Wes and others employed. In <u>How To Play Chordal Bebop Lines</u> it is my hope that guitar students who are seeking a more pianistic approach in improvisation – and hence realize the full capabilities of our instrument – will find a path for the development of a chordal vocabulary that can be used in improvisation, much in the style that Wes employed.

Improvising using lines of chords is an advanced craft. This book is intended for the jazz guitarist who is familiar with music theory, has developed at least a basic vocabulary in bebop and jazz improvisation, has studied some ear training, and is now beginning to explore the technique of playing lines of chords. Specifically, this book is a collection of patterns that demonstrate how lines of chords can be created and used to express improvised melodies. The patterns are arranged by tonal centers of the dominant 7th, the minor, and the major. A section is included in the front which illustrates (1) frequently used voicings; (2) four note chords in their inversions; and (3) different types of chord scales. These are the building blocks from which melodic lines in chords can be created. These should be practiced in all keys before proceeding to the patterns which follow.

Each pattern is notated with the melody line on the staff, a corresponding chord symbol above each note, and a fingering diagram (fret box) below the note. If the chord is played as shown, the highest voice sounds as the written note.

Therefore, for ease of reading and playing:

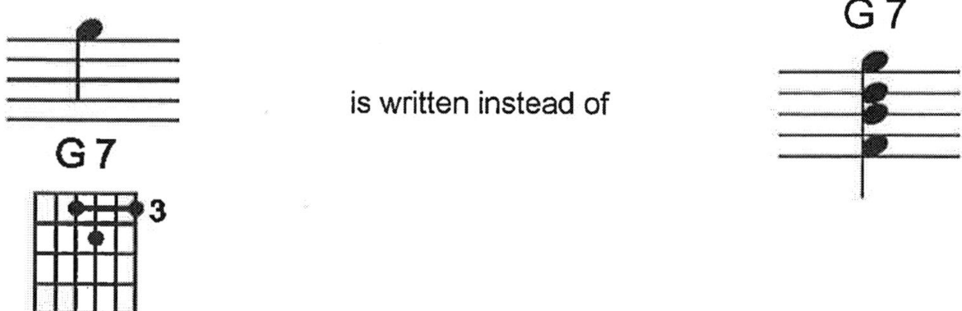

This manner of writing also allows students who do not read well to navigate this book and play the patterns.

Fret numbers are written to the right of the fretboard box throughout this book.

Once mastered, it is possible to play through the entire set of patterns in about half an hour. If done regularly, this is a great way to continually reinforce the patterns. Until that mastery is achieved, the proven way to develop the technique is one pattern at a time practiced slowly and repetitively. As other teachers have established......patience, commitment to a long-term goal, and acceptance of progress made are the helpful attributes to embrace.

The Author

Jim Bastian currently lives on the east coast where he is an active performer on both guitar and electric bass. Mr. Bastian received the Master of Arts degree in guitar performance from Indiana University of Pennsylvania in 1986, and the Master of Divinity degree from the Methodist Theological School in Ohio in 1990. In his diverse career Mr. Bastian has been a drug and alcohol counselor, a youth minister, a designer, and, most recently, a college-level jazz program director and professor. He continues to author resource materials for college-level jazz programs.

Following are sixty chord forms that are used heavily throughout this book. In each section – Dominant 7, Minor, and Major – the examples shown start with the root on top, and progress through the chromatic scale (or in scale-wise fashion) up the neck. This is not an exhaustive glossary, but is meant as an exercise to warm up the student to the idea of paying attention to the movement of the highest sounding voice (the melody note).

- The chords should be practiced in all keys.

- Regarding the chord diagram boxes: Only those strings sound which have a fingering mark. Strings with no fingering mark remain silent or are muted.

- As you practice the chords, be sure to memorize which interval sounds on top of the chord....root, ninth, third, etc.

- When you try these exercises in different keys, try "jumping" string sets, from 5432 to 4321. Start the progression on 5432 and finish it on 4321.

- Remember, this book is one system....there are many "right" ways to do things. As you develop your own sound you will find your own unique ways to organize the material you use. Jazz Guitarist and educator Mark Boling in his book Creative Comping Concepts for Jazz Guitar, suggests keeping an idea book, wherein you can write down phrases and ideas that you want to incorporate into your personal vocabulary.

Dominant 7 Voicings. Key of C. Highest voice on B string. Chromatic movement.

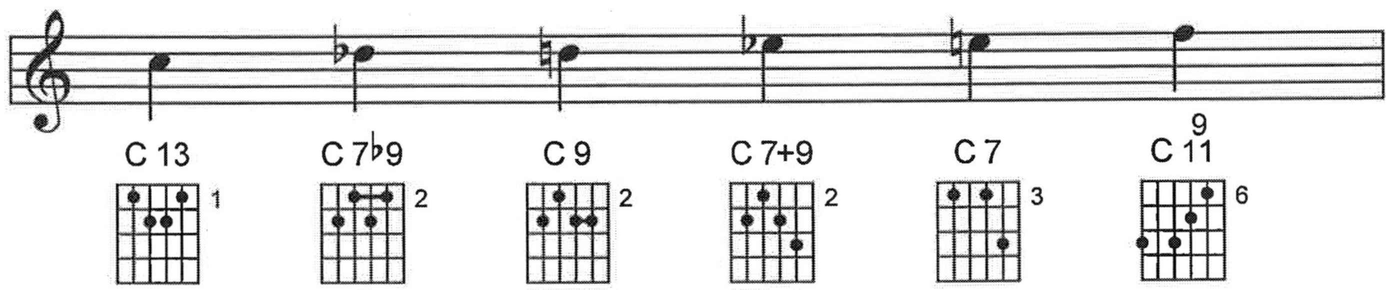
C 13   1
C 7♭9   2
C 9   2
C 7+9   2
C 7   3
C 11 9 6

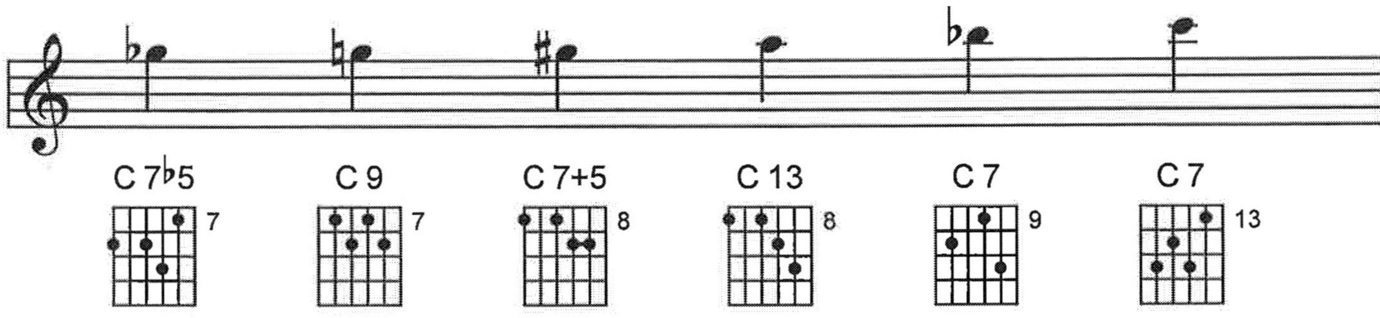
C 7♭5   7
C 9   7
C 7+5   8
C 13   8
C 7   9
C 7   13

Dominant 7 Voicings. Key of F. Highest voice on E string. Chromatic movement.

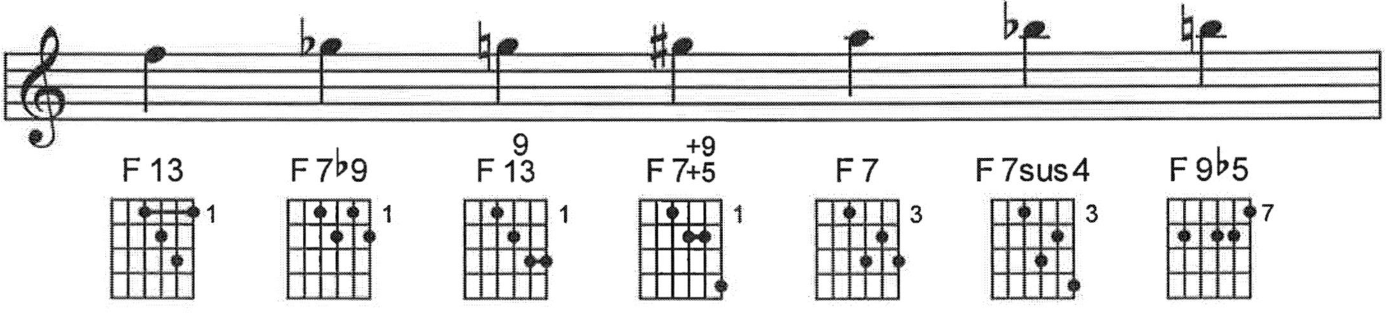
F 13   1
F 7♭9   1
F 13 9   1
F 7+5 +9   1
F 7   3
F 7sus 4   3
F 9♭5   7

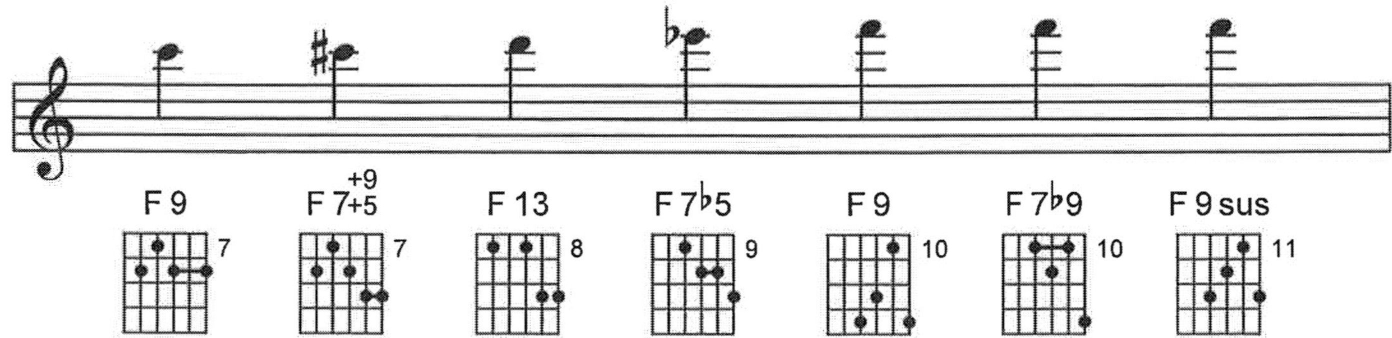
F 9   7
F 7+5 +9   7
F 13   8
F 7♭5   9
F 9   10
F 7♭9   10
F 9 sus   11

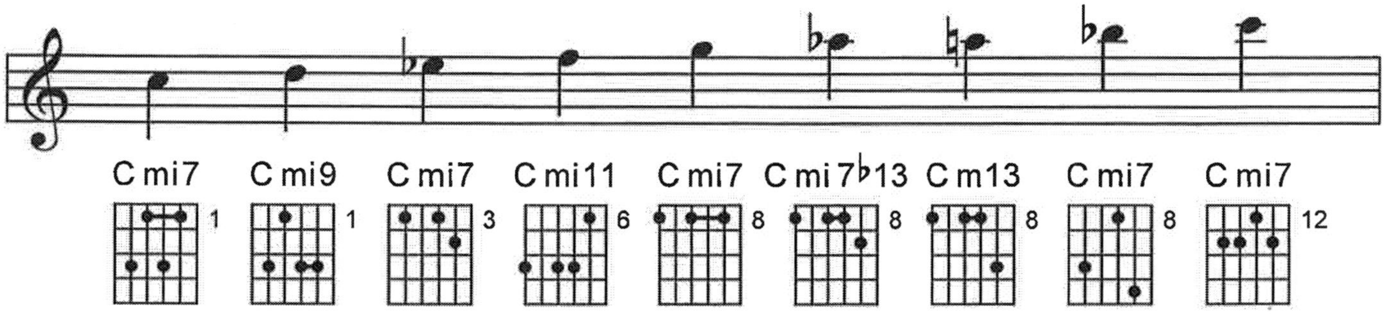

C mi7 — C mi9 — C mi7 — C mi11 — C mi7 — C mi7♭13 — C m13 — C mi7 — C mi7

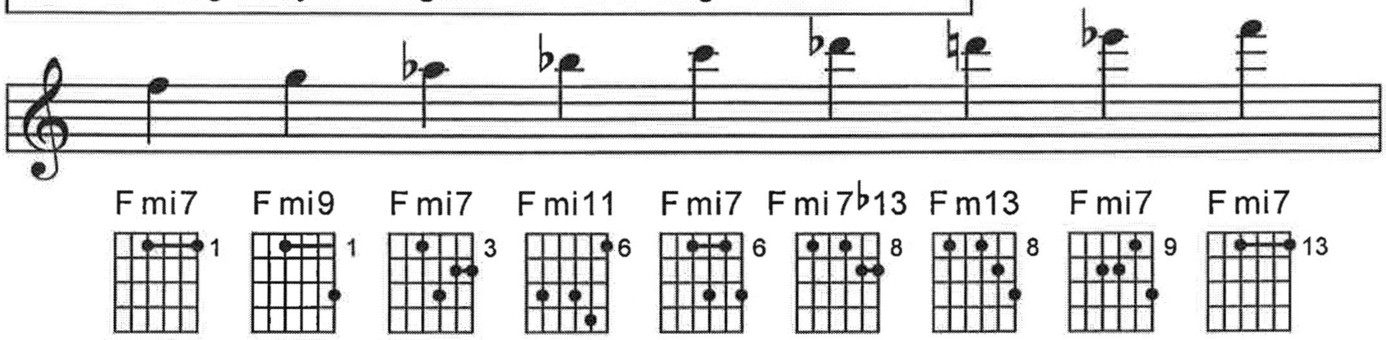

F mi7 — F mi9 — F mi7 — F mi11 — F mi7 — F mi7♭13 — F m13 — F mi7 — F mi7

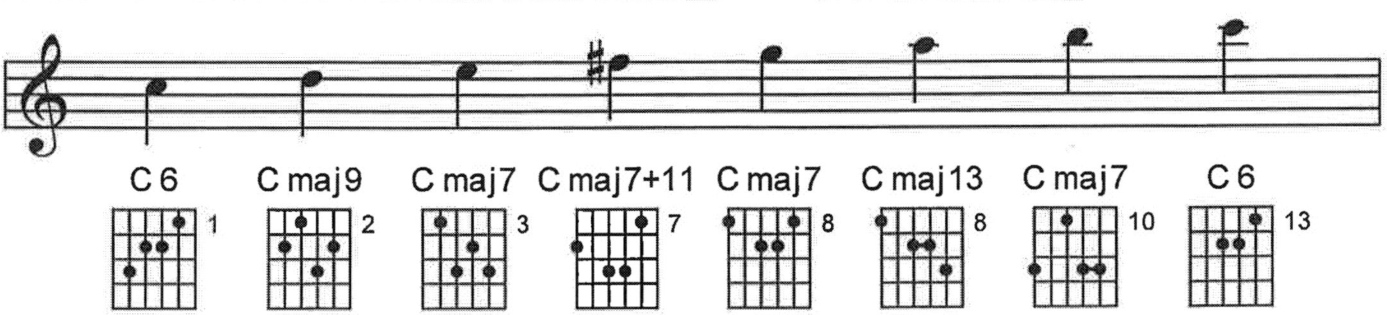

C 6 — C maj9 — C maj7 — C maj7+11 — C maj7 — C maj13 — C maj7 — C 6

F maj7 — F maj9 — F 6 — F maj7+11 — F maj9 — F maj13 — F maj9 — F 6

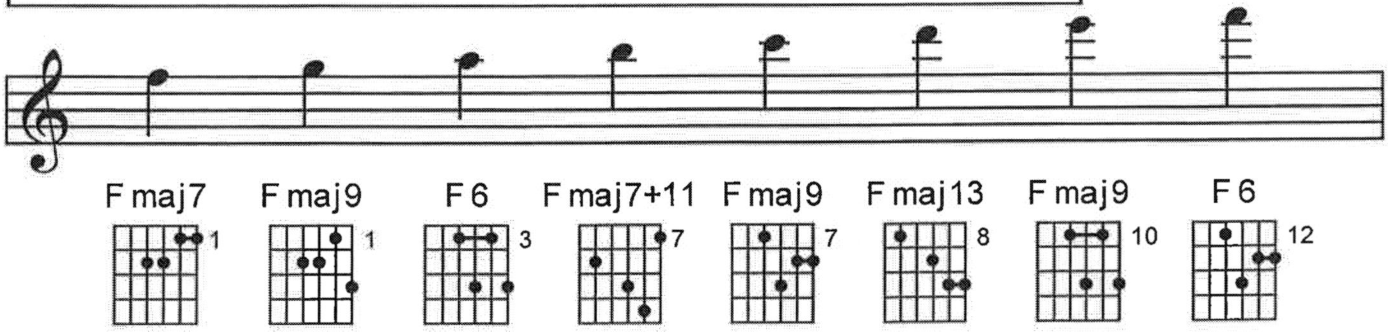

In this section there are fret diagrams which show twenty-eight positions to play a particular chord. (Some educators refer to these as "drop two voicings"). There are seven string combinations and four inversions for each. The obvious value of this for the chord work we are pursuing is that the inversions allow us to keep the root, third, fifth, or seventh on top of the chord (highest sounding melody note). ***The success of being able to play an improvised chord line lies in our being able, at will, to put any melody note we need on top of the chord.***

- *Practice the chords in all keys.*

- *Memorize which interval is on top and how it sounds.*

- *Practice the chords in various progressions, in their inversions, including:*

  - ii – V – I

  - I – vi – ii – V – I

  - iii – VI – ii – V – I

  - vii(m7♭5) – I

  - ii(m7♭5) – V – I

- *Other chord qualities (not pictured) also work well:*

  - Minor (#7) – [root, flat third, fifth, major seven]
  - Dominant 9 – [ninth, third, fifth, flat seven]
  - Dominant 7, #5 – [root, third, sharp five, flat seven]

- *Regarding the chord diagrams: Only the fingered notes sound. Strings with no fingering are silent.*

Inversions of Gmaj7

⊙ = Root

4321	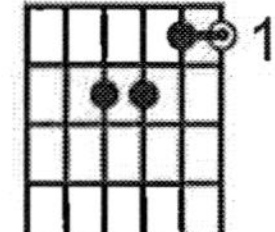 1	5	8	12
5432	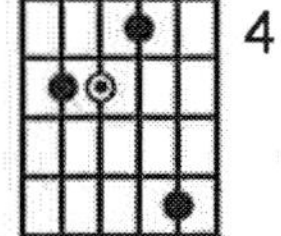 4	7	10	12
6543	3	5	9	12
5321	3	7	10	12
6432	3	5	8	12
5421	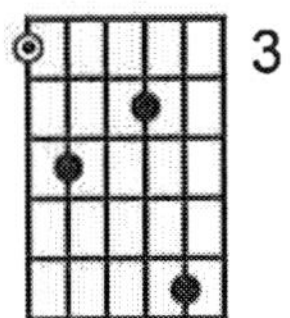 2	5	8	10
6532	3	7	10	12

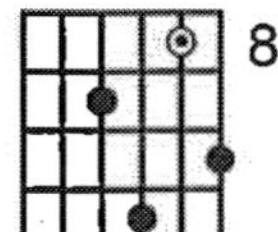
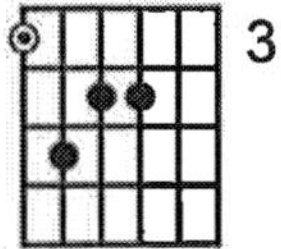
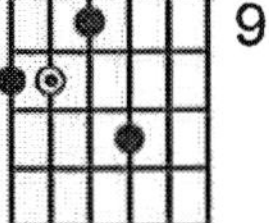
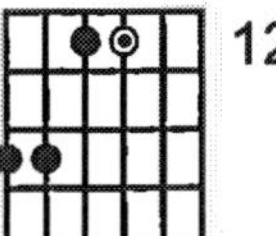
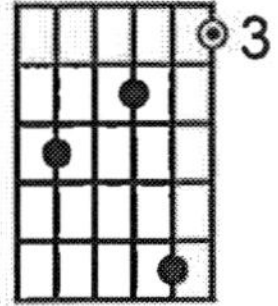
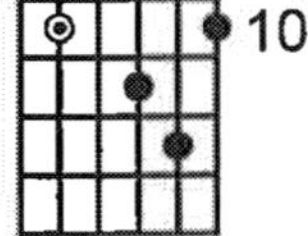
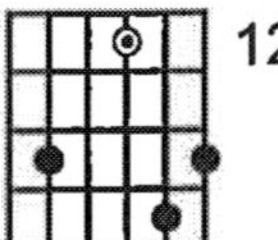
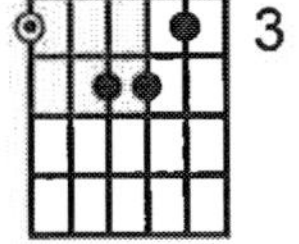
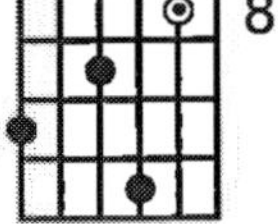
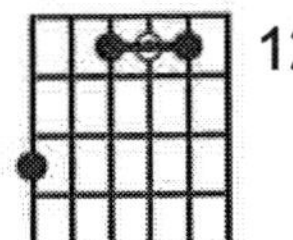
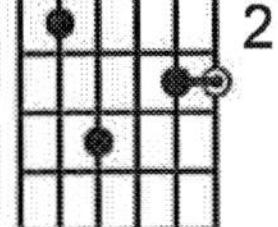
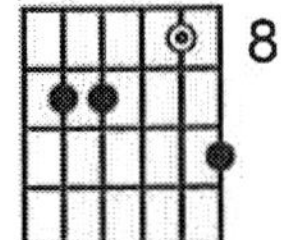
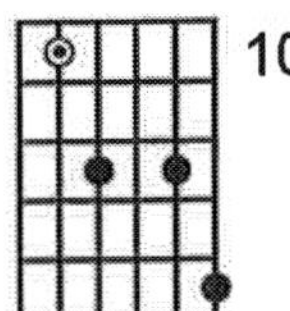
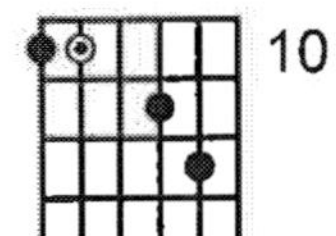

Inversions of G7

4321

5432

6543

5321

6432

5421

6532

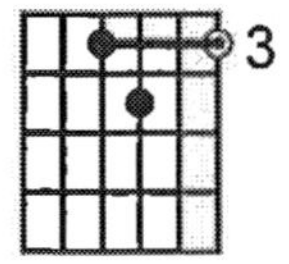

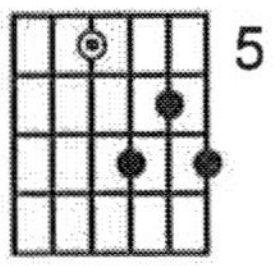

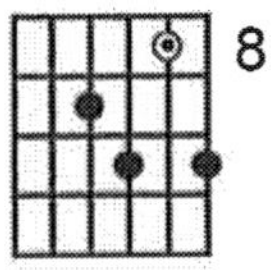

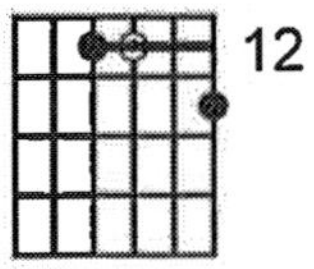

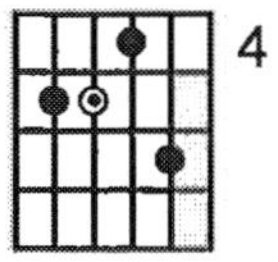

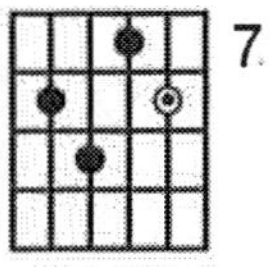

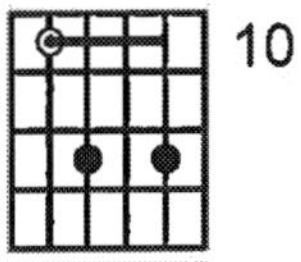

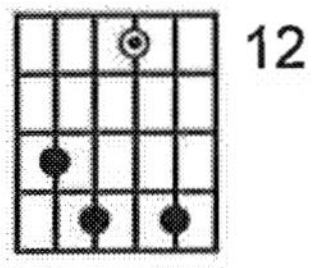

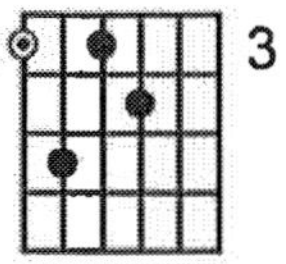

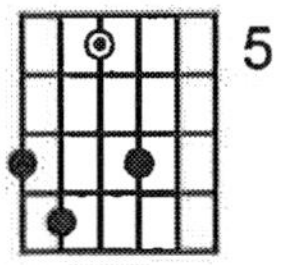

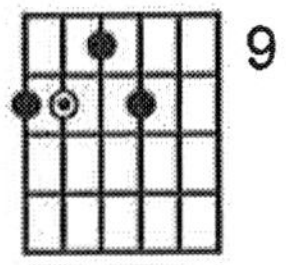

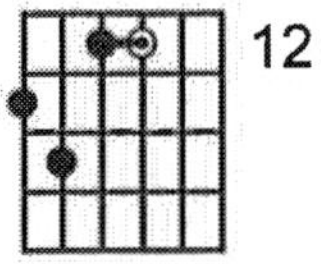

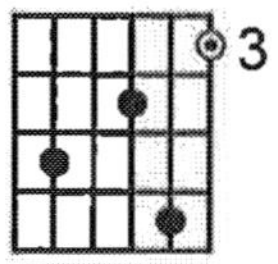

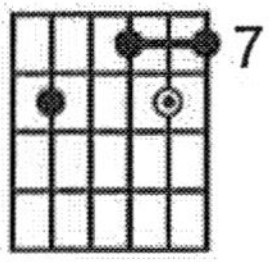

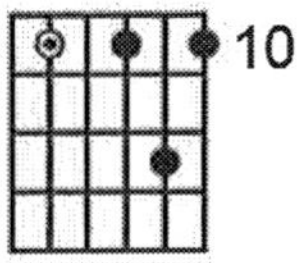

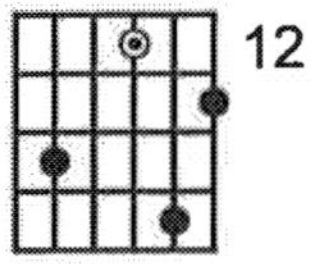

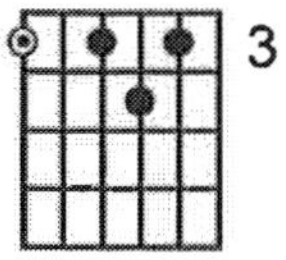

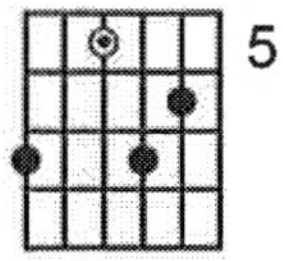

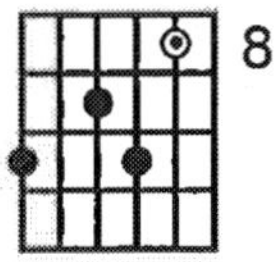

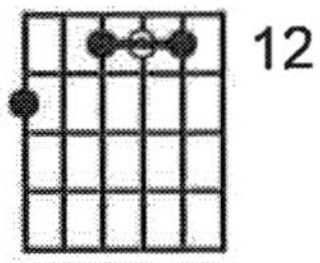

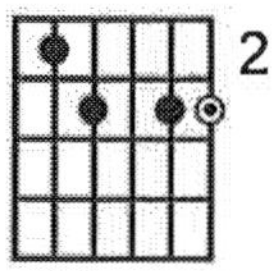

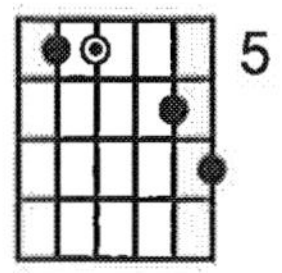

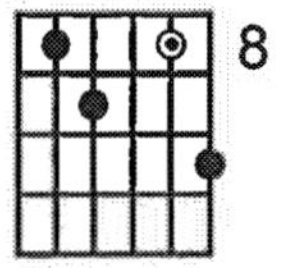

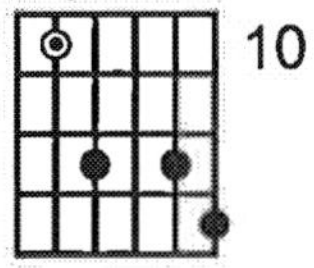

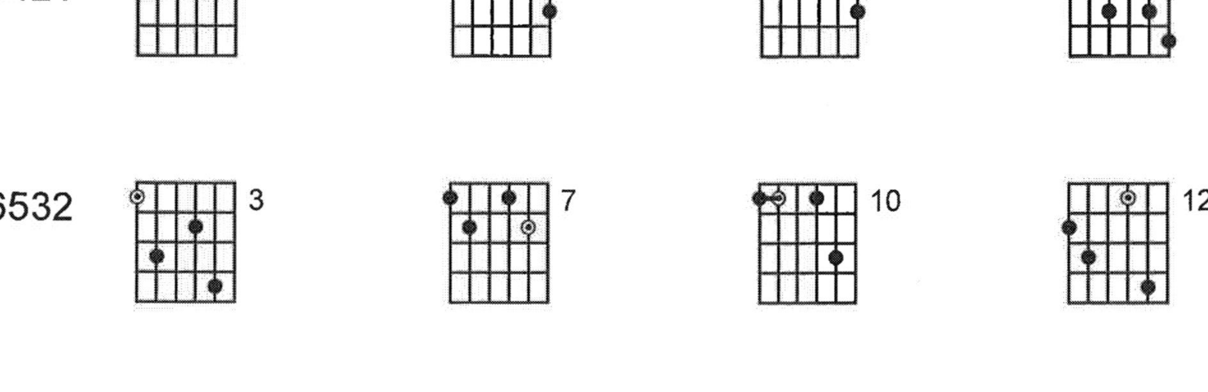

Inversions of Gmi7

4321	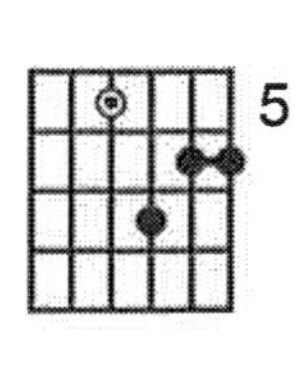 3	5	8	11
5432	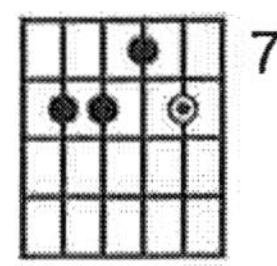 3	7	10	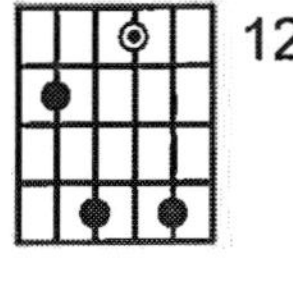 12
6543	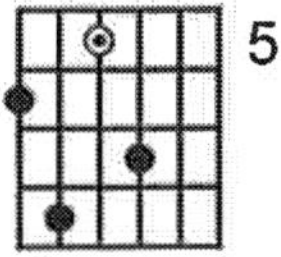 3	5	8	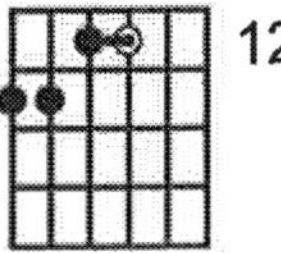 12
5321	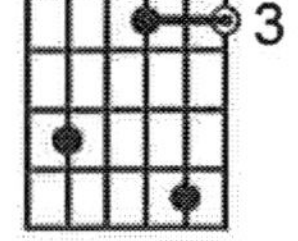 3	6	10	12
6432	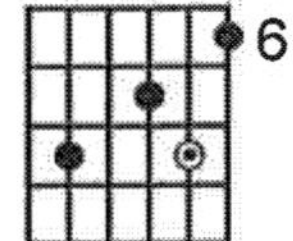 3	5	8	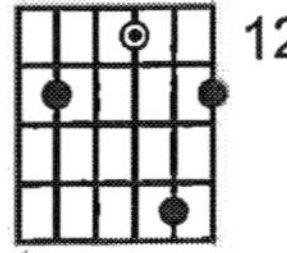 11
5421	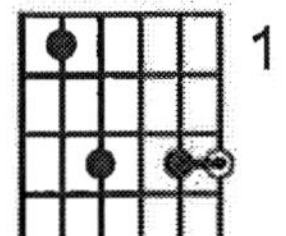 1	5	8	10
6532	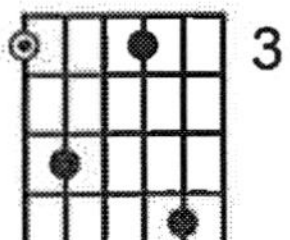 3	6	10	12

Inversions of Gmi7♭5

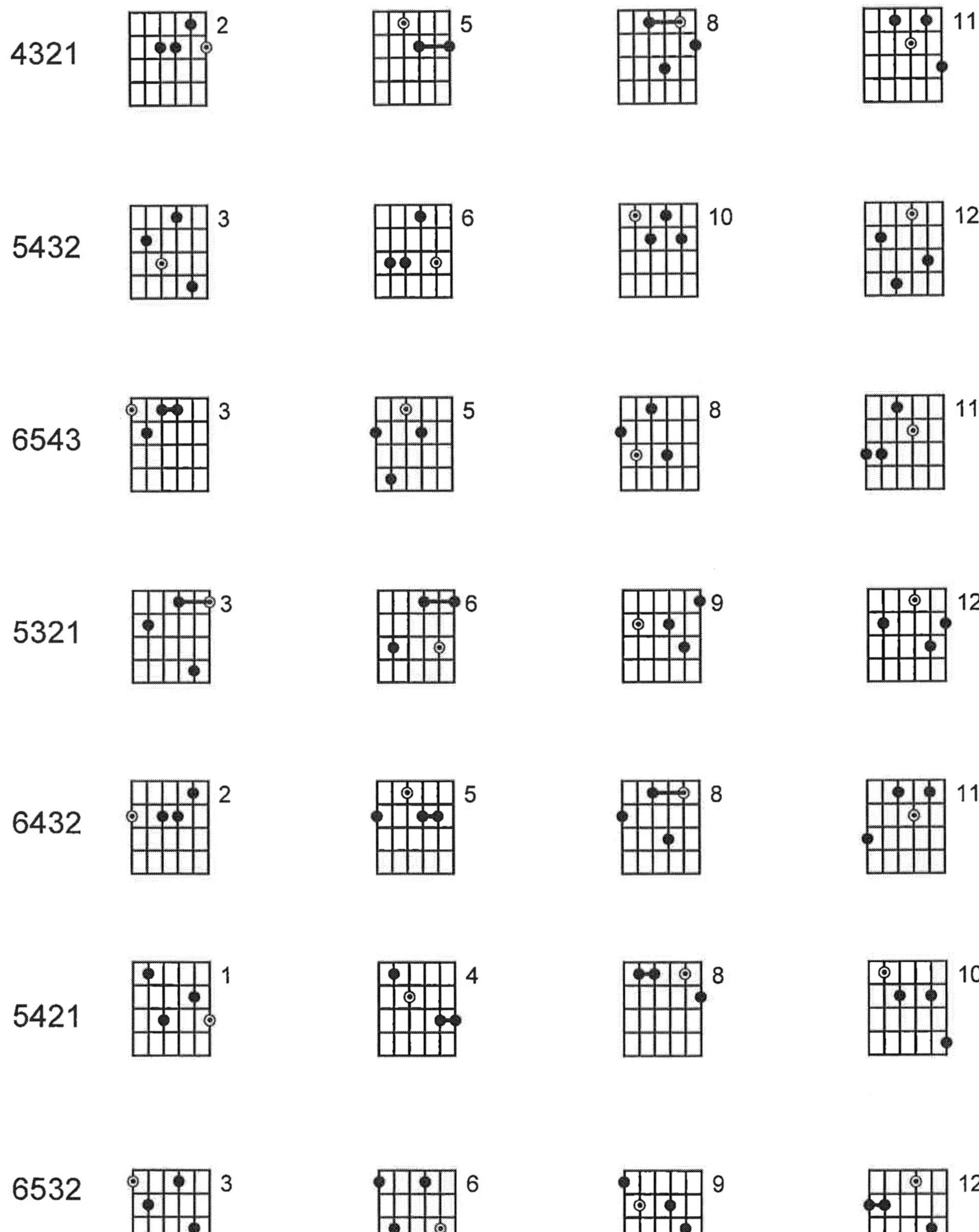

Inversions of Gdim7

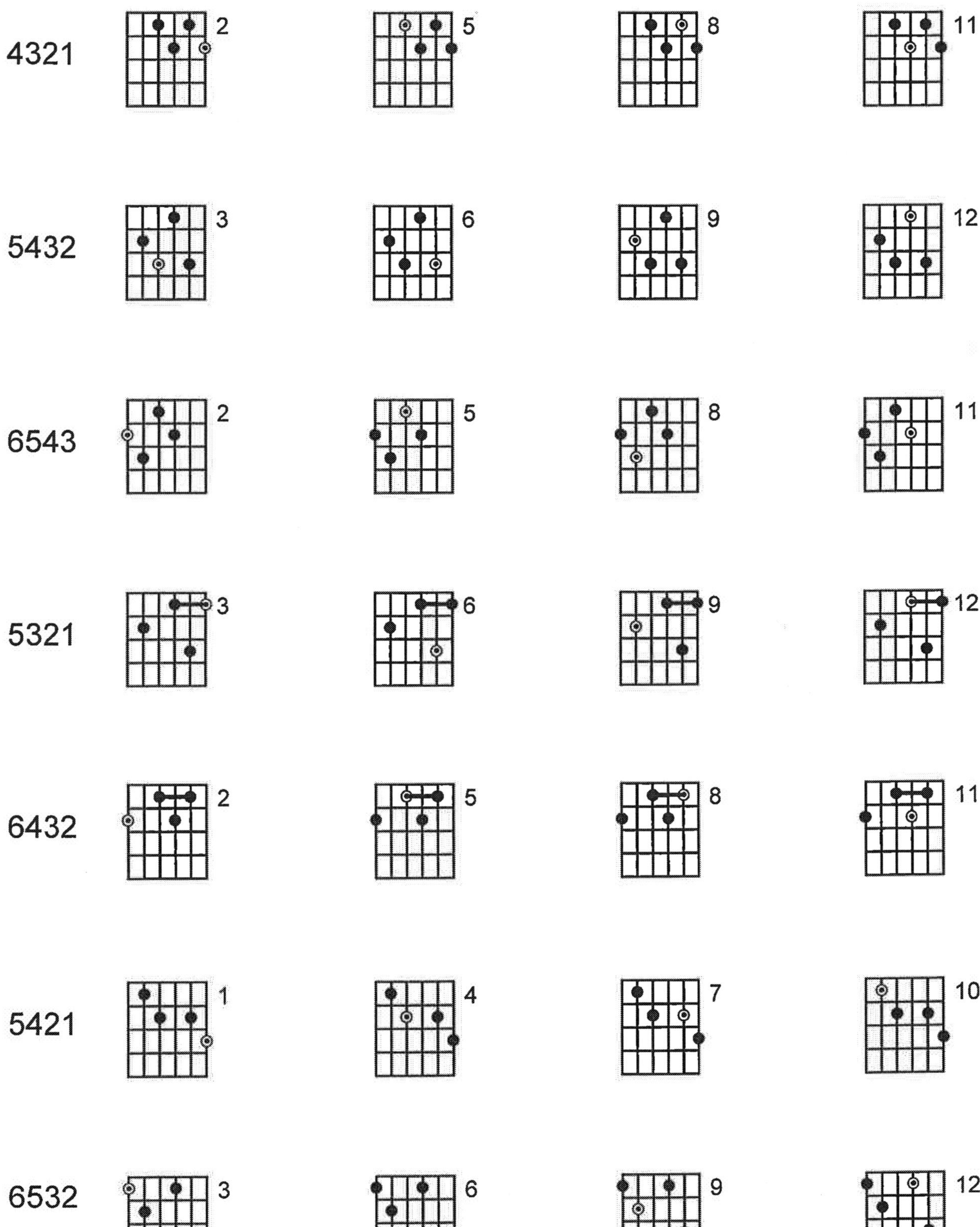

Inversions of G7♭5

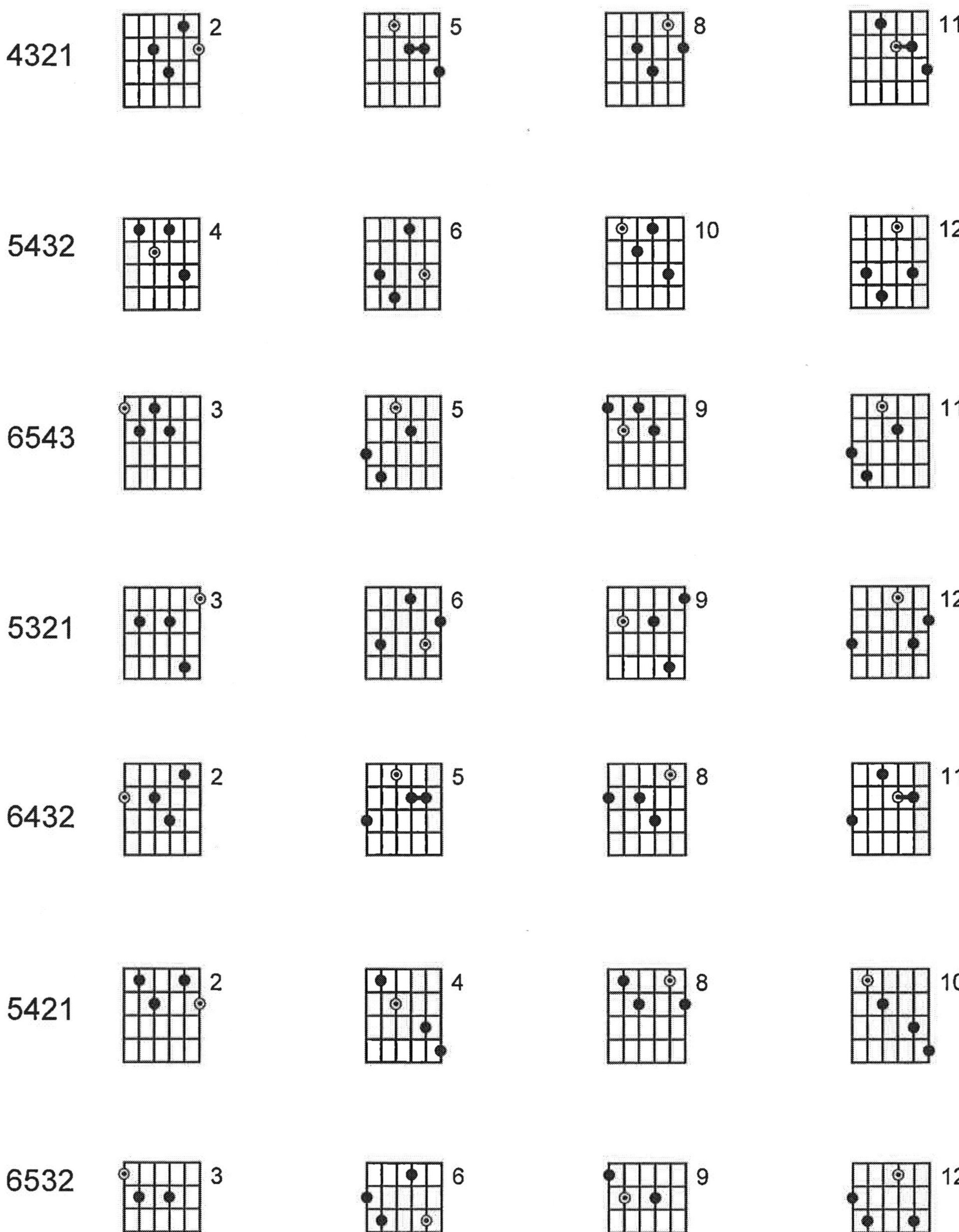

The following chord scales offer just a few of the possibilities for harmonizing major and minor scales. Using the inversions found in the previous section, there are no less than twenty-eight different inversions/string sets that you could start on when you play a particular chord scale. On the various string sets, the root can be the highest sounding voice of each chord, or the third, or the fifth, or the seventh. Some of the following examples will illustrate this.

I show only a few examples of the traditional (classical) scale harmonization; e.g., I – ii – iii – IV – V – vi – vii. Other examples employ alternating chords as a way to harmonize a scale; e.g., I – V – I – V – I – V – V, or alternating between I and ii. Among the examples are illustrations of how to "jump" string sets; e.g., starting a chord scale on string set 6-4-3-2 and completing it on string set 4-3-2-1.

As you practice, focus on the sounds presented rather than feeling the need to practice every possible combination (they are endless!). A player like Cal Collins, when improvising chords, had a well-worn path through his favorite chord licks ("stock" chordal passages). In clinics Cal had difficulty explaining what he was doing when he played his improvised cascading chordal passages. This shows that, for Cal, the theoretical took a back seat to what he could hear and feel. Nevertheless, he certainly had an established chordal vocabulary on which he relied.

A player can develop "chord licks" just as he/she can develop a stock vocabulary of single-line bebop licks (and this book is filled with them!). Don't kid yourself....all players use them. The material that we practice repeatedly is the material that will come out in our solos. One needs only to glance through the Charlie Parker solos in the Omnibook to see that Charlie Parker had a stockpile of licks that he used, sometimes to exhaustion, and often over the same measures every time they came up. All three players mentioned on the cover of this book have their pet chord licks that worked over particular underlying harmonies. For all of us as jazz players the creativity lies in our ability to take that stockpile that we develop – or that vocabulary – and alter it to meet various situations, over changing chords, and to create new improvised melodies with it.

The following chord scales offer some of the necessary pieces useful in the development of such a vocabulary.

G Major

G 6   A mi7   B mi7   A mi7   B mi7   E mi7   F#m7b5   G maj7
2   3   5   7   9   7   8   10

G Major (with Roots on Top)
G maj7   A mi7   B mi7   C maj7   D 7   E mi7   F#m7b5   G 6
3   5   7   8   10   12   13   14

G Major (with I, ii, and iii)
G 6   A mi7   B mi7   A mi7   B mi7   A mi7   B mi7   G 6
2   5   7   7   9   10   12   14
parallel   parallel   parallel

G Major (Adding Extensions to Chord)
G maj7   A mi7   A mi9   A mi7   A mi11   E mi7   E mi9   G 6
3   5   5   7   7   12   12   14

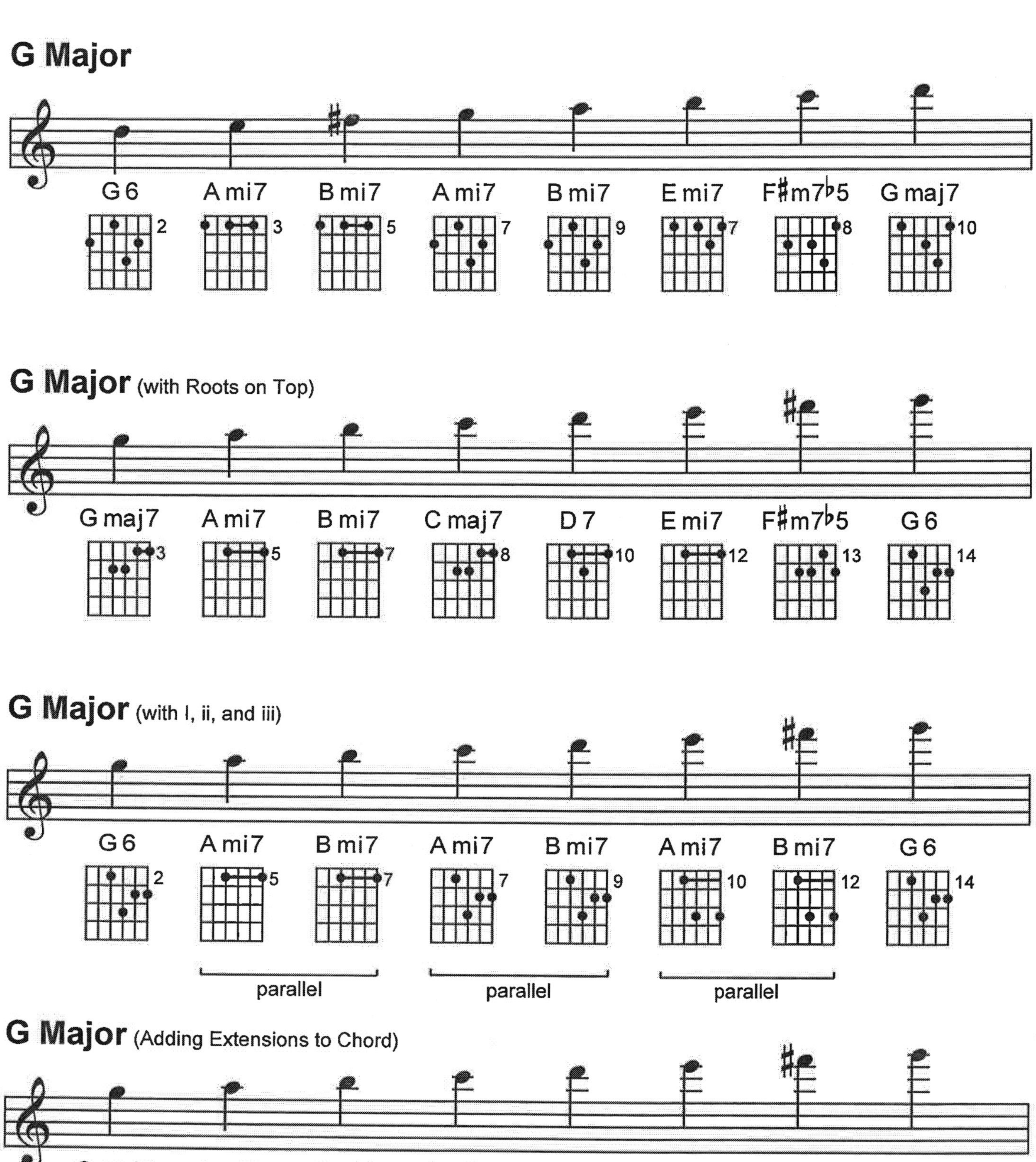

C Major (Roots on Top)

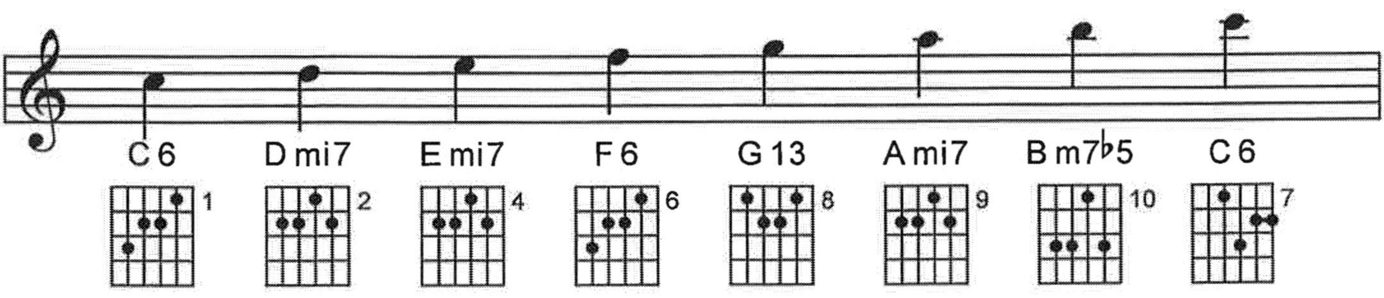

C Major (Thirds on Top)

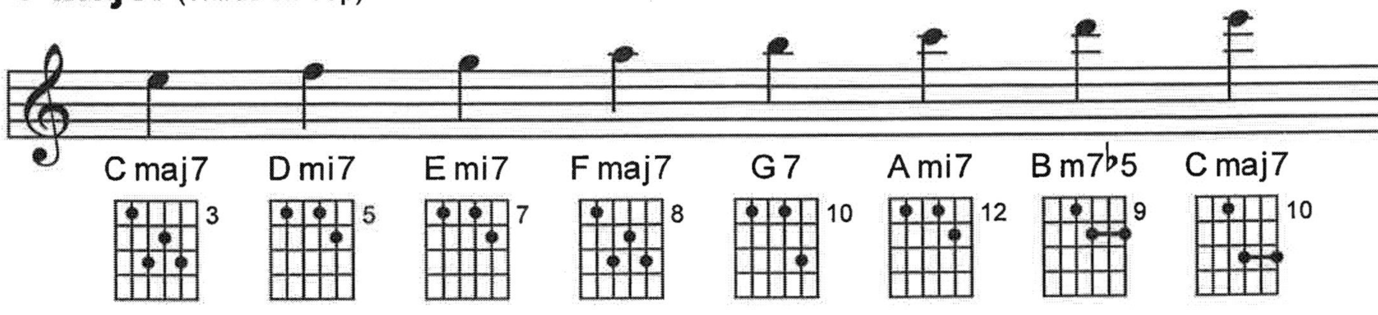

C Major (Fifths on Top)

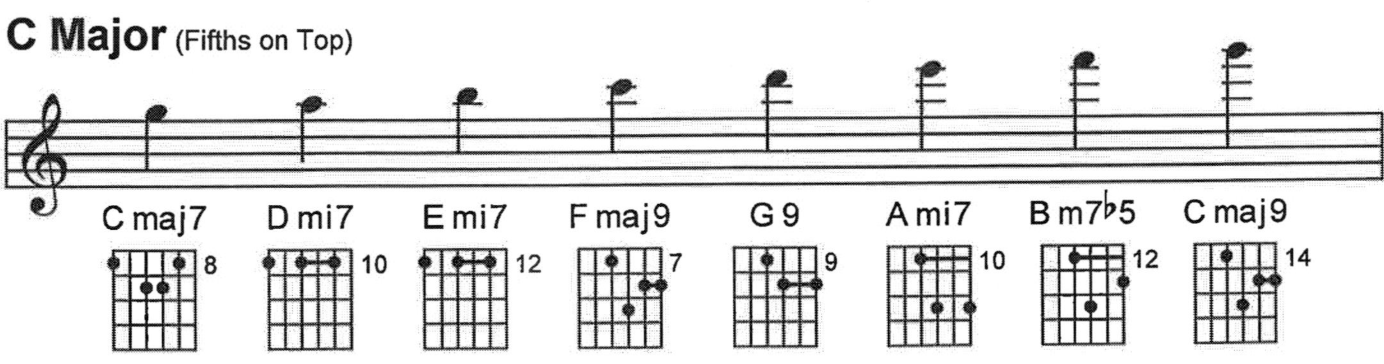

C Major (Sevenths on Top)

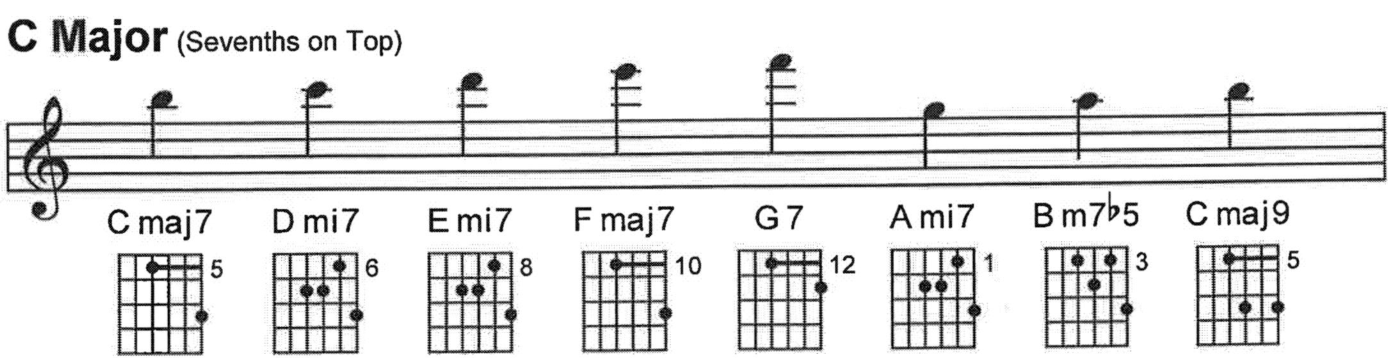

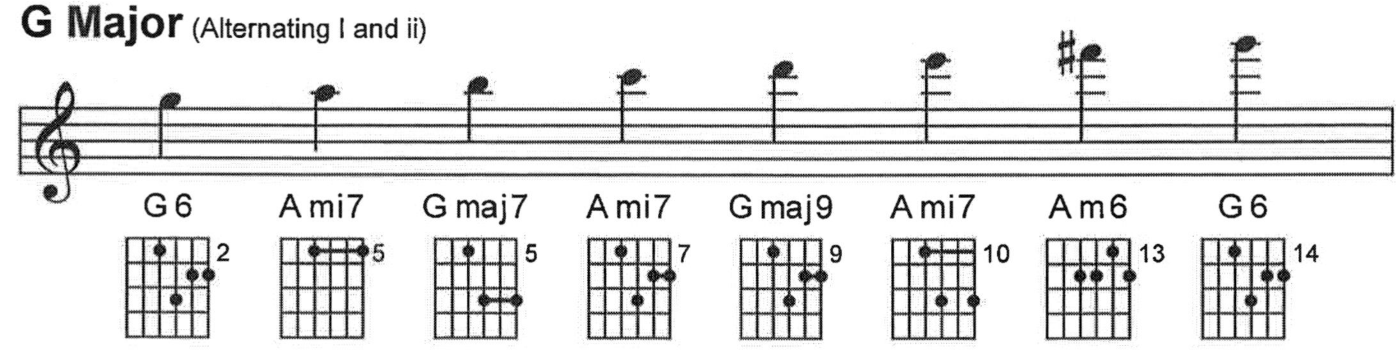

G Major (Alternating I and ii)
G 6   A mi7   G maj7   A mi7   G maj9   A mi7   A m6   G 6
2   5   5   7   9   10   13   14

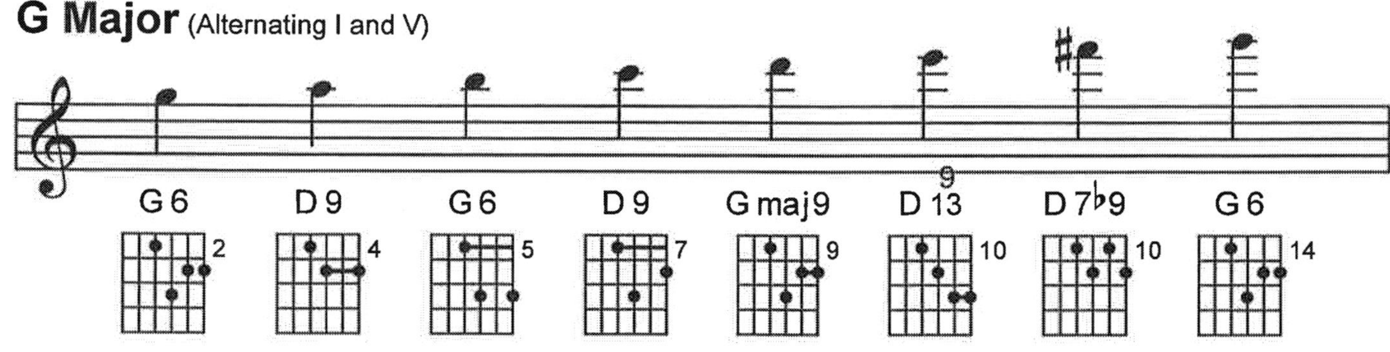

G Major (Alternating I and V)
G 6   D 9   G 6   D 9   G maj9   D 13   D 7♭9   G 6
2   4   5   7   9   10   10   14

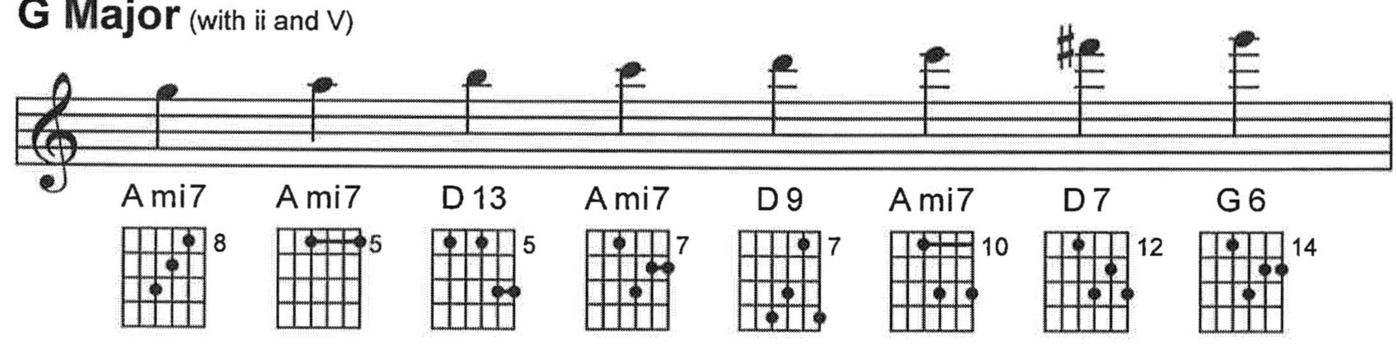

G Major (with ii and V)
A mi7   A mi7   D 13   A mi7   D 9   A mi7   D 7   G 6
8   5   5   7   7   10   12   14

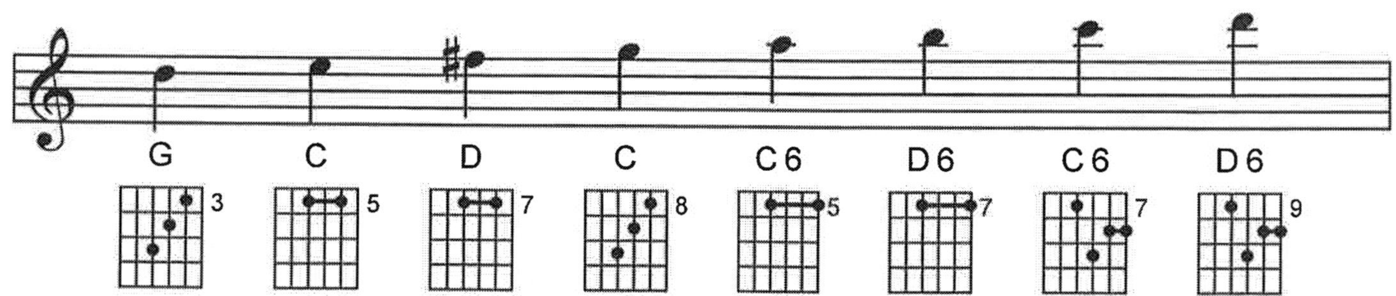

G Major (with I, IV, and V.....or I, ii, and iii!)
G   C   D   C   C 6   D 6   C 6   D 6
3   5   7   8   5   7   7   9

F Major (Three Note Voicings with I, IV, and V)

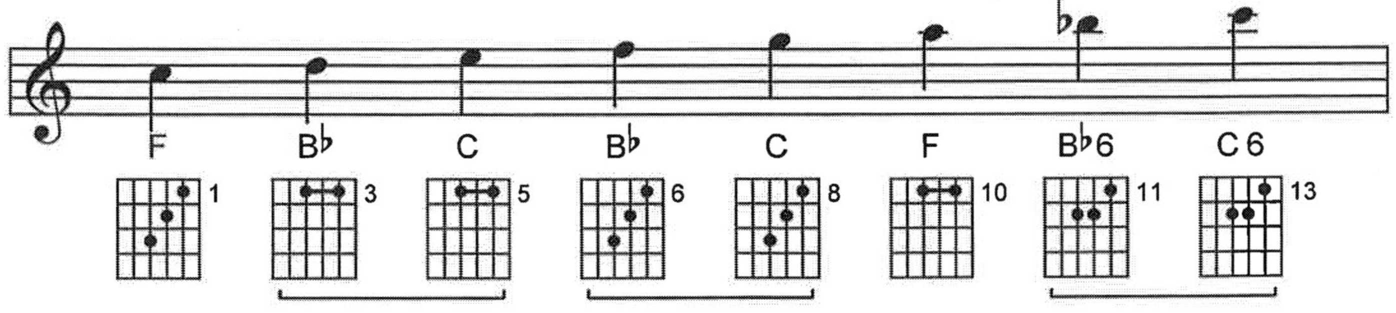

To add chromaticism, play the same form in between

F Major (Thirds on Top)

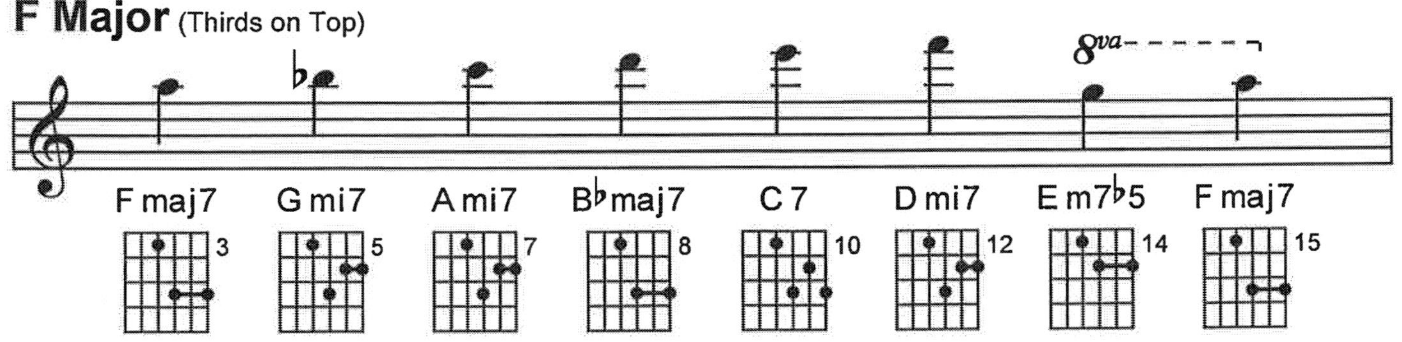

F Major (Alternating I and V)

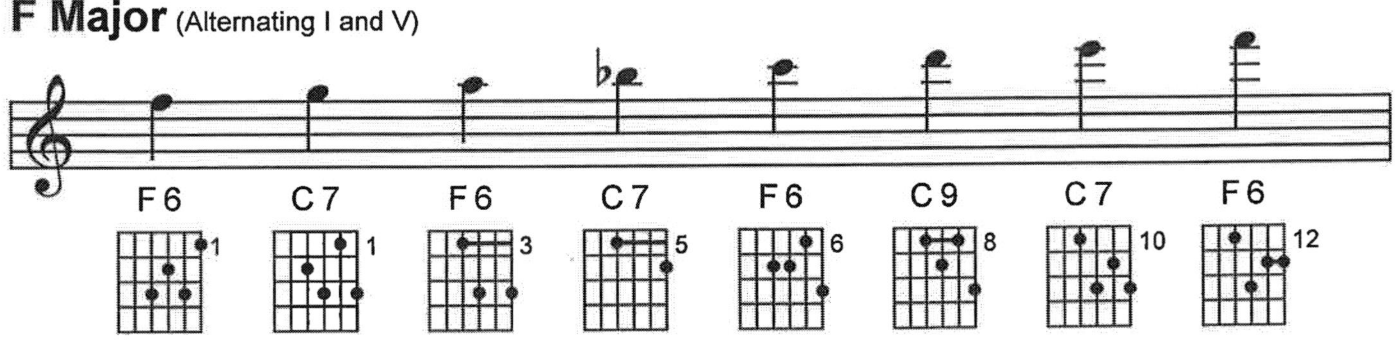

F Major (With Three Note Voicings)

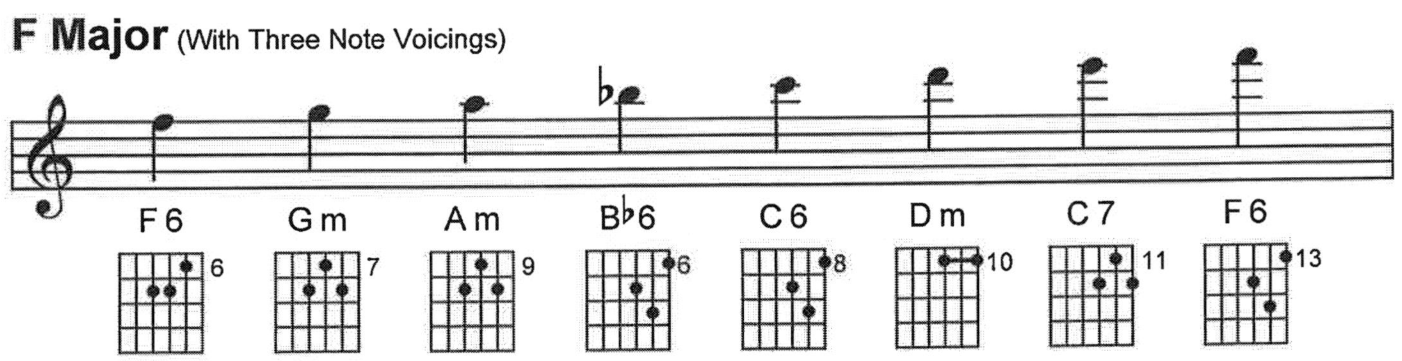

G Harmonic Minor (Alternating Gmi7 and D7)

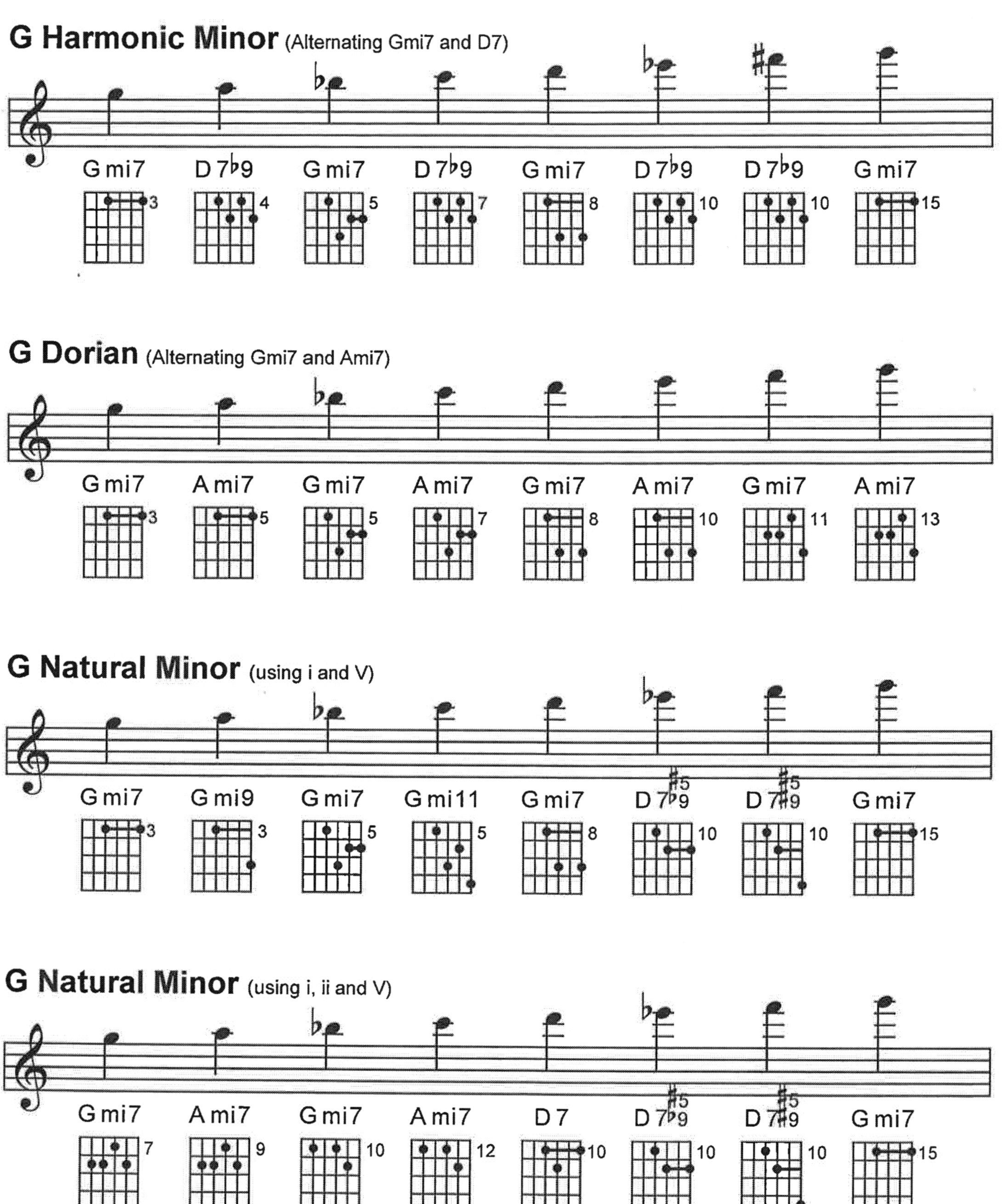

G Dorian (Alternating Gmi7 and Ami7)

G Natural Minor (using i and V)

G Natural Minor (using i, ii and V)

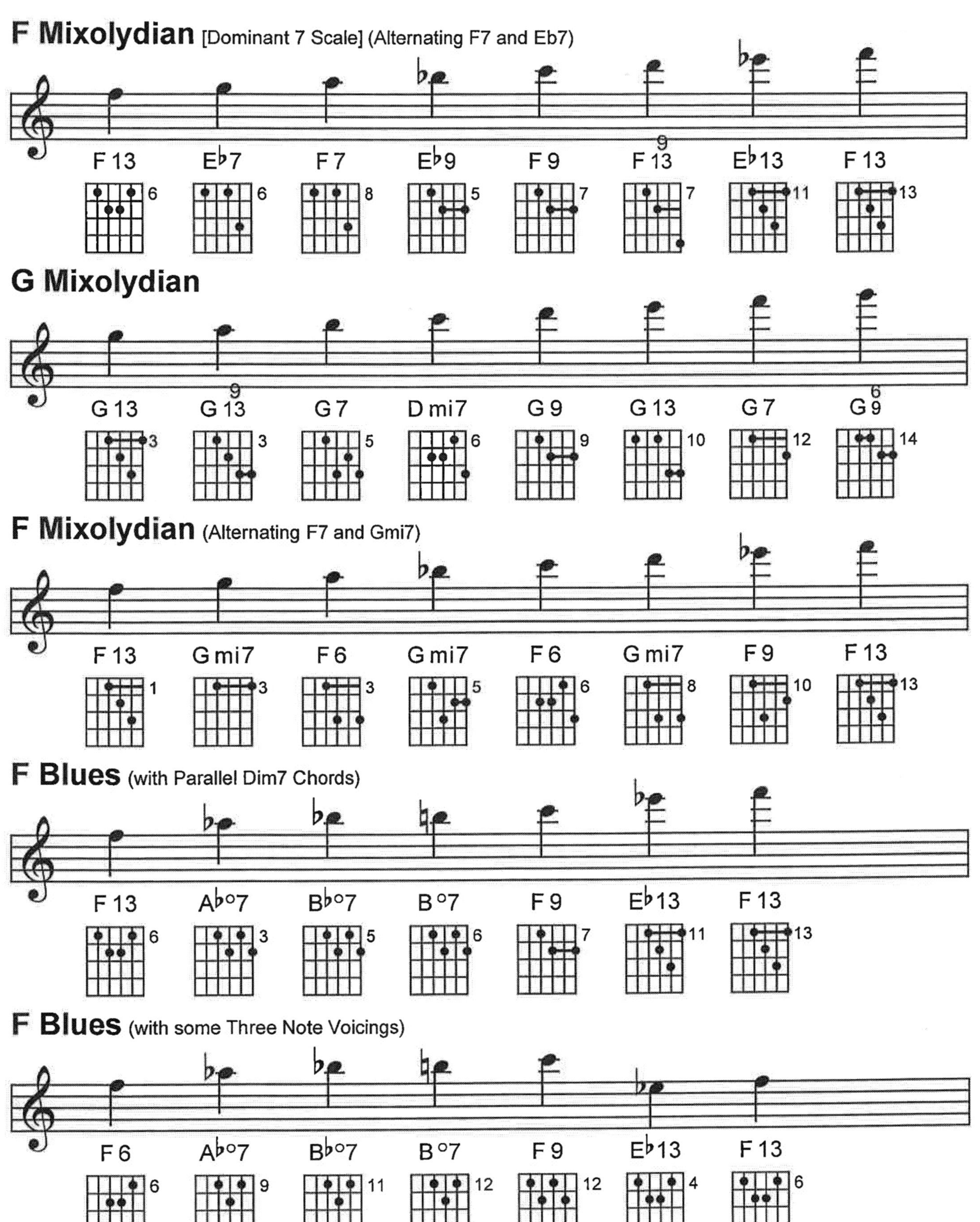

F Mixolydian [Dominant 7 Scale] (Alternating F7 and Eb7)
F13 Eb7 F7 Eb9 F9 F13 Eb13 F13

G Mixolydian
G13 G13 G7 Dmi7 G9 G13 G7 G9

F Mixolydian (Alternating F7 and Gmi7)
F13 Gmi7 F6 Gmi7 F6 Gmi7 F9 F13

F Blues (with Parallel Dim7 Chords)
F13 Ab°7 Bb°7 B°7 F9 Eb13 F13

F Blues (with some Three Note Voicings)
F6 Ab°7 Bb°7 B°7 F9 Eb13 F13

The first chord scale on the following page is the C Dorian minor scale, as harmonized in fourths (string set 5-4-3-2). The stacked fourths give a modern open sound and can offer a whole new direction for chordal improvisation. We might also think about this scale as being made up entirely of Cmi7 and F7 voicings, which allow us to see how well it fits over ii-V situations (see scale #2 below). This same quartal C Dorian scale can be used with great results over an F7 chord or over a C minor tonal center. Try using this chord scale over the first four bars of an F Blues, then switch to the F minor quartal chord scale over the Bb7 chord......some very modern and colorful possibilities emerge.

It goes without saying that this scale can be approached modally. For example, treat the C Dorian quartal chord scale as an Eb major7 (#11) chord scale; (Eb becomes tonic instead of C). In this way the chord scale has application to a major tonal center instead of minor.

The scale is also shown in F Dorian, to illustrate string set 4-3-2-1 (scale #3 below). This is followed by an illustration (scale #4) of the C Dorian scale played over 2 string sets (5-4-3-2 shifting to 4-3-2-1).

- *Practice the chord scales with a metronome, in half notes*

- *Play scales in all keys, and practice shifting string sets.*

- *Practice improvising on the blues form, using the appropriate quartal scale on each changing 7th chord.*

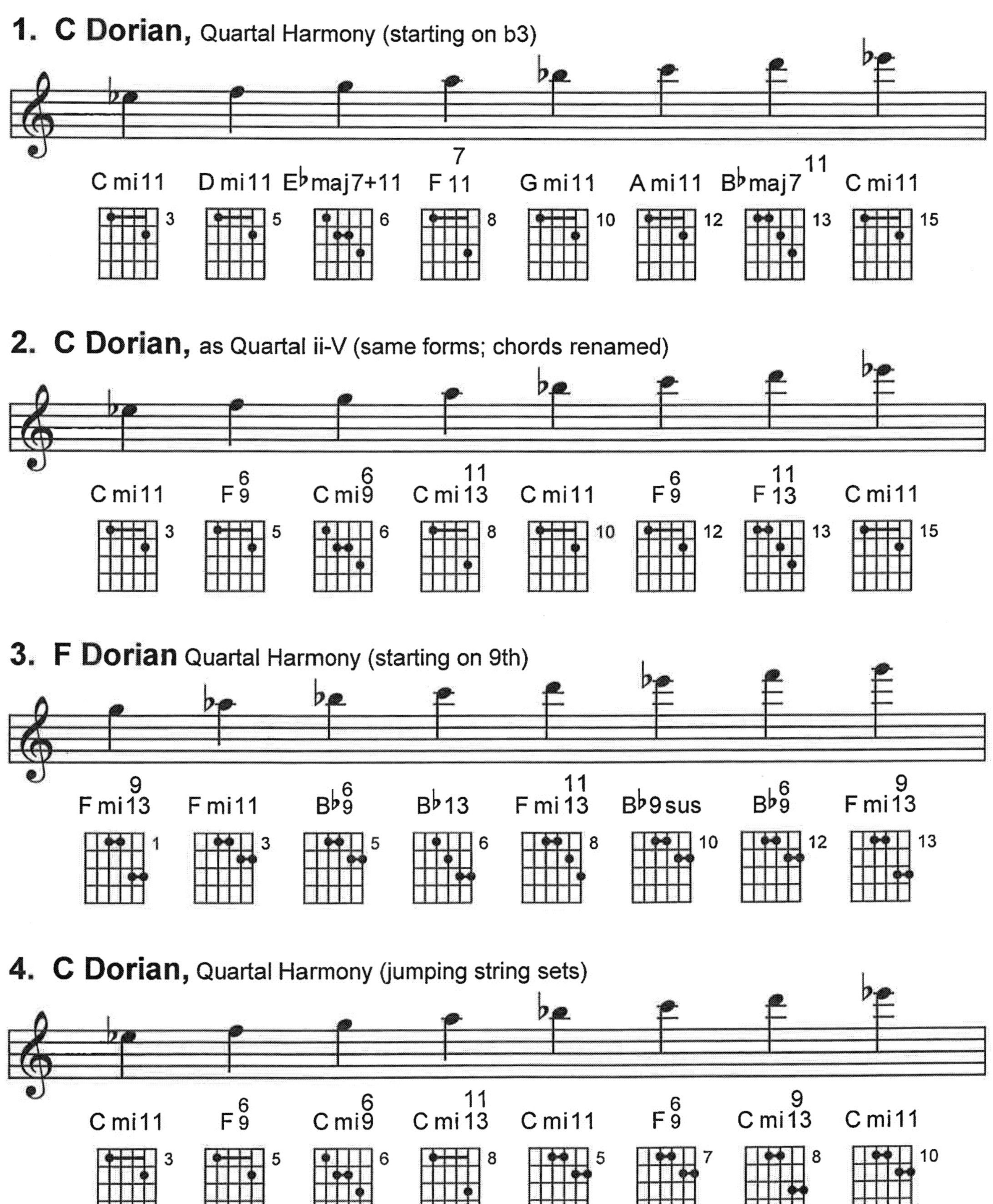

1. C Dorian, Quartal Harmony (starting on b3)
C mi11   D mi11   E♭maj7+11   F 11   G mi11   A mi11   B♭maj7 11   C mi11
3   5   6   8   10   12   13   15

2. C Dorian, as Quartal ii-V (same forms; chords renamed)
C mi11   F 9 6   C mi9 6   C mi13 11   C mi11   F 9 6   F 13 11   C mi11
3   5   6   8   10   12   13   15

3. F Dorian Quartal Harmony (starting on 9th)
F mi13 9   F mi11   B♭9 6   B♭13   F mi13 11   B♭9 sus   B♭9 6   F mi13 9
1   3   5   6   8   10   12   13

4. C Dorian, Quartal Harmony (jumping string sets)
C mi11   F 9 6   C mi9 6   C mi13 11   C mi11   F 9 6   C mi13 9   C mi11
3   5   6   8   5   7   8   10

Now we come to the most exciting part of the book. What follows are fifty-five pages of harmonized melodic patterns composed around Dominant 7, Minor, and Major tonalities. These patterns are intended to illustrate in depth the possibilities for harmonizing melodic phrases on the guitar.....without stopping to return to single lines! Wes showed us that this is possible.....that a guitarist can play an entire solo with chords – chords which support an exciting and well-composed upper melody line.

- Each phrase is numbered and ends with a double bar.

- Play the single line melody first by itself in order to hear the melody you are harmonizing.

- Many of the phrases are short melodic fragments which can be linked together.

- In some of the phrases a sense of time is absent. Such phrases can be used rhythmically as the player chooses.

- Each phrase suggests a broad tonal area, but the phrases may actually fit several tonal areas. For example, many of the Gmi7 phrases would fit over a C7 tonal center.

- Once internalized, the patterns can be modified, linked and used as the improviser chooses.

- Practice the phrases slowly and repetitively.

- Pay special attention to how chromaticism can be accomplished in moving chords; for example (1) by using the same chord up (or down) a half step [parallel forms]; (2) by using the diminished chord as a passing chord to connect things chromatically; (3) by actually changing chords on every chromatic melody note. Following are three harmonizations of one melodic fragment using these three techniques:

1. Parallel Forms

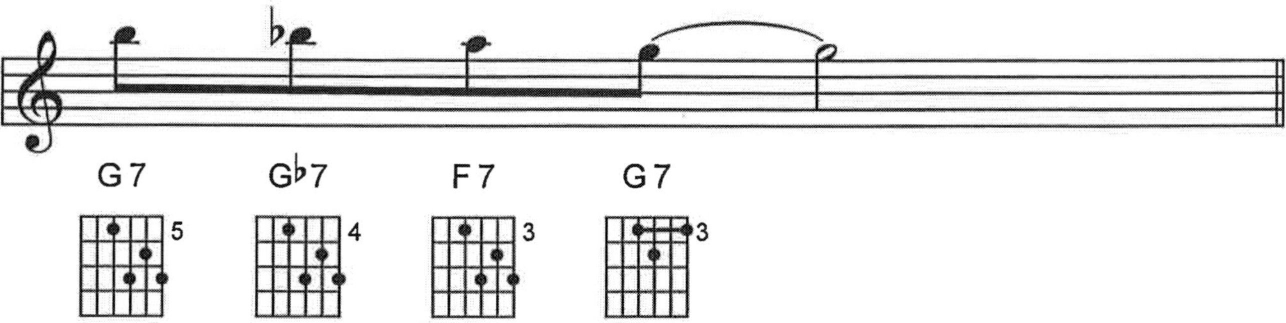

2. Using the Diminished Chord

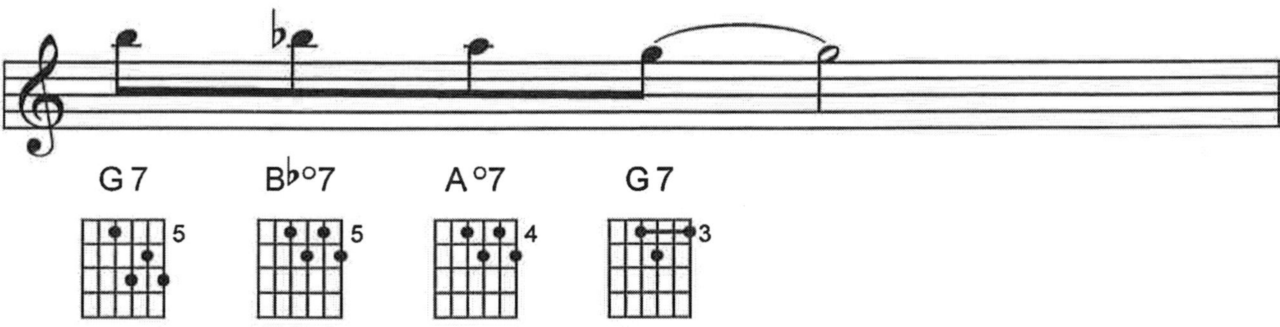

3. Changing Chords on Every Chromatic Melody Note

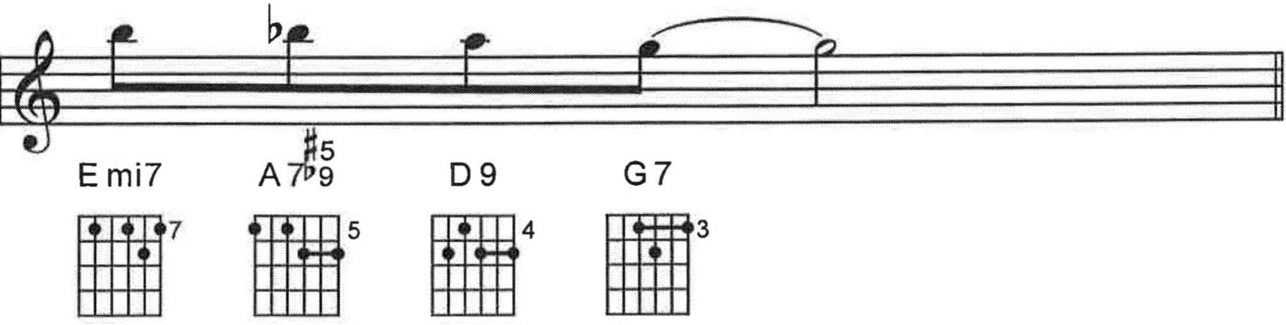

Dominant 7 Phrases

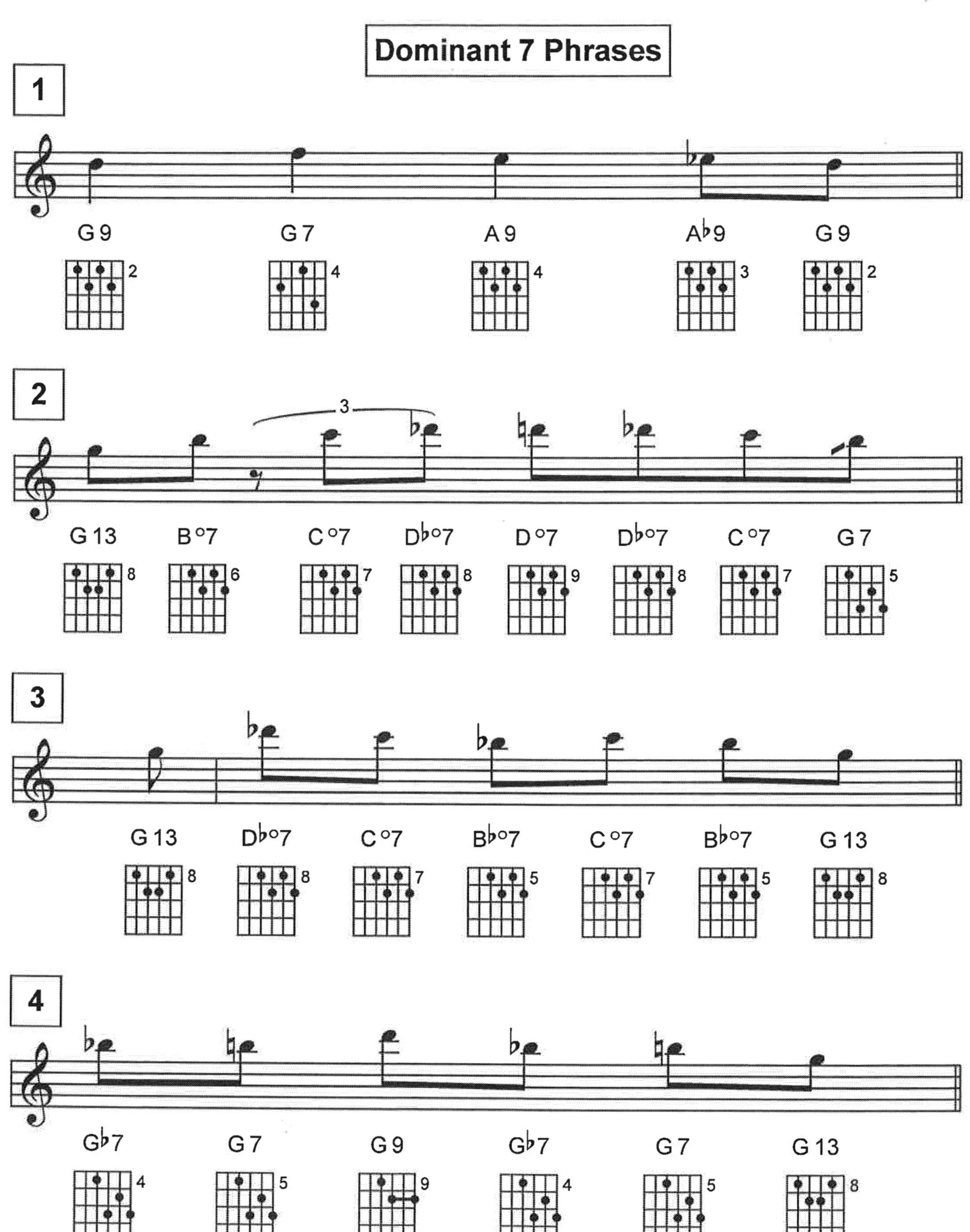

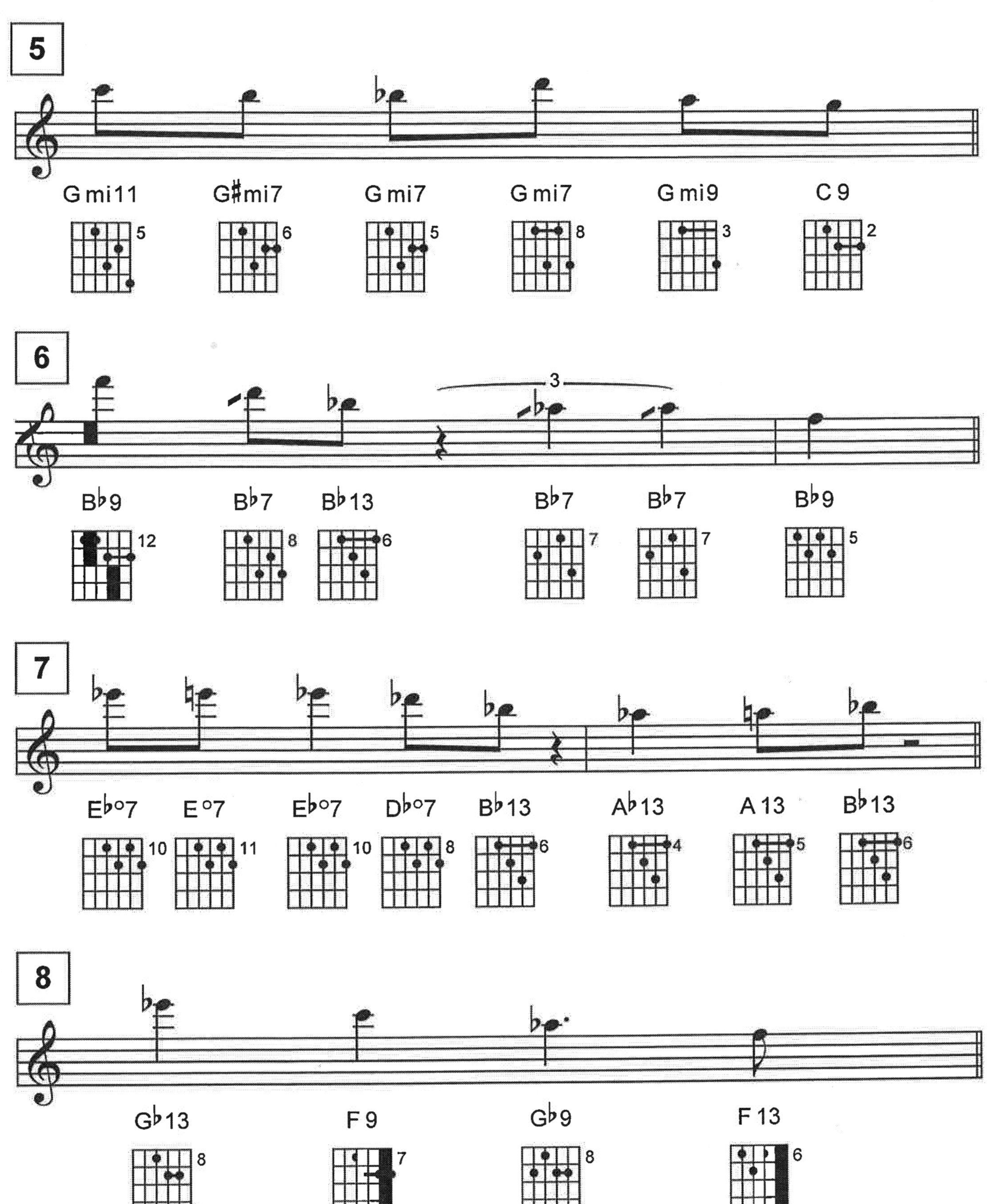

5
G mi11
G#mi7
G mi7
G mi7
G mi9
C 9
6
Bb9
Bb7
Bb13
Bb7
Bb7
Bb9
7
Ebo7
E o7
Ebo7
Dbo7
Bb13
Ab13
A 13
Bb13
8
Gb13
F 9
Gb9
F 13

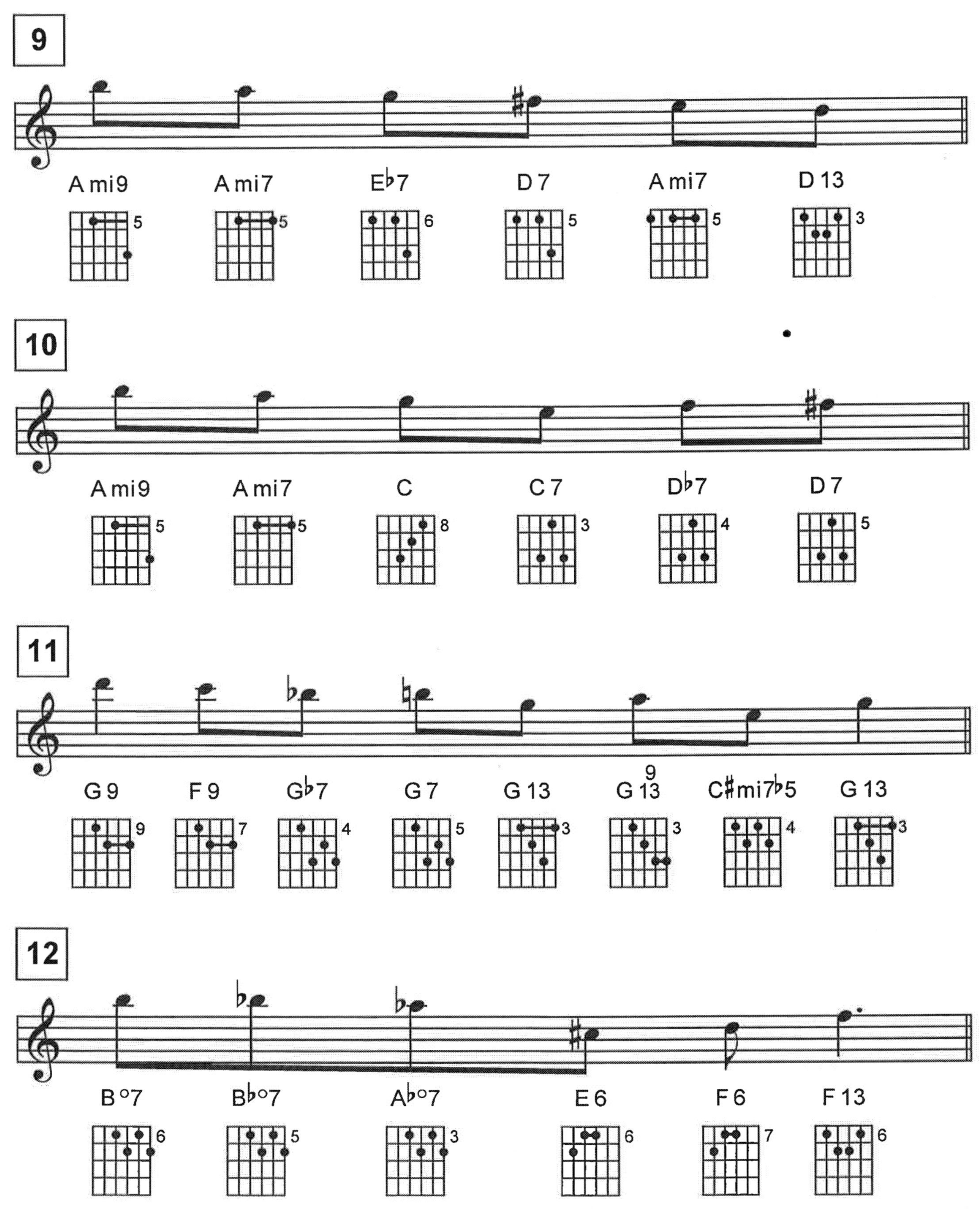

9
A mi9   A mi7   E♭7   D 7   A mi7   D 13
5   5   6   5   5   3

10
A mi9   A mi7   C   C 7   D♭7   D 7
5   5   8   3   4   5

11
G 9   F 9   G♭7   G 7   G 13   G 13(9)   C♯mi7♭5   G 13
9   7   4   5   3   3   4   3

12
B °7   B♭°7   A♭°7   E 6   F 6   F 13
6   5   3   6   7   6

Three Note Voicings

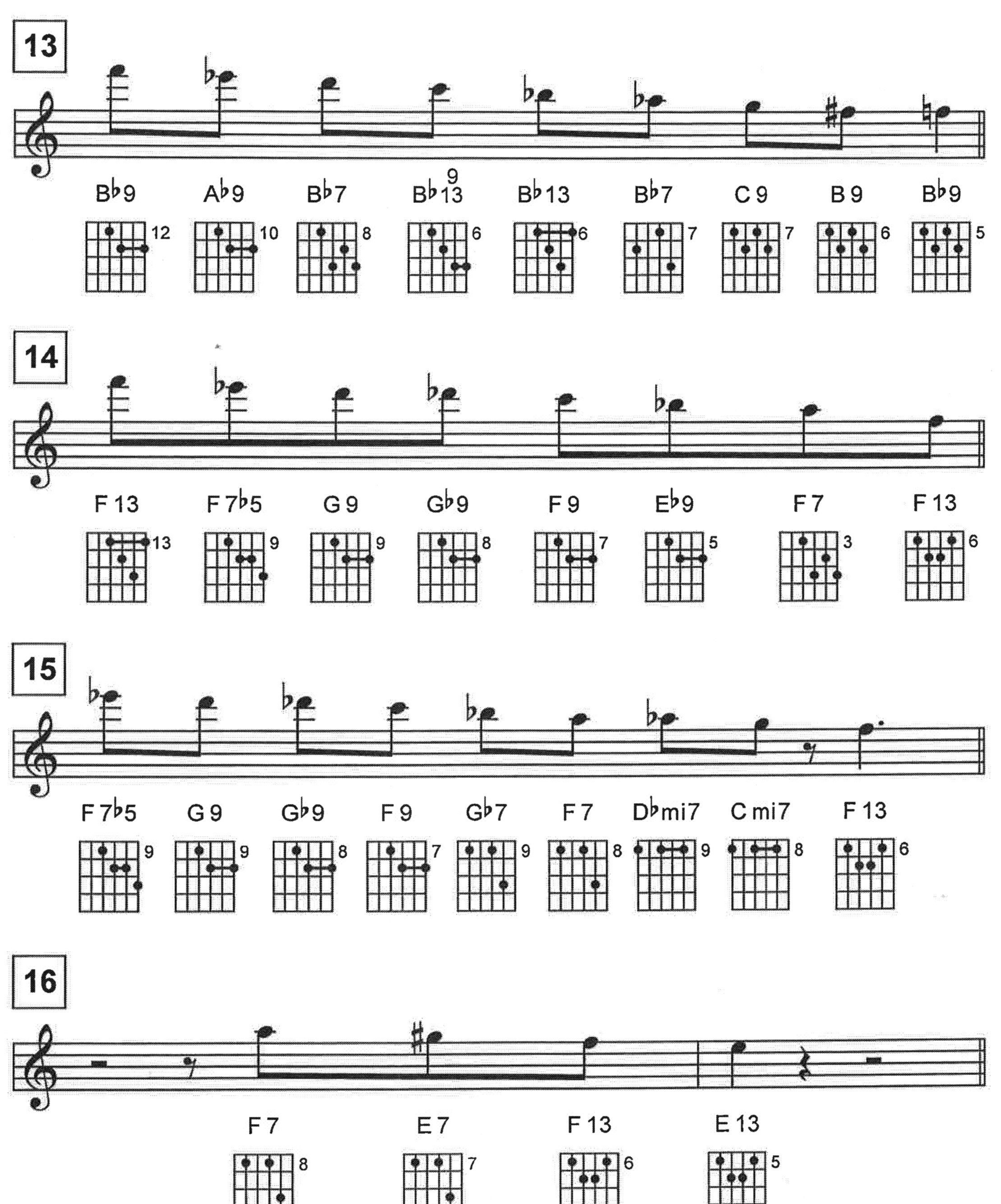
13
Bb9   Ab9   Bb7   Bb13   Bb13   Bb7   C9   B9   Bb9
14
F13   F7b5   G9   Gb9   F9   Eb9   F7   F13
15
F7b5   G9   Gb9   F9   Gb7   F7   Dbmi7   Cmi7   F13
16
F7   E7   F13   E13

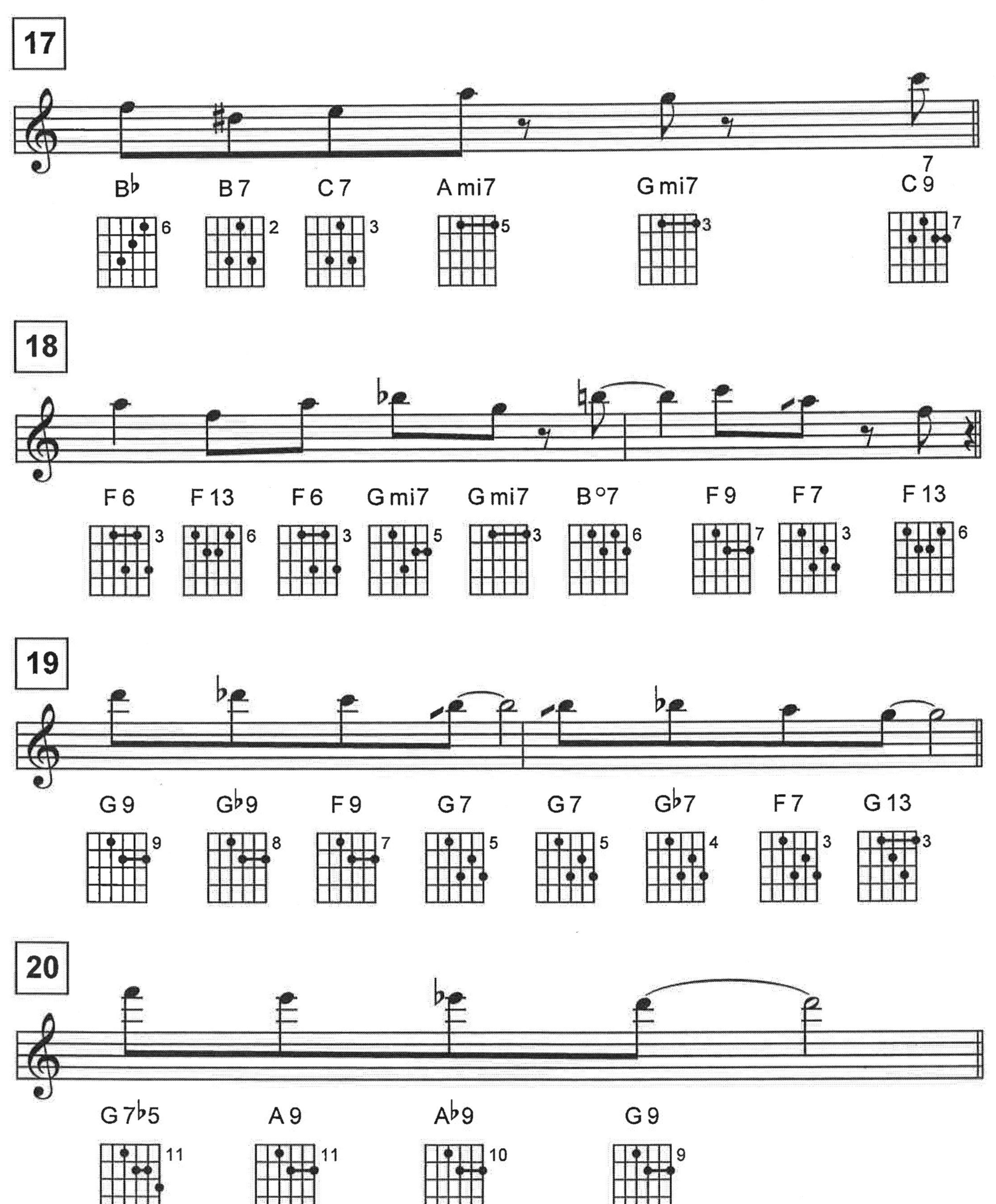

17
B♭   B 7   C 7   A mi7   G mi7   C 9

18
F 6   F 13   F 6   G mi7   G mi7   B °7   F 9   F 7   F 13

19
G 9   G♭9   F 9   G 7   G 7   G♭7   F 7   G 13

20
G 7♭5   A 9   A♭9   G 9

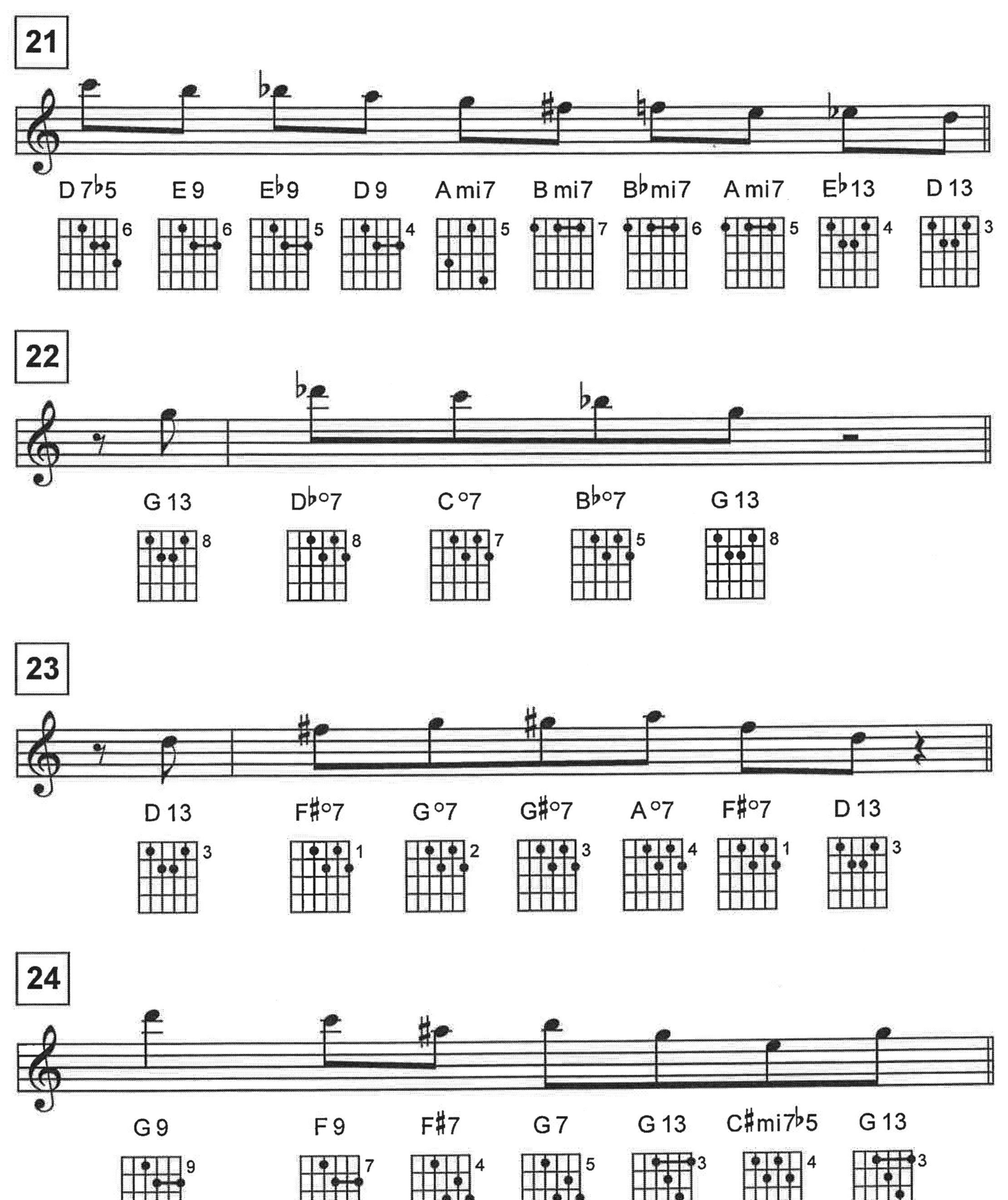

21
D 7♭5   E 9   E♭9   D 9   A mi7   B mi7   B♭mi7   A mi7   E♭13   D 13
6   6   5   4   5   7   6   5   4   3

22
G 13   D♭°7   C °7   B♭°7   G 13
8   8   7   5   8

23
D 13   F#°7   G °7   G#°7   A °7   F#°7   D 13
3   1   2   3   4   1   3

24
G 9   F 9   F#7   G 7   G 13   C#mi7♭5   G 13
9   7   4   5   3   4   3

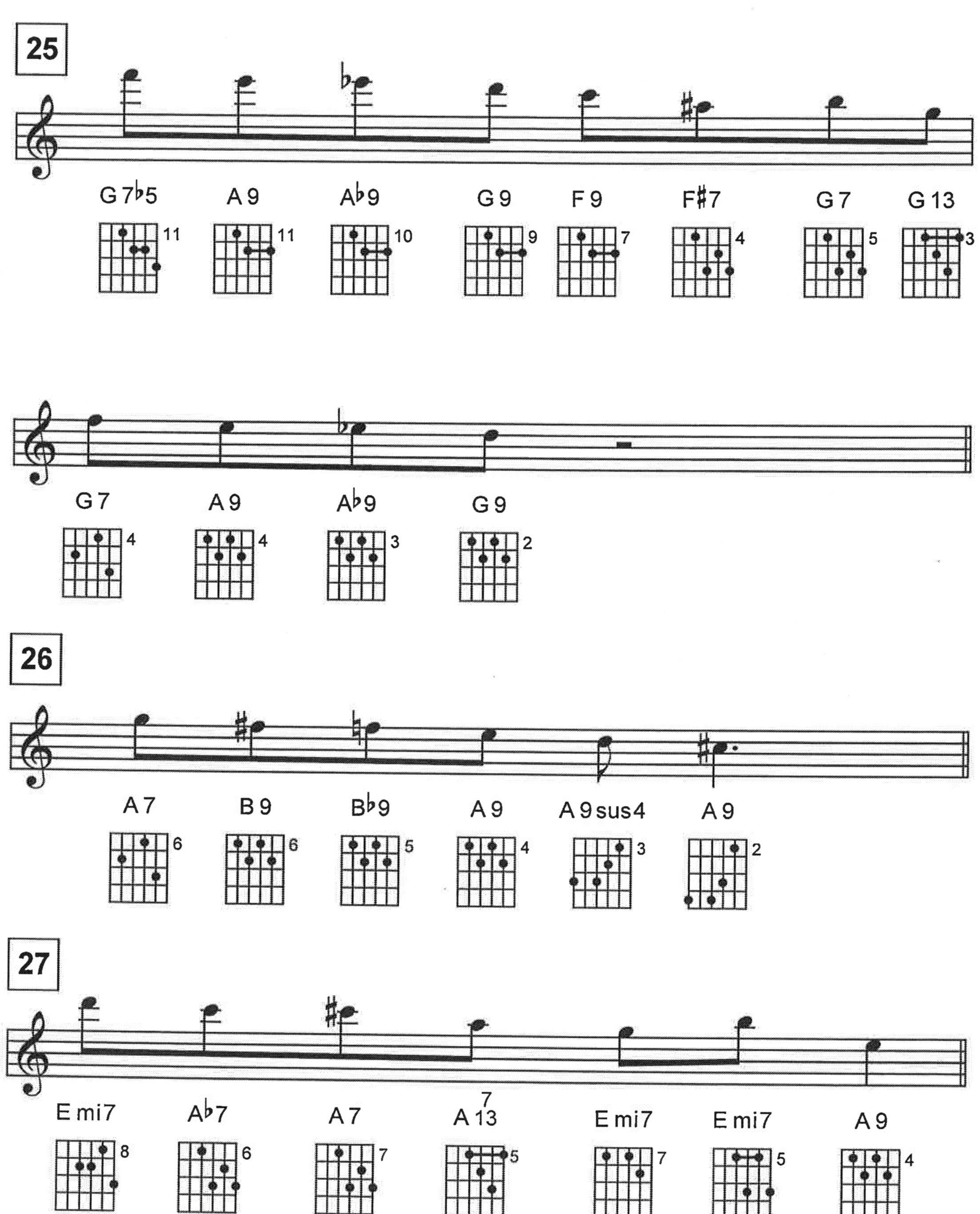

25
G 7♭5   A 9   A♭9   G 9   F 9   F#7   G 7   G 13
11   11   10   9   7   4   5   3
G 7   A 9   A♭9   G 9
4   4   3   2
26
A 7   B 9   B♭9   A 9   A 9 sus 4   A 9
6   6   5   4   3   2
27
E mi7   A♭7   A 7   A 13   E mi7   E mi7   A 9
8   6   7   7   5   5   4

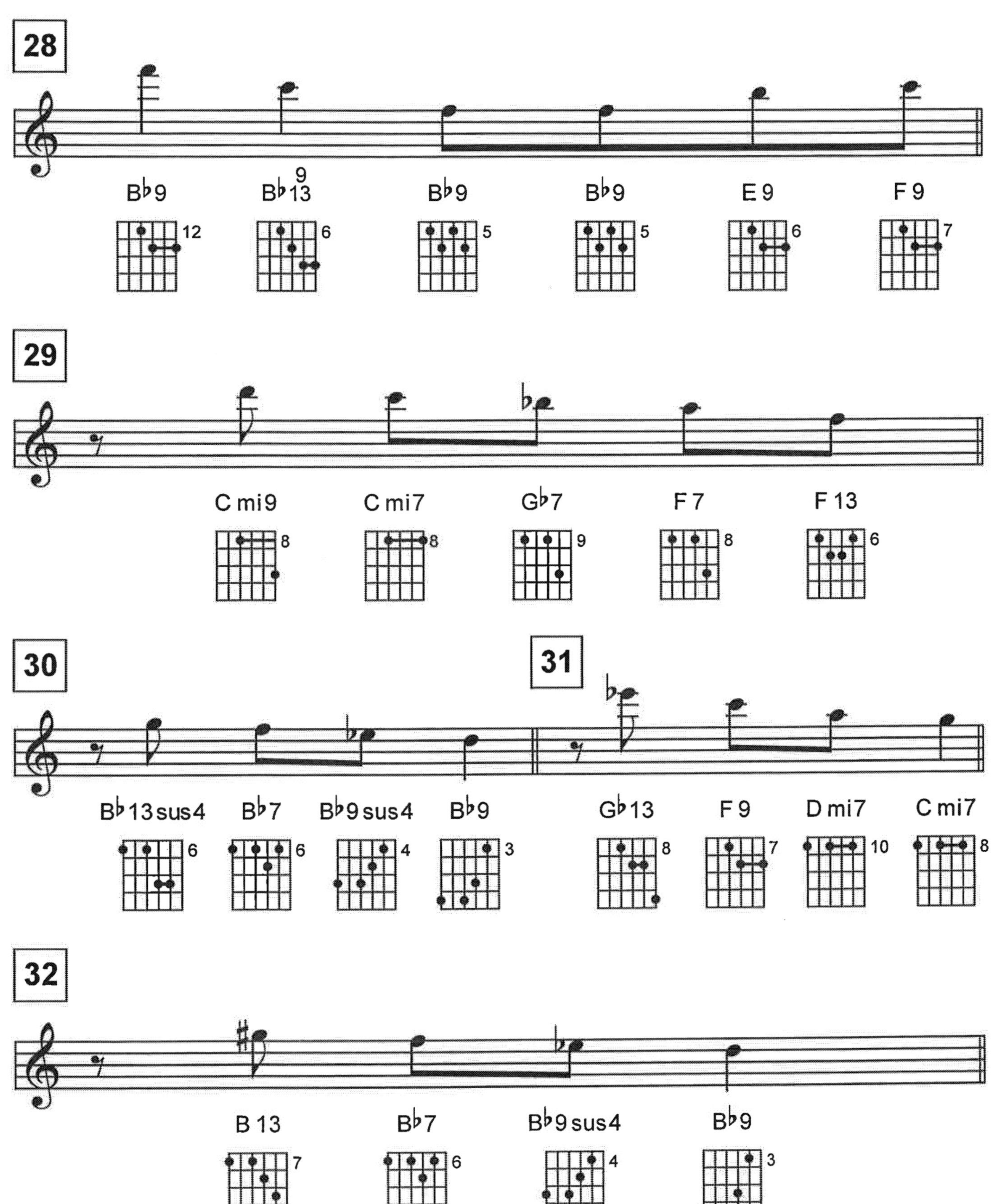

28
B♭9
B♭13
9
B♭9
B♭9
E9
F9
12
6
5
5
6
7

29
C mi9
C mi7
G♭7
F7
F13
8
8
9
8
6

30
B♭13 sus 4
B♭7
B♭9 sus 4
B♭9
6
6
4
3

31
G♭13
F9
D mi7
C mi7
8
7
10
8

32
B13
B♭7
B♭9 sus 4
B♭9
7
6
4
3

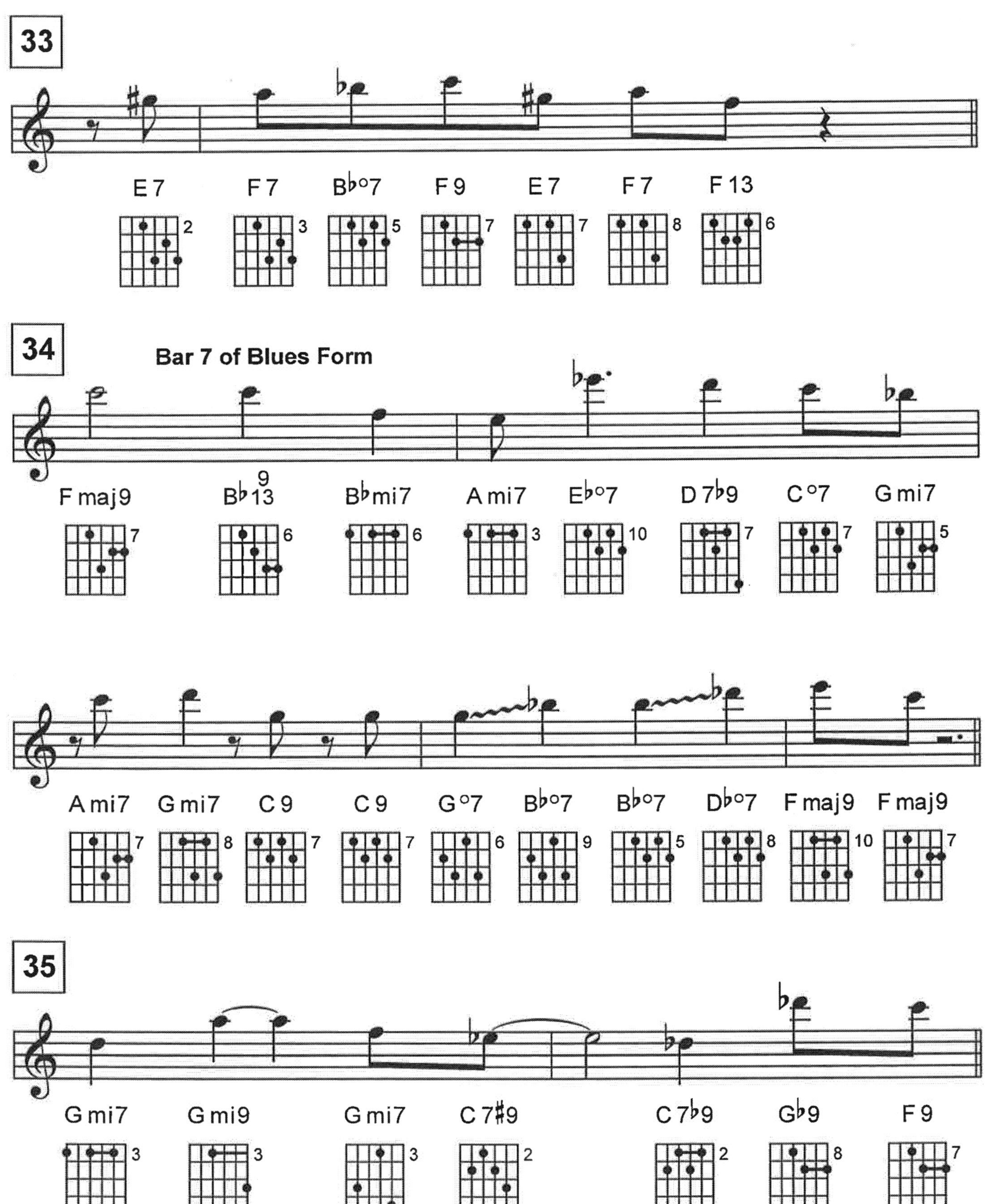

33
E 7   F 7   B♭°7   F 9   E 7   F 7   F 13
2   3   5   7   7   8   6

34
Bar 7 of Blues Form
F maj9   B♭13   B♭mi7   A mi7   E♭°7   D 7♭9   C °7   G mi7
7   6   6   3   10   7   7   5

A mi7   G mi7   C 9   C 9   G °7   B♭°7   B♭°7   D♭°7   F maj9   F maj9
7   8   7   7   6   9   5   8   10   7

35
G mi7   G mi9   G mi7   C 7♯9   C 7♭9   G♭9   F 9
3   3   3   2   2   8   7

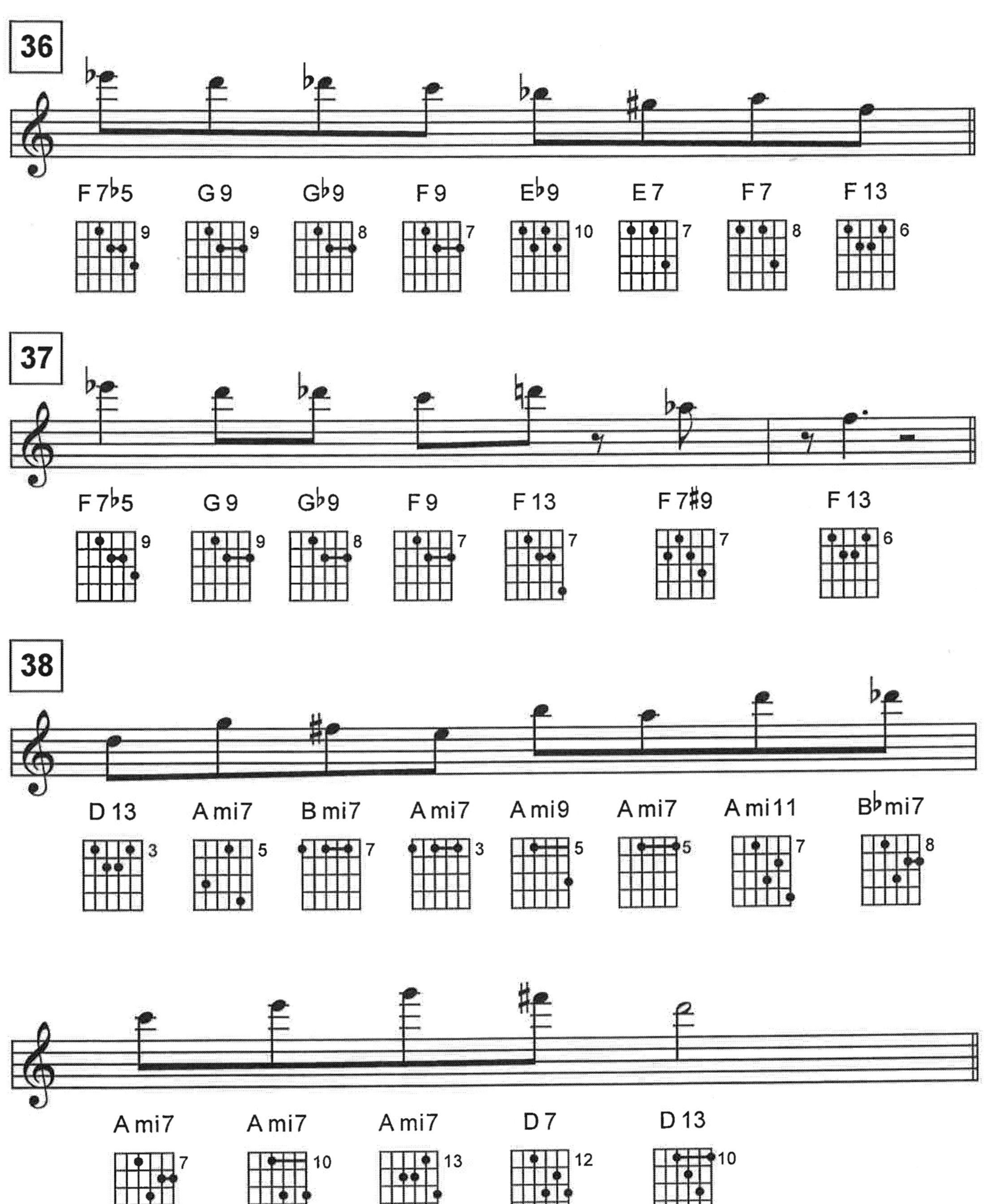

36
F 7b5   G 9   Gb9   F 9   Eb9   E 7   F 7   F 13
9   9   8   7   10   7   8   6

37
F 7b5   G 9   Gb9   F 9   F 13   F 7#9   F 13
9   9   8   7   7   7   6

38
D 13   A mi7   B mi7   A mi7   A mi9   A mi7   A mi11   Bb mi7
3   5   7   3   5   5   7   8

A mi7   A mi7   A mi7   D 7   D 13
7   10   13   12   10

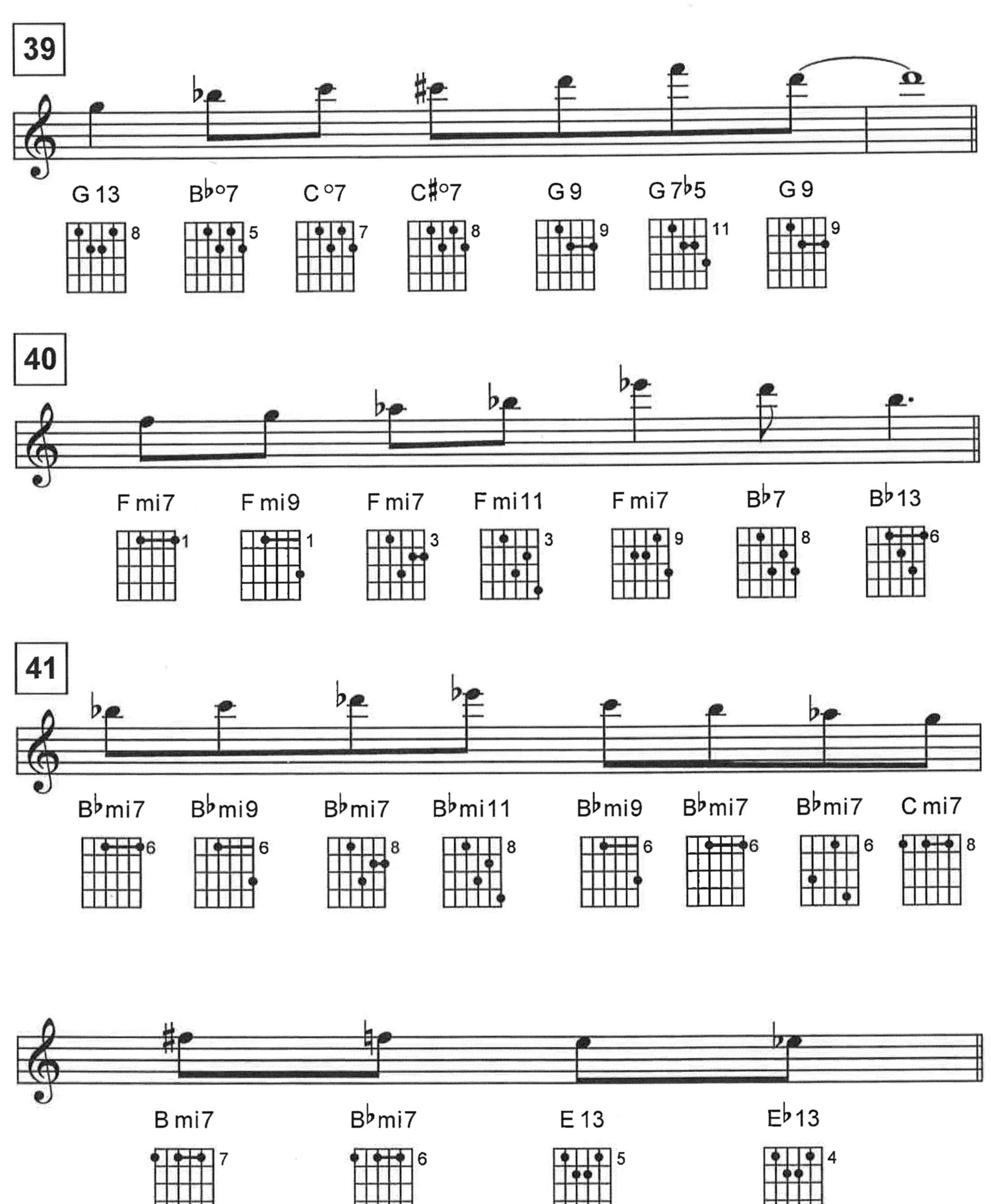

39
G 13   B♭°7   C °7   C#°7   G 9   G 7♭5   G 9
8   5   7   8   9   11   9

40
F mi7   F mi9   F mi7   F mi11   F mi7   B♭7   B♭13
1   1   3   3   9   8   6

41
B♭mi7   B♭mi9   B♭mi7   B♭mi11   B♭mi9   B♭mi7   B♭mi7   C mi7
6   6   8   8   6   6   6   8

B mi7   B♭mi7   E 13   E♭13
7   6   5   4

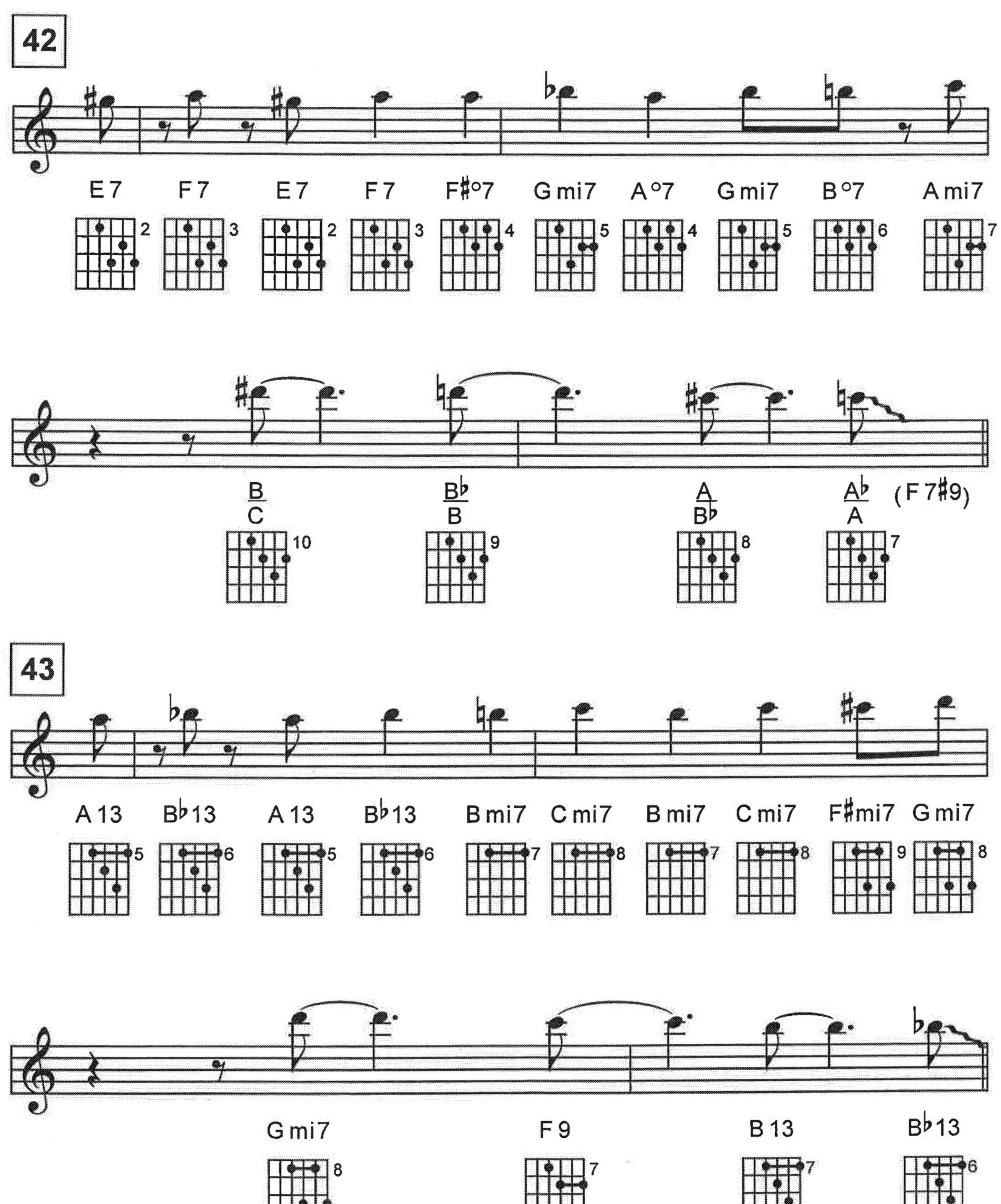
42
E7   F7   E7   F7   F#o7   Gmi7   Ao7   Gmi7   Bo7   Ami7
2   3   2   3   4   5   4   5   6   7
B/C   Bb/B   A/Bb   Ab/A   (F7#9)
10   9   8   7
43
A13   Bb13   A13   Bb13   Bmi7   Cmi7   Bmi7   Cmi7   F#mi7   Gmi7
5   6   5   6   7   8   7   8   9   8
Gmi7   F9   B13   Bb13
8   7   7   6

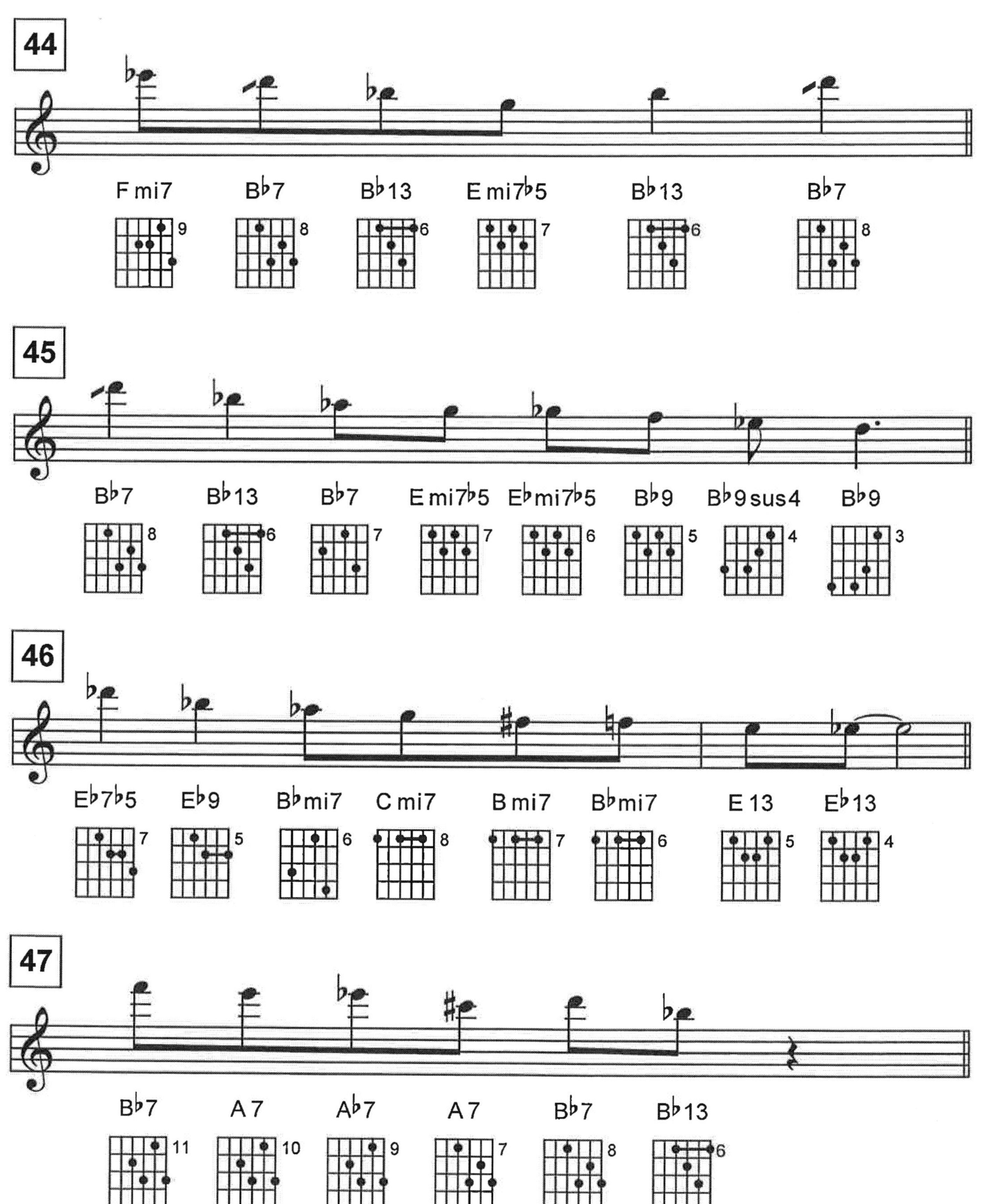

44
F mi7   B♭7   B♭13   E mi7♭5   B♭13   B♭7
9   8   6   7   6   8

45
B♭7   B♭13   B♭7   E mi7♭5   E♭mi7♭5   B♭9   B♭9sus4   B♭9
8   6   7   7   6   5   4   3

46
E♭7♭5   E♭9   B♭mi7   C mi7   B mi7   B♭mi7   E 13   E♭13
7   5   6   8   7   6   5   4

47
B♭7   A 7   A♭7   A 7   B♭7   B♭13
11   10   9   7   8   6

48
C 9   B 9   B♭9   C 7   B 7   B♭7   C 13   C 7   D 9   D♭9
14   13   12   10   9   8   8   9   9   8
C 9   B♭9   B 7   C 7   C 13
7   5   2   3   1
49
F 7♭5   G 9   G♭9   F 9   E♭9   E 7
9   9   8   7   5   2
F 7   F 13   E♭13   E 13   F 13
3   6   4   5   6

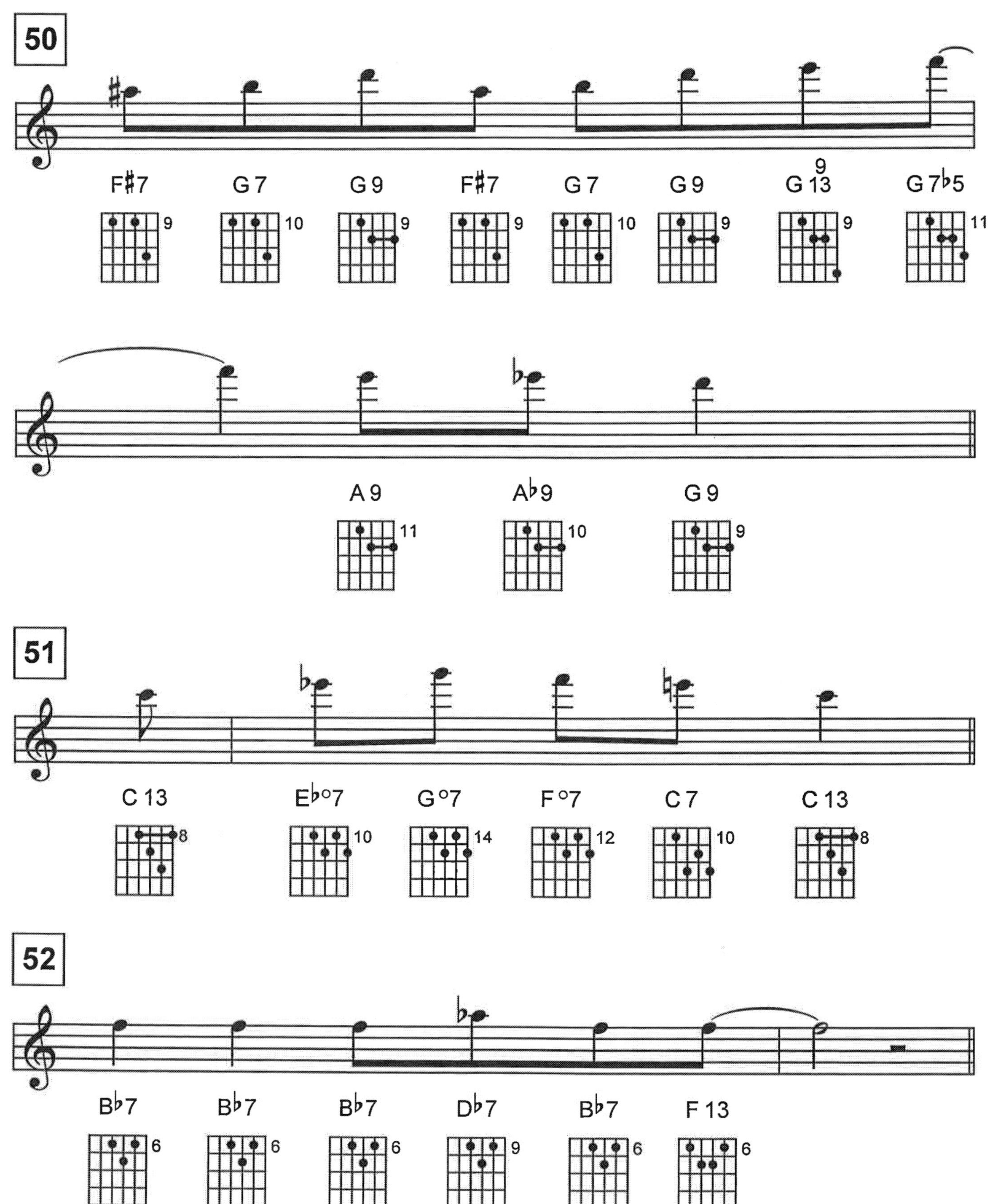

50
F#7 G7 G9 F#7 G7 G9 G13(9) G7b5
A9 Ab9 G9
51
C13 Eb°7 G°7 F°7 C7 C13
52
Bb7 Bb7 Bb7 Db7 Bb7 F13

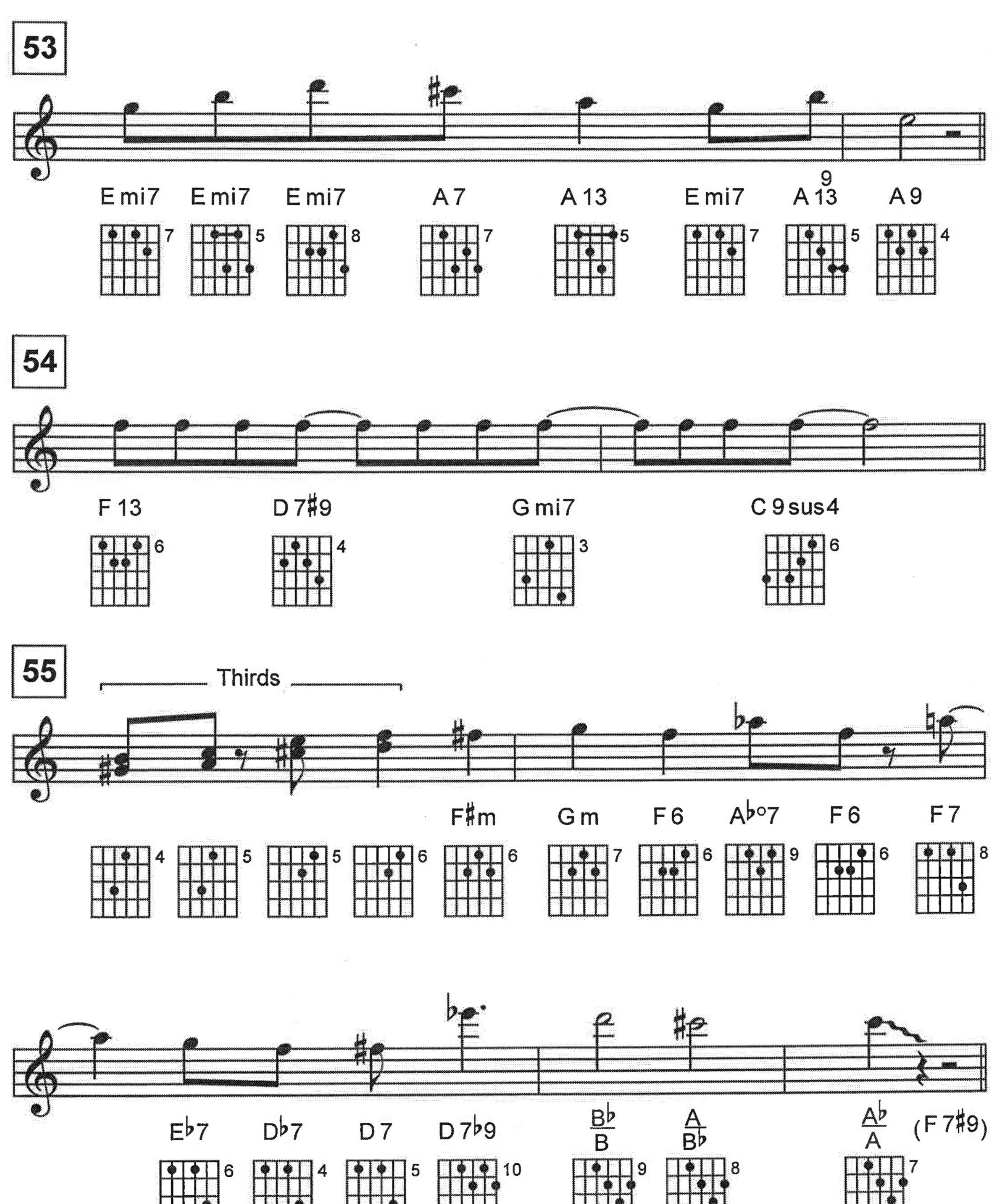

53
E mi7   E mi7   E mi7   A 7   A 13   E mi7   A 13 9   A 9
7   5   8   7   5   7   5   4
54
F 13   D 7#9   G mi7   C 9 sus4
6   4   3   6
55
Thirds
F#m   Gm   F 6   Ab°7   F 6   F 7
4   5   5   6   6   7   6   9   6   8
Eb7   Db7   D 7   D 7b9   Bb/B   A/Bb   Ab/A   (F 7#9)
6   4   5   10   9   8   7

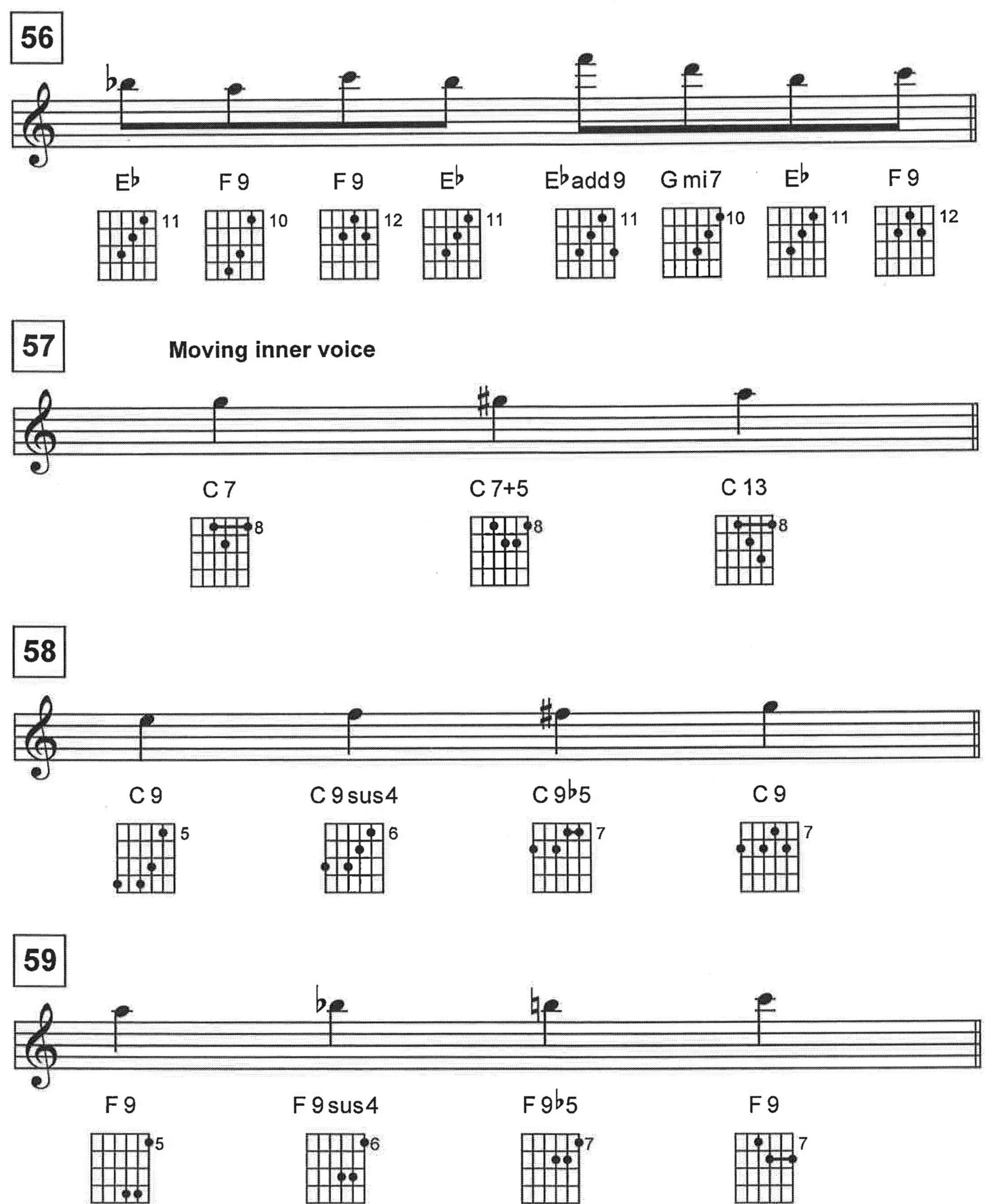

56
E♭   F 9   F 9   E♭   E♭add9   G mi7   E♭   F 9
11   10   12   11   11   10   11   12

57
Moving inner voice
C 7   C 7+5   C 13
8   8   8

58
C 9   C 9sus4   C 9♭5   C 9
5   6   7   7

59
F 9   F 9sus4   F 9♭5   F 9
5   6   7   7

Phrases In Minor

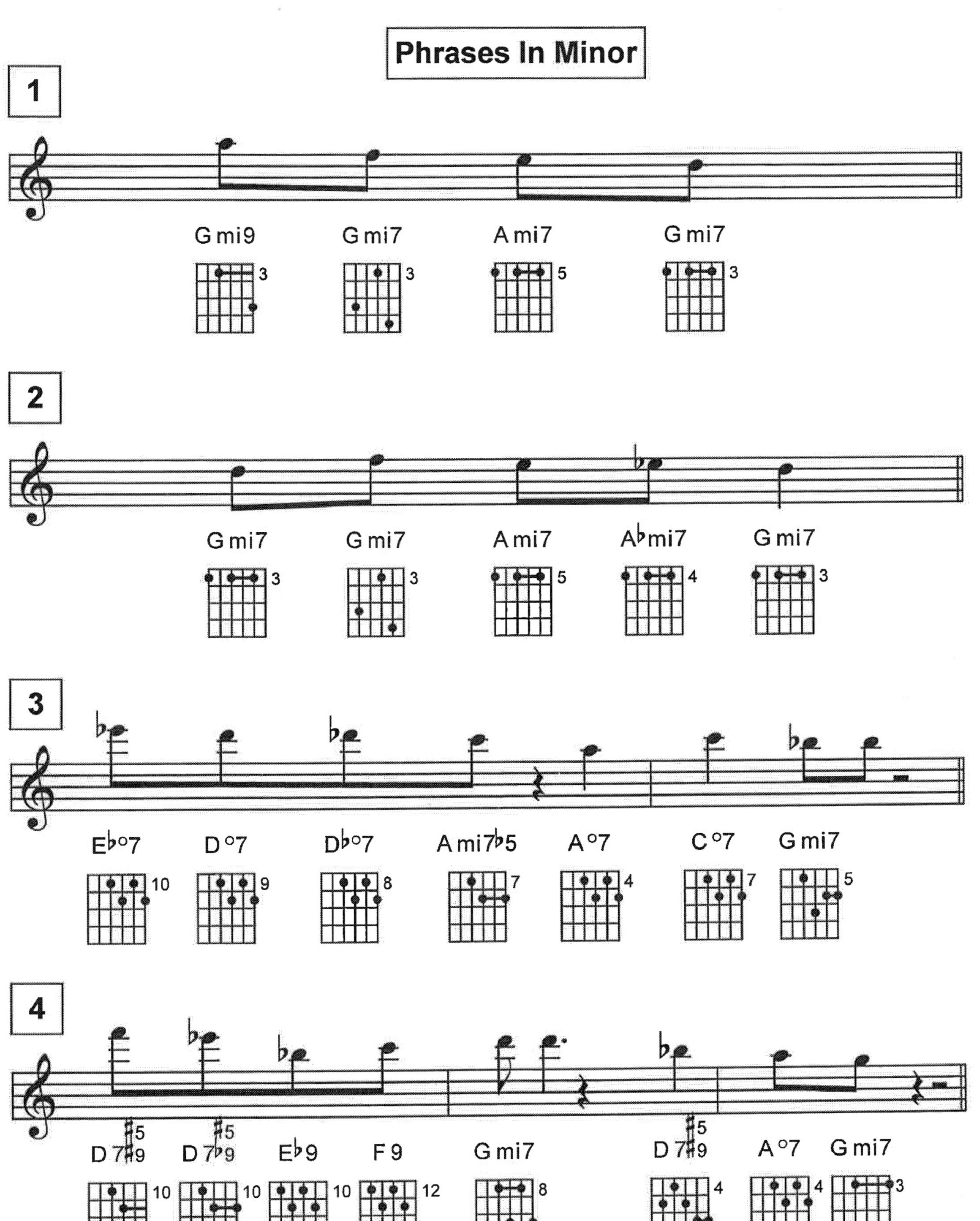

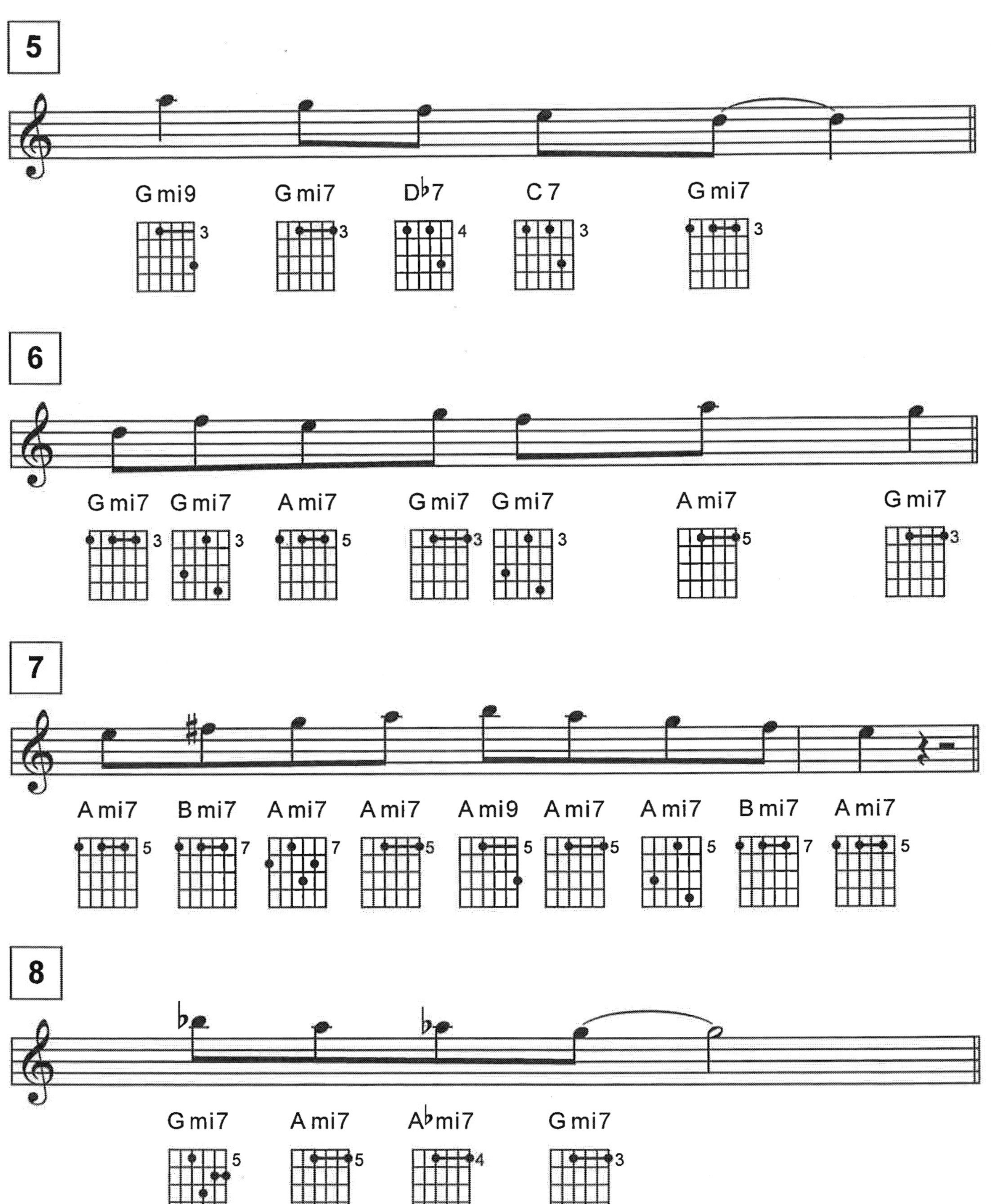

5
G mi9
G mi7
D♭7
C 7
G mi7
6
G mi7
G mi7
A mi7
G mi7
G mi7
A mi7
G mi7
7
A mi7
B mi7
A mi7
A mi7
A mi9
A mi7
A mi7
B mi7
A mi7
8
G mi7
A mi7
A♭mi7
G mi7

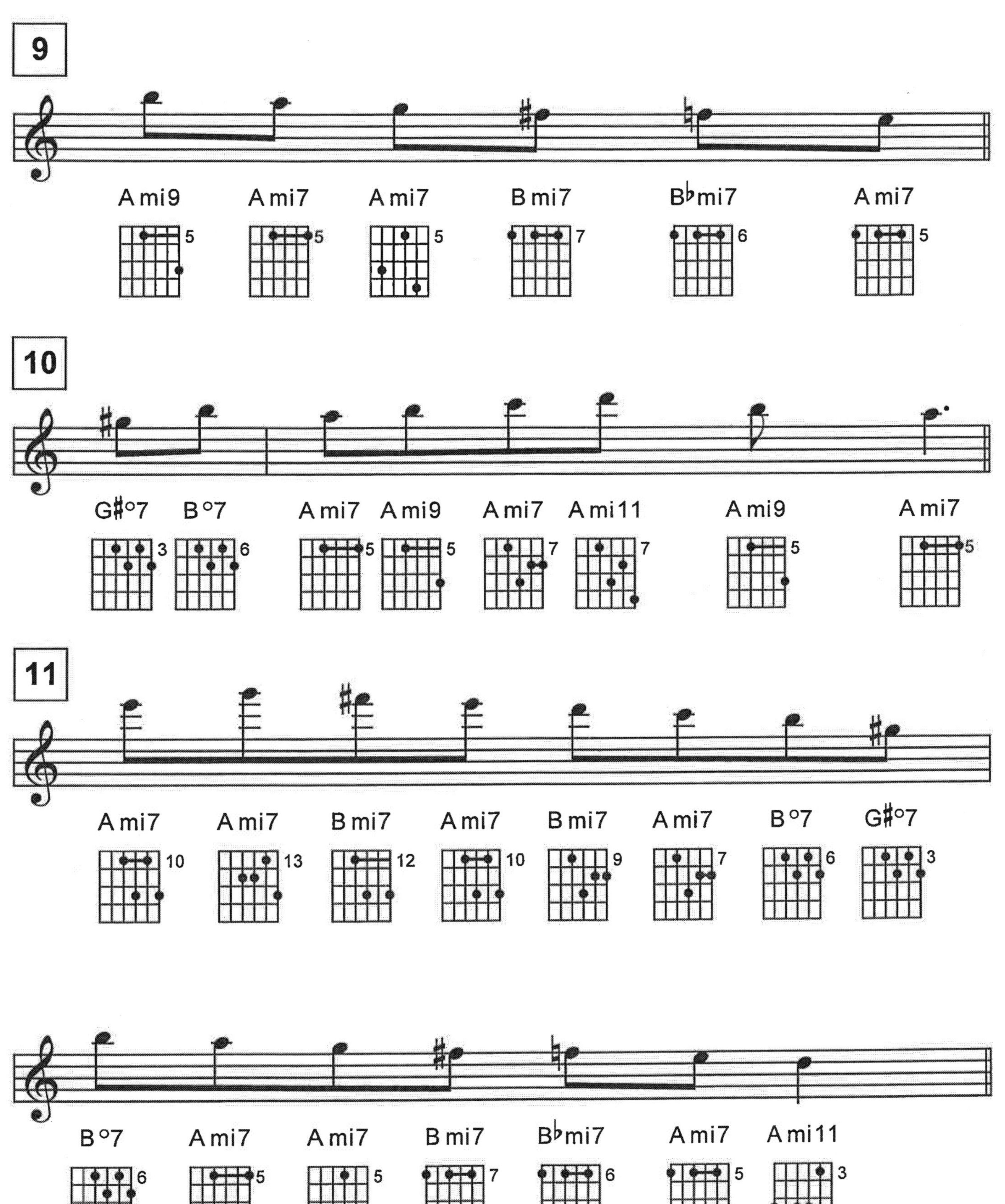

9
A mi9   A mi7   A mi7   B mi7   B♭mi7   A mi7
10
G#°7   B°7   A mi7   A mi9   A mi7   A mi11   A mi9   A mi7
11
A mi7   A mi7   B mi7   A mi7   B mi7   A mi7   B°7   G#°7
B°7   A mi7   A mi7   B mi7   B♭mi7   A mi7   A mi11

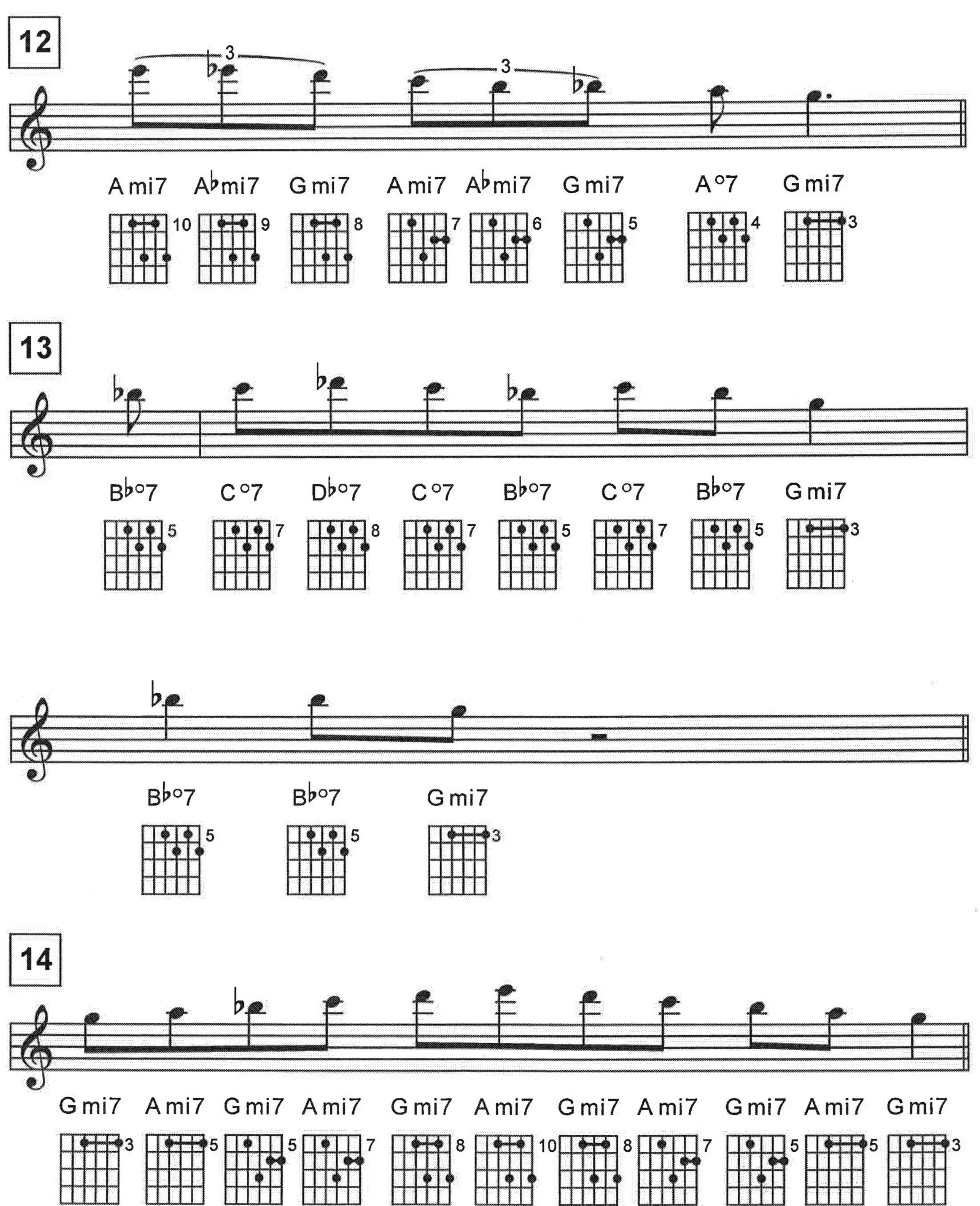

12
A mi7   A♭mi7   G mi7   A mi7   A♭mi7   G mi7   A°7   G mi7
10   9   8   7   6   5   4   3
13
B♭°7   C°7   D♭°7   C°7   B♭°7   C°7   B♭°7   G mi7
5   7   8   7   5   7   5   3
B♭°7   B♭°7   G mi7
5   5   3
14
G mi7   A mi7   G mi7   A mi7   G mi7   A mi7   G mi7   A mi7   G mi7   A mi7   G mi7
3   5   5   7   8   10   8   7   5   5   3

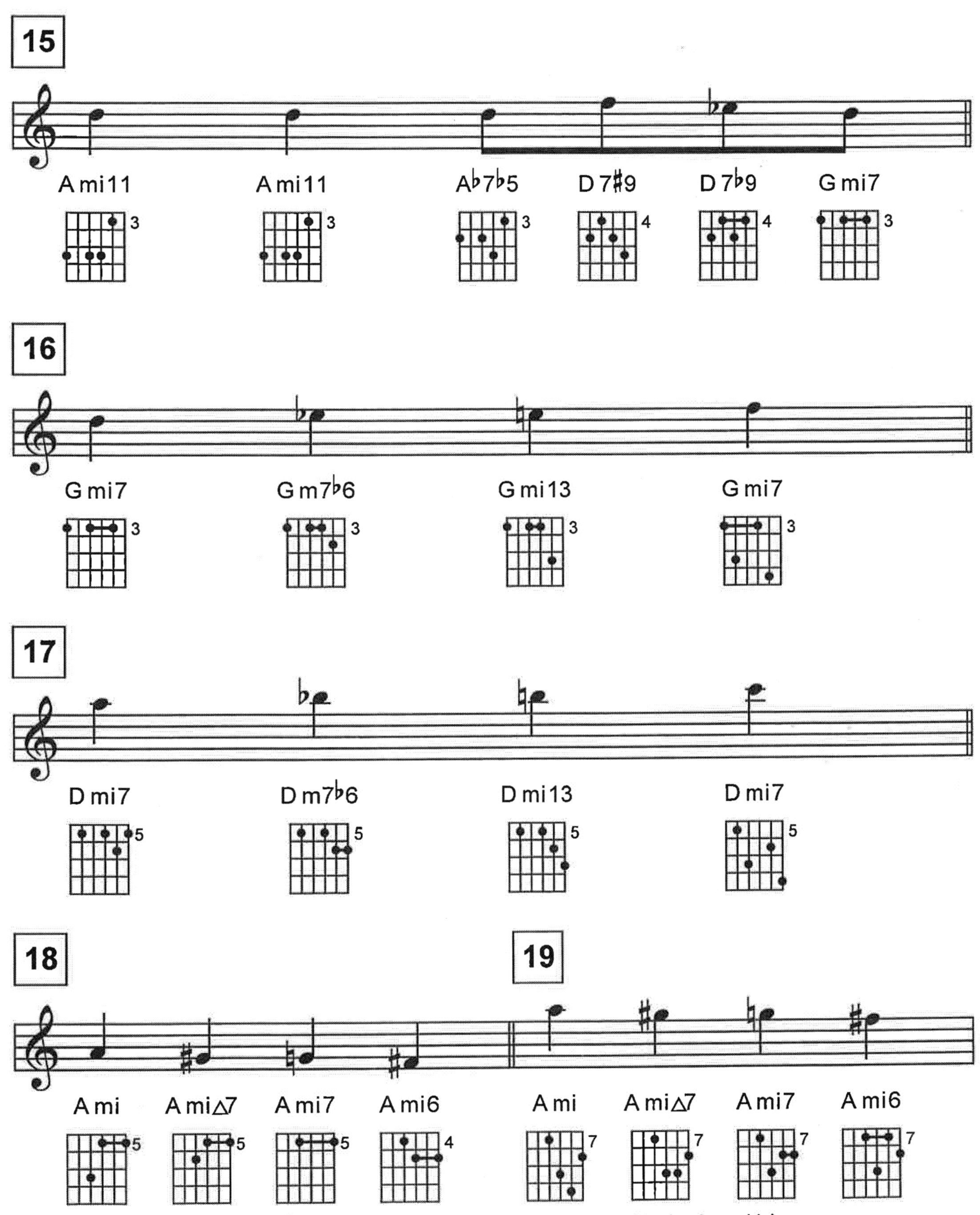

15
A mi11   A mi11   Ab7b5   D 7#9   D 7b9   G mi7

16
G mi7   G m7b6   G mi13   G mi7

17
D mi7   D m7b6   D mi13   D mi7

18
A mi   A mi△7   A mi7   A mi6
Moving Bass Voice

19
A mi   A mi△7   A mi7   A mi6
Moving Inner Voice

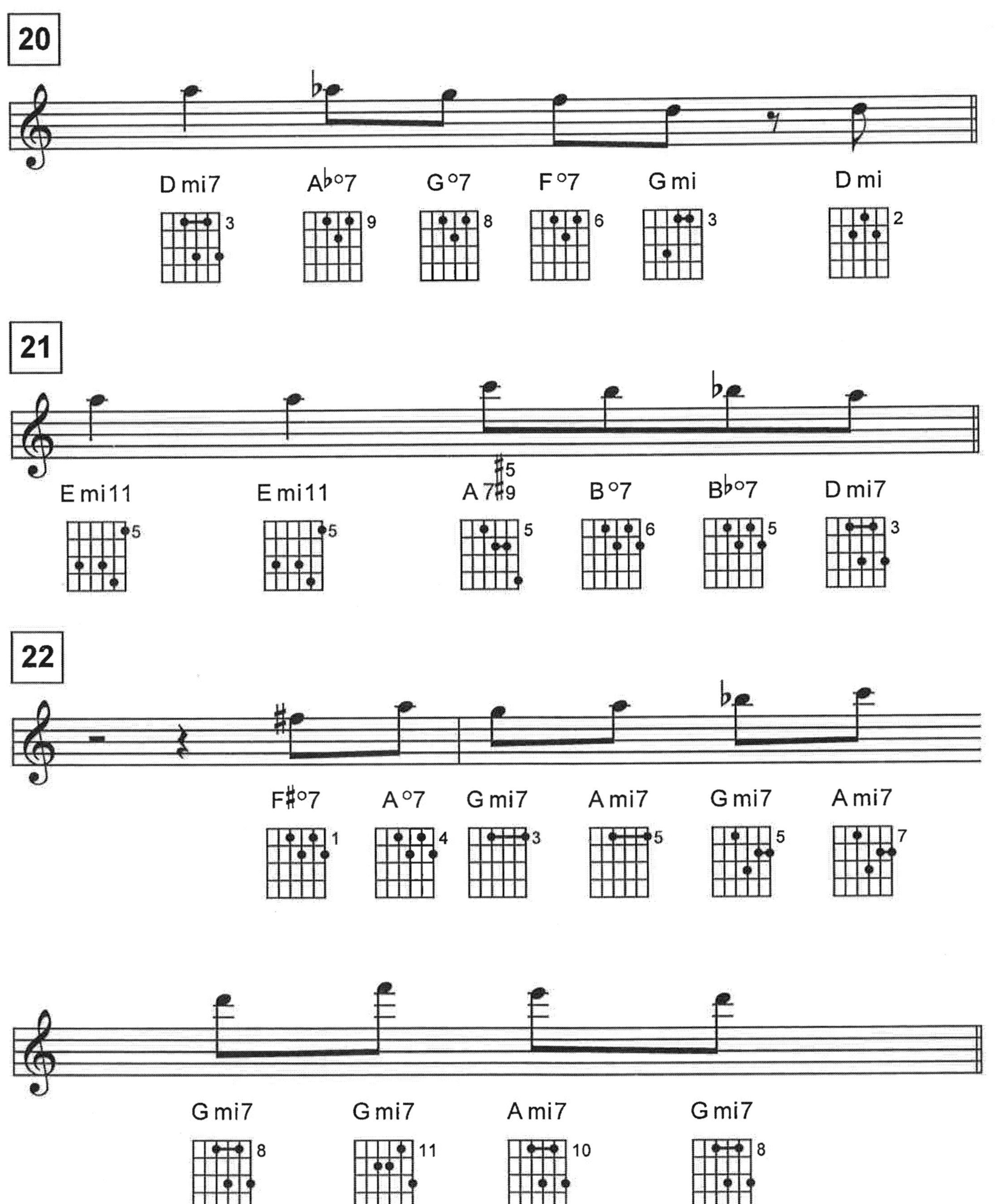

20
D mi7   Ab°7   G°7   F°7   G mi   D mi
3   9   8   6   3   2

21
E mi11   E mi11   A 7#9   B°7   Bb°7   D mi7
5   5   5   6   5   3

22
F#°7   A°7   G mi7   A mi7   G mi7   A mi7
1   4   3   5   5   7

G mi7   G mi7   A mi7   G mi7
8   11   10   8

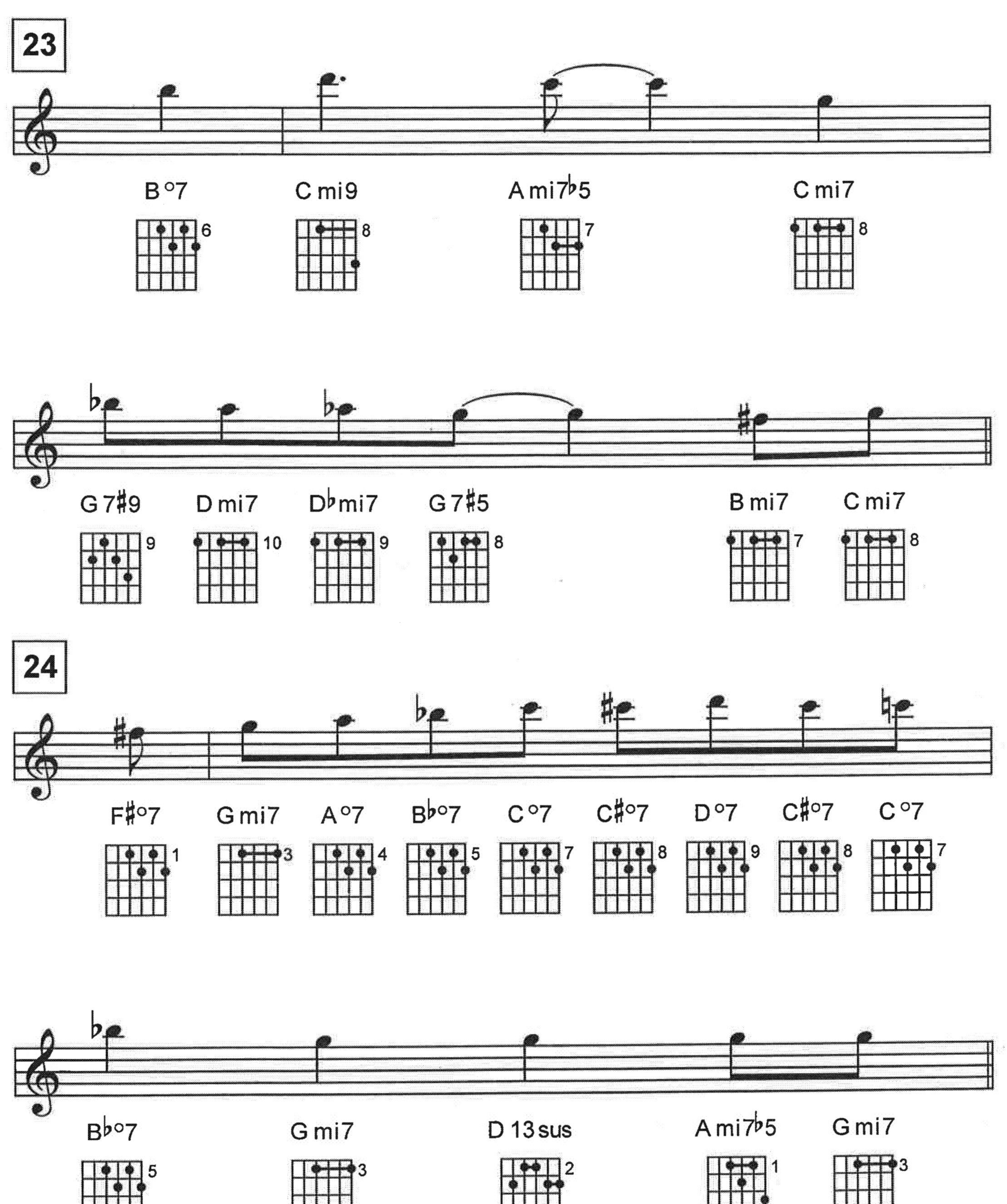
23
B °7
C mi9
A mi7♭5
C mi7
G 7♯9
D mi7
D♭mi7
G 7♯5
B mi7
C mi7
24
F♯°7
G mi7
A °7
B♭°7
C °7
C♯°7
D °7
C♯°7
C °7
B♭°7
G mi7
D 13sus
A mi7♭5
G mi7

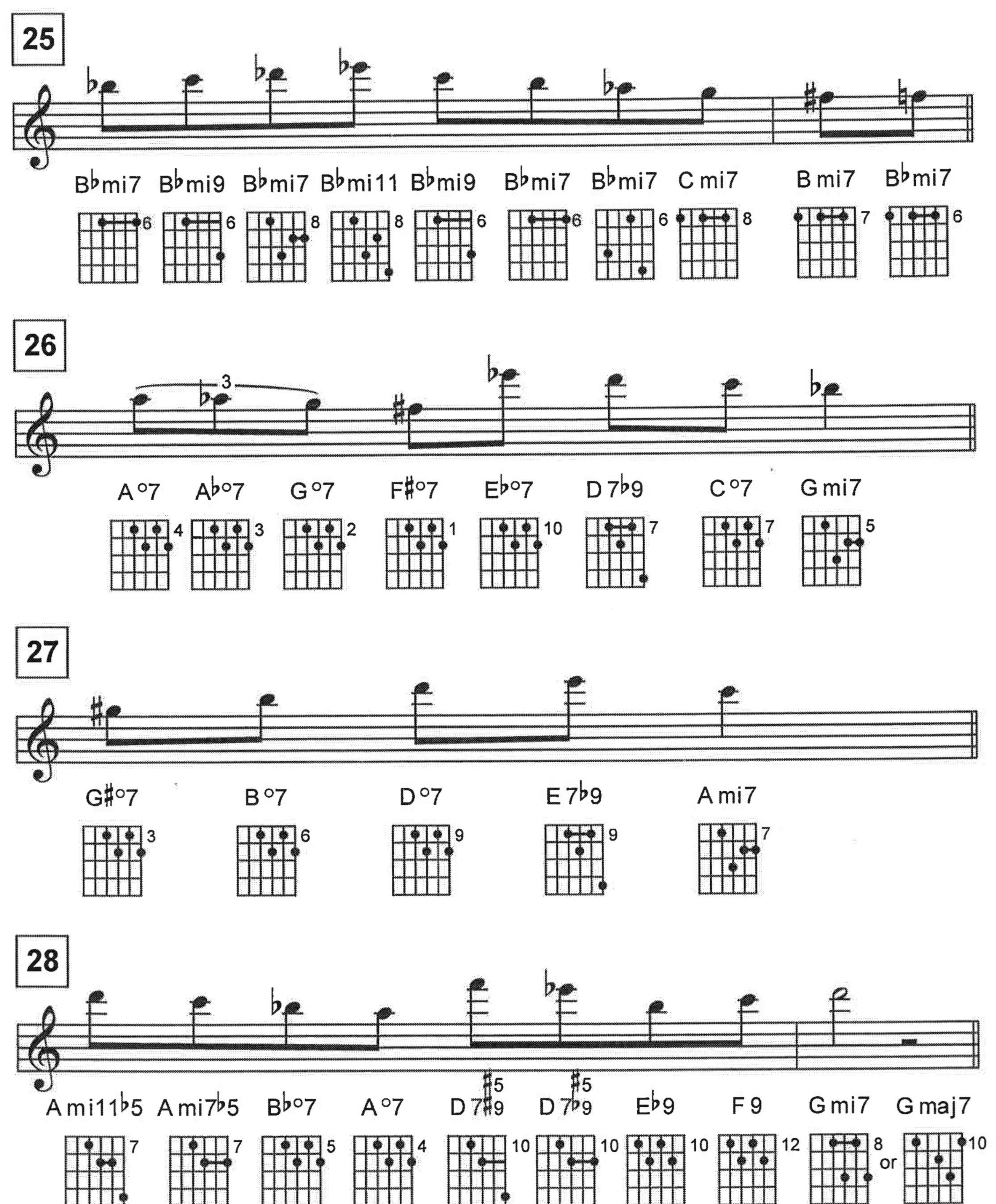

25
Bbmi7 Bbmi9 Bbmi7 Bbmi11 Bbmi9 Bbmi7 Bbmi7 C mi7 B mi7 Bbmi7
26
A°7 Ab°7 G°7 F#°7 Eb°7 D 7b9 C°7 G mi7
27
G#°7 B°7 D°7 E 7b9 A mi7
28
A mi11b5 A mi7b5 Bb°7 A°7 D 7#9 D 7b9 Eb9 F 9 G mi7 G maj7
or

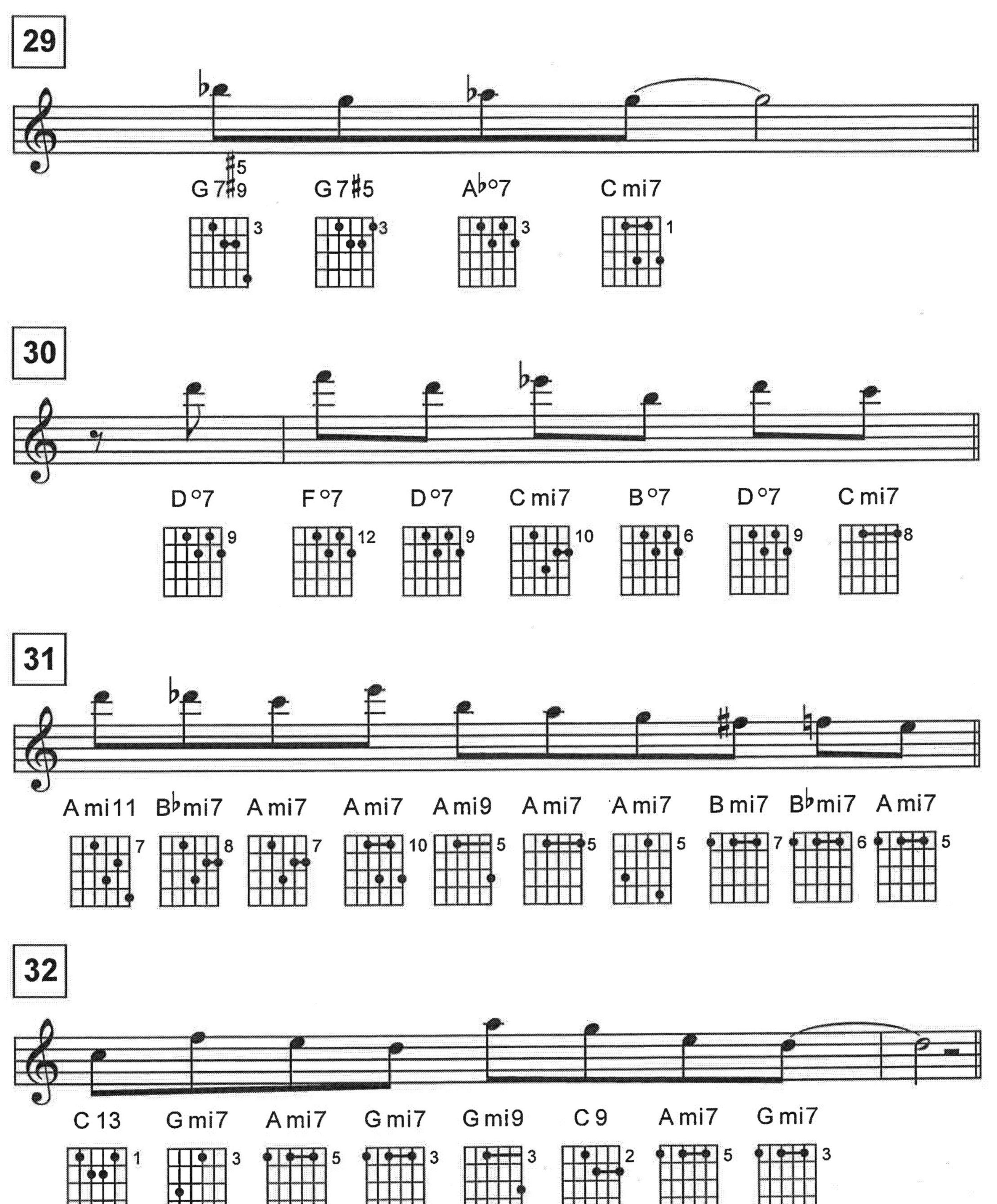

29
G7#9
G7#5
Ab°7
C mi7
30
D°7
F°7
D°7
C mi7
B°7
D°7
C mi7
31
A mi11
Bb mi7
A mi7
A mi7
A mi9
A mi7
A mi7
B mi7
Bb mi7
A mi7
32
C 13
G mi7
A mi7
G mi7
G mi9
C 9
A mi7
G mi7

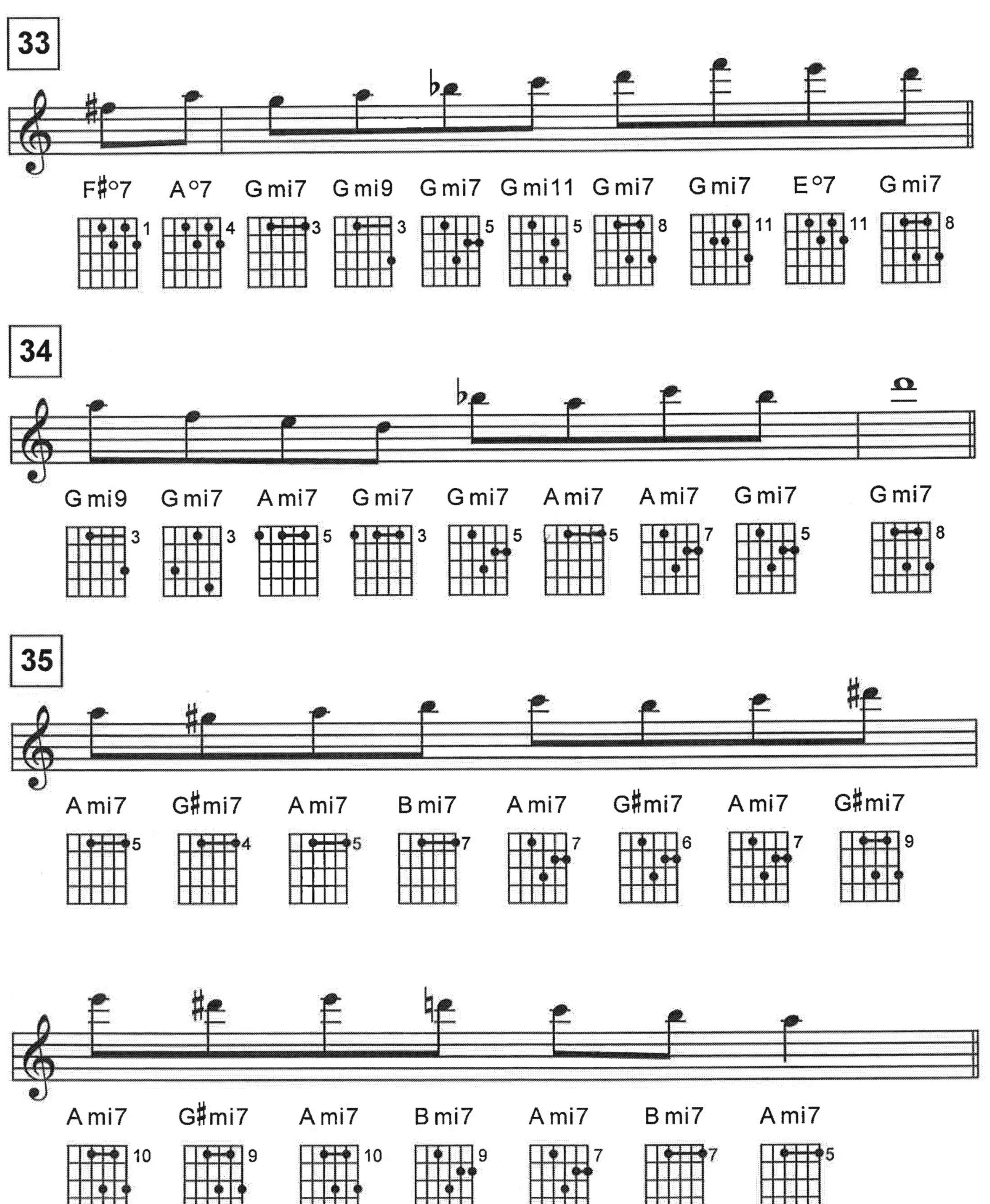

33
F#°7   A°7   G mi7   G mi9   G mi7   G mi11   G mi7   G mi7   E°7   G mi7
1   4   3   3   5   5   8   11   11   8

34
G mi9   G mi7   A mi7   G mi7   G mi7   A mi7   A mi7   G mi7   G mi7
3   3   5   3   5   5   7   5   8

35
A mi7   G#mi7   A mi7   B mi7   A mi7   G#mi7   A mi7   G#mi7
5   4   5   7   7   6   7   9

A mi7   G#mi7   A mi7   B mi7   A mi7   B mi7   A mi7
10   9   10   9   7   7   5

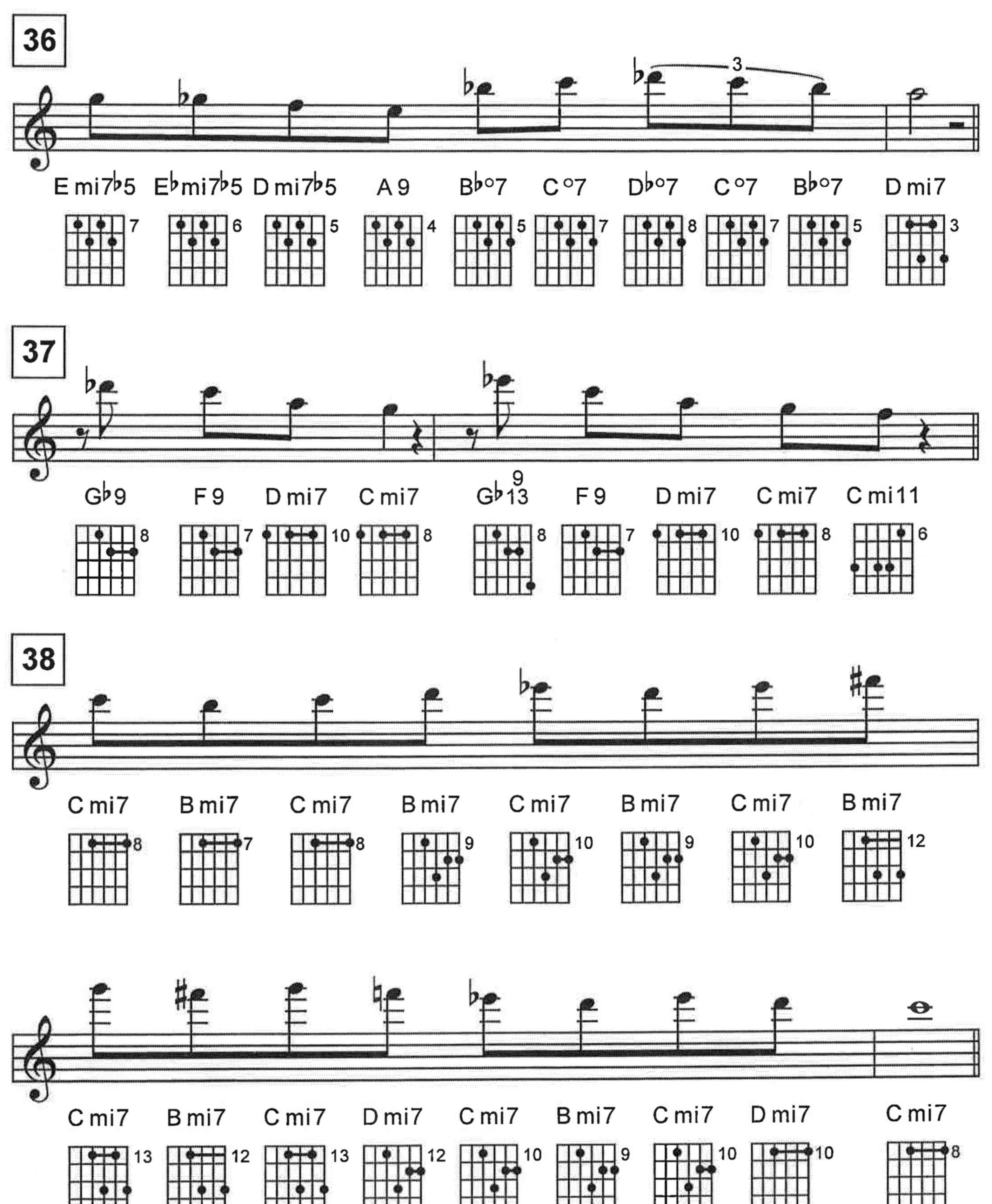

36
E mi7♭5 E♭mi7♭5 D mi7♭5 A 9 B♭°7 C°7 D♭°7 C°7 B♭°7 D mi7
37
G♭9 F 9 D mi7 C mi7 G♭13 F 9 D mi7 C mi7 C mi11
38
C mi7 B mi7 C mi7 B mi7 C mi7 B mi7 C mi7 B mi7
C mi7 B mi7 C mi7 D mi7 C mi7 B mi7 C mi7 D mi7 C mi7

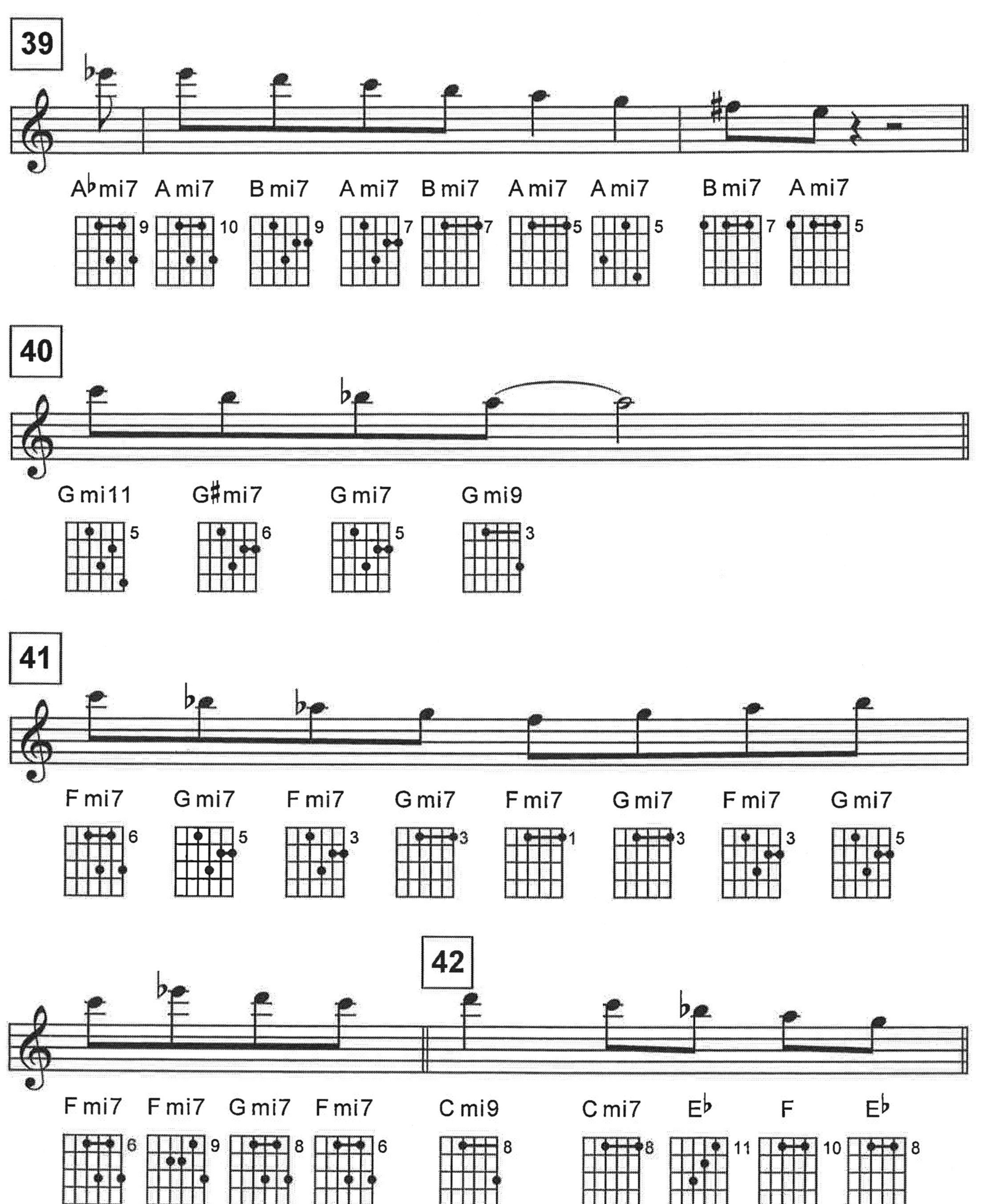

39
A♭mi7 A mi7 B mi7 A mi7 B mi7 A mi7 A mi7 B mi7 A mi7
40
G mi11 G♯mi7 G mi7 G mi9
41
F mi7 G mi7 F mi7 G mi7 F mi7 G mi7 F mi7 G mi7
42
F mi7 F mi7 G mi7 F mi7 C mi9 C mi7 E♭ F E♭

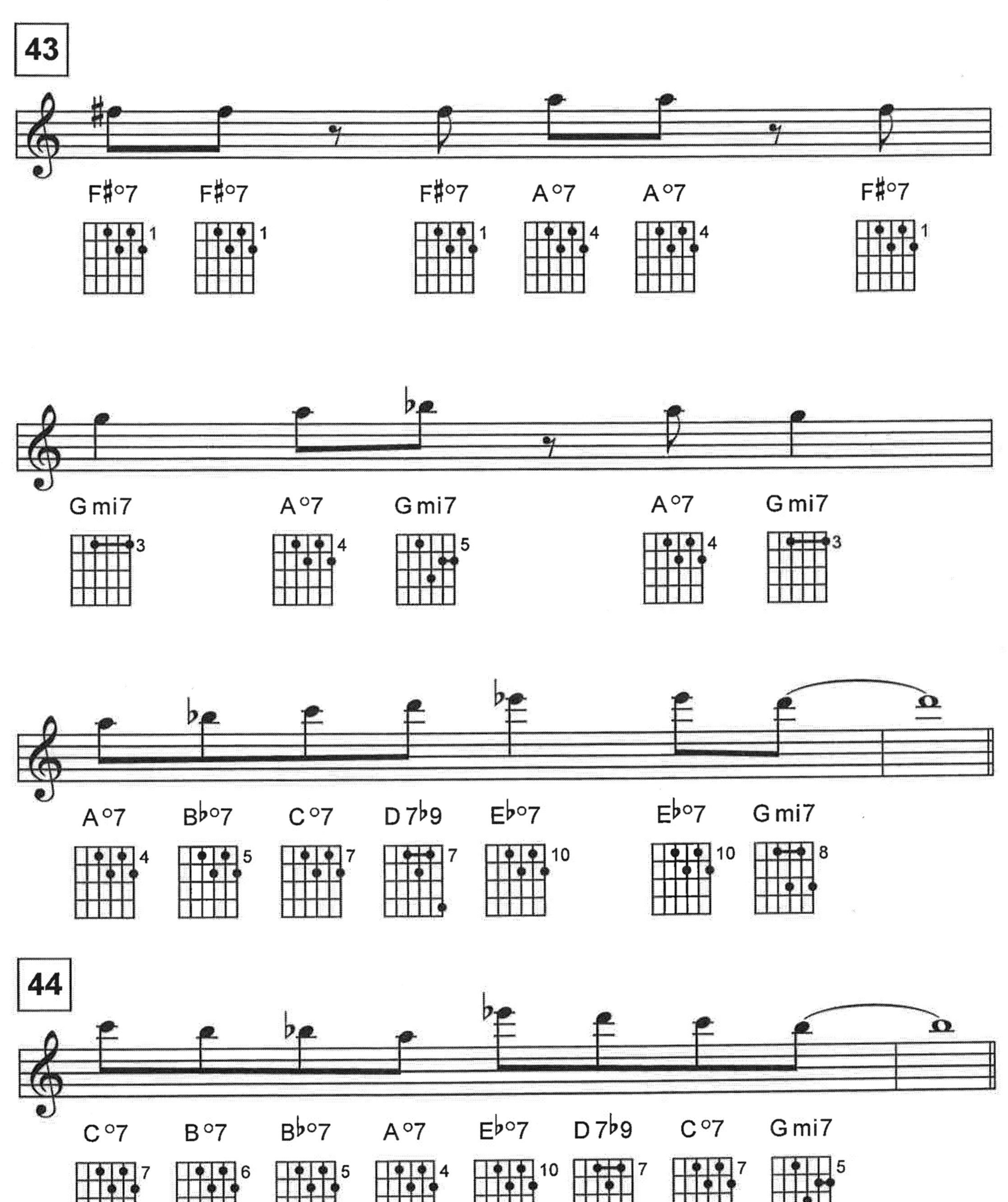

43
F#°7   F#°7   F#°7   A°7   A°7   F#°7
G mi7   A°7   G mi7   A°7   G mi7
A°7   B♭°7   C°7   D 7♭9   E♭°7   E♭°7   G mi7
44
C°7   B°7   B♭°7   A°7   E♭°7   D 7♭9   C°7   G mi7

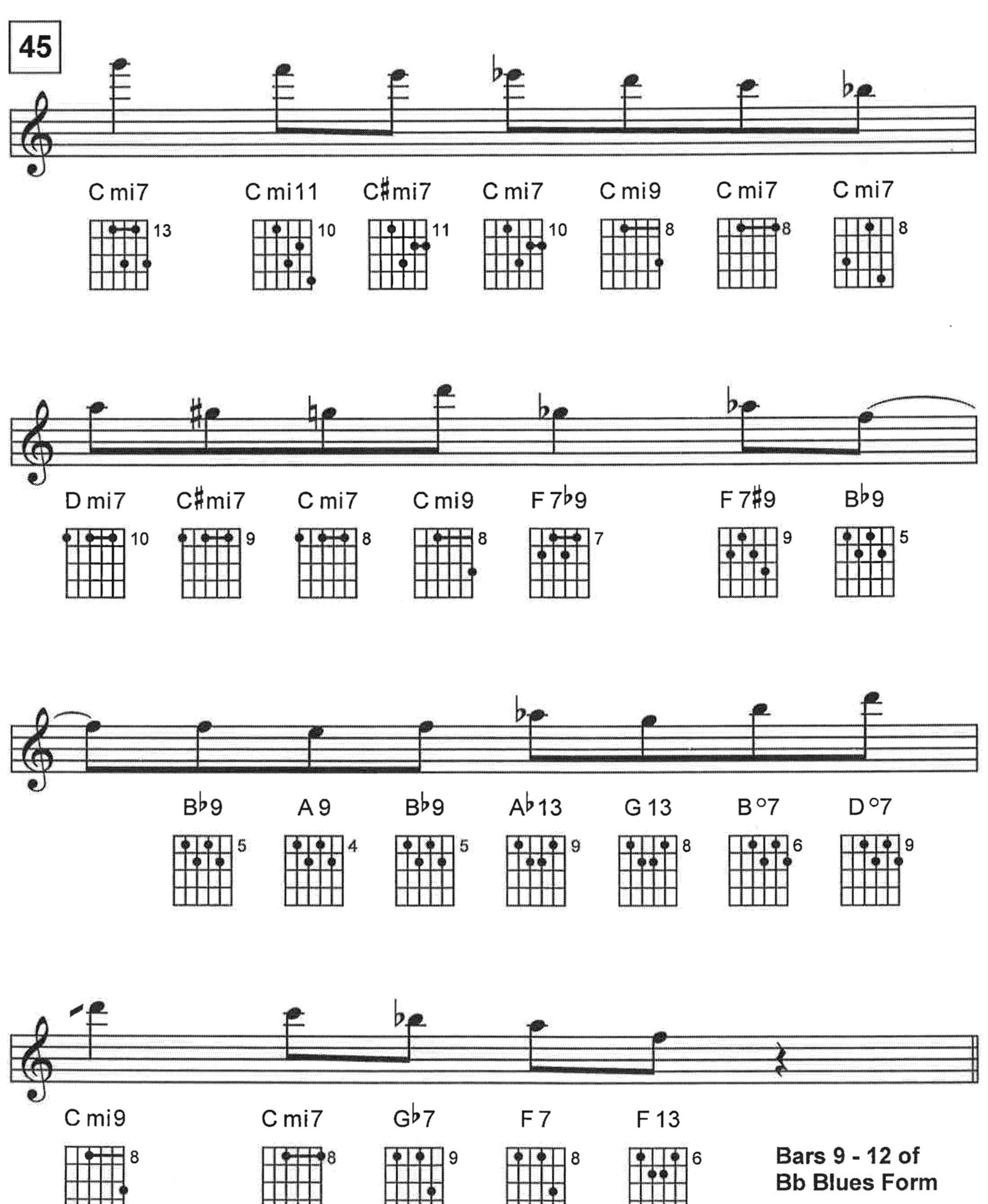

45

C mi7   C mi11   C#mi7   C mi7   C mi9   C mi7   C mi7
13   10   11   10   8   8   8

D mi7   C#mi7   C mi7   C mi9   F 7b9   F 7#9   Bb9
10   9   8   8   7   9   5

Bb9   A 9   Bb9   Ab13   G 13   B °7   D °7
5   4   5   9   8   6   9

C mi9   C mi7   Gb7   F 7   F 13
8   8   9   8   6

Bars 9 - 12 of
Bb Blues Form

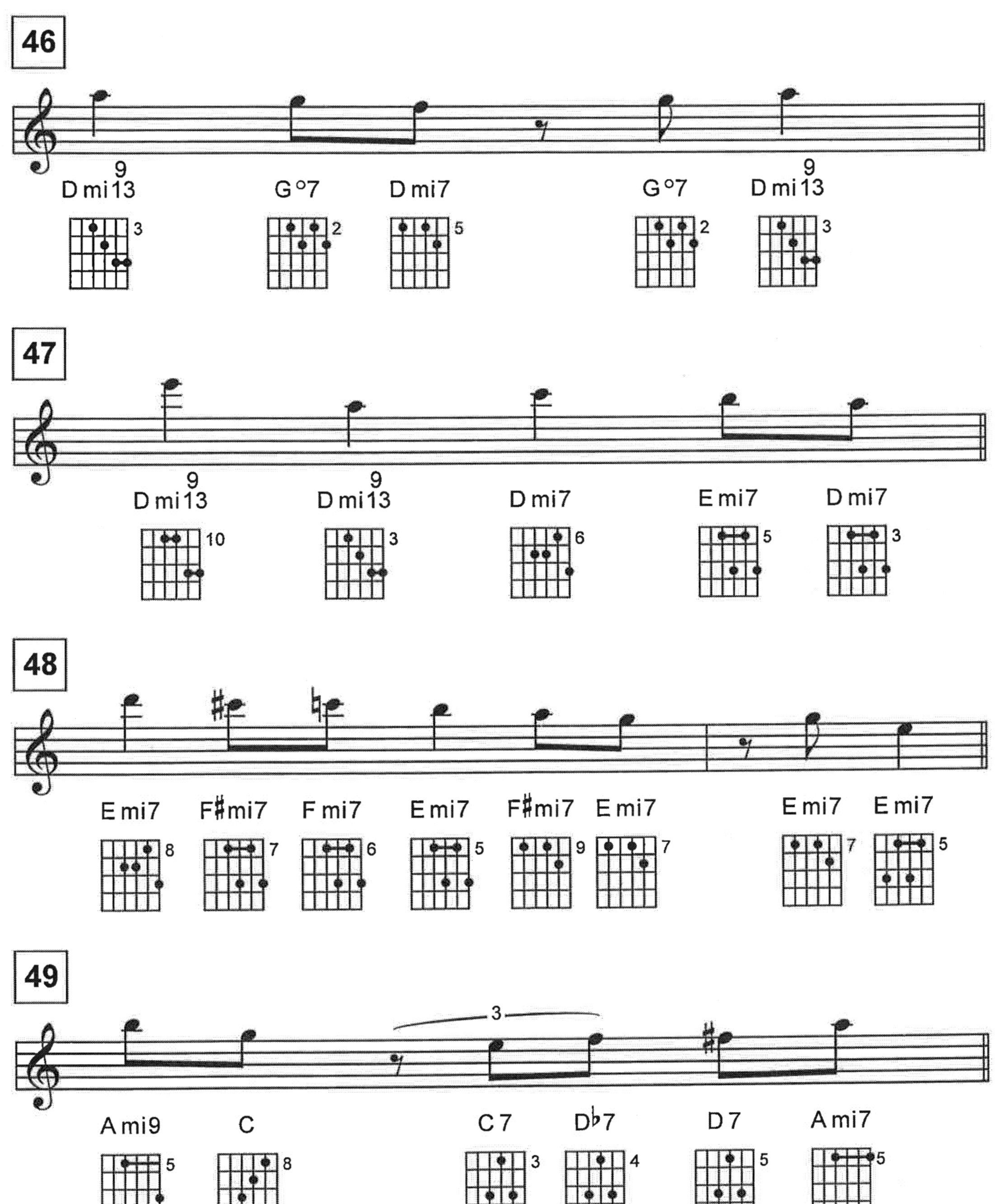

46
D mi13
G°7
D mi7
G°7
D mi13
3
2
5
2
3
9
9
47
D mi13
D mi13
D mi7
E mi7
D mi7
10
3
6
5
3
9
9
48
E mi7
F#mi7
F mi7
E mi7
F#mi7
E mi7
E mi7
E mi7
8
7
6
5
9
7
7
5
49
A mi9
C
C 7
Db7
D 7
A mi7
5
8
3
4
5
5
3

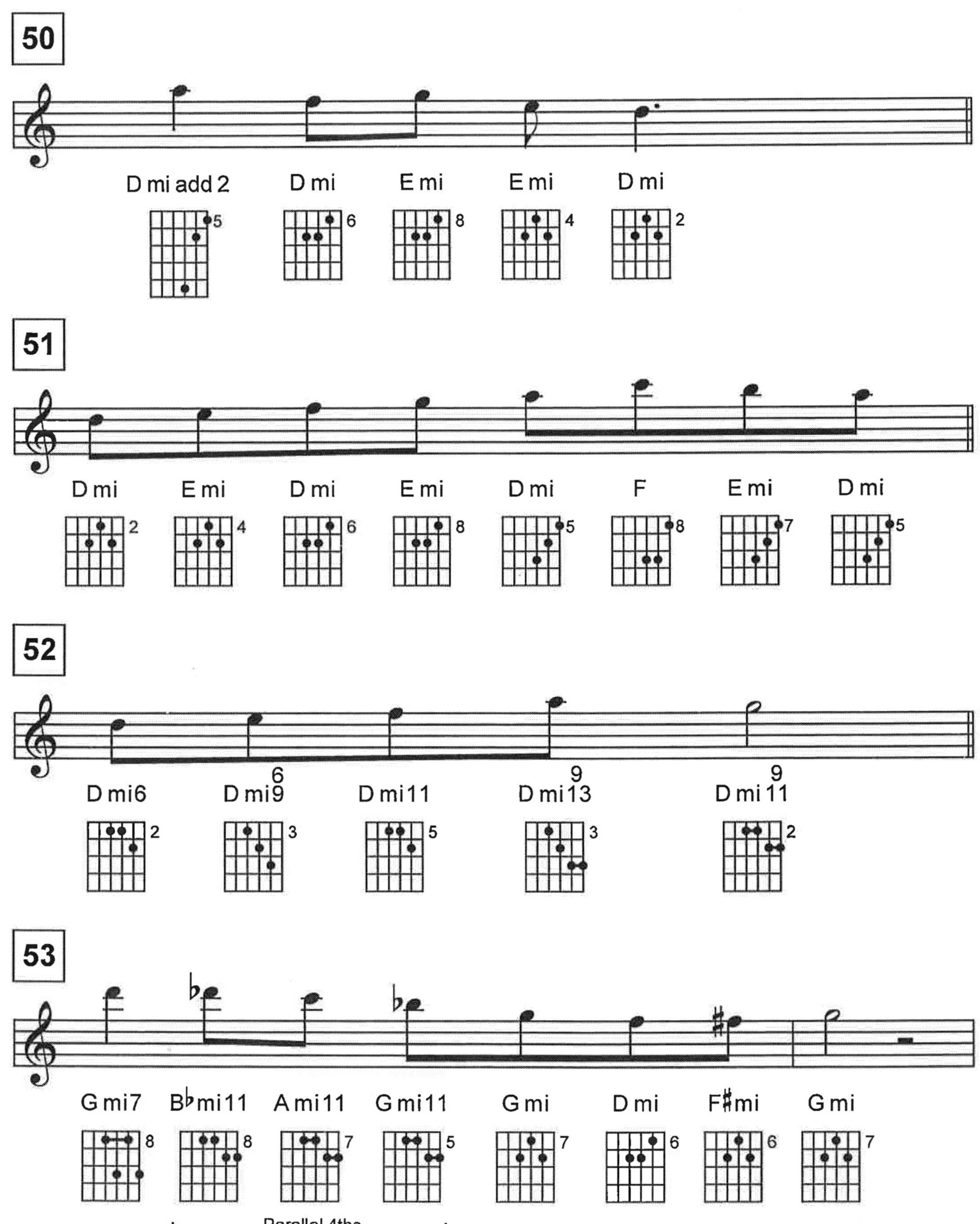
50
D mi add 2   D mi   E mi   E mi   D mi

51
D mi   E mi   D mi   E mi   D mi   F   E mi   D mi

52
D mi6   D mi9   D mi11   D mi13   D mi11

53
G mi7   B♭mi11   A mi11   G mi11   G mi   D mi   F#mi   G mi
Parallel 4ths

Phrases In Major

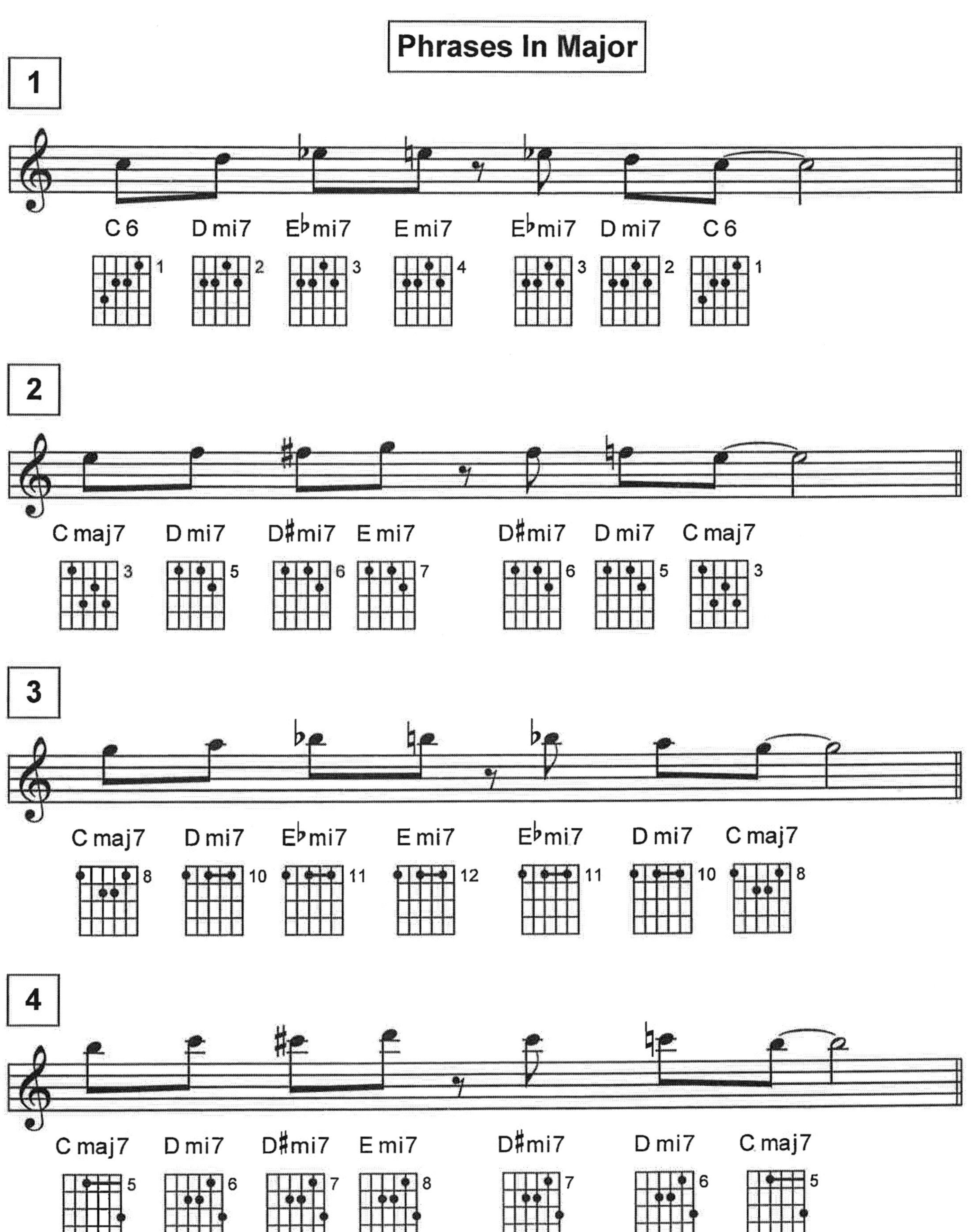

5
F maj7
A mi11
B♭ mi7
A mi7
G mi7
A °7
10
7
8
7
5
4
G mi7
B♭
B♭7
B 7
C 7
C 9
3
6
1
2
3
7
6
C maj9
C maj9
C 6
C 6
2
5
7
10
Alternating parallel forms
7
C maj9
D mi7
C maj9
C 6
D mi7
C 6
2
3
5
7
10
10
Alternating I and ii

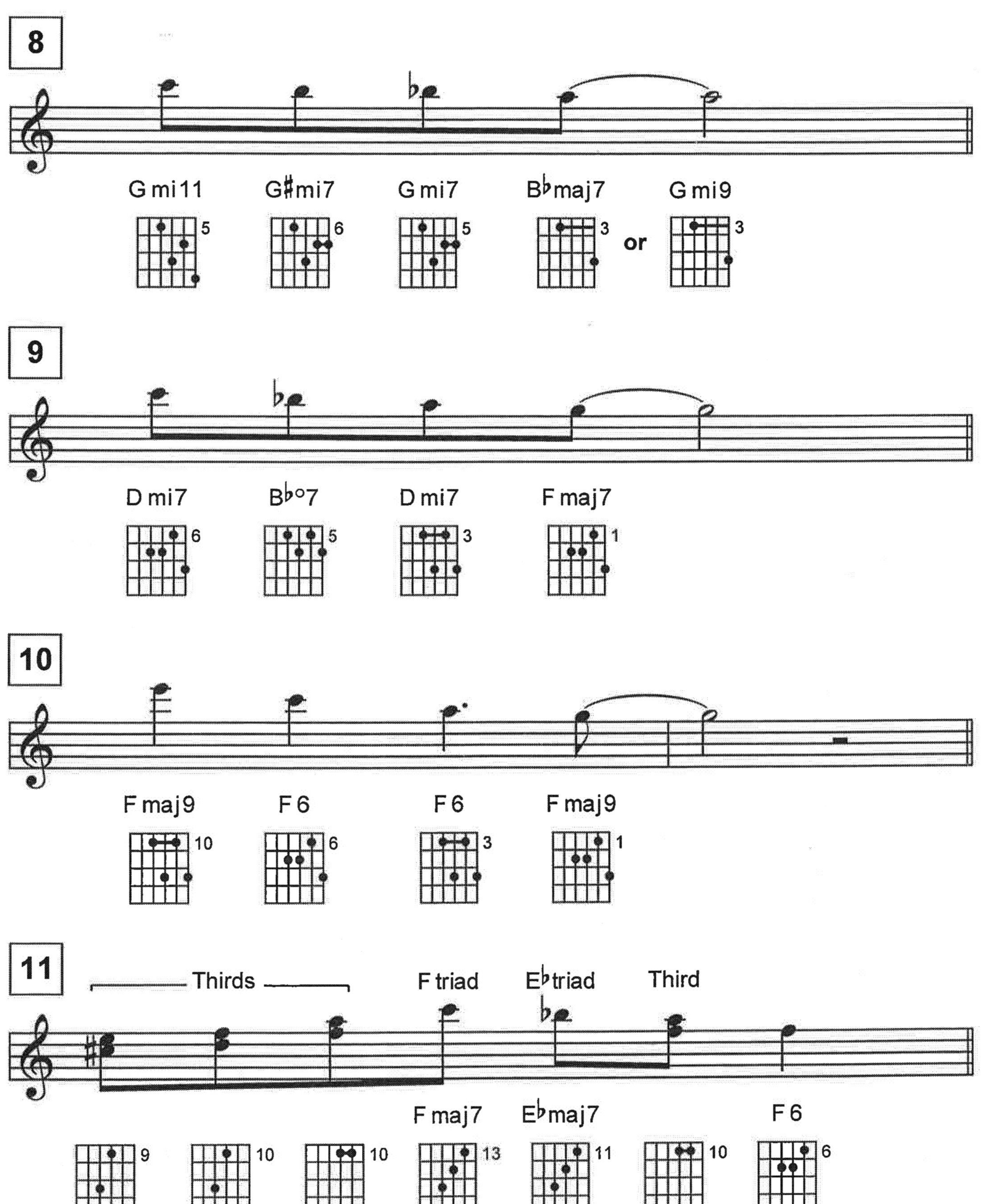

8
G mi11
G#mi7
G mi7
Bbmaj7
or
G mi9
5
6
5
3
3

9
D mi7
Bbo7
D mi7
F maj7
6
5
3
1

10
F maj9
F 6
F 6
F maj9
10
6
3
1

11
Thirds
F triad
Eb triad
Third
F maj7
Ebmaj7
F 6
9
10
10
13
11
10
6

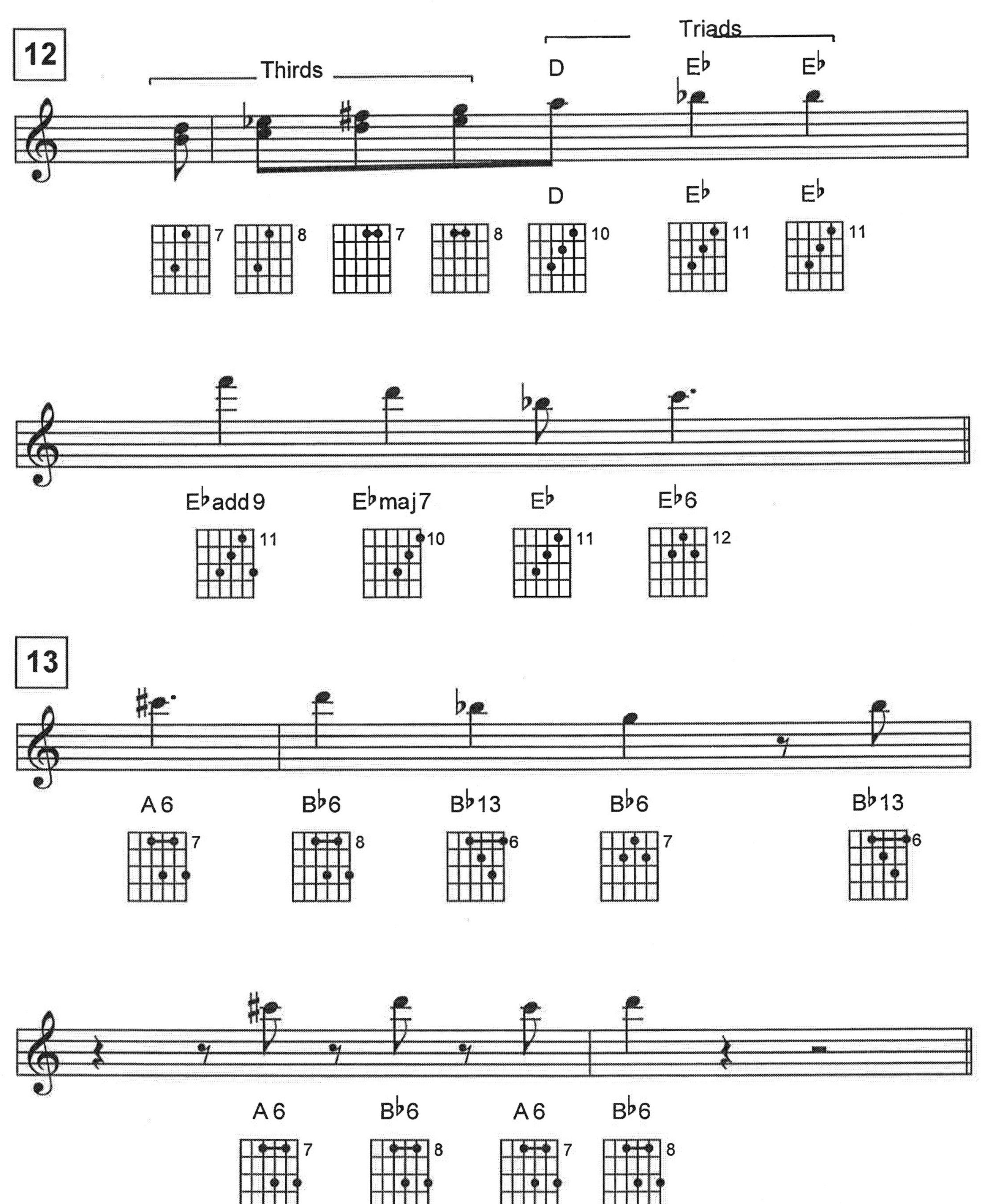

12
Thirds
Triads
D
E♭
E♭
D
E♭
E♭
7 8 7 8 10 11 11
E♭add9
E♭maj7
E♭
E♭6
11 10 11 12
13
A6
B♭6
B♭13
B♭6
B♭13
7 8 6 7 6
A6
B♭6
A6
B♭6
7 8 7 8

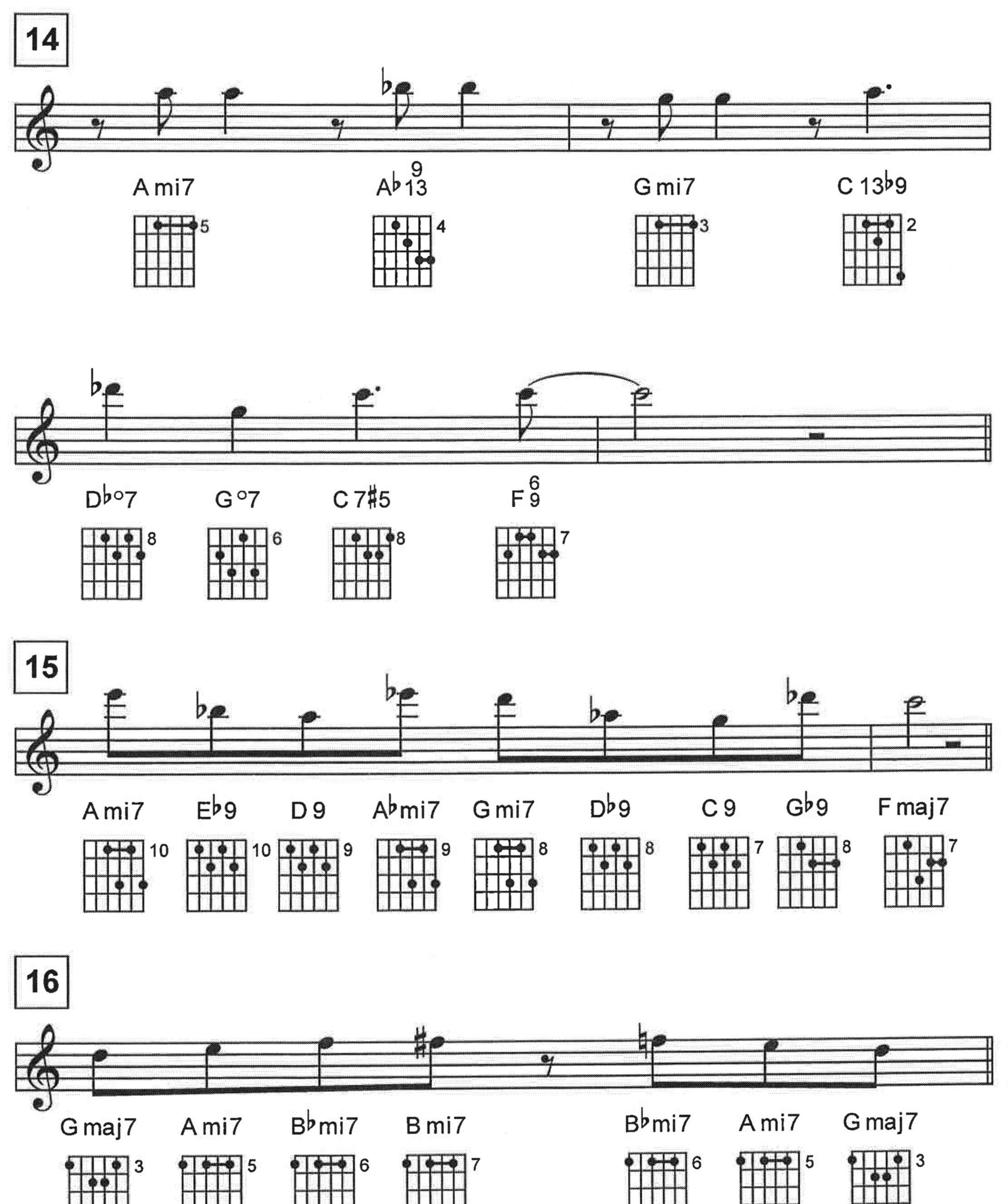

14
A mi7
Ab13 9
G mi7
C 13b9
Db o7
G o7
C 7#5
F 9 6
15
A mi7
Eb9
D 9
Ab mi7
G mi7
Db9
C 9
Gb9
F maj7
16
G maj7
A mi7
Bb mi7
B mi7
Bb mi7
A mi7
G maj7

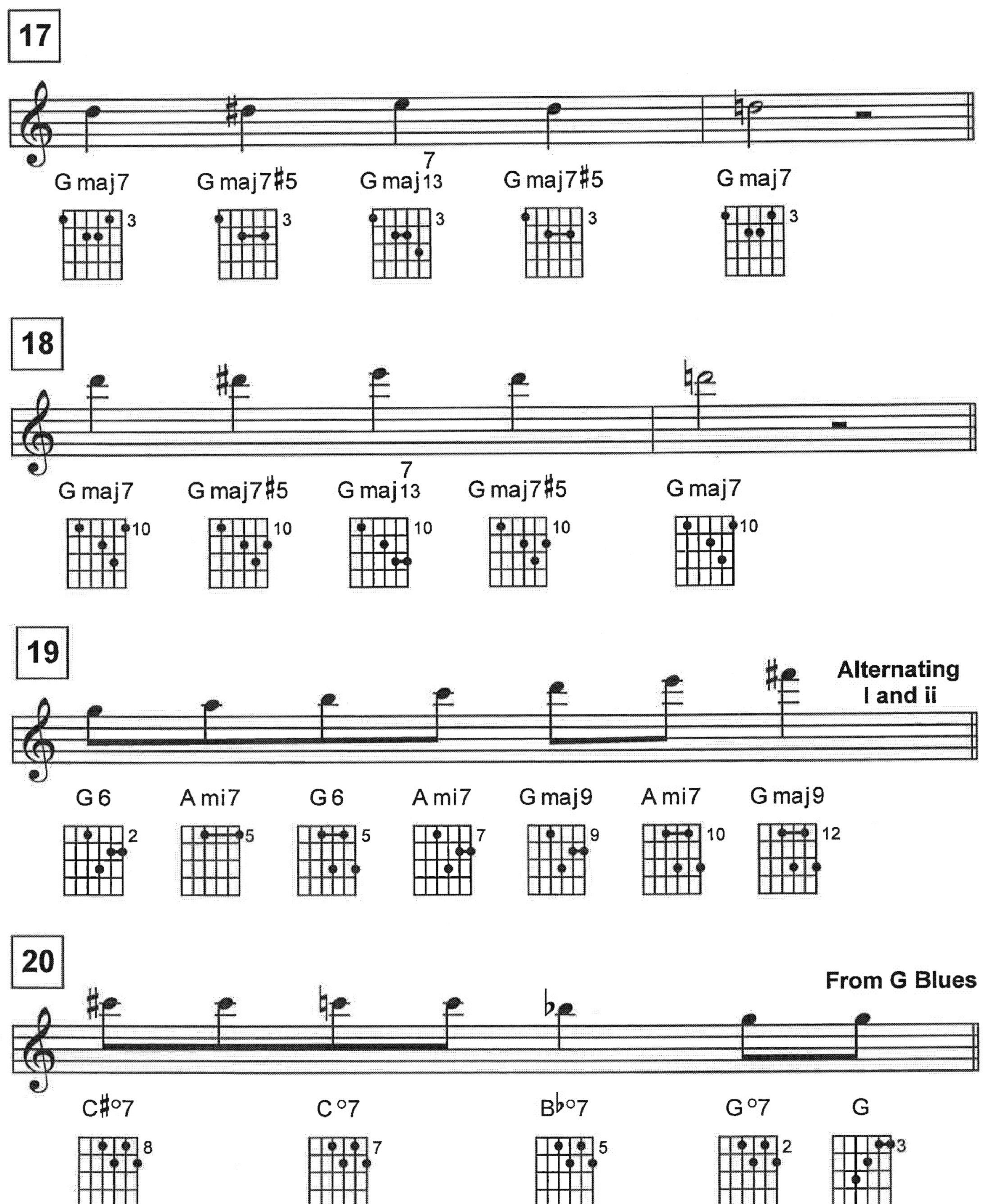

17
G maj7
G maj7#5
G maj13
G maj7#5
G maj7
18
G maj7
G maj7#5
G maj13
G maj7#5
G maj7
19
Alternating I and ii
G 6
A mi7
G 6
A mi7
G maj9
A mi7
G maj9
20
From G Blues
C#°7
C °7
Bb°7
G °7
G

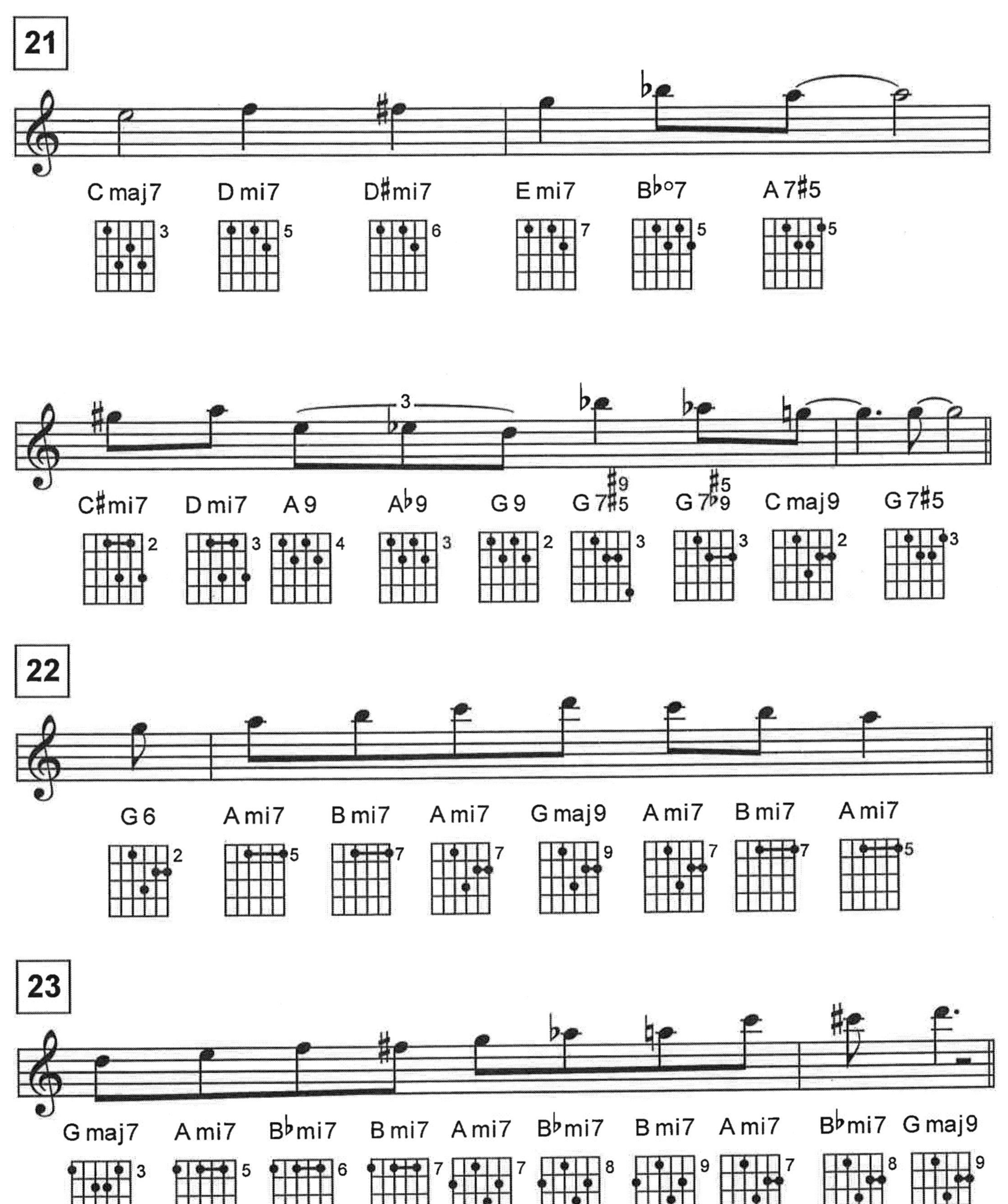

21
C maj7   D mi7   D#mi7   E mi7   Bb°7   A 7#5
C#mi7   D mi7   A 9   Ab9   G 9   G 7#5   G 7b9#5   C maj9   G 7#5
22
G 6   A mi7   B mi7   A mi7   G maj9   A mi7   B mi7   A mi7
23
G maj7   A mi7   Bbmi7   B mi7   A mi7   Bbmi7   B mi7   A mi7   Bbmi7   G maj9

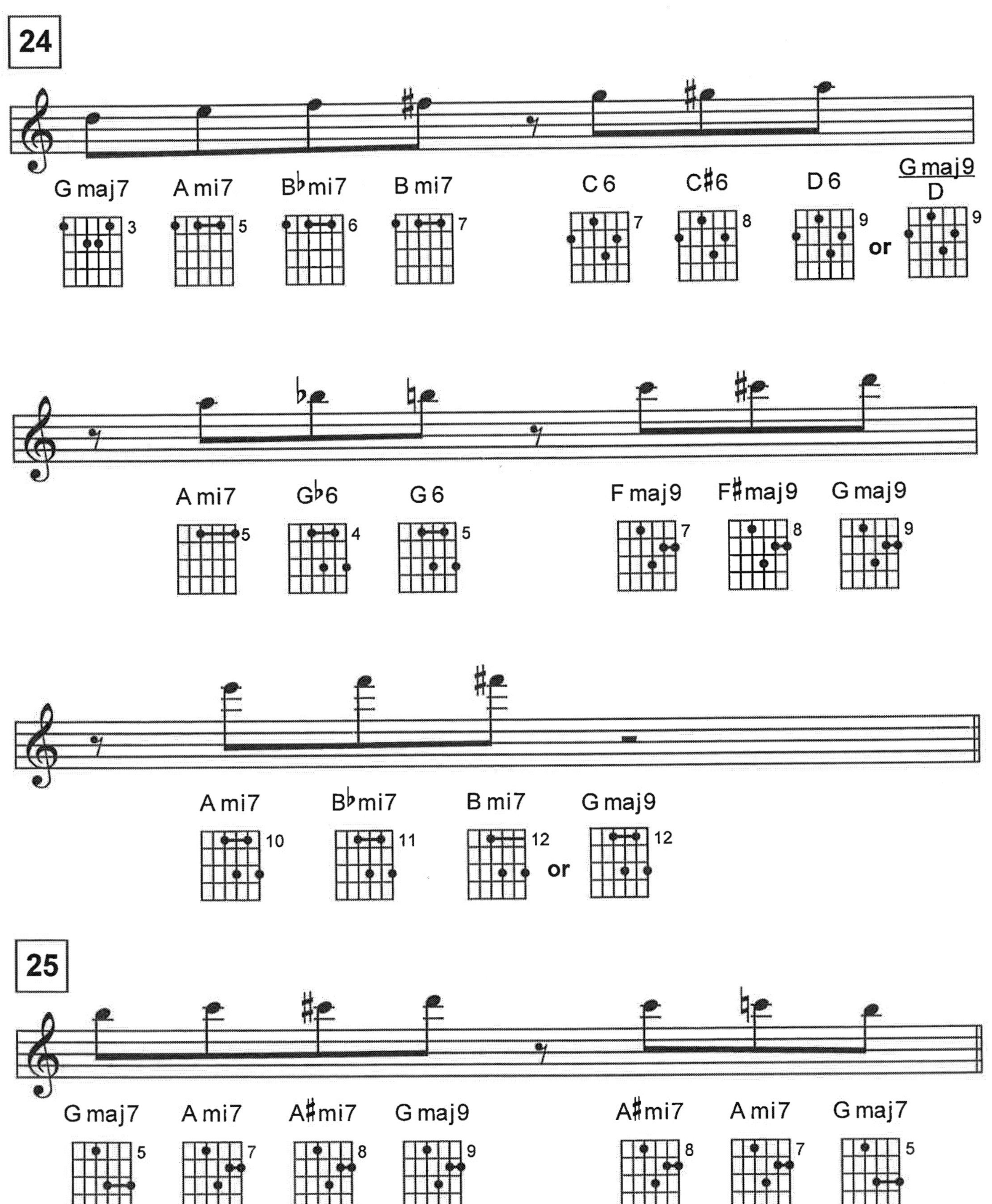
24
G maj7   A mi7   B♭mi7   B mi7   C 6   C#6   D 6   G maj9 / D
3   5   6   7   7   8   9   or   9
A mi7   G♭6   G 6   F maj9   F#maj9   G maj9
5   4   5   7   8   9
A mi7   B♭mi7   B mi7   G maj9
10   11   12   or   12
25
G maj7   A mi7   A#mi7   G maj9   A#mi7   A mi7   G maj7
5   7   8   9   8   7   5

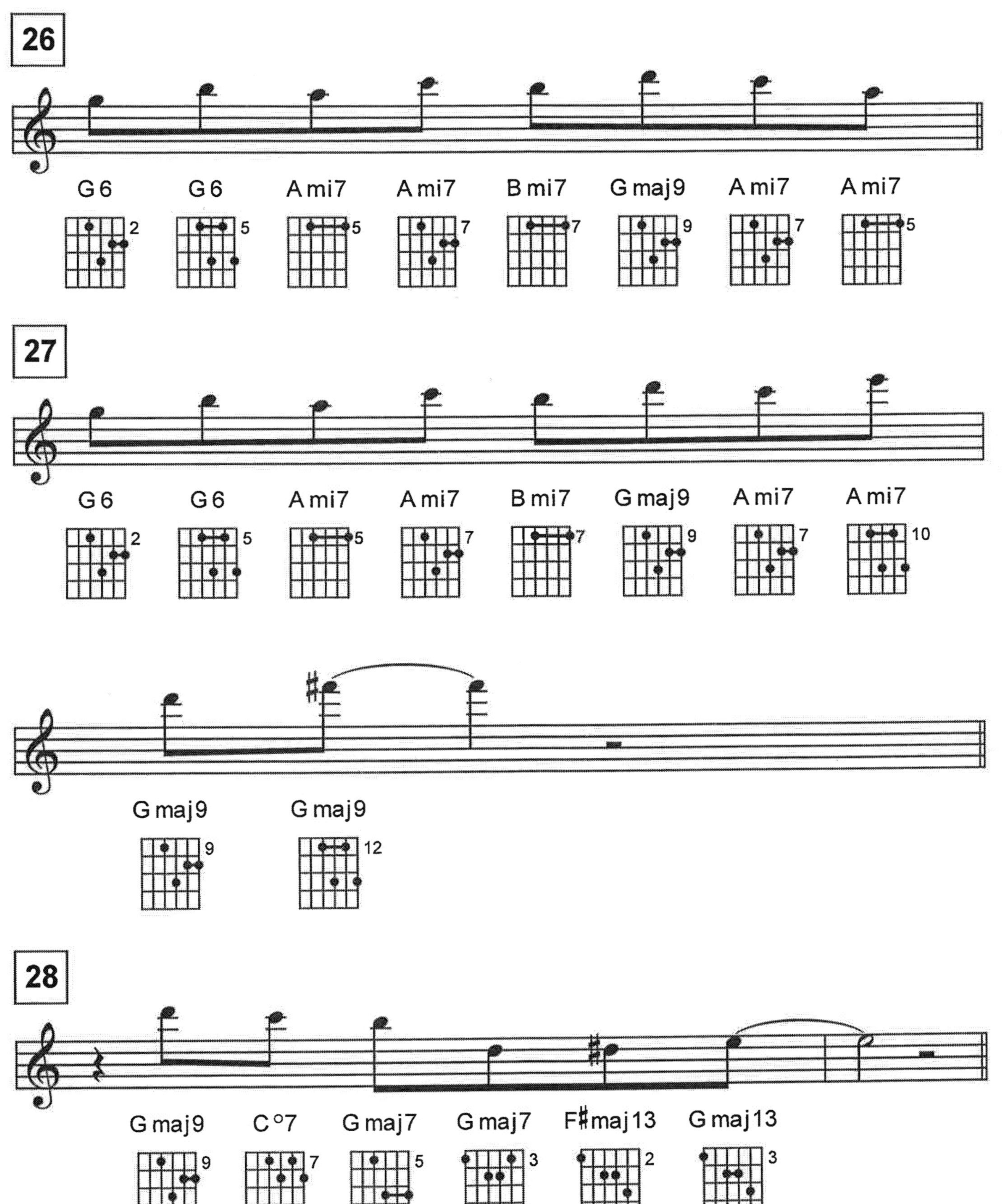
26
G 6   G 6   A mi7   A mi7   B mi7   G maj9   A mi7   A mi7
2   5   5   7   7   9   7   5

27
G 6   G 6   A mi7   A mi7   B mi7   G maj9   A mi7   A mi7
2   5   5   7   7   9   7   10

G maj9   G maj9
9   12

28
G maj9   C°7   G maj7   G maj7   F#maj13   G maj13
9   7   5   3   2   3

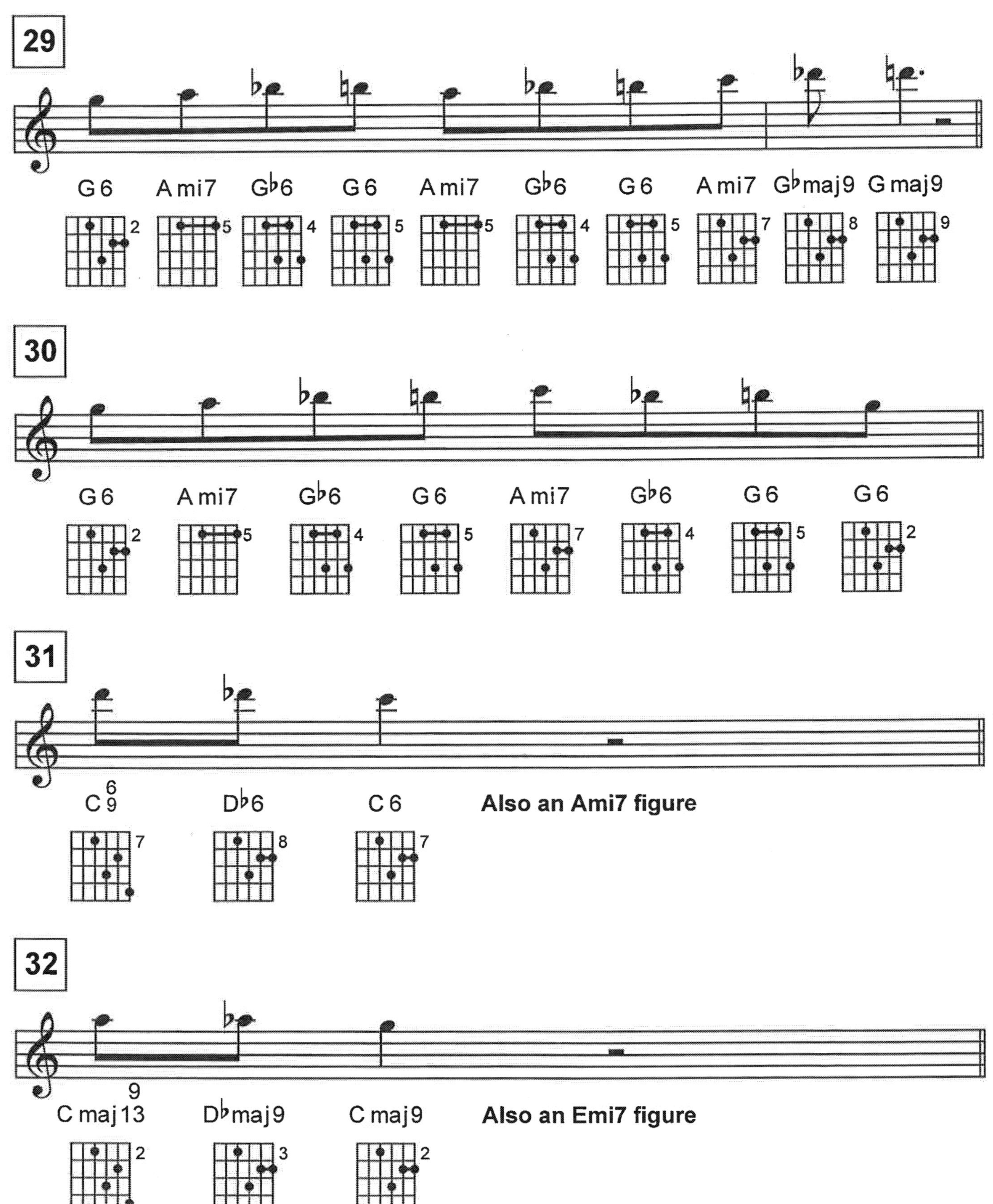

29

G 6   A mi7   G♭6   G 6   A mi7   G♭6   G 6   A mi7   G♭maj9   G maj9

30

G 6   A mi7   G♭6   G 6   A mi7   G♭6   G 6   G 6

31

C 6/9   D♭6   C 6   Also an Ami7 figure

32

C maj13   D♭maj9   C maj9   Also an Emi7 figure

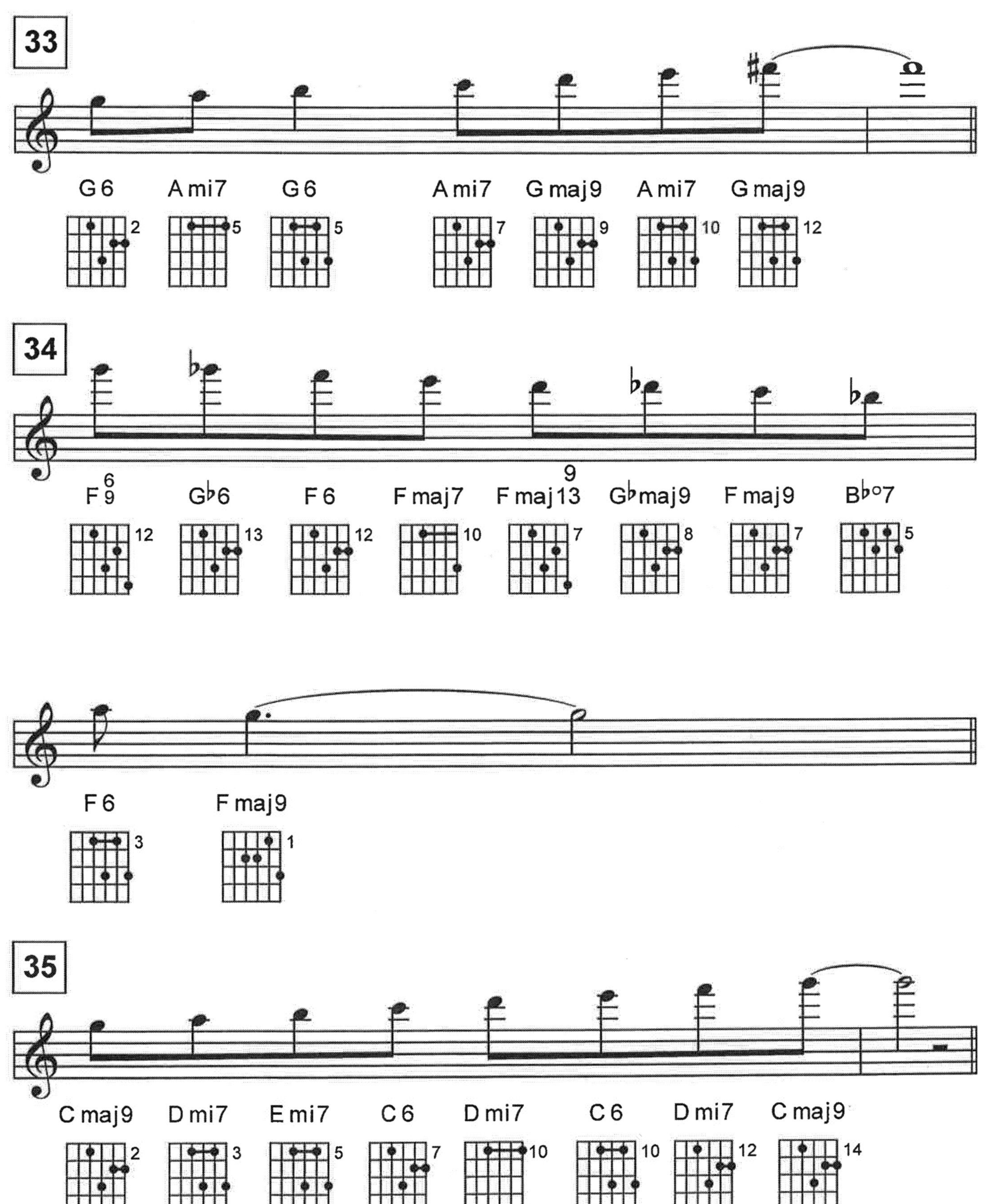

33
G 6   A mi7   G 6   A mi7   G maj9   A mi7   G maj9
2   5   5   7   9   10   12

34
F 6/9   G♭6   F 6   F maj7   F maj13/9   G♭maj9   F maj9   B♭°7
12   13   12   10   7   8   7   5

F 6   F maj9
3   1

35
C maj9   D mi7   E mi7   C 6   D mi7   C 6   D mi7   C maj9
2   3   5   7   10   10   12   14

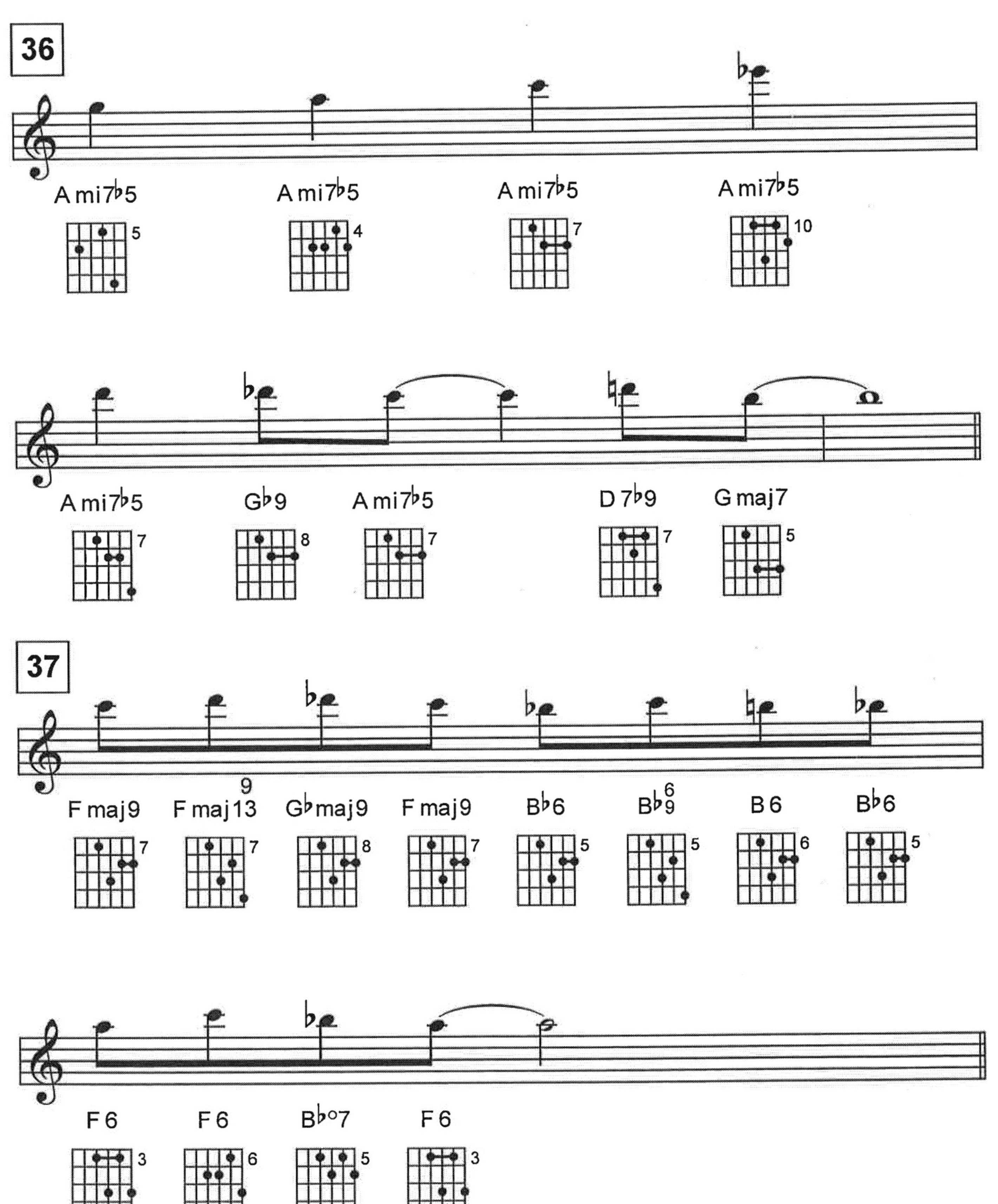

36
A mi7♭5   A mi7♭5   A mi7♭5   A mi7♭5
5   4   7   10
A mi7♭5   G♭9   A mi7♭5   D 7♭9   G maj7
7   8   7   7   5
37
F maj9   F maj13   G♭maj9   F maj9   B♭6   B♭9/6   B 6   B♭6
7   7   8   7   5   5   6   5
9
F 6   F 6   B♭°7   F 6
3   6   5   3

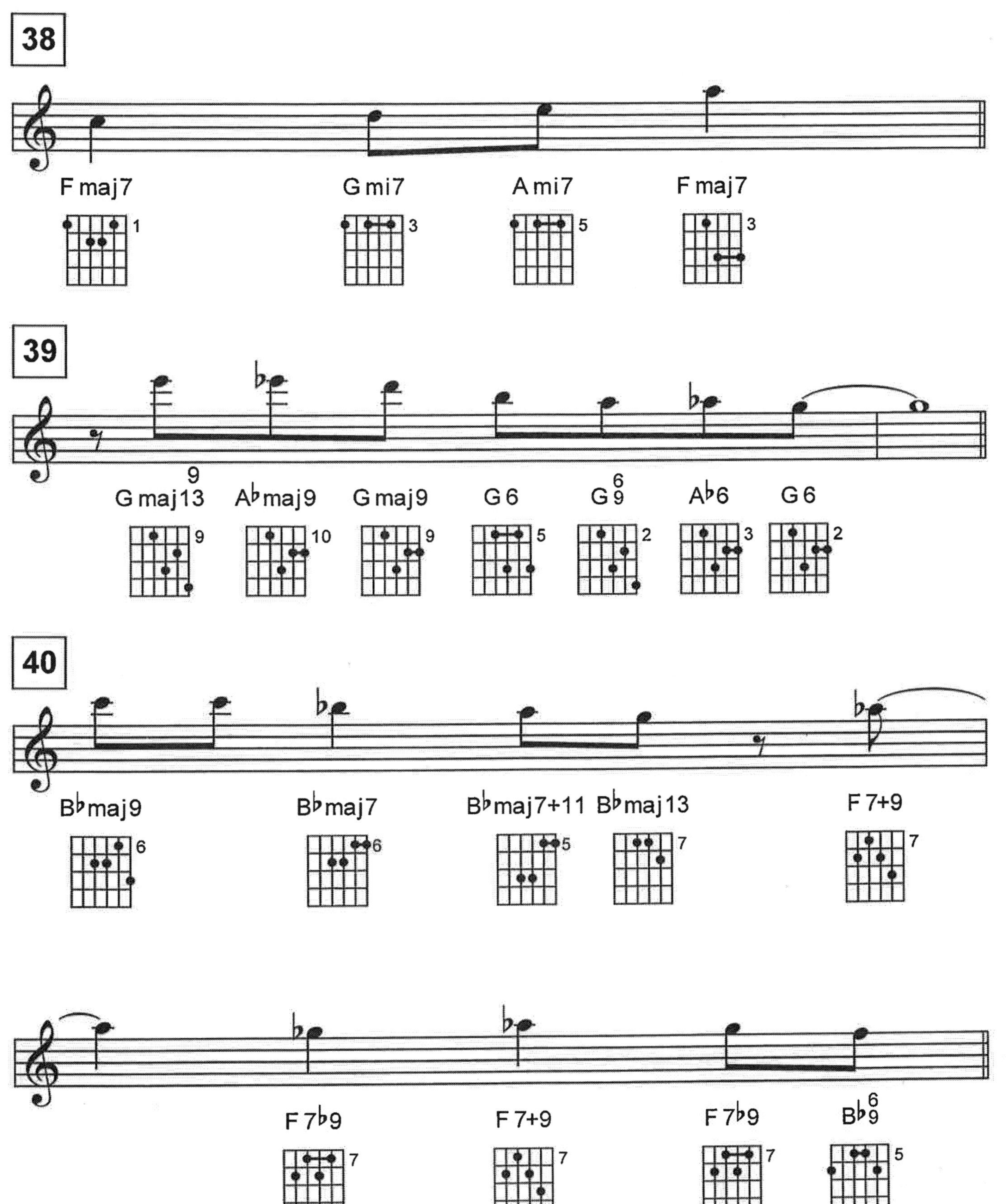

38
F maj7   G mi7   A mi7   F maj7
1   3   5   3

39
G maj13   A♭maj9   G maj9   G 6   G 6/9   A♭6   G 6
9   10   9   5   2   3   2

40
B♭maj9   B♭maj7   B♭maj7+11   B♭maj13   F 7+9
6   6   5   7   7

F 7♭9   F 7+9   F 7♭9   B♭6/9
7   7   7   5

41
A mi9   A mi7   A mi9   A mi7   A mi7
B mi7   A mi7   D 7♭9   G maj7
42
G maj9   G maj7   G maj7+11   C 7   B mi7   F 13   E 13
A mi7   A mi9   A mi7   A mi11   D 7#9#5   D 7♭9#5   G maj9

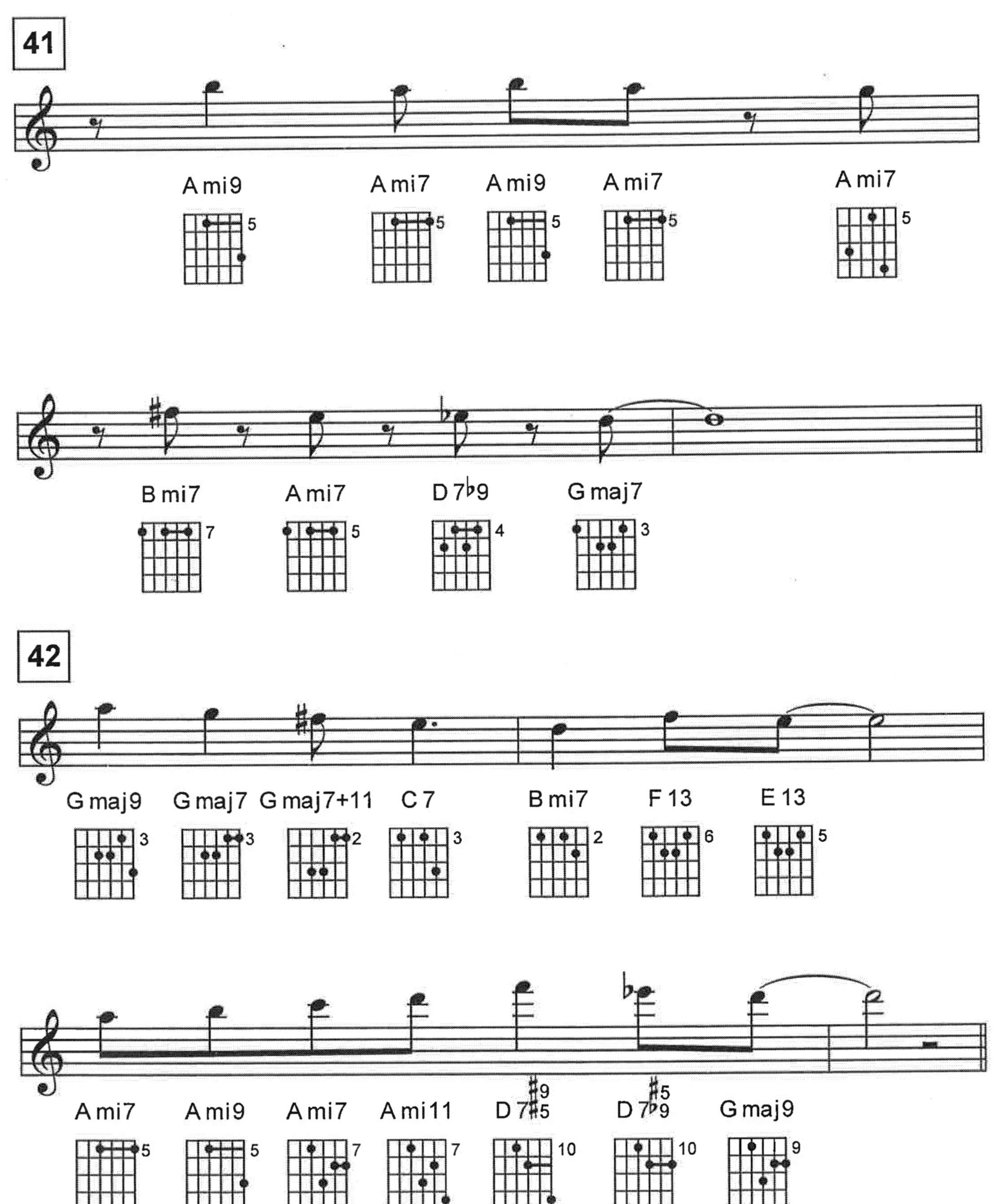

72

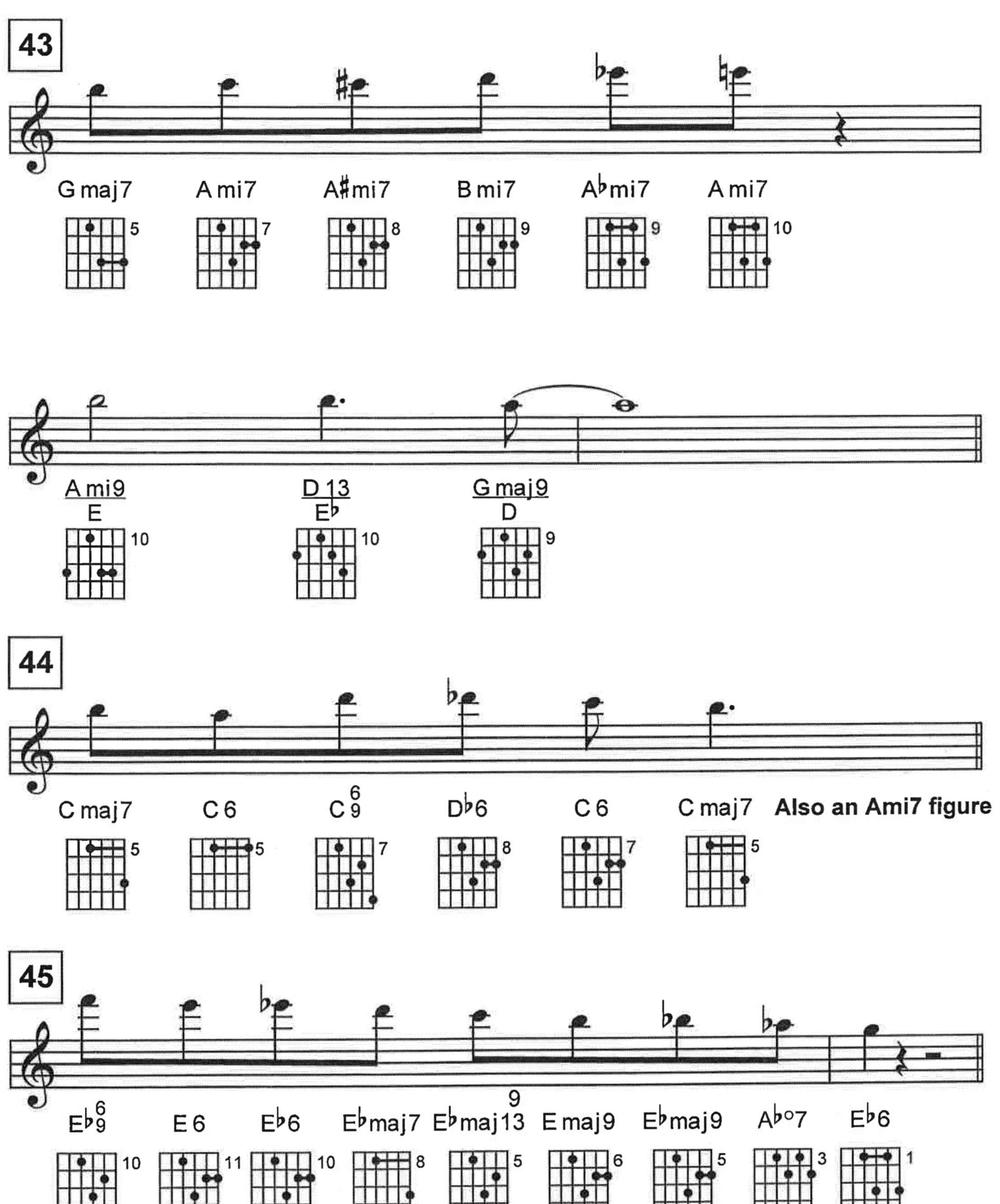
43
G maj7   A mi7   A#mi7   B mi7   Abmi7   A mi7
A mi9   D 13   G maj9
E   Eb   D
44
C maj7   C 6   C 6/9   Db6   C 6   C maj7   Also an Ami7 figure
45
Eb 6/9   E 6   Eb 6   Ebmaj7   Ebmaj13   E maj9   Ebmaj9   Abo7   Eb6

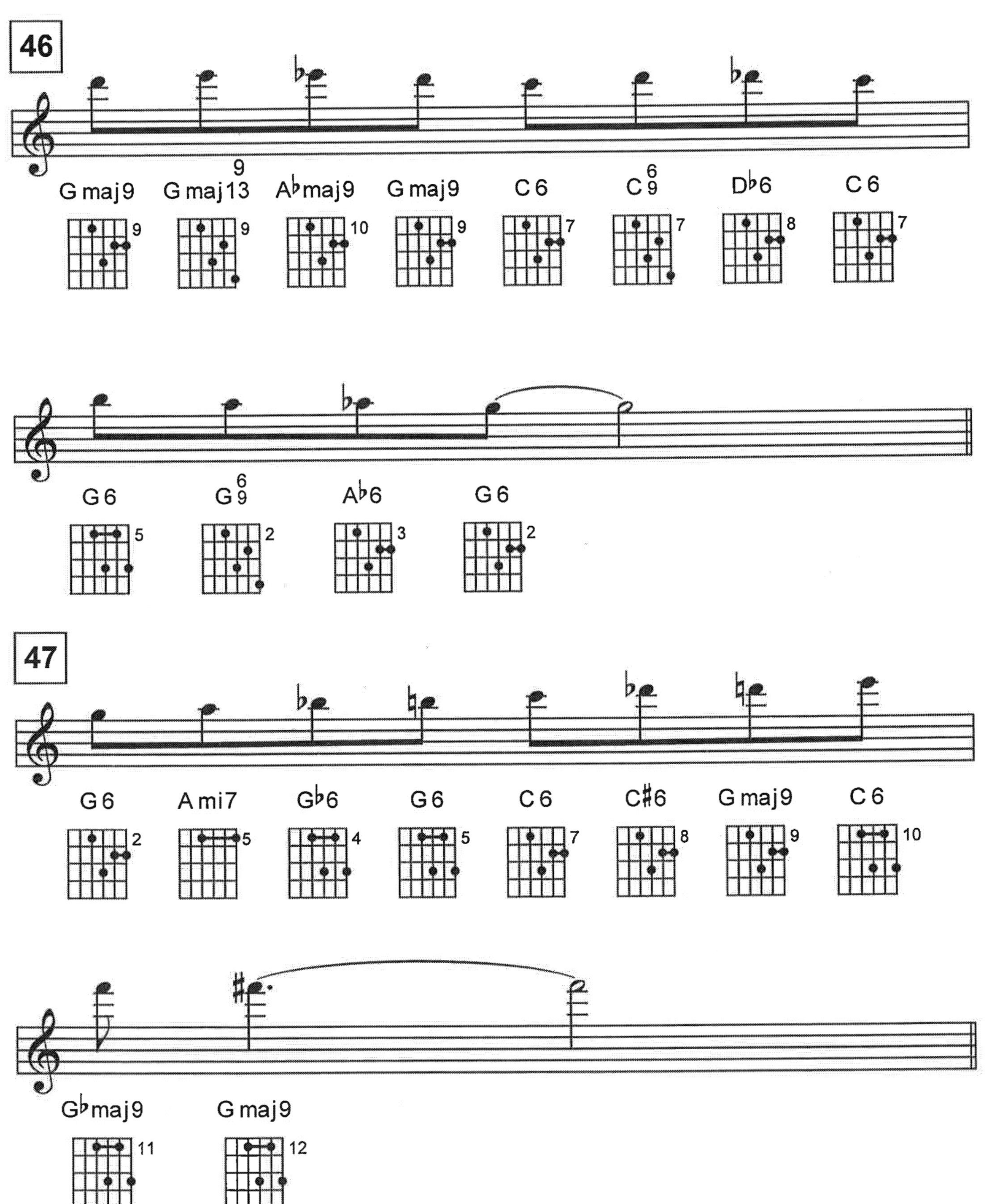

46
G maj9   G maj13   A♭maj9   G maj9   C 6   C 6/9   D♭6   C 6
G 6   G 6/9   A♭6   G 6
47
G 6   A mi7   G♭6   G 6   C 6   C#6   G maj9   C 6
G♭maj9   G maj9

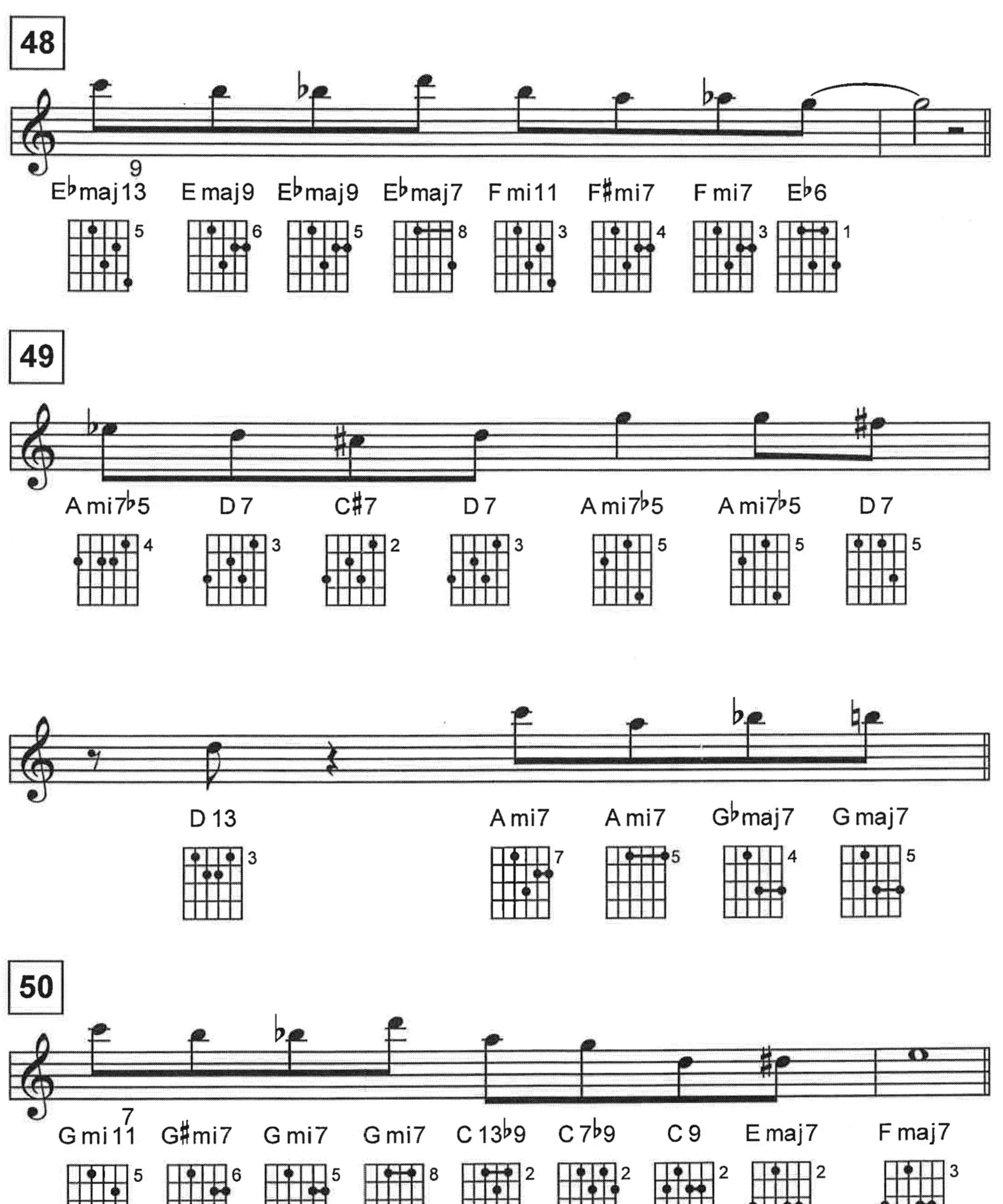
48
Ebmaj13   Emaj9   Ebmaj9   Ebmaj7   Fmi11   F#mi7   Fmi7   Eb6
49
Ami7b5   D7   C#7   D7   Ami7b5   Ami7b5   D7
D13   Ami7   Ami7   Gbmaj7   Gmaj7
50
Gmi11   G#mi7   Gmi7   Gmi7   C13b9   C7b9   C9   Emaj7   Fmaj7

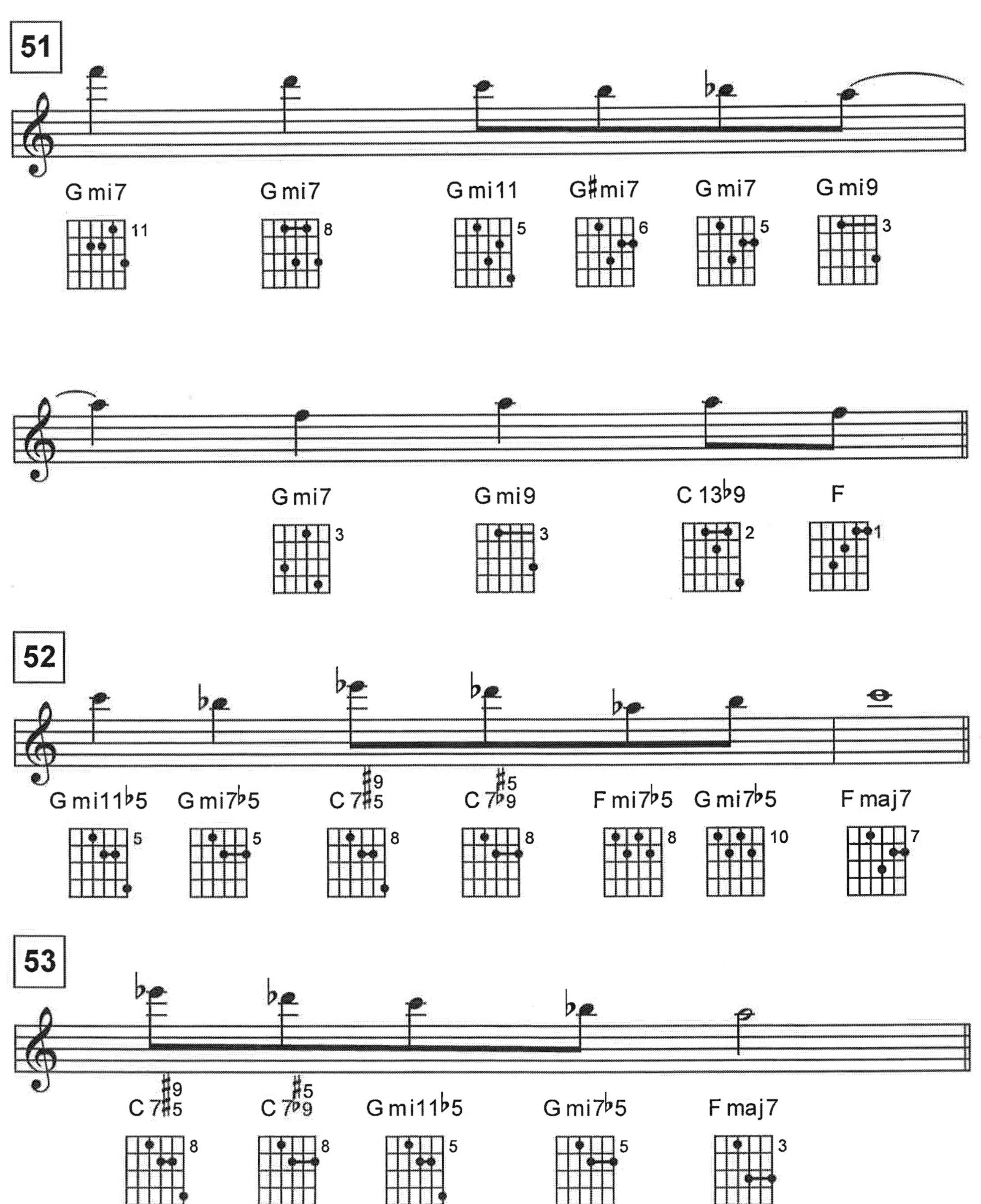
51
G mi7   G mi7   G mi11   G#mi7   G mi7   G mi9
11   8   5   6   5   3
G mi7   G mi9   C 13b9   F
3   3   2   1
52
G mi11b5   G mi7b5   C 7#5 #9   C 7#5 b9   F mi7b5   G mi7b5   F maj7
5   5   8   8   8   10   7
53
C 7#5 #9   C 7#5 b9   G mi11b5   G mi7b5   F maj7
8   8   5   5   3

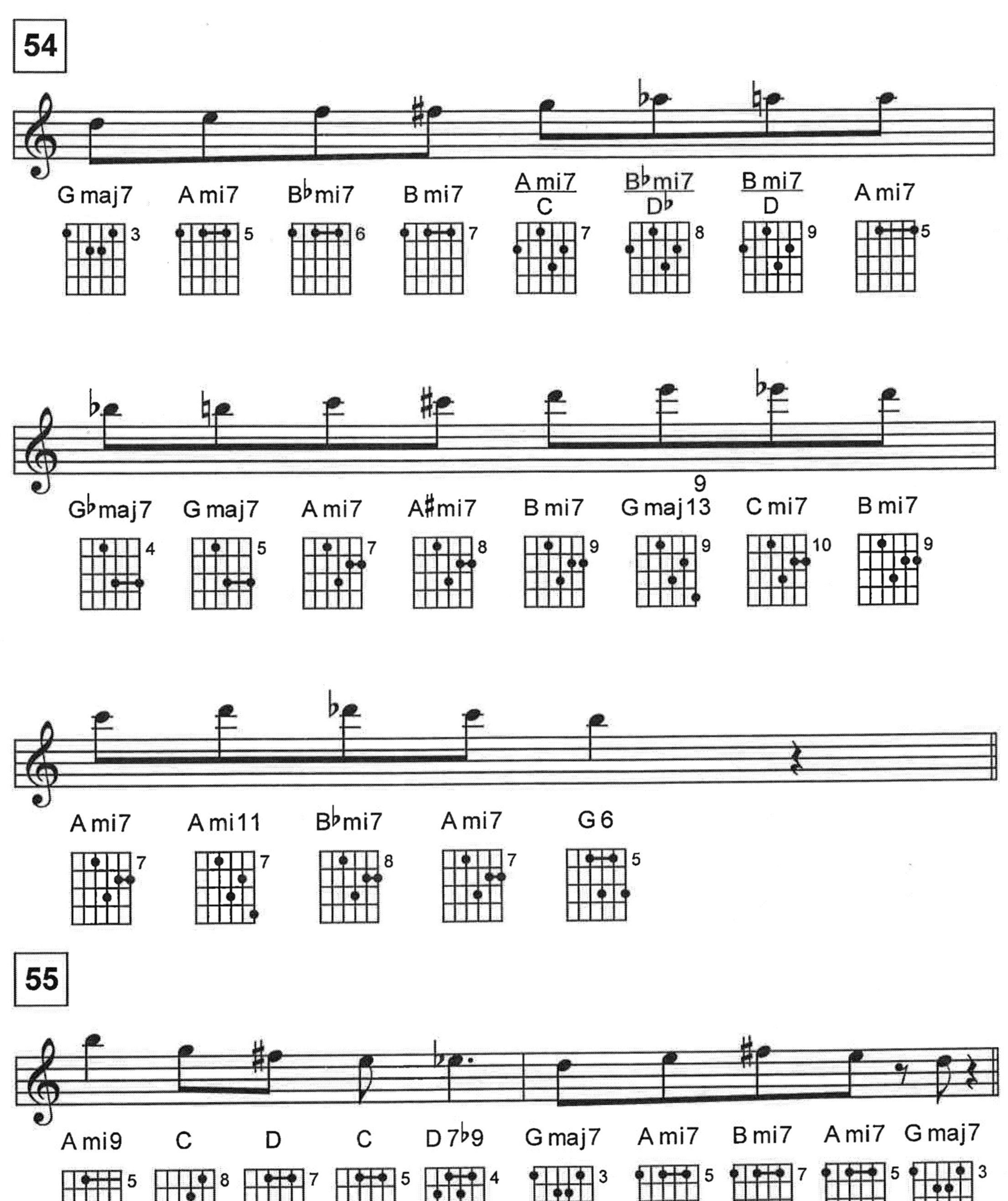

54
G maj7   A mi7   B♭mi7   B mi7   A mi7/C   B♭mi7/D♭   B mi7/D   A mi7
G♭maj7   G maj7   A mi7   A#mi7   B mi7   G maj13   C mi7   B mi7
A mi7   A mi11   B♭mi7   A mi7   G 6
55
A mi9   C   D   C   D 7♭9   G maj7   A mi7   B mi7   A mi7   G maj7

56
D mi9
D mi7
E mi7
E♭mi7
D mi7
G 7♭9
C maj7
57
B °7
A mi7
C
D 9
A mi7
G maj7
A mi7
G maj7
58
B♭13 9
B♭9
D °7
E♭maj9
A♭°7
A♭°7
E♭6

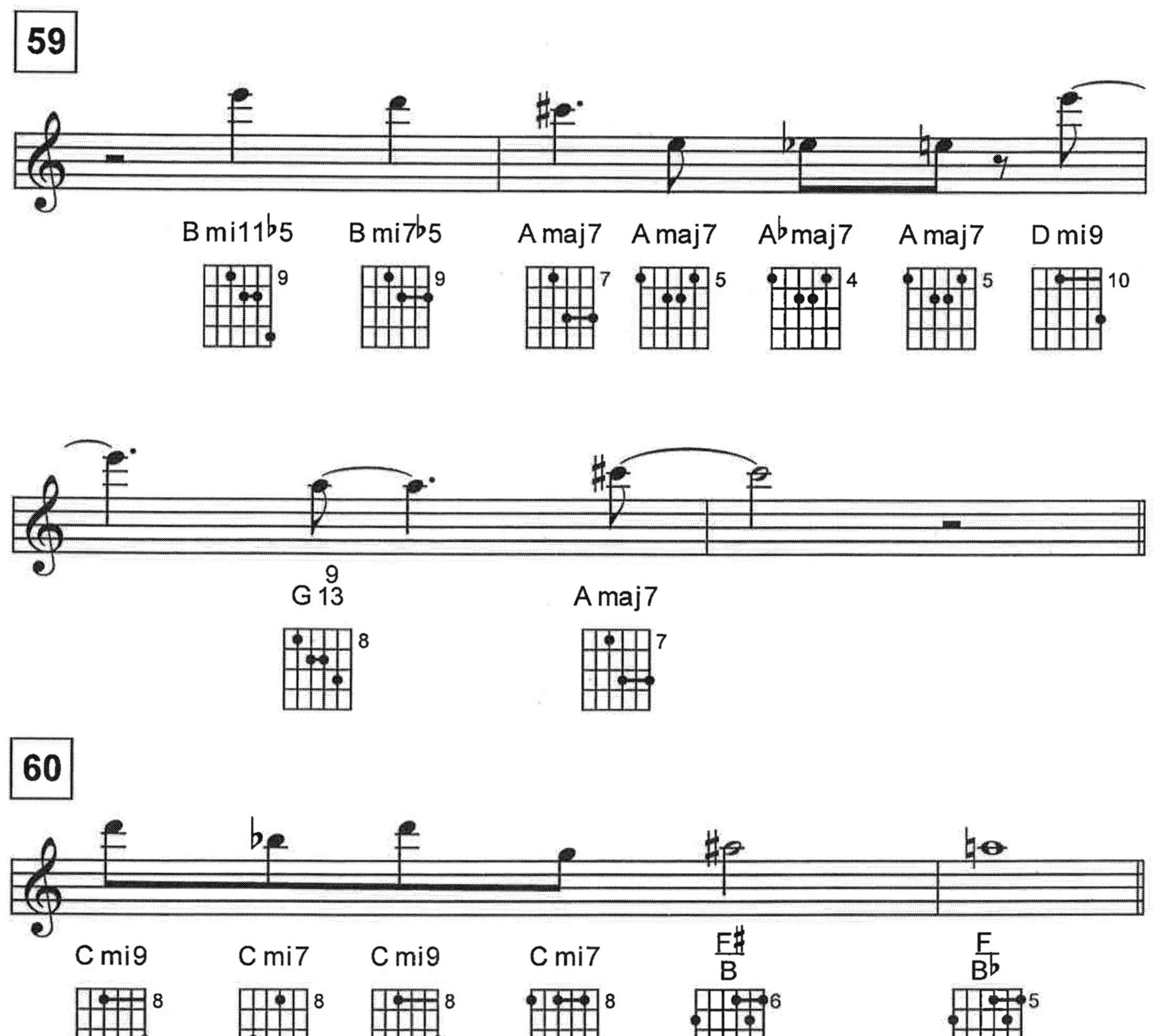
59
B mi11♭5
B mi7♭5
A maj7
A maj7
A♭maj7
A maj7
D mi9
9
G 13
A maj7
60
C mi9
C mi7
C mi9
C mi7
F#/B
F/B♭

Conclusions on Developing a Chordal Vocabulary

Below are some examples of chord progressions you might self-record. (You can record at the tempo you feel comfortable with. Try them in different grooves: latin, swing, ballad tempo, etc.). Record just a bass line, then practice improvising chordal patterns on top of it, in a play-along fashion. I have found it helpful to record a metronome beat along with the bass line.

* You may want to sketch out a melody line underneath the chords, and harmonize it.

* Write out (and record) your own sequences/bass lines. Play them in different keys.

* Begin recording bass lines on the blues form and standard tunes, and improvise chordally over those bass lines.

* It takes a long time to develop a personalized chordal vocabulary. Begin writing down chord licks in your "idea book" - to be practiced repetitively - as a way to develop your own unique voice in this style.

* Remember that as you practice and perform your are contributing - in whatever small or large measure - to the evolution of jazz guitar playing! Good Luck!

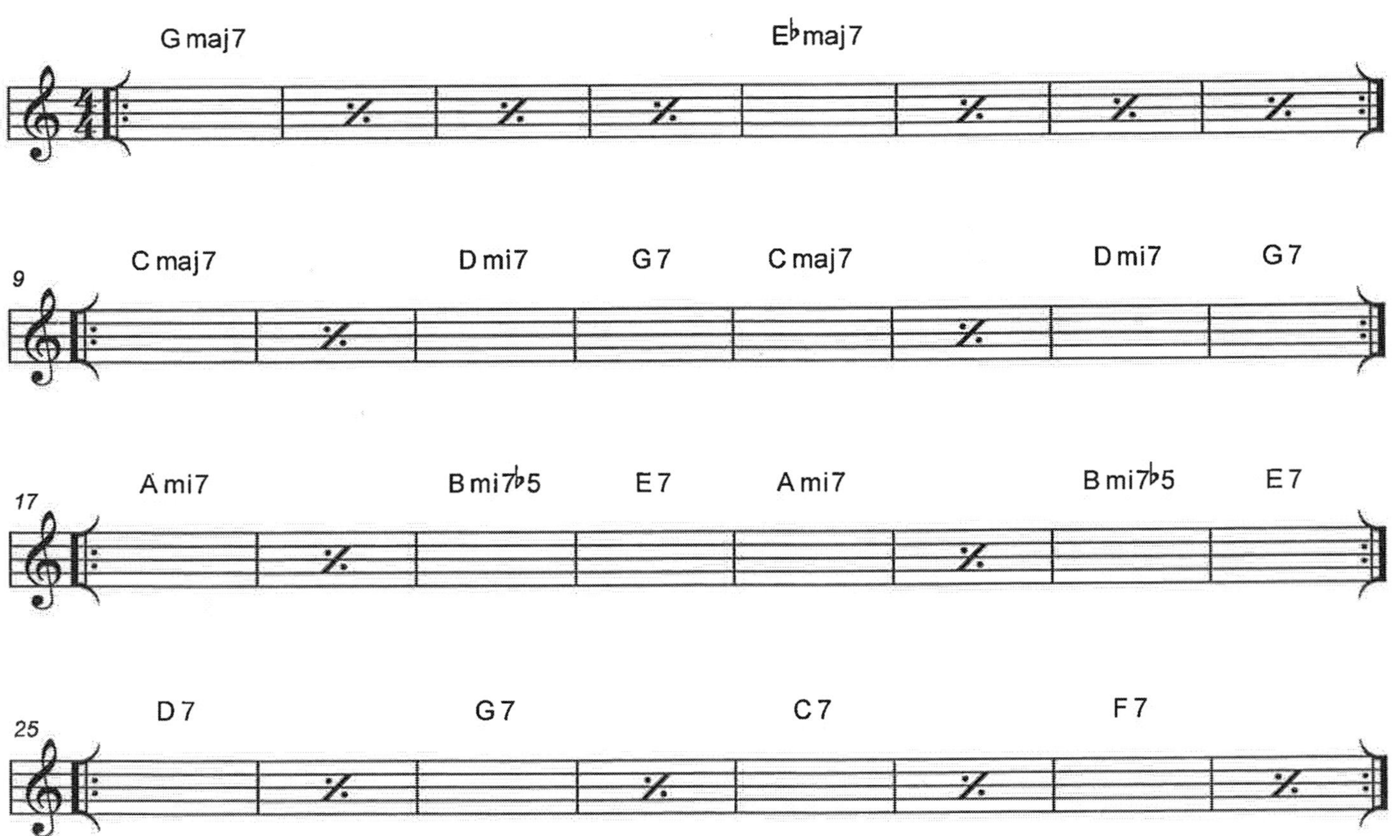

HOW TO PLAY
ADVANCED
CHORDAL BEBOP LINES
FOR GUITAR.
VOLUME II
Book Two in a New Series: An advanced guide for developing a linear chordal vocabulary for improvisation. Written with the styles of Wes Montgomery, Cal Collins, and Barney Kessel in mind! Complete with chordal patterns and solo excerpts!
A NEW APPROACH!
BY JIM BASTIAN (with graphics by JOHN ALEXANDER)
COASTAL PUBLISHING

How To Play

ADVANCED CHORDAL BEBOP LINES

For Guitar
VOLUME II

Jim Bastian

Layout by John Alexander

SpeakPeace Press

Educational Resources Division

All rights reserved. No part of this book may be reproduced or copied in any manner whatsoever without written permission.

Copyright 2017 by
SpeakPeace Press and Jim Bastian
Original Copyright Registration 2008; Library of Congress,
U.S. Copyright Office, Washington, D.C.

Printed in the United States of America

Table of Contents

Introduction 3

Part I - *Exercises in Voice Leading*...5

Part II - *Chordal Patterns*..14

Part III - *Interpretations of Solo Excerpts**...57

- Barney's phrases, based on the chords from "Autumn Leaves" 59

- Barney's phrases, based on the chords from "You're the One for Me" 65

- Barney's phrases, based on the chords from "The Look of Love" 68

- Wes' chorus 8: based on the chords from "West Coast Blues".......................69

- Wes' phrases, based on the 12 bar blues chords from "Missile Blues" 74

- Wes solo excerpt, based on the chords from "Delilah Take 3" 78

- Wes solo excerpt, based on the chords from "Delilah Take 4" 82

Conclusion 87

* The original songs and their copyrighted melodies are not presented in this text but are available elsewhere.

Coastal Publishing takes great pride in presenting <u>Advanced Chordal Bebop Lines for Guitar Volume II</u>. Over the past several years, Volume I has aided many serious practitioners in developing a chordal vocabulary for improvisation, and it has been praised in both on-line forums and various guitar magazines for its groundbreaking methodology. Previously, there have been many texts available that teach chord systems and comping approaches, but none exist on the market that so comprehensively teach how to execute improvised eighth-note lines of chords in the style of Wes, as do these two volumes. It is the hope of the publisher that this set of texts will advance jazz guitar performance on its evolutionary path. It is a further hope that the books will democratize - and remove the mystery from - the process of improvising in chords in the Wes style, making the technique accessible to anyone who wants to devote serious study to this craft.

<u>Advanced Chordal Bebop Lines for Guitar Volume II</u> provides the next logical step, following Volume I, for guitarists who are seriously engaged in developing a chordal approach to improvisation, in the styles of Wes Montgomery, Barney Kessel, and Cal Collins. Whereas Volume I lays a foundation for this style, and includes studies of patterns, chord scales, and chord inversions, Volume II devotes more space to longer and more complex patterns. This volume contains more advanced linear examples, exercises in voice leading (which utilize more modern voicings), extended solo excerpts from the masters of this style, and a widening vocabulary of chords that builds on those found in Volume I.

The same principle from Volume I is applied in Volume II as well: In memorizing the chordal patterns, fragments, and riffs, the goal is for the player to be able to weave these together, at will, in whole or part, to fit any changing improvisatory situation. The goal of both volumes is to develop a chordal vocabulary, which can be applied over underlying chord, changes, much the same as single-line patterns and scales are <u>internalized</u> and *able to be applied without thinking about them.*

Volume II utilizes the same easily readable system of presentation that players enjoyed in Volume I: A single melody line is provided, along with a corresponding chord box. When the chords are played in sequence, the melody line sounds as the highest voice. Throughout this text, the melody line is always the highest sounding voice, with harmony underneath. Persons with poor reading skills can still navigate this text by simply playing the consecutive chord boxes.

Within the chord diagrams used in this book, only those strings are played that have a fingering dot. In a few cases, the "o" underneath the string signifies an open string that is played. All other strings (with no marking) are muted or silent. When playing any of the chords found in this book, it is suggested that the player be aware of at all times - and memorize - which interval note is sounding on top of each chord at any given moment...root, ninth, third, etc.

Many of the patterns are written without a time signature. This approach is supported by the idea that the patterns are to be used by the player in any rhythmic variance that a situation may call for. The goal is to have long scalar lines of chords - and patterns of chords - that can be used, at will, in any key and in any rhythmic configuration that the player chooses. *The memorized patterns are to be used as a basis from which to improvise.* For that reason some of the sequences do not show a time signature. With other patterns, a time signature *is* shown. These patterns often use guide tones or have typical bebop note placements that necessarily fall in certain parts of the measure. This book presupposes the player's knowledge of the bebop melodic style.

The player's vocabulary of chordal patterns - which becomes very individualized over time - needs to be "under the fingers" in the same way that basic single-note scales are: *played almost unconsciously and with the ability to move freely through changing keys.* This happens only through slow repetitive practice. It is also therefore necessary to practice the patterns in other keys, and up and down the neck, when possible. This book also presupposes the player's knowledge of music theory and his/her ability to discern what key a pattern is written in.

With regard to the long solo excerpts found at the end of the book, shorter fragments and phrases within these solos can be isolated for further internalization.

Barney Kessel has described the guitar as having the same capability as an orchestra, with the inherent possibilities of subtlety, ferocity, smooth reed-section-like sounds, loud brass-section-shout-chorus-type effects…a world of color in six strings. Anyone who has heard him describe the guitar thusly, and illustrate his examples on the guitar, quickly becomes a believer in the boundless possibilities of the expressiveness of the instrument. Mastering the chordal bebop lines approach can help in the full realization of that limitless capability.

Daily repetitive slow practice, commitment to this project over the long term, and applying what is learned to actual performance situations will result in the development of a unique chordal vocabulary and in the player's growth as a more exciting performer.

Since the time of the printing of the hand-written first edition, this second edition has compiled additional phrases and has been painstakingly computerized and edited with assistance from John Alexander. It is our hope that future generations of guitarists will greatly benefit from this unique project, and that the role of the guitar will move ever more closely to the highly evolved harmonic role the piano has enjoyed for decades.

The Author

    Jim Bastian lives on the east coast where he is an active perfomer on both guitar and electric bass. Mr. Bastian received the Master of Arts degree in guitar performance from Indiana University of Pennsylvania in 1986, and the Master of Divinity degree from The Methodist Theological School in Delaware, Ohio, in 1990. He was the founding director of the jazz program at the College of Charleston, Charleston, SC, and has written the texts <u>Chet Baker's Greatest Scat Solos</u>, <u>The Trumpet Artistry of Chet Baker</u>, and <u>The Boss Guitar of Wes Montgomery, Volumes 1 and 2</u>. In 2005, Volume 1 of <u>Chordal Bebop Lines for Guitar</u> was published. He continues to teach and to author resource materials for practicing jazz artists and college-level programs.

Following are seven pages of voice leading exercises (many of which are ii-V-I function). These exercises serve several purposes: (1) to teach a newer, more modern vocabulary of chords that is a natural extension to the vocabulary taught in Volume I; (2) to demonstrate that good voice leading can take place while simultaneously paying attention to a logical melodic movement in the highest sounding voice; and (3) to practice these chords in common applications and associate them with fitting 'family members'.

When practicing these, the simple upper melody can be used as a basis for further improvisation, such as you might do in a chord-melody.

For example, the phrase

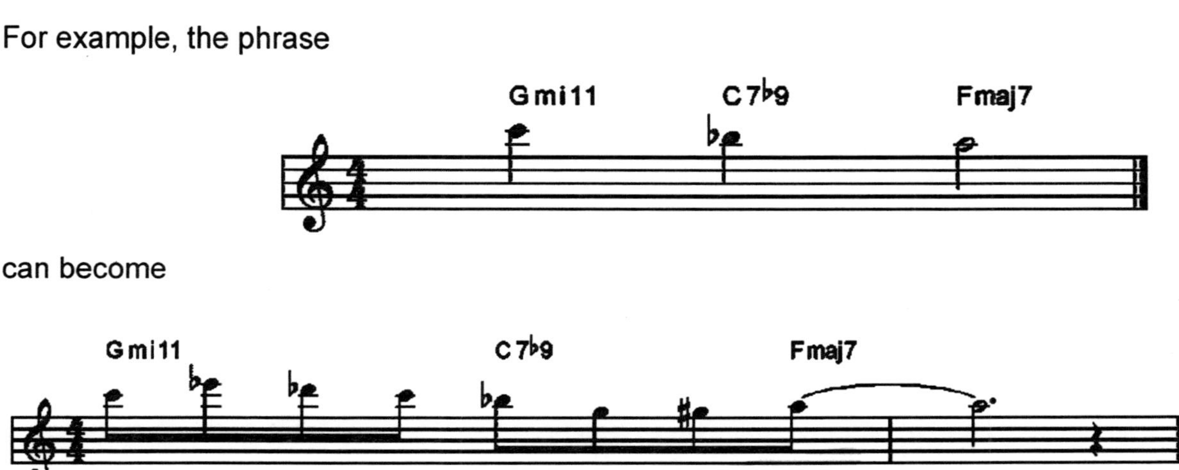

can become

Many of the voicings in this section offer a more modern-sounding harmony than the traditional four-part harmony. These voicings have a place in both chord-melody work and chordal bebop lines, although, depending on the context, the more complex and 'thick-sounding' voicings may be impractical to 'grab' within a line of eighth-note chords. They are nevertheless presented here as another harmonic color that is perfect for certain applications, when more of a dissonant "chill-factor" is called for. The chord diagrams in this section remind us that some chord shapes work better than others for being strung together and played consecutively in an eighth-note line. Some of the modern-sounding voicings, with their spread fingerings, are often better used in shorter fragmentary riff playing, in laying on one note for awhile, and in shorter shout-chorus type phrases. The modern voicings also lend themselves well to solo-guitar chord-melody work where richer, more colorful harmonies can allow for greater expressiveness.

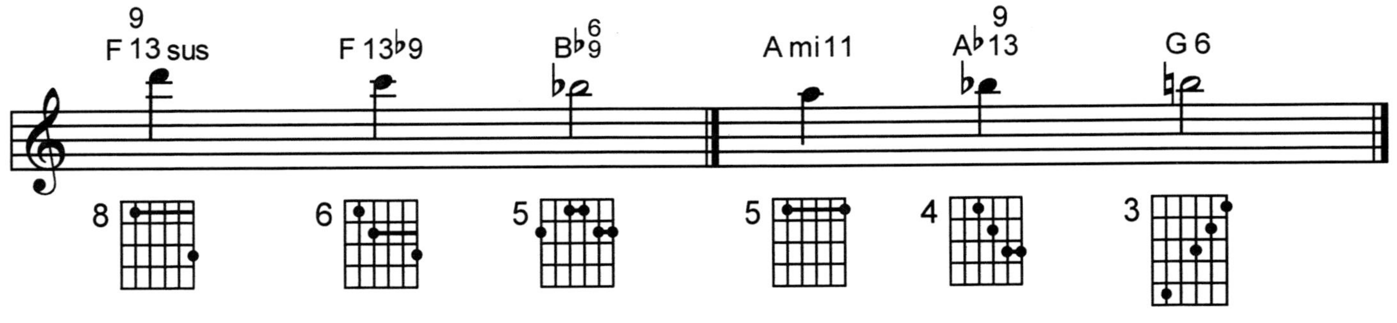
F 13 sus
F 13♭9
B♭9 6
A mi11
A♭13 9
G 6
8
6
5
5
4
3

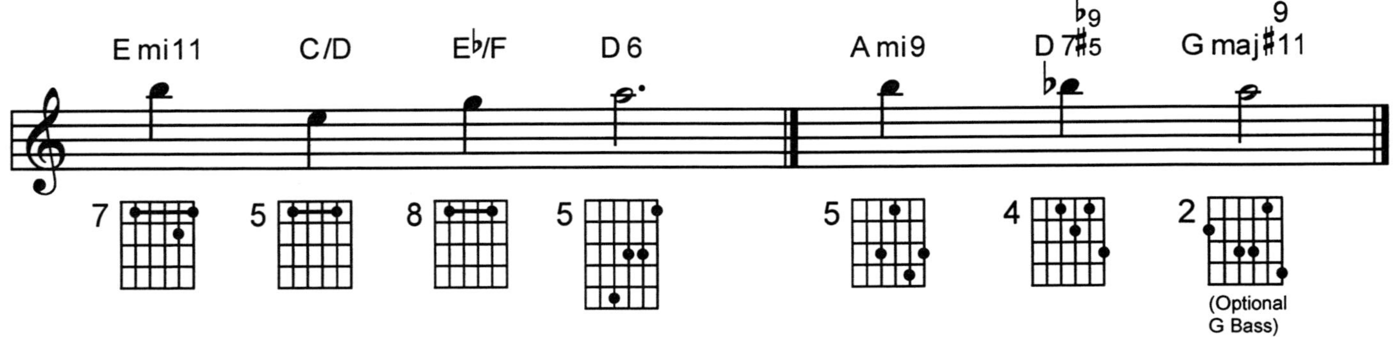
E mi11
C/D
E♭/F
D 6
A mi9
D 7#5 ♭9
G maj#11 9
7
5
8
5
5
4
2
(Optional G Bass)

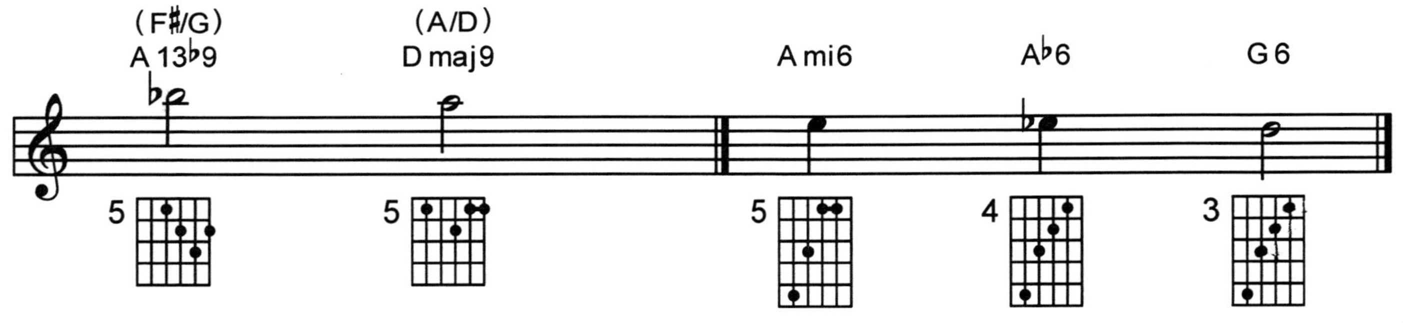
(F#/G)
A 13♭9
(A/D)
D maj9
A mi6
A♭6
G 6
5
5
5
4
3

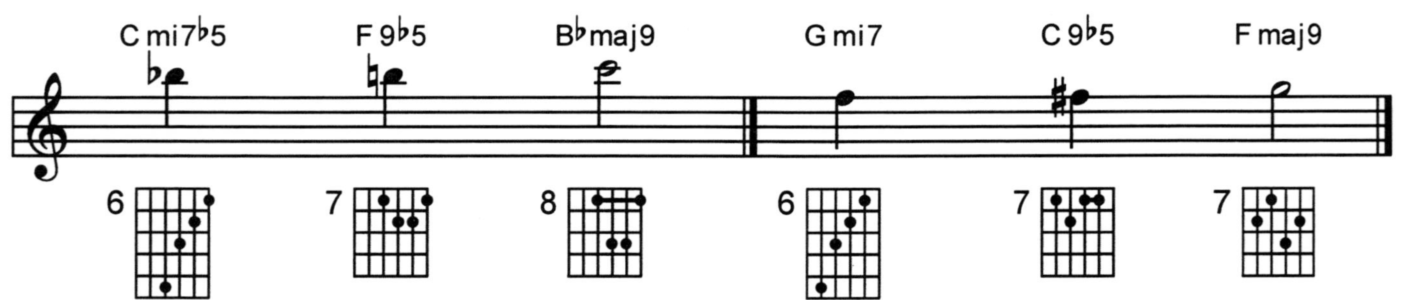
C mi7♭5
F 9♭5
B♭maj9
G mi7
C 9♭5
F maj9
6
7
8
6
7
7

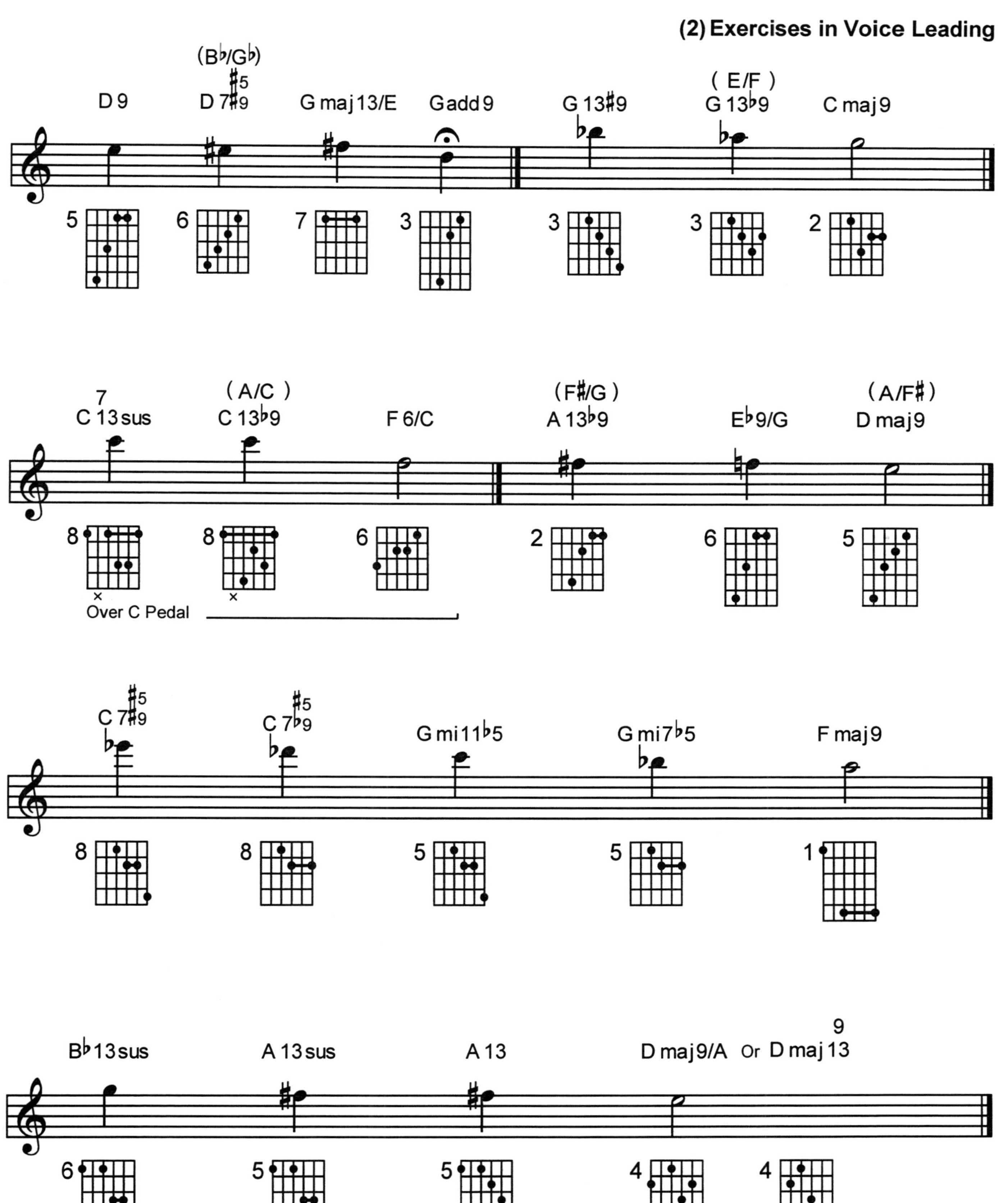

(2) Exercises in Voice Leading
D 9
(B♭/G♭)
D 7#9 #5
G maj13/E
G add 9
G 13#9
(E/F)
G 13♭9
C maj9
5
6
7
3
3
3
2
7
C 13sus
(A/C)
C 13♭9
F 6/C
(F#/G)
A 13♭9
E♭9/G
(A/F#)
D maj9
8
8
6
2
6
5
Over C Pedal
#5
C 7#9
#5
C 7♭9
G mi11♭5
G mi7♭5
F maj9
8
8
5
5
1
B♭13sus
A 13sus
A 13
D maj9/A Or D maj9 13
6
5
5
4
4

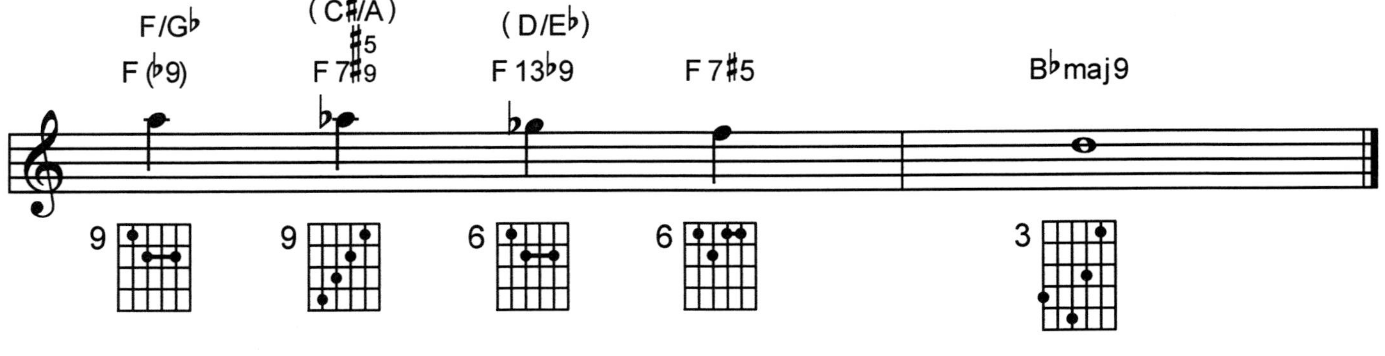
F/G♭
F (♭9)
(C#/A)
#5
F 7#9
(D/E♭)
F 13♭9
F 7#5
B♭maj9
9
9
6
6
3

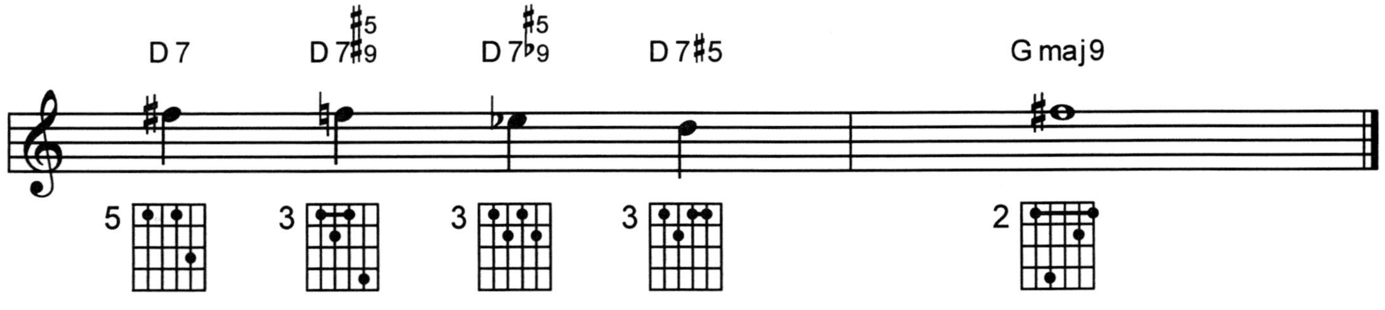
D 7
D 7#9
#5
D 7♭9
#5
D 7#5
G maj9
5
3
3
3
2

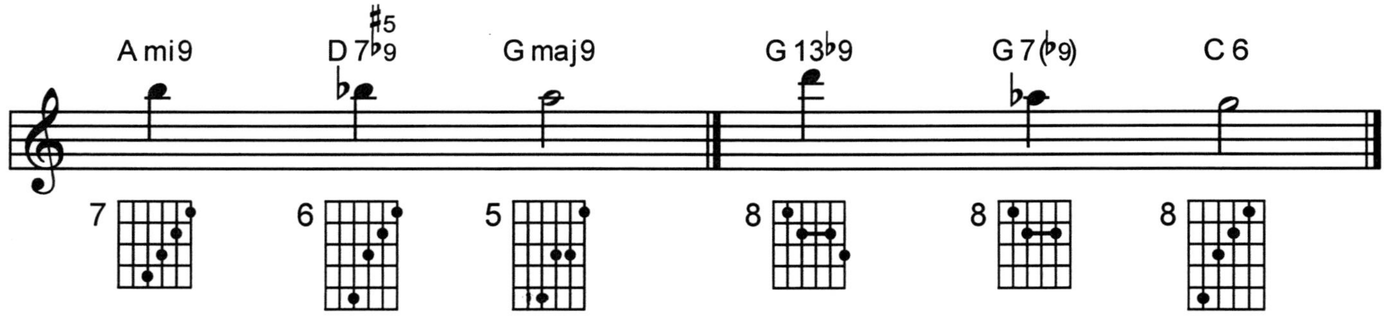
A mi9
D 7♭9
#5
G maj9
G 13♭9
G 7(♭9)
C 6
7
6
5
8
8
8

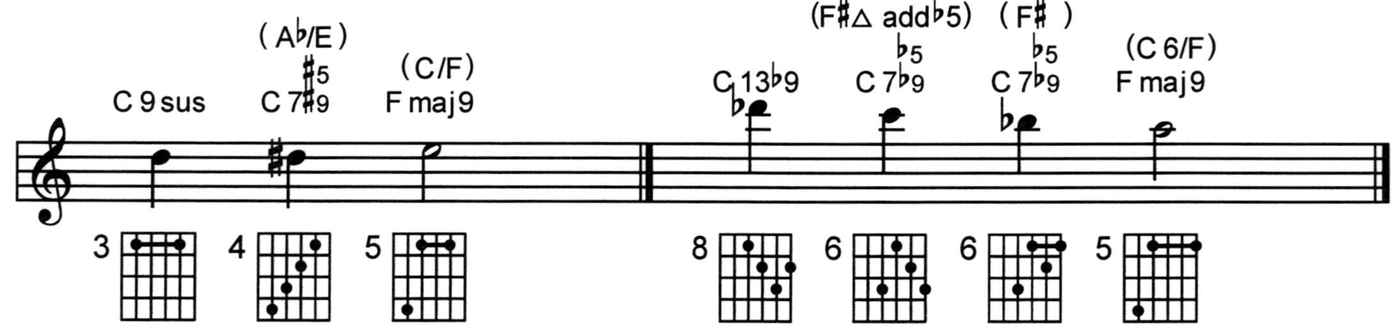
C 9 sus
(A♭/E)
#5
C 7#9
(C/F)
F maj9
(F#△ add♭5)
♭5
C 13♭9
(F#)
♭5
C 7♭9
C 7♭9
(C 6/F)
F maj9
3
4
5
8
6
6
5

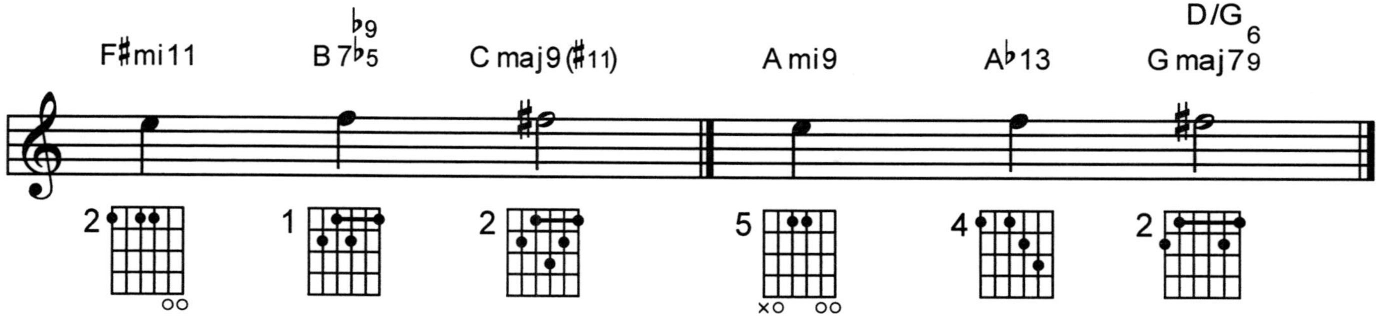
F#mi11
B 7b5 b9
C maj9 (#11)
A mi9
Ab13
D/G
G maj7 9 6

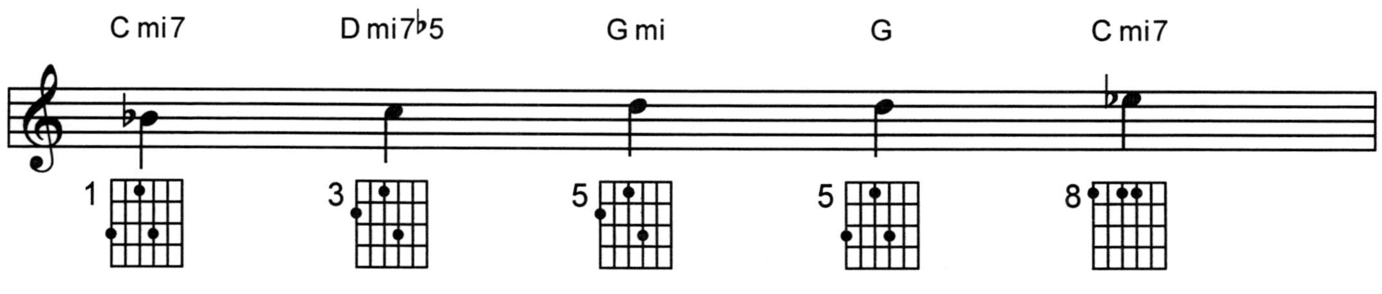
C mi7
D mi7b5
G mi
G
C mi7

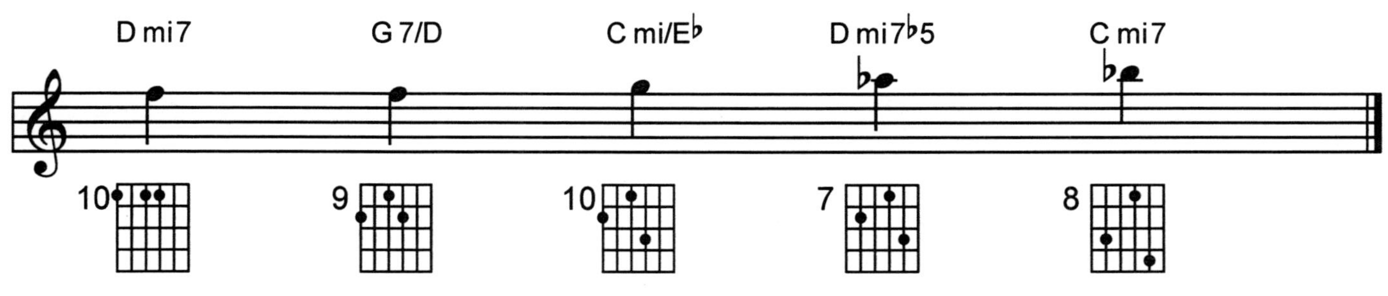
D mi7
G 7/D
C mi/Eb
D mi7b5
C mi7

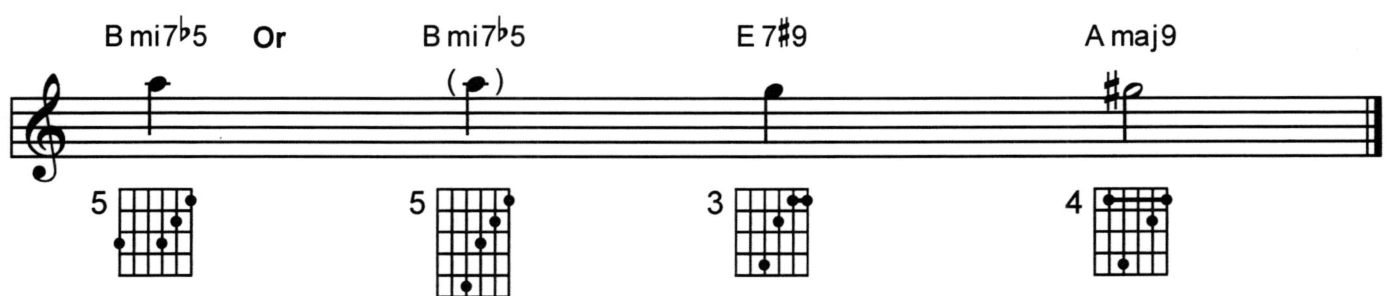
B mi7b5   Or
B mi7b5
E 7#9
A maj9

(5) Exercises in Voice Leading
Intro/Ending
Riff Figure
Over D (V) Pedal

G 6
G dim
C
G dim
G 6
3
3
3
3
3

G
G dim
C 6
G dim
G
3
2
1
2
3

A mi6
(D sus♭9)
C mi/D
G maj7(♯11)
G 6
D mi6
G 13♭9
C maj7(♯11)
9
8
7
9
5
8
7

(G 13)
D mi9
G 7(♭9)
C 9
D mi9 (♯7)
D mi9 (♯7)
G(♭9)
C maj7(♯11)
Or
8
8
7
3
5
3
2

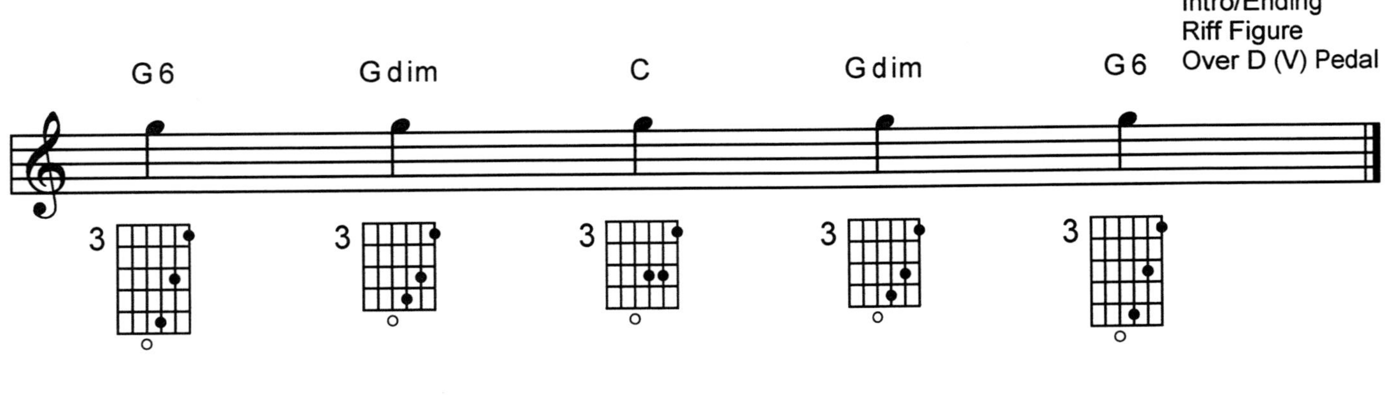

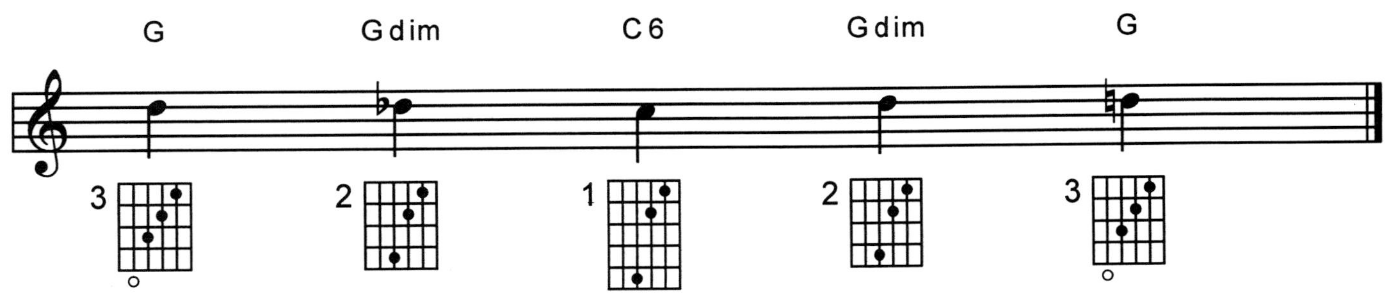

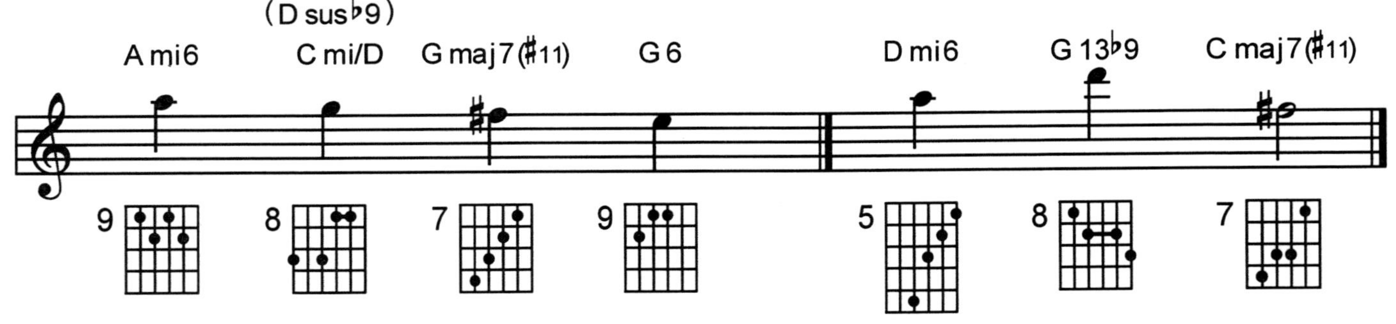

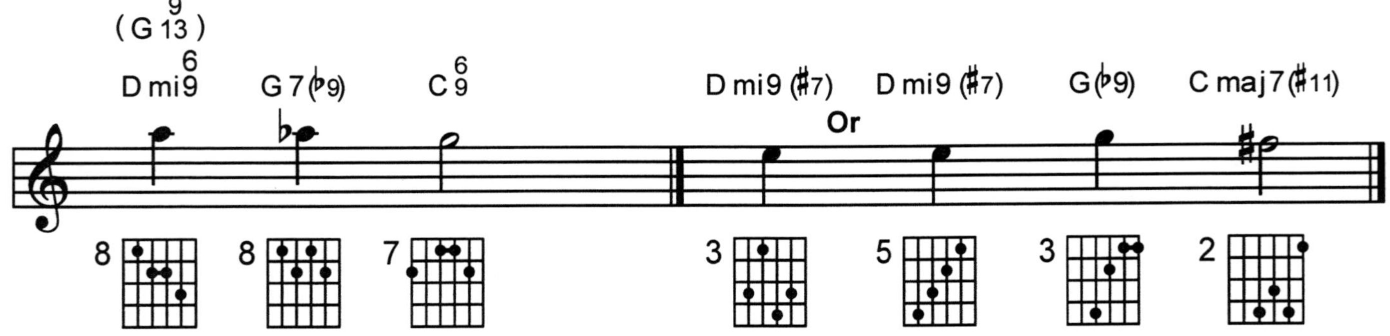

10

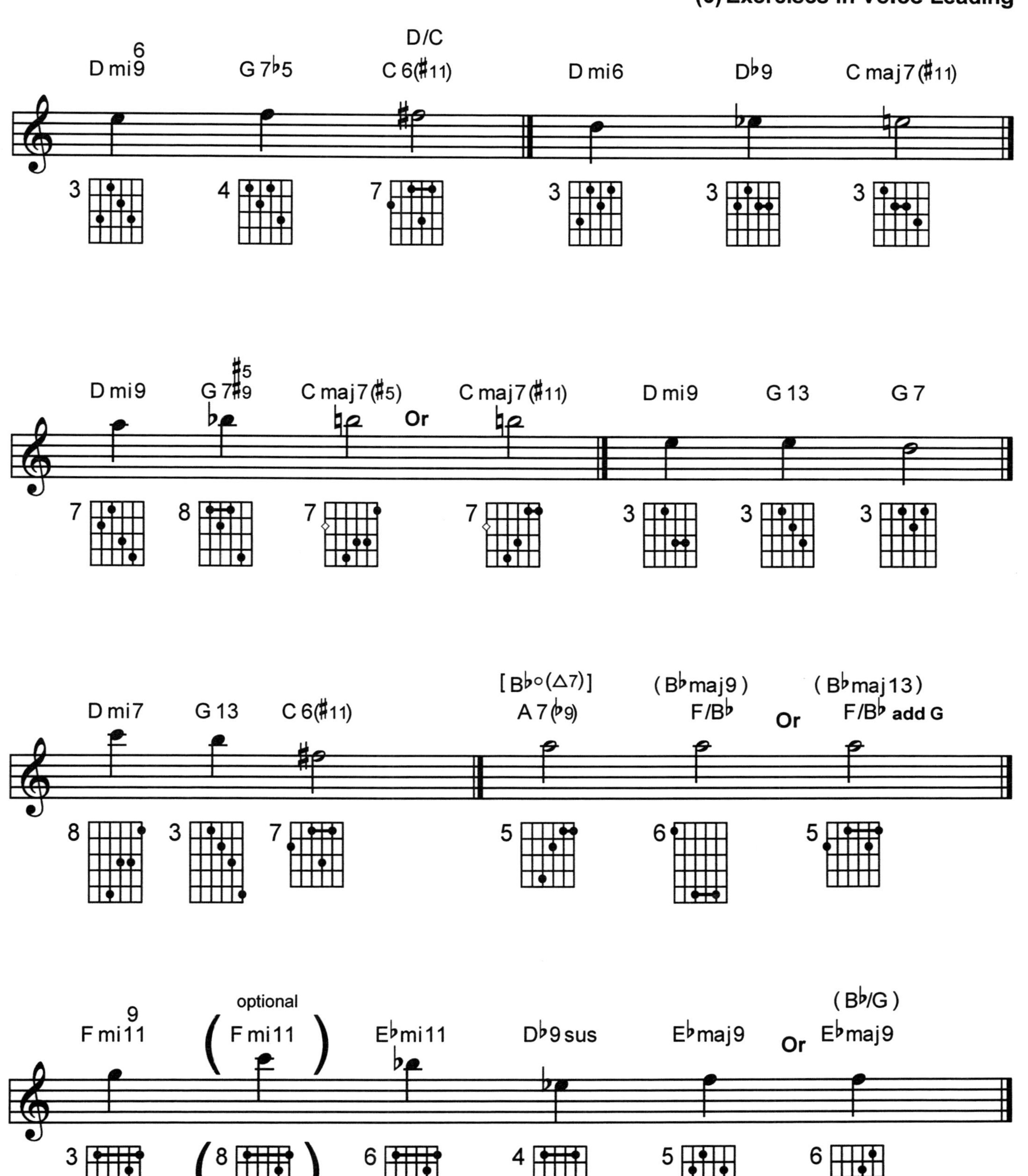
D mi9
G 7♭5
D/C
C 6(♯11)
D mi6
D♭9
C maj7 (♯11)
3
4
7
3
3
3

D mi9
G 7♯9
♯5
C maj7(♯5)
Or
C maj7(♯11)
D mi9
G 13
G 7
7
8
7
7
3
3
3

D mi7
G 13
C 6(♯11)
[B♭○(△7)]
A 7(♭9)
(B♭maj9)
F/B♭
Or
(B♭maj13)
F/B♭ add G
8
3
7
5
6
5

F mi11
9
optional
(F mi11)
E♭mi11
D♭9 sus
E♭maj9
Or
(B♭/G)
E♭maj9
3
(8)
6
4
5
6

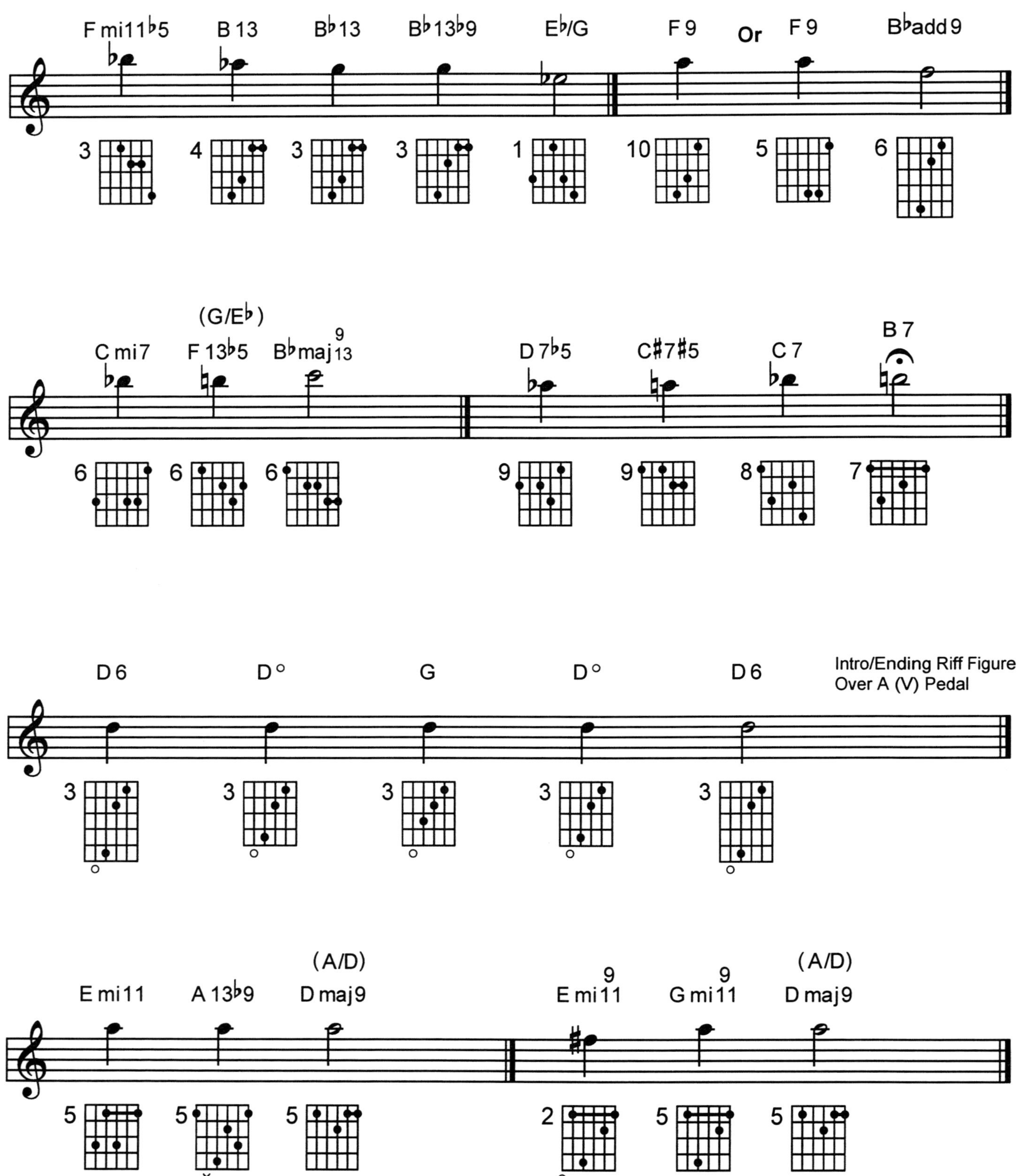
F mi11♭5   B 13   B♭ 13   B♭ 13♭9   E♭/G   F 9   Or   F 9   B♭ add 9
C mi7   (G/E♭)   F 13♭5   B♭ maj13 9   D 7♭5   C#7#5   C 7   B 7
D 6   D°   G   D°   D 6   Intro/Ending Riff Figure Over A (V) Pedal
E mi11   A 13♭9   D maj9   (A/D)   E mi11 9   G mi11 9   D maj9   (A/D)

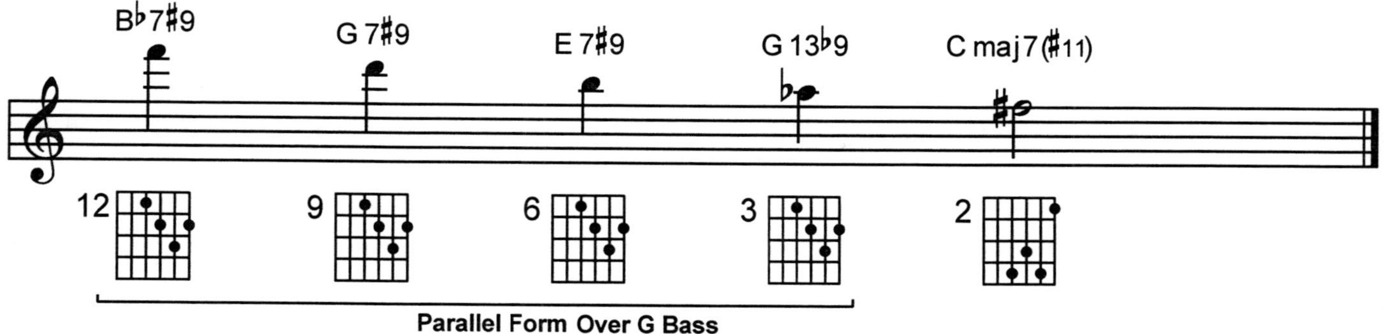
B♭7♯9
G 7♯9
E 7♯9
G 13♭9
C maj7 (♯11)
12
9
6
3
2
Parallel Form Over G Bass

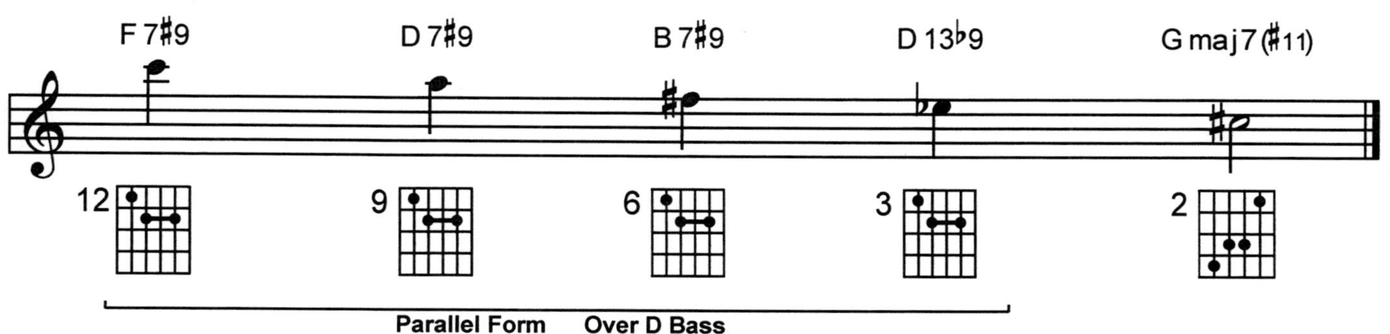
F 7♯9
D 7♯9
B 7♯9
D 13♭9
G maj7 (♯11)
12
9
6
3
2
Parallel Form   Over D Bass

THE PATTERNS

In Volume I, the patterns are divided into three broad tonal areas: Major, Minor and Dominant 7 functions. In Volume II, since the patterns are often long and go through several tonal areas, it will simply be assumed that the advancing player has the ability to discern in what harmonic situations each pattern could be applied. The patterns are therefore not divided up into particular areas of function.

- Each phrase is numbered and ends with a double bar.

- Play the single-line melody first by itself in order to hear the melody you are harmonizing.

- As in Volume I, practice with the goal in mind of being able to link phrases and fragments together.

- Once internalized, the patterns can be modified, linked, and used as the player chooses.

- Practice the phrases slowly and repetitively.

- Pay special attention to how chromaticism can be accomplished in a moving chordal line: (1) by using the same chord up (or down) a half step [parallel forms]; (2) by using the diminished chord as a passing chord to connect things chromatically; and (3) by actually changing chords on every chromatic melody note.

The guitarists named on the cover - along with virtually every major jazz player including Charlie Parker - have their own unique lexicon of stock 'pet' licks and phrases that they repeatedly turn to. These pet phrases are often heard repeatedly and verbatim, even within one solo (Charlie Parker is notorious for repeating exact phrases over the same set of changes whenever they come up in a solo). The aim of this section is to assist players in developing such a vocabulary of phrases - albeit with chords - that can be linked, changed, lengthened, rhythmically altered, and otherwise adapted to meet any improvisatory situation. This is not a new approach. One of the earliest definitive texts for development of a vocabulary for improvisation was the 1970 text <u>Patterns for Jazz</u>, by Jerry Coker.

For Wes, use of chordal bebop lines usually came after single lines and octaves. For Cal Collins and Barney Kessel, chordal bebop lines could be interspersed with single lines, thirds, and octaves. How the chordal patterns will be used stylistically in the development of a solo is the free choice of the player. Internalizing these patterns gives the player this powerful choice!

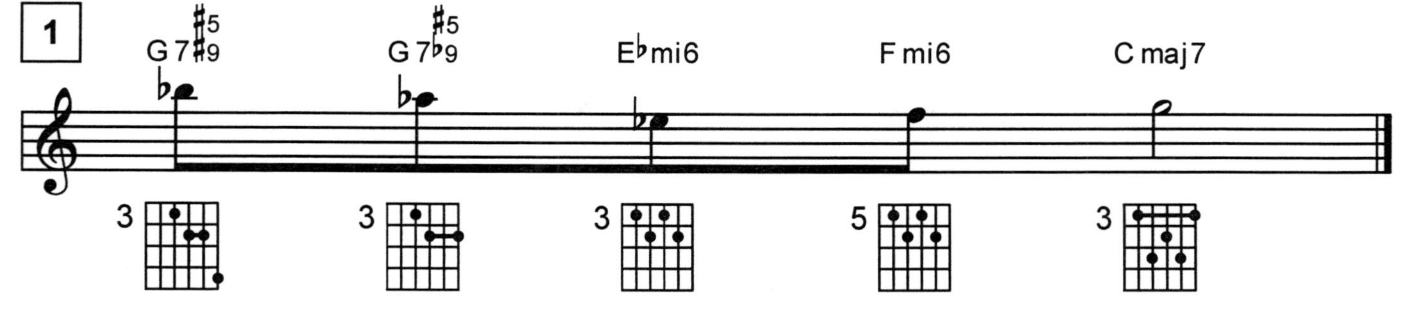

1
G 7#5#9
G 7#5b9
Eb mi6
F mi6
C maj7
3
3
3
5
3

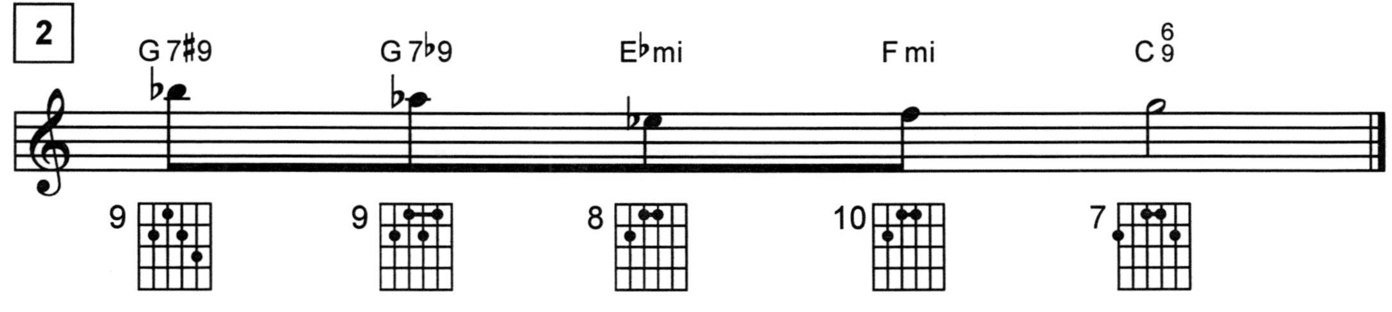

2
G 7#9
G 7b9
Eb mi
F mi
C 6/9
9
9
8
10
7

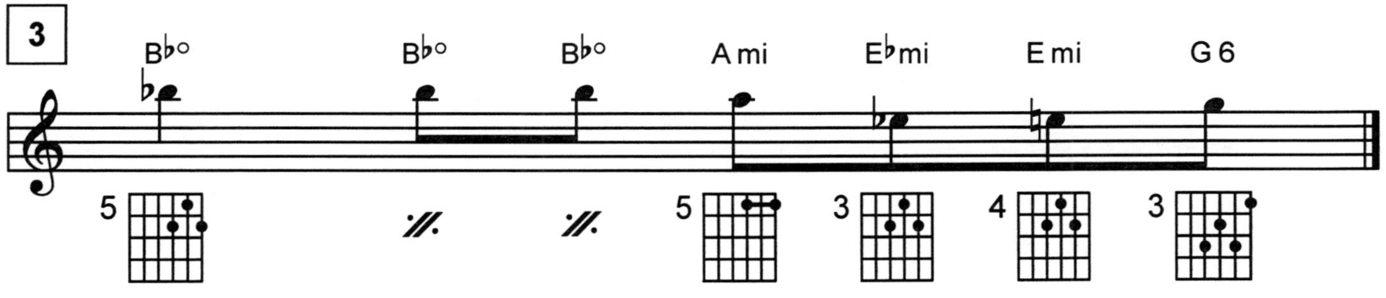

3
Bb o
Bb o
Bb o
A mi
Eb mi
E mi
G 6
5
//.
//.
5
3
4
3

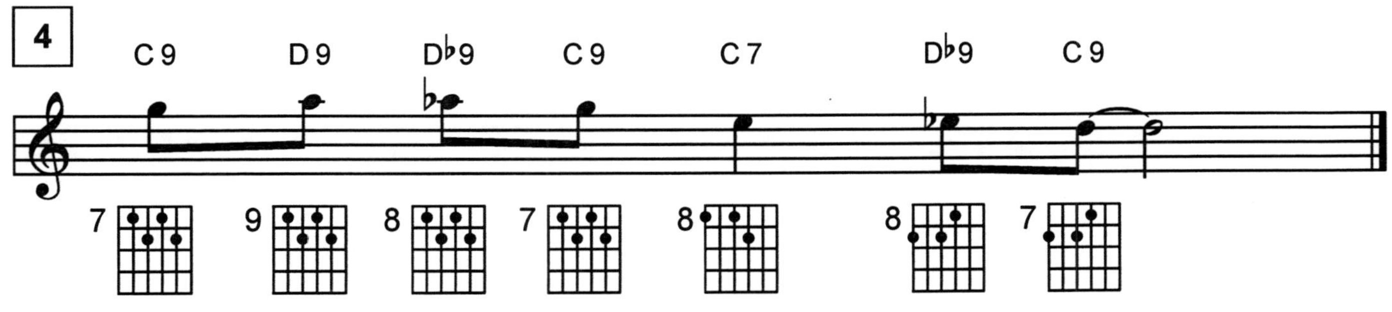

4
C 9
D 9
Db 9
C 9
C 7
Db 9
C 9
7
9
8
7
8
8
7

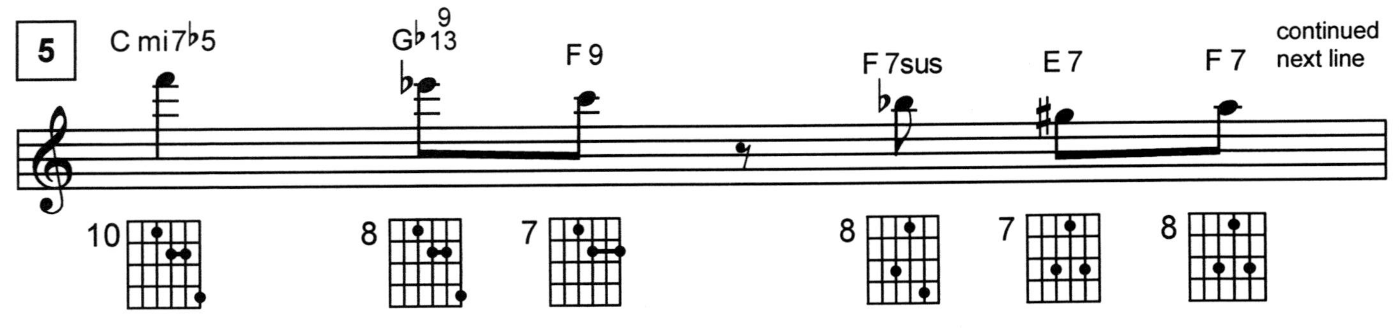

5
continued next line
C mi7♭5
G♭13 9
F 9
F 7sus
E 7
F 7
10
8
7
8
7
8

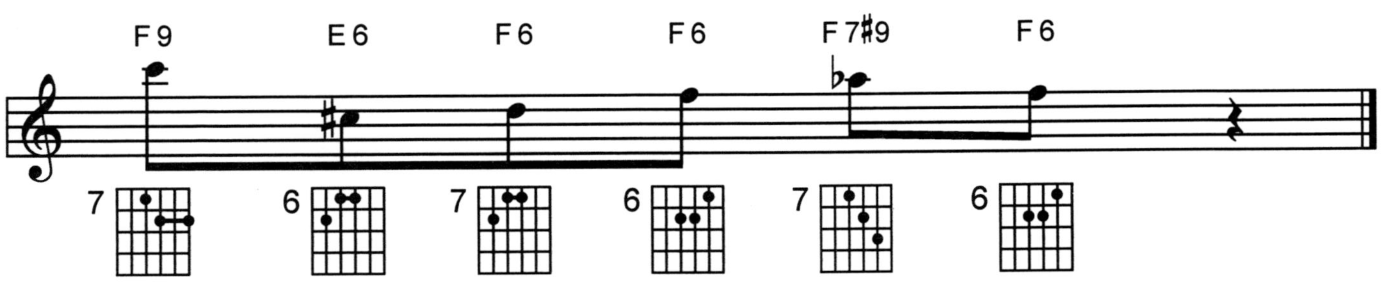

F 9
E 6
F 6
F 6
F 7♯9
F 6
7
6
7
6
7
6

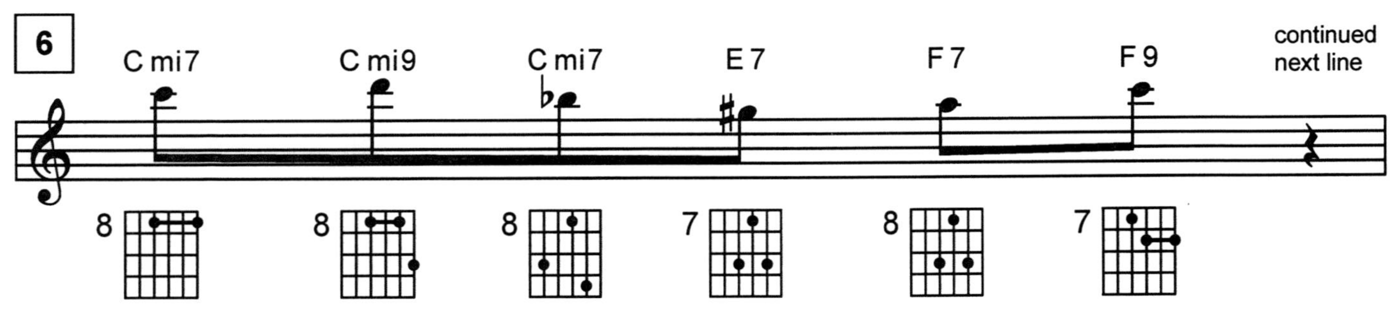

6
continued next line
C mi7
C mi9
C mi7
E 7
F 7
F 9
8
8
8
7
8
7

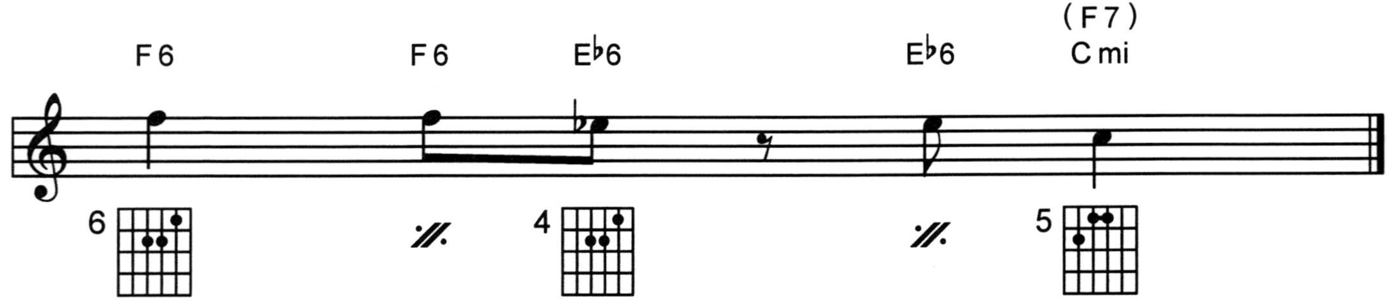

F 6
F 6
E♭6
E♭6
(F 7)
C mi
6
4
5

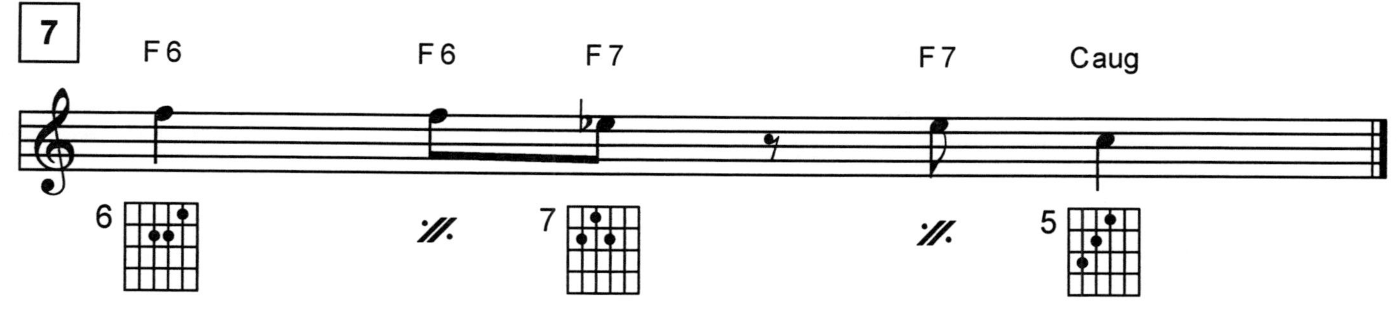

7
F 6   F 6   F 7   F 7   Caug
6   7   5

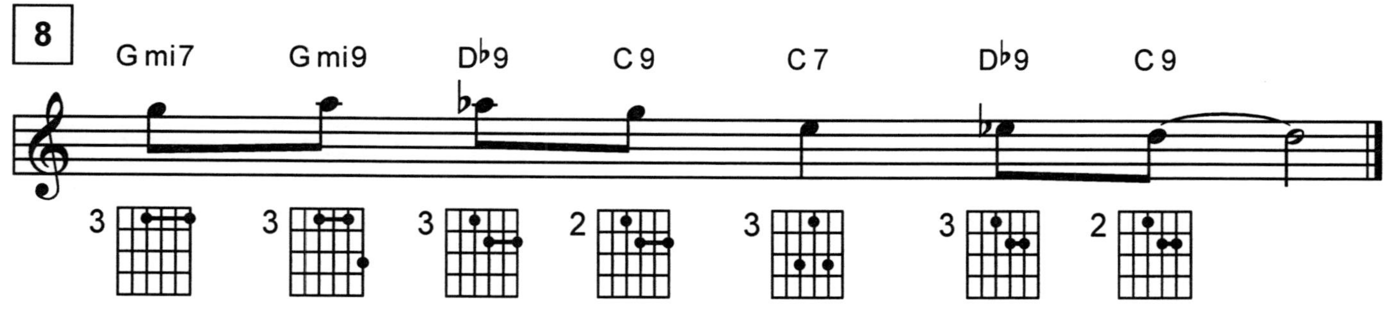

8
G mi7   G mi9   Db9   C 9   C 7   Db9   C 9
3   3   3   2   3   3   2

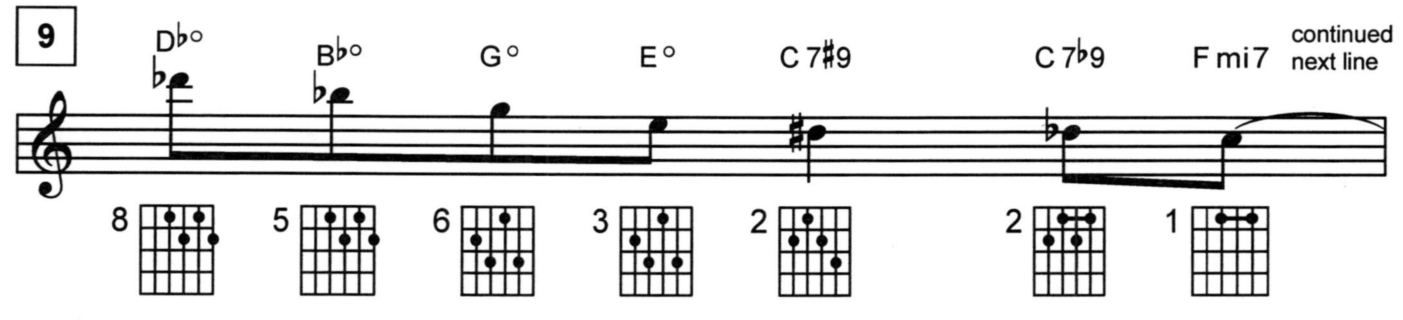

9
Dbo   Bbo   G°   E°   C 7#9   C 7b9   F mi7   continued next line
8   5   6   3   2   2   1

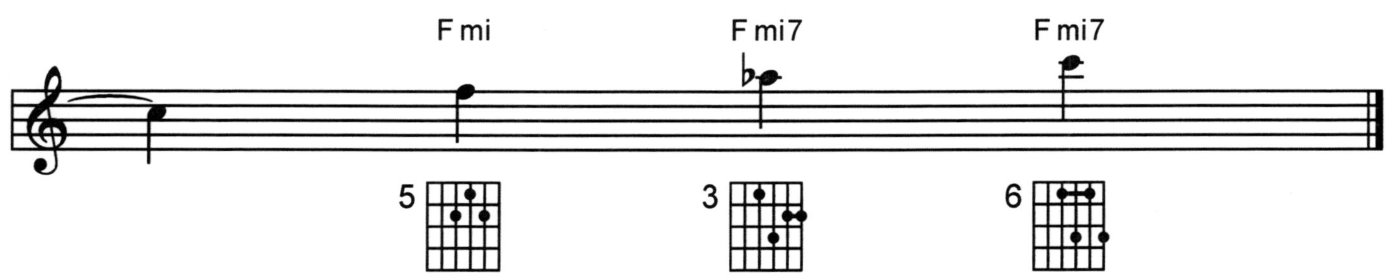

F mi   F mi7   F mi7
5   3   6

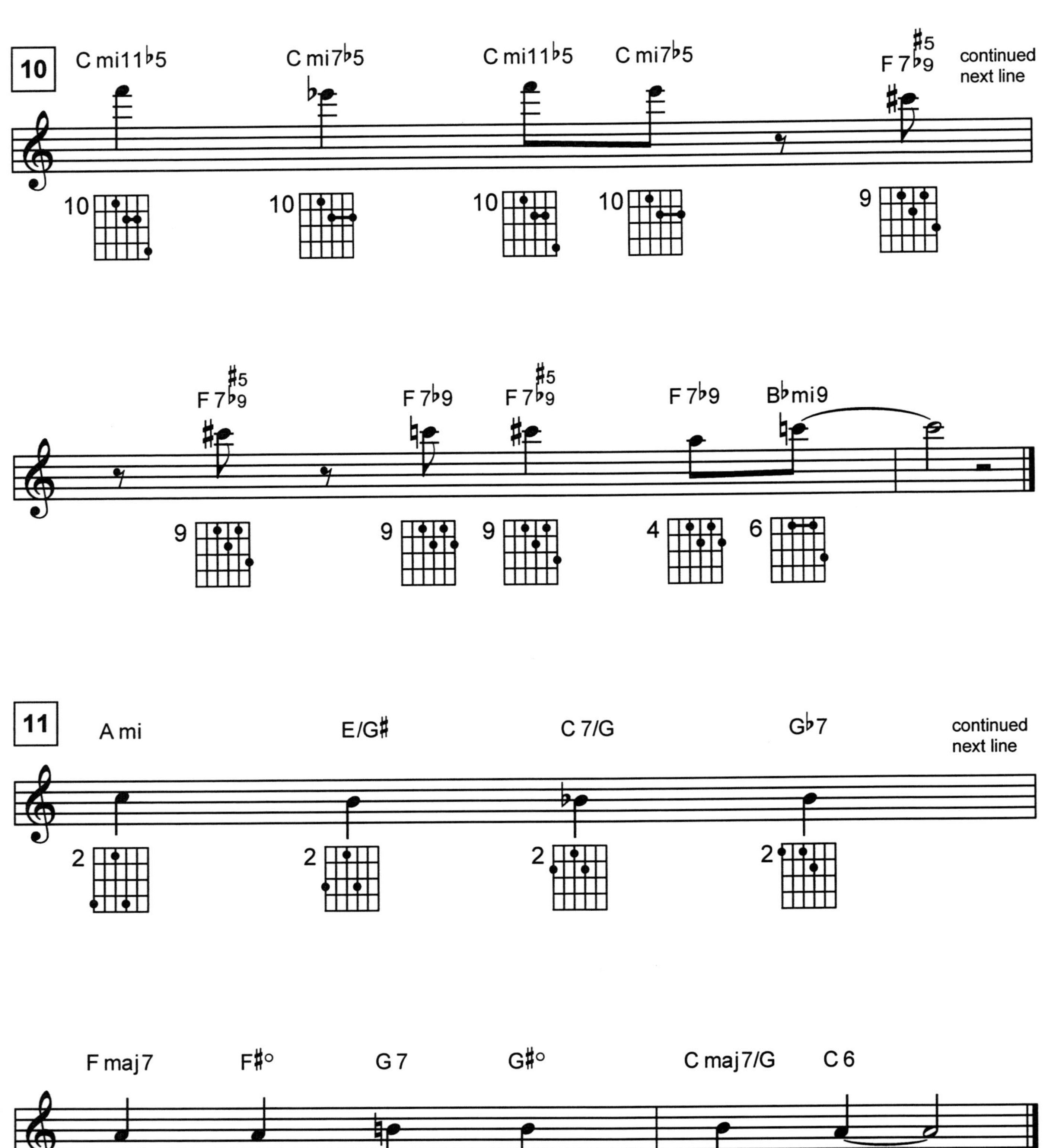

10
C mi11♭5   C mi7♭5   C mi11♭5   C mi7♭5   F 7♭9 #5   continued next line
10   10   10   10   9

F 7♭9 #5   F 7♭9   F 7♭9 #5   F 7♭9   B♭mi9
9   9   9   4   6

11
A mi   E/G#   C 7/G   G♭7   continued next line
2   2   2   2

F maj7   F#°   G 7   G#°   C maj7/G   C 6
1   1   3   3   2   2

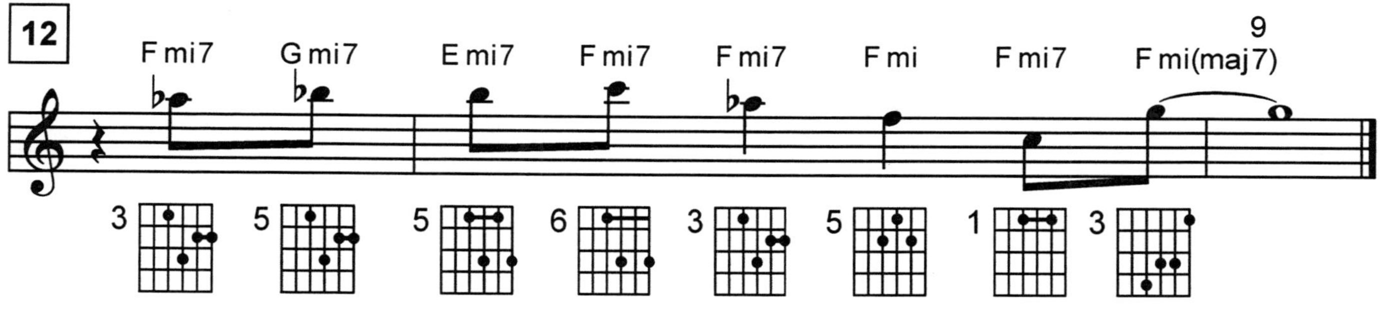

12
F mi7   G mi7   E mi7   F mi7   F mi7   F mi
F mi7   F mi(maj7)   9
3   5   5   6   3   5   1   3

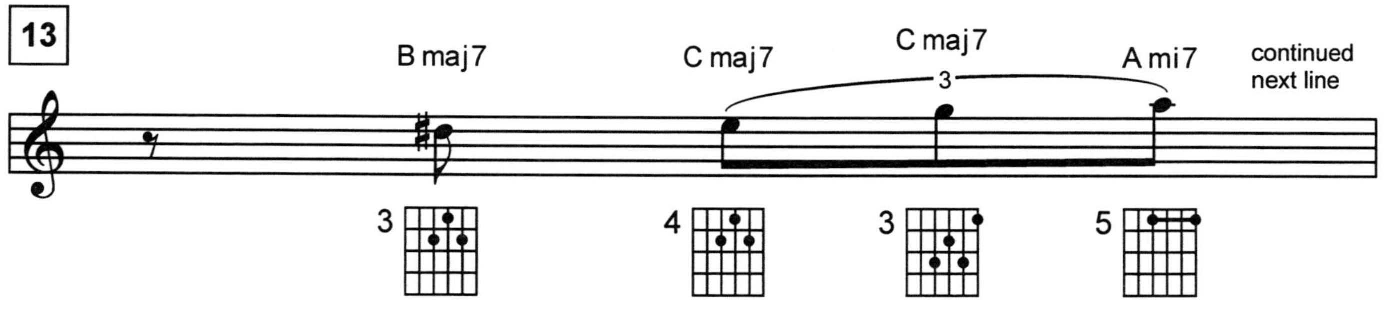

13
B maj7   C maj7   C maj7   A mi7   continued next line
3
3   4   3   5

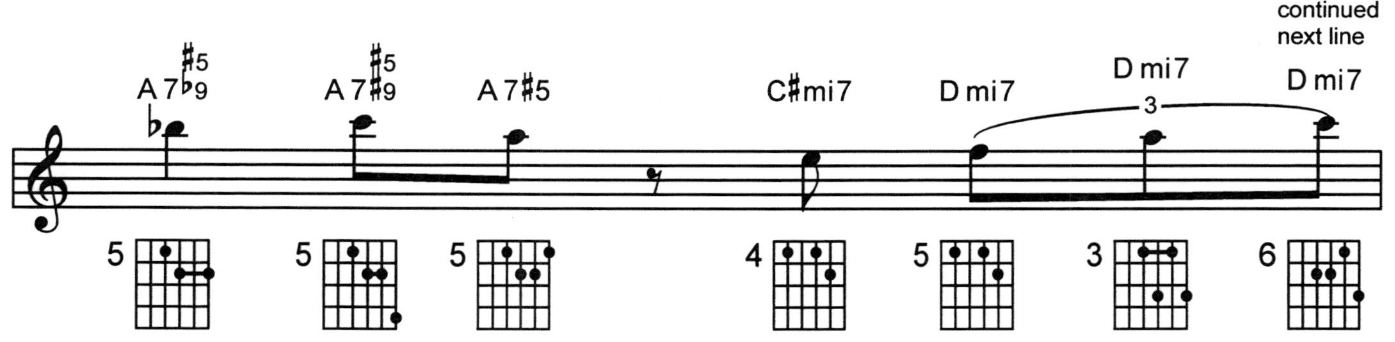

A 7♭9 ♯5   A 7♯9 ♯5   A 7♯5   C♯mi7   D mi7   D mi7   continued next line   D mi7
3
5   5   5   4   5   3   6

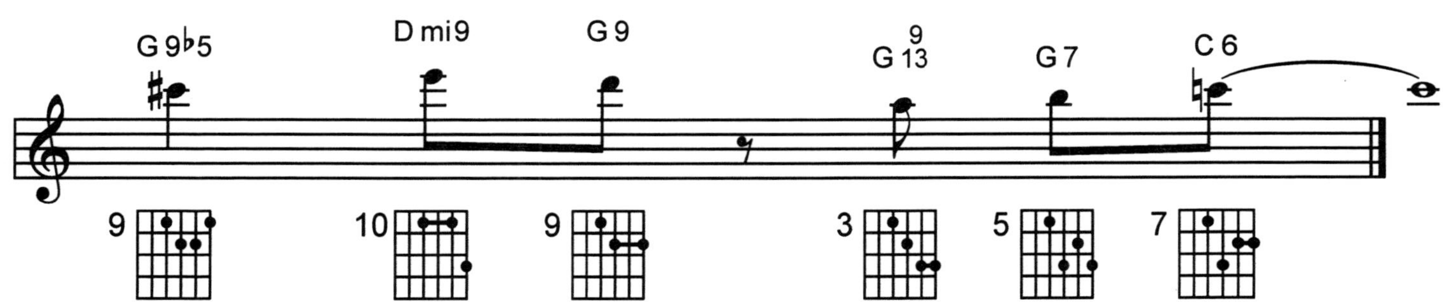

G 9♭5   D mi9   G 9   G 13 9   G 7   C 6
9   10   9   3   5   7

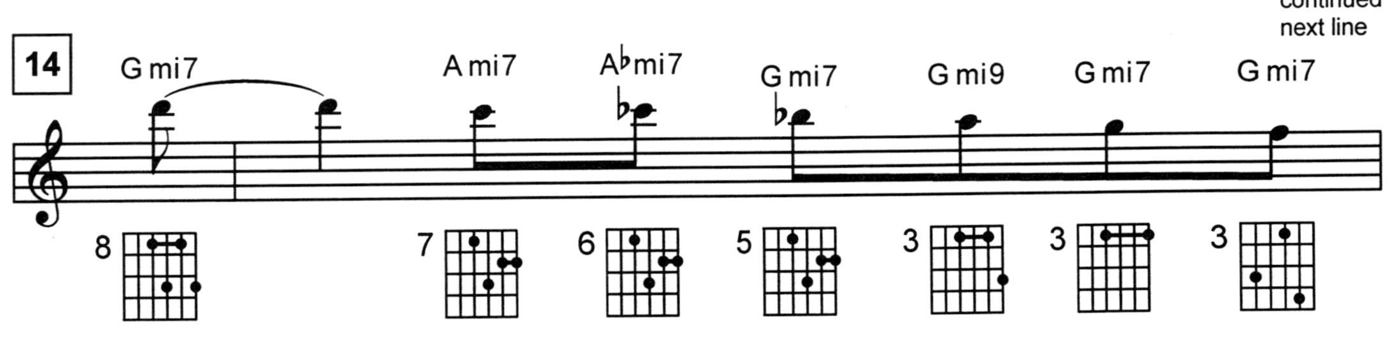
14
G mi7
A mi7
A♭mi7
G mi7
G mi9
G mi7
G mi7
8
7
6
5
3
3
3

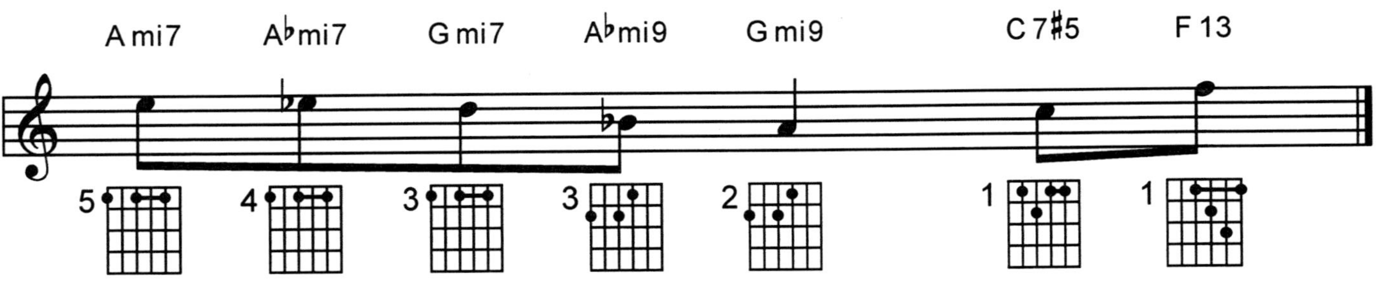
A mi7
A♭mi7
G mi7
A♭mi9
G mi9
C 7♯5
F 13
5
4
3
3
2
1
1

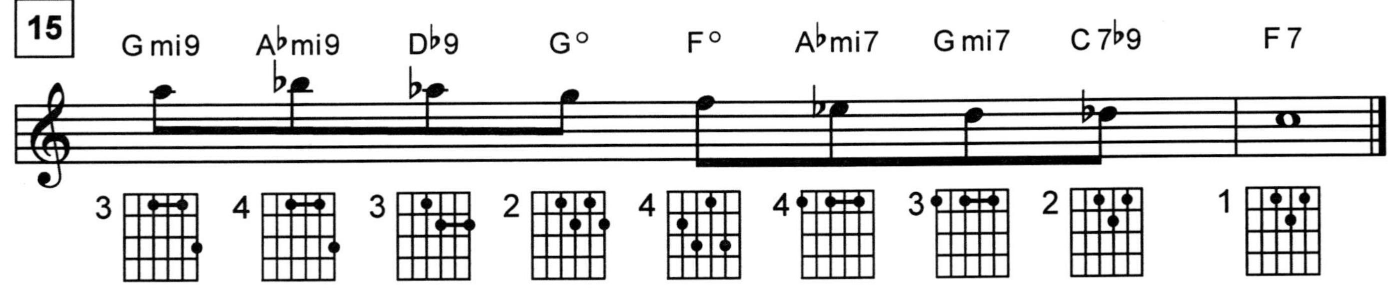
15
G mi9
A♭mi9
D♭9
G°
F°
A♭mi7
G mi7
C 7♭9
F 7
3
4
3
2
4
4
3
2
1

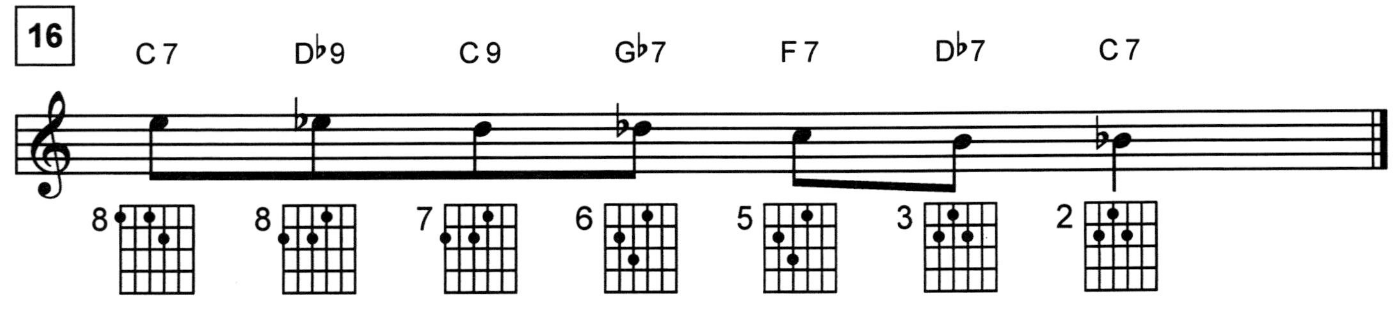
16
C 7
D♭9
C 9
G♭7
F 7
D♭7
C 7
8
8
7
6
5
3
2

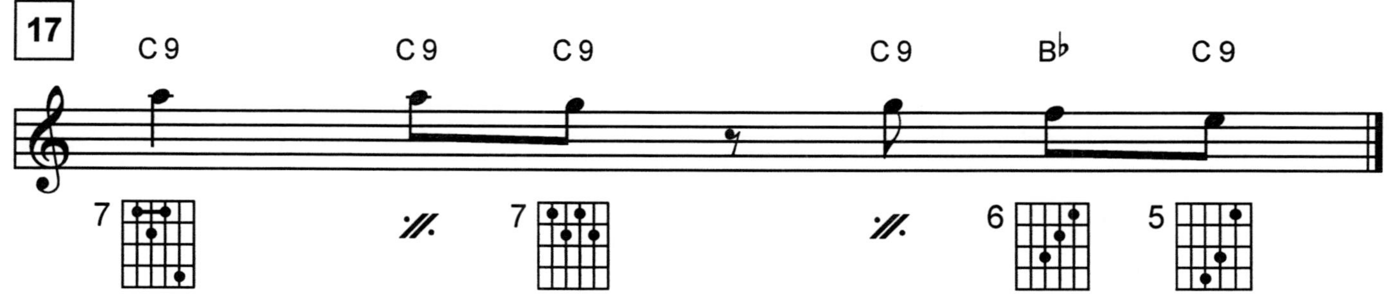

17
C 9
C 9
C 9
C 9
Bb
C 9
7
7
6
5

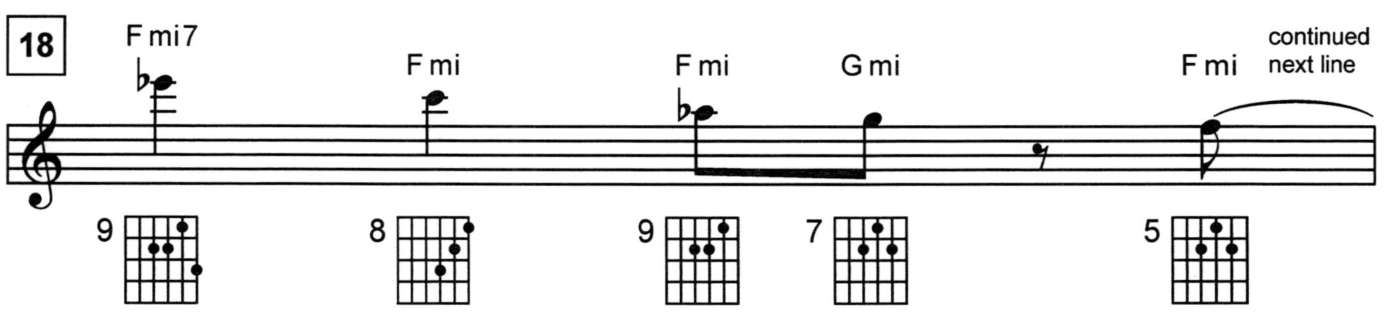

18
F mi7
F mi
F mi
G mi
F mi
continued
next line
9
8
9
7
5

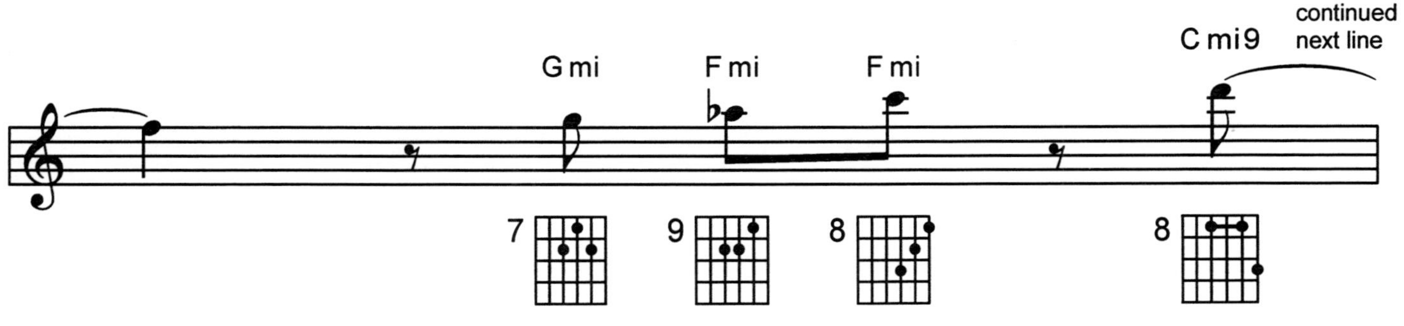

G mi
F mi
F mi
C mi9
continued
next line
7
9
8
8

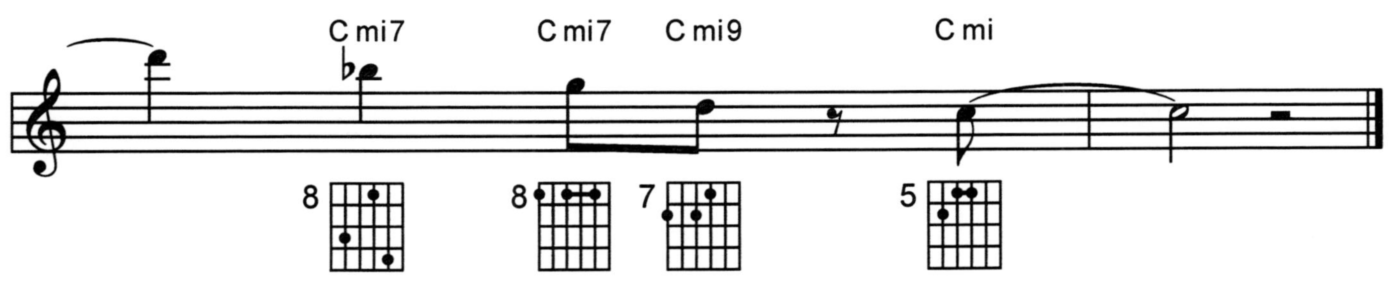

C mi7
C mi7
C mi9
C mi
8
8
7
5

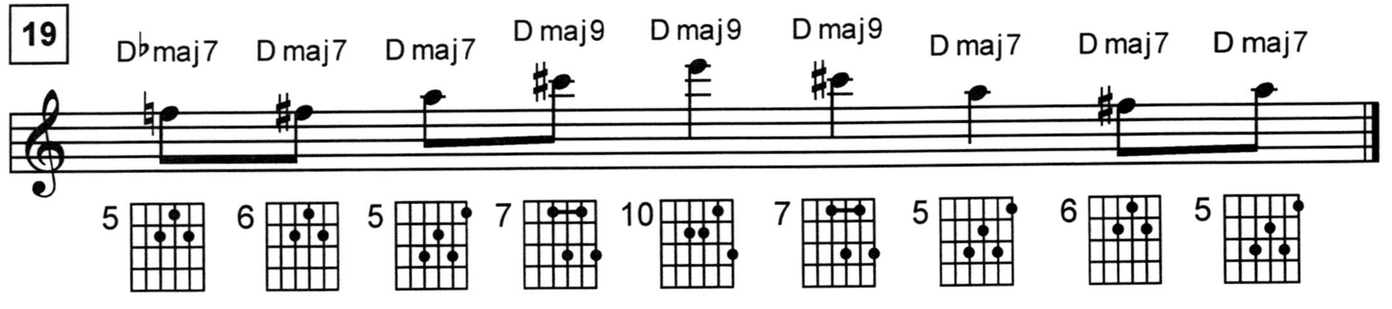

19
D♭maj7   D maj7   D maj7   D maj9   D maj9   D maj9   D maj7   D maj7   D maj7
5   6   5   7   10   7   5   6   5

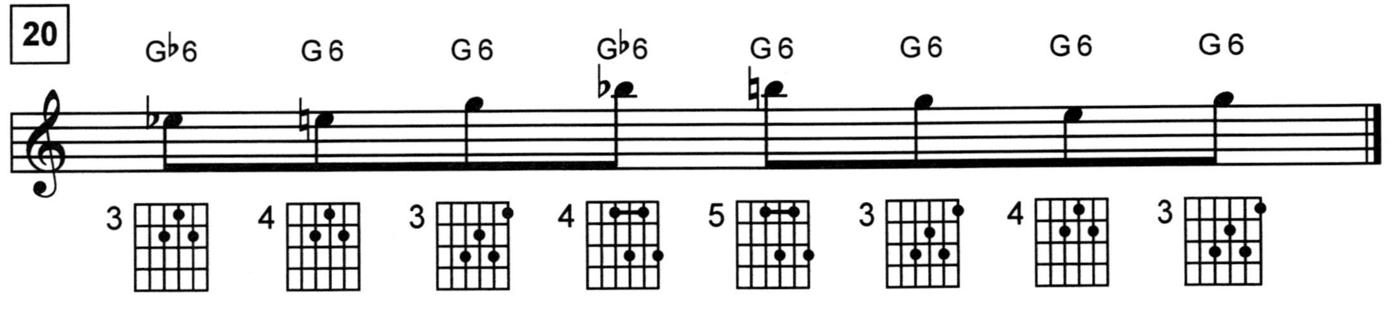

20
G♭6   G 6   G 6   G♭6   G 6   G 6   G 6   G 6
3   4   3   4   5   3   4   3

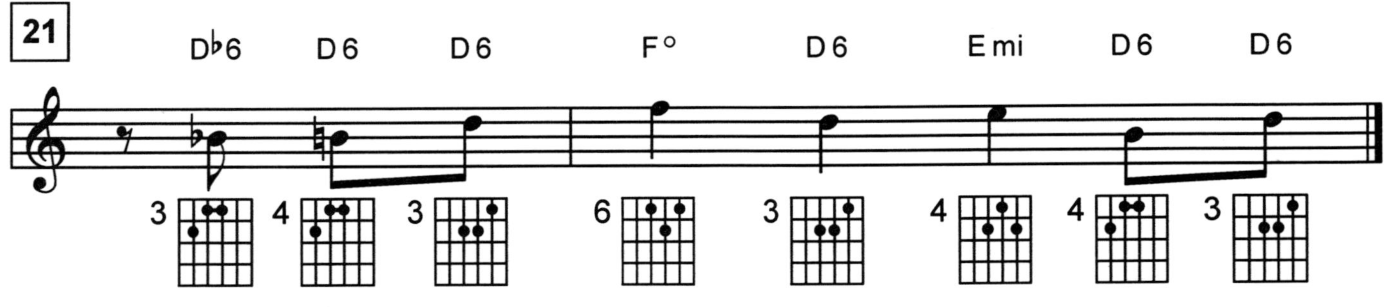

21
D♭6   D 6   D 6   F°   D 6   E mi   D 6   D 6
3   4   3   6   3   4   4   3

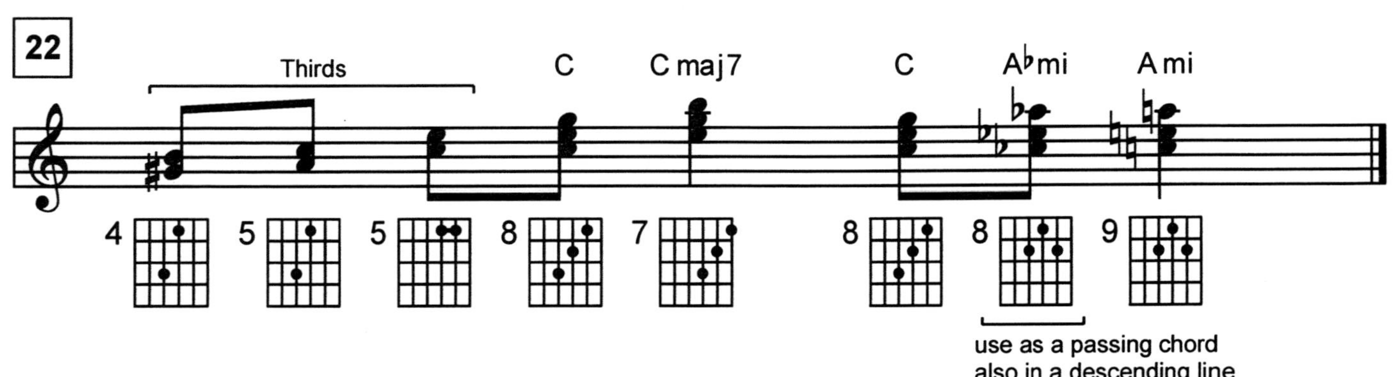

22
Thirds   C   C maj7   C   A♭mi   A mi
4   5   5   8   7   8   8   9
use as a passing chord
also in a descending line

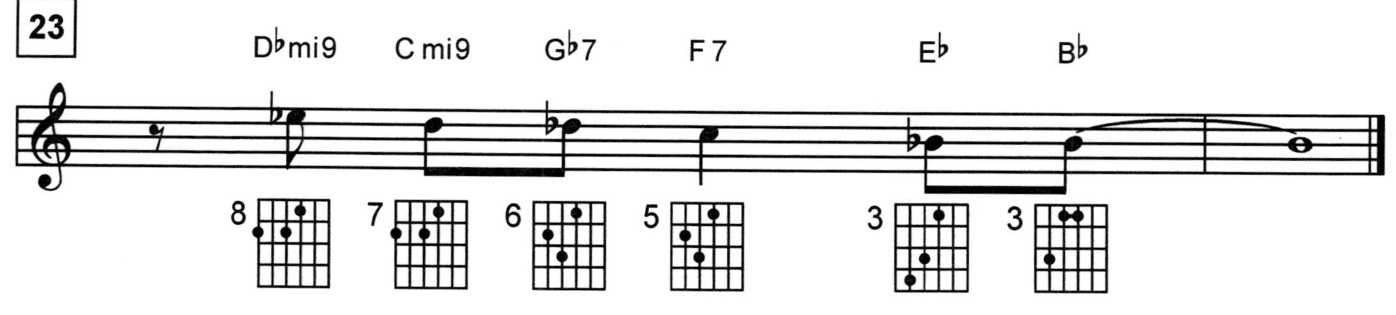

23
Db mi9   C mi9   Gb7   F 7   Eb   Bb
8 7 6 5   3 3

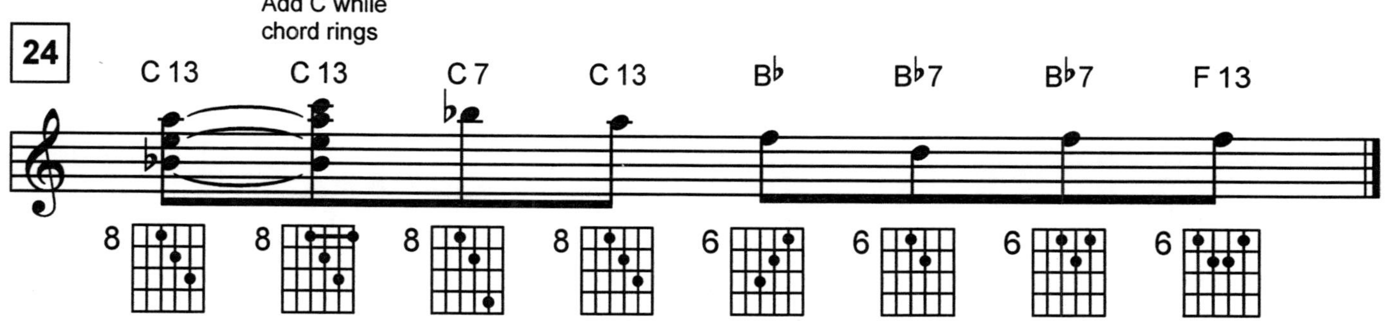

24
Add C while
chord rings
C 13   C 13   C 7   C 13   Bb   Bb7   Bb7   F 13
8 8 8 8 6 6 6 6

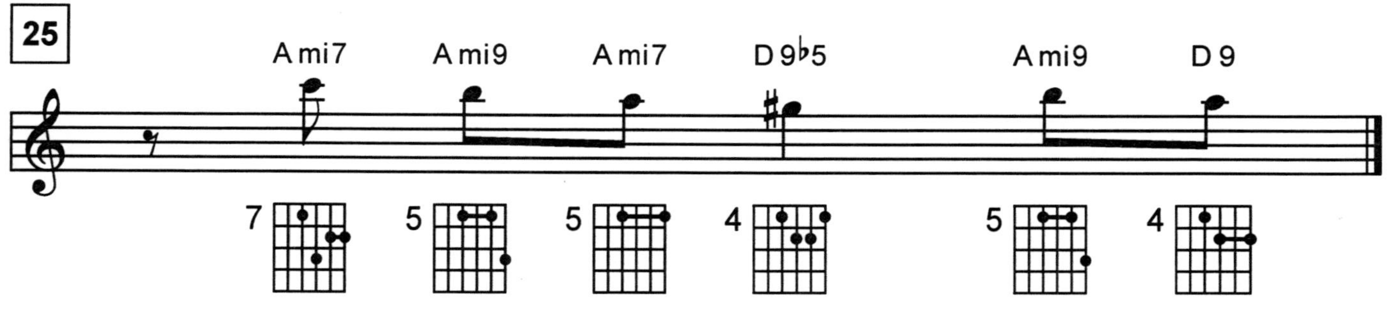

25
A mi7   A mi9   A mi7   D 9b5   A mi9   D 9
7 5 5 4   5 4

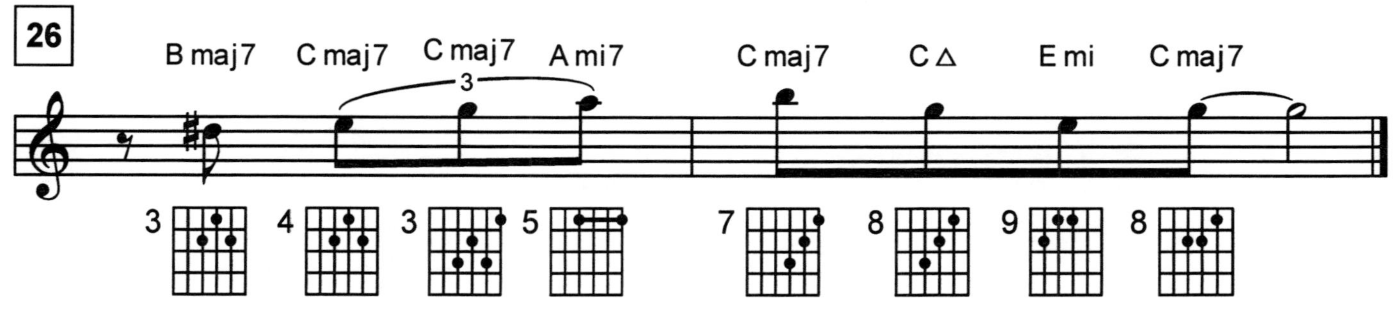

26
B maj7   C maj7   C maj7   A mi7   C maj7   C △   E mi   C maj7
3   3
3 4 3 5   7 8 9 8

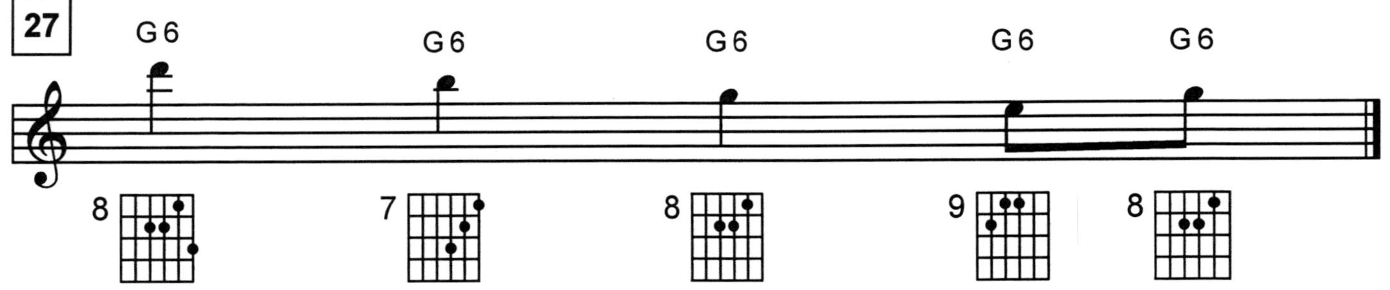

The chord set in example 27 can be renamed as members of the C major family, as in example 28.

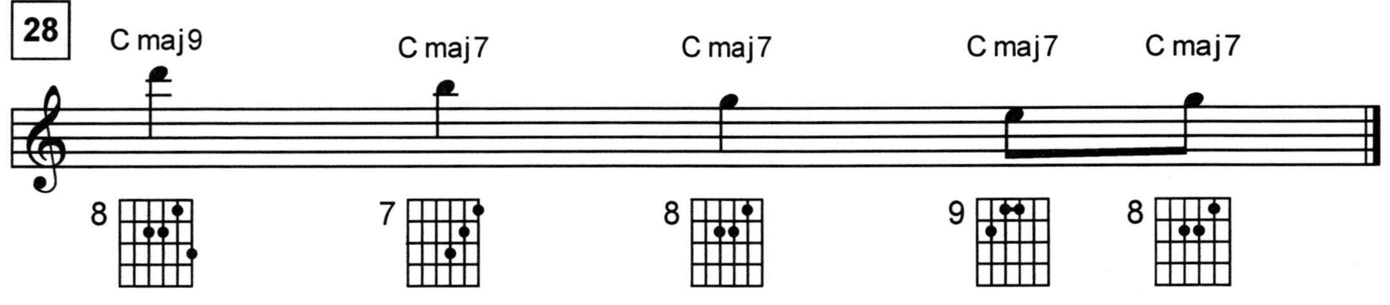

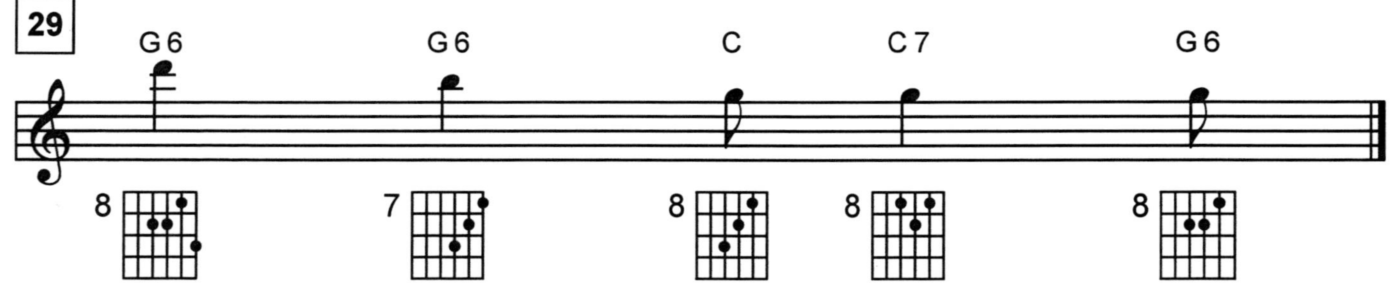

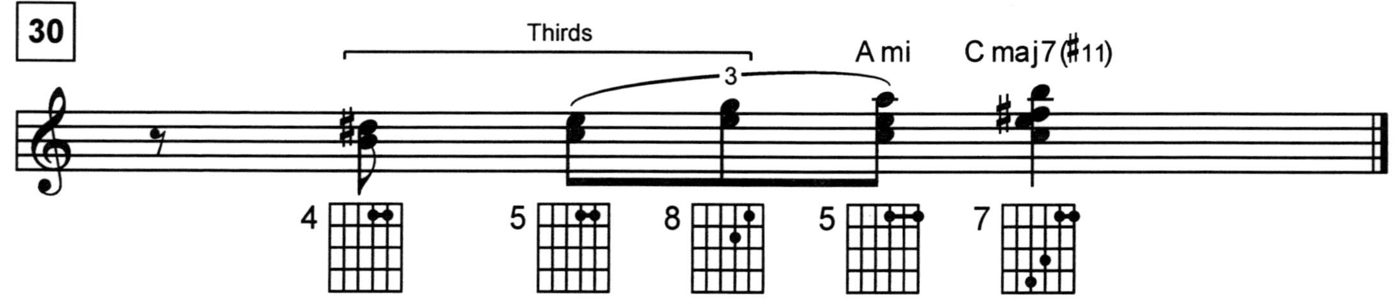

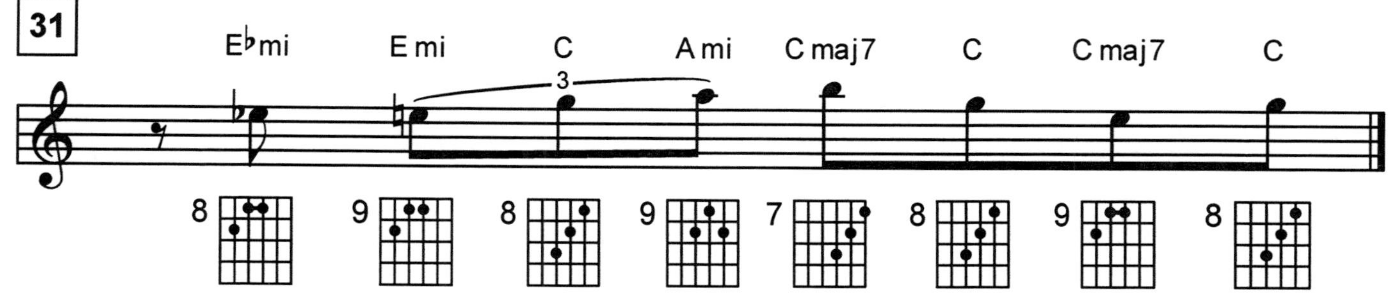

31
Eb mi   E mi   C   A mi   C maj7   C   C maj7   C
3
8   9   8   9   7   8   9   8

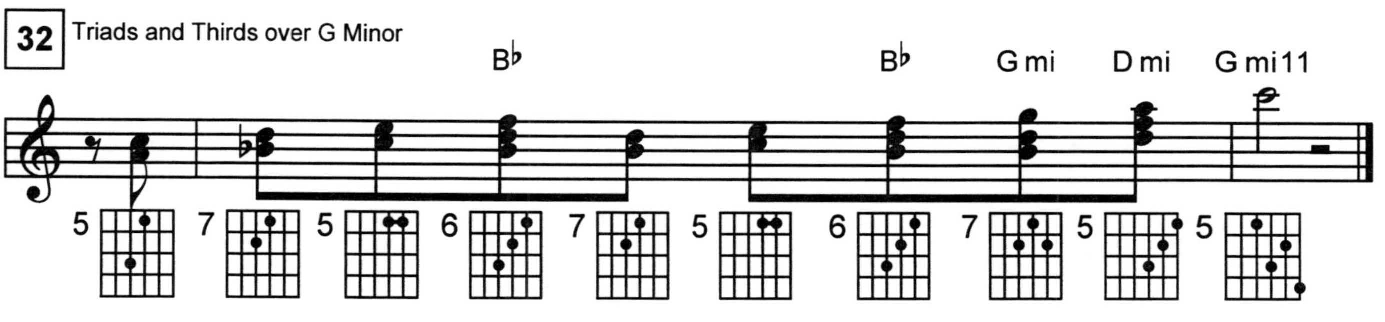

32   Triads and Thirds over G Minor
Bb   Bb   G mi   D mi   G mi 11
5   7   5   6   7   5   6   7   5   5

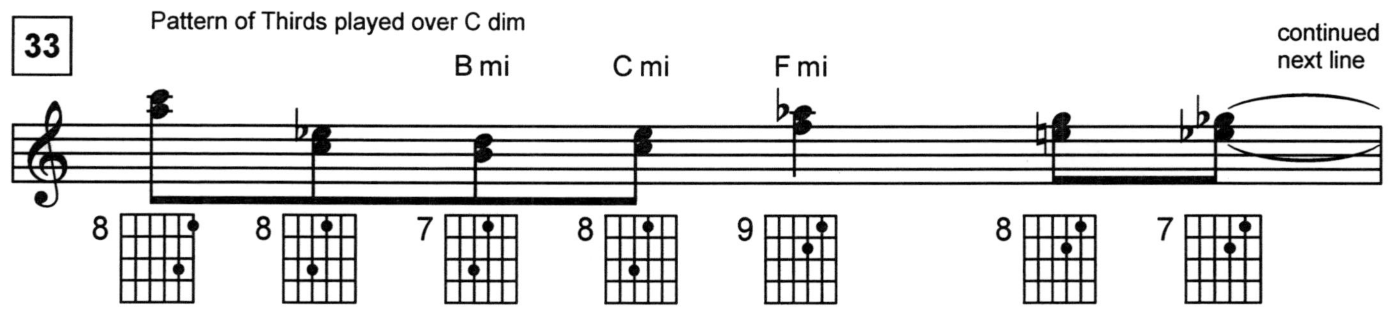

33   Pattern of Thirds played over C dim
B mi   C mi   F mi   continued next line
8   8   7   8   9   8   7

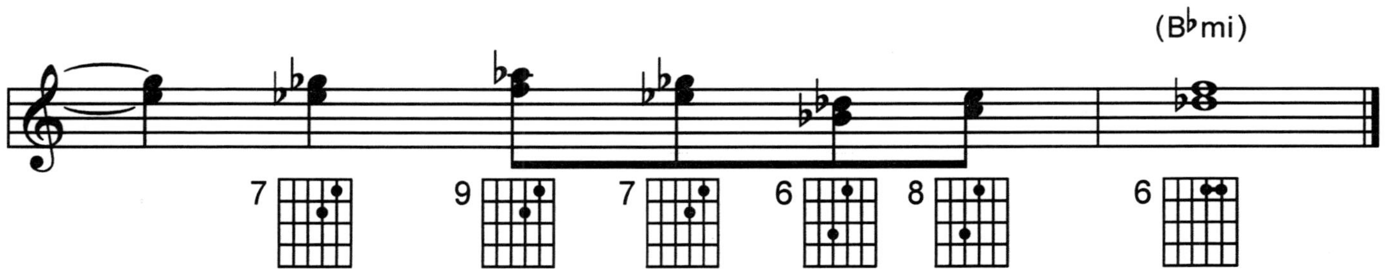

(Bb mi)
7   9   7   6   8   6

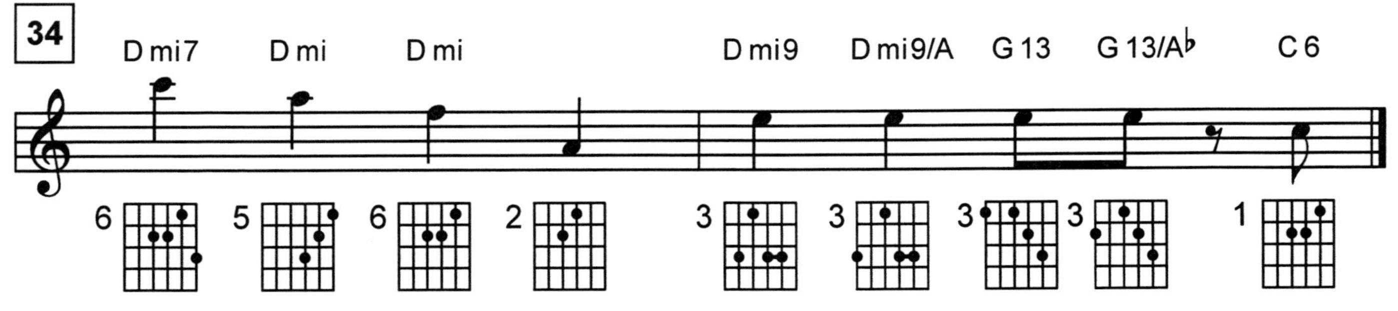

34
D mi7   D mi   D mi   D mi9   D mi9/A   G 13   G 13/Ab   C 6
6   5   6   2   3   3   3   3   1

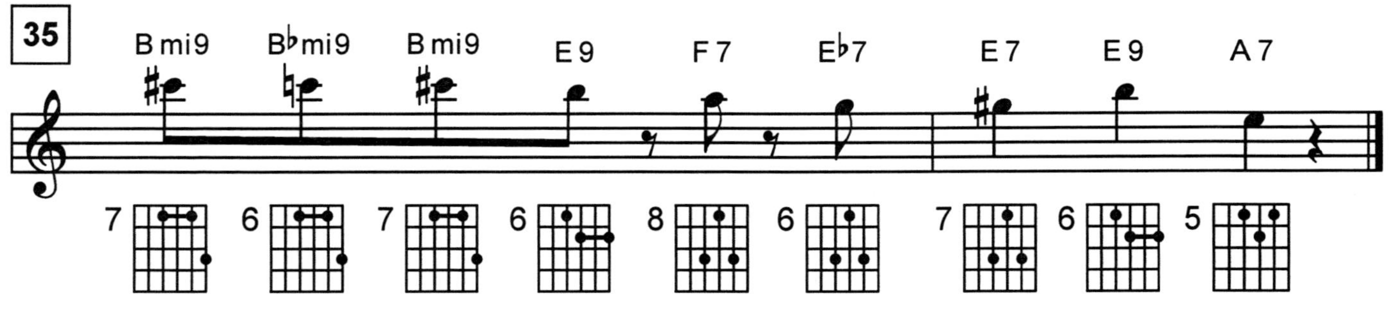

35
B mi9   Bb mi9   B mi9   E 9   F 7   Eb 7   E 7   E 9   A 7
7   6   7   6   8   6   7   6   5

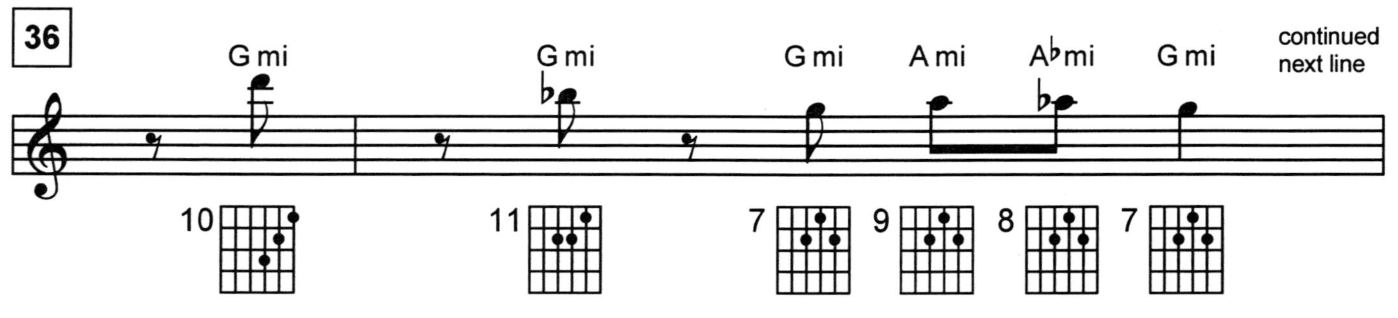

36
G mi   G mi   G mi   A mi   Ab mi   G mi   continued next line
10   11   7   9   8   7

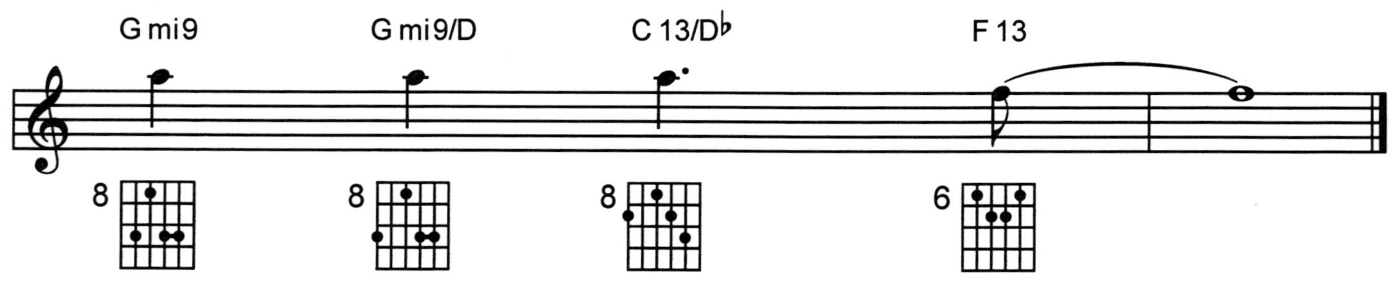

G mi9   G mi9/D   C 13/Db   F 13
8   8   8   6

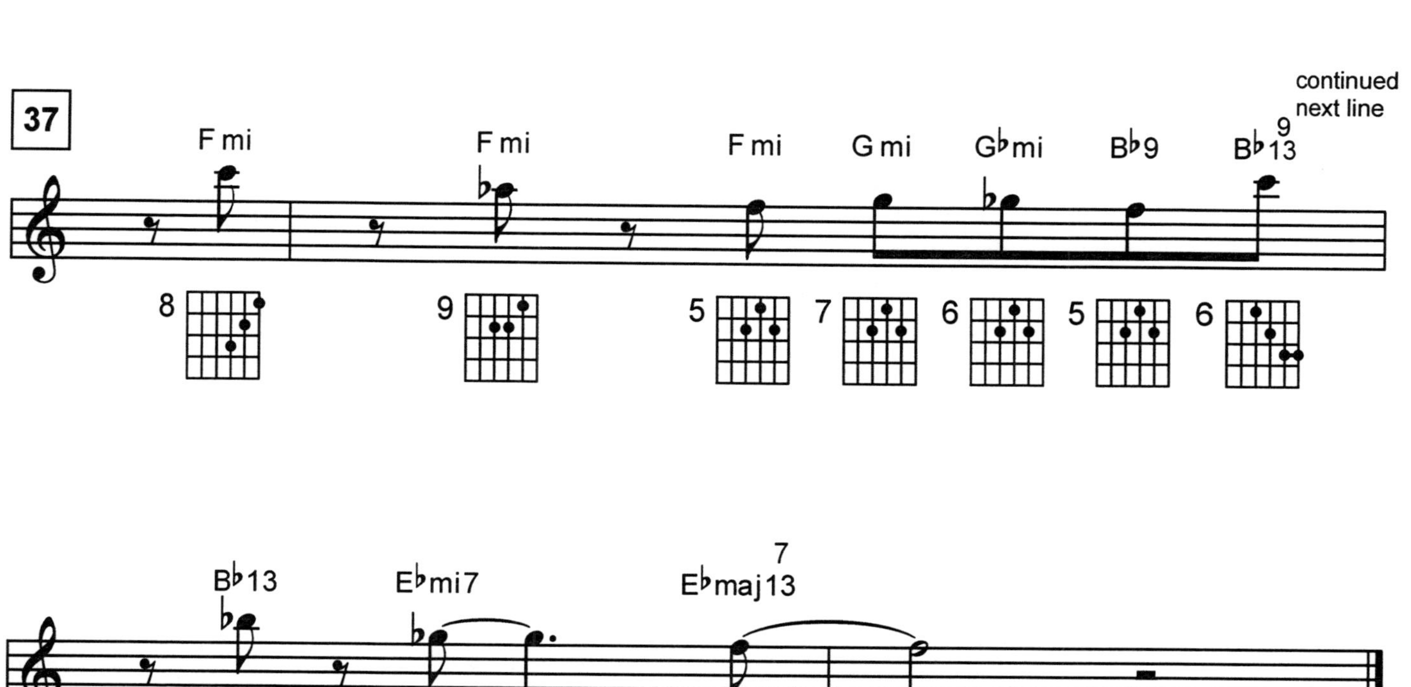

37
continued next line
F mi   F mi   F mi   G mi   Gb mi   Bb9   Bb13 9
8   9   5   7   6   5   6

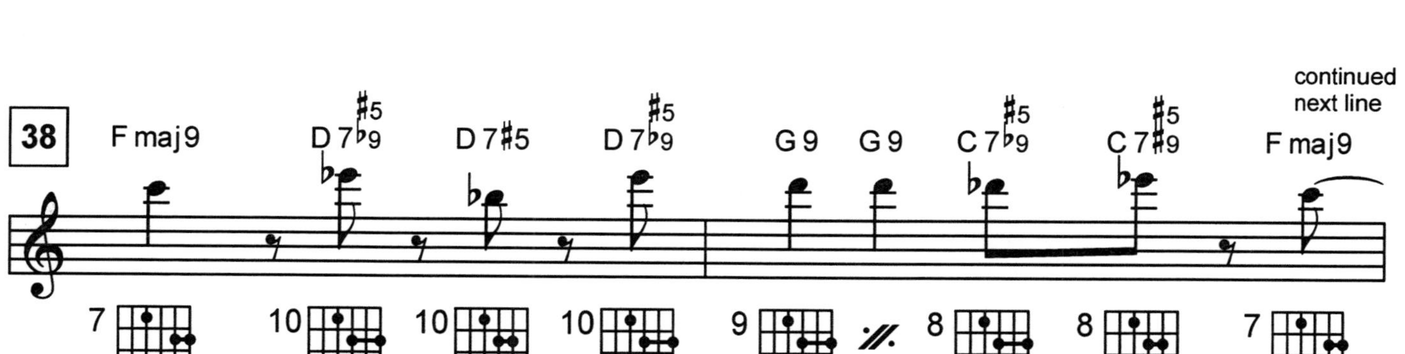

Bb13   Eb mi7   Eb maj13 7
6   6   5

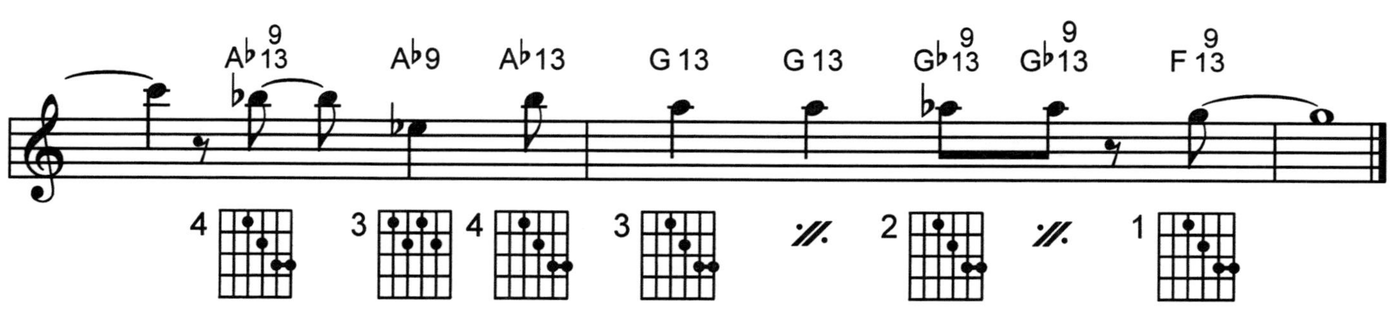

continued next line
38
F maj9   D7#5 b9   D7#5   D7#5 b9   G9   G9   C7#5 b9   C7#5 #9   F maj9
7   10   10   10   9   //.   8   8   7

Ab13 9   Ab9   Ab13   G13   G13   Gb13 9   Gb13 9   F13 9
4   3   4   3   //.   2   //.   1

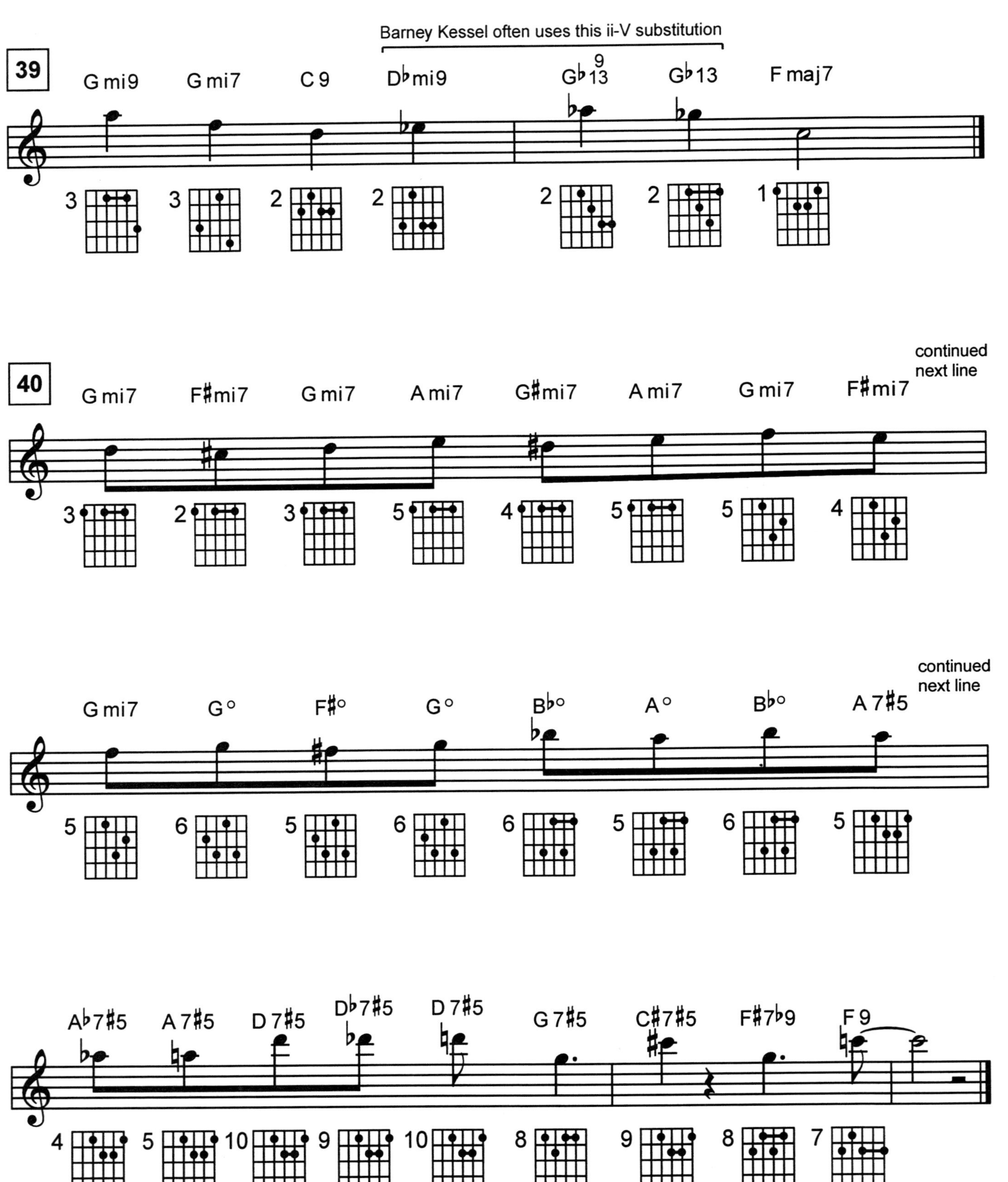

Barney Kessel often uses this ii-V substitution

39
G mi9   G mi7   C 9   D♭mi9   G♭13(9)   G♭13   F maj7

40
G mi7   F#mi7   G mi7   A mi7   G#mi7   A mi7   G mi7   F#mi7
continued next line

G mi7   G°   F#°   G°   B♭°   A°   B♭°   A 7#5
continued next line

A♭7#5   A 7#5   D 7#5   D♭7#5   D 7#5   G 7#5   C#7#5   F#7♭9   F 9

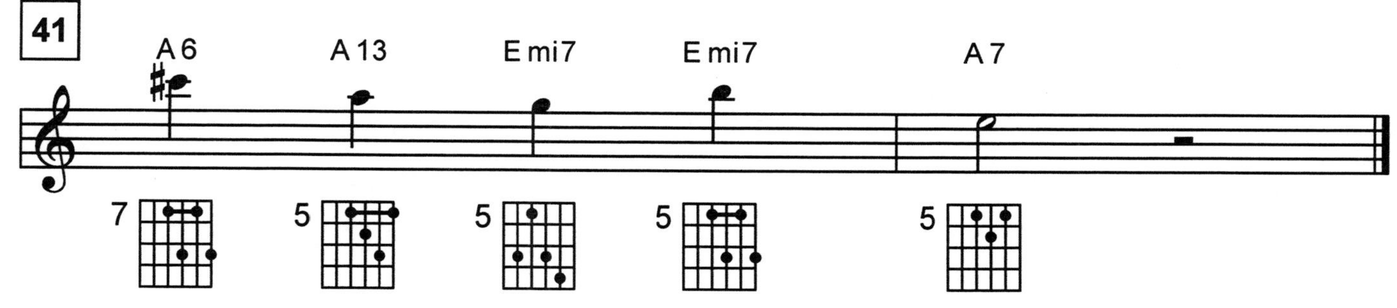

41
A 6
A 13
E mi7
E mi7
A 7
7
5
5
5
5

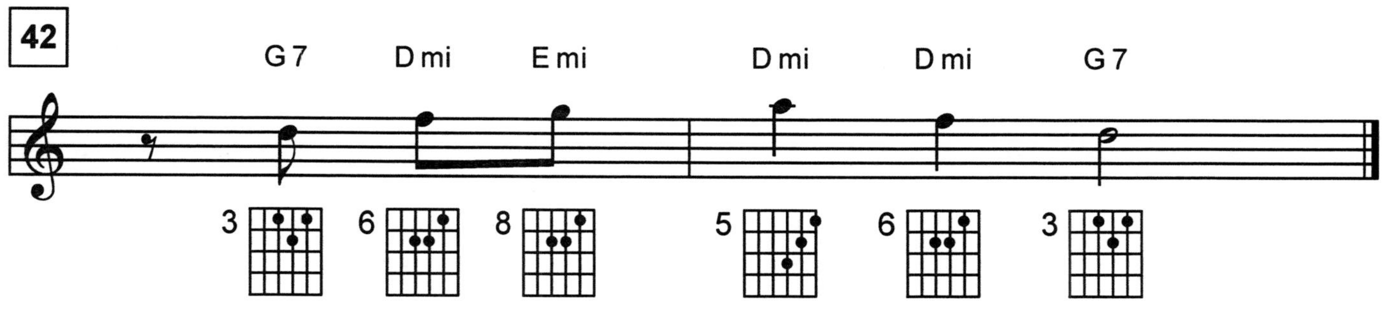

42
G 7
D mi
E mi
D mi
D mi
G 7
3
6
8
5
6
3

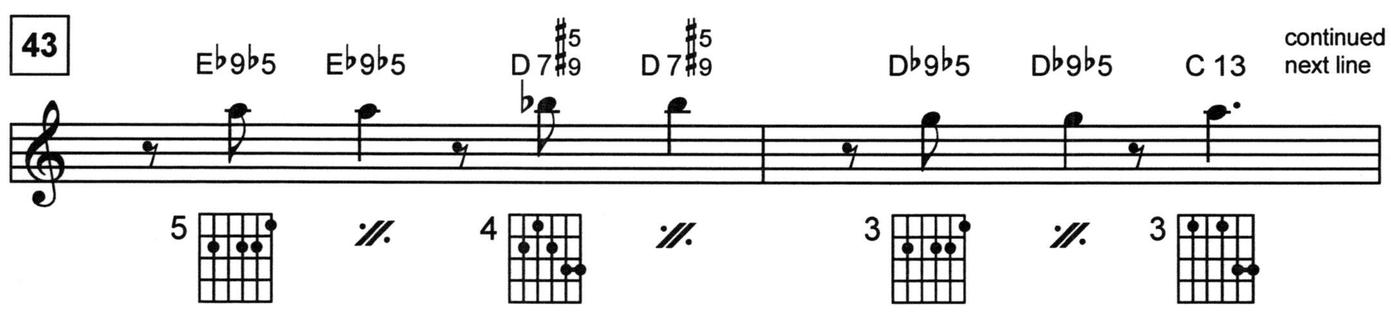

43
continued
next line
Eb9b5
Eb9b5
D 7#5#9
D 7#5#9
Db9b5
Db9b5
C 13
5
4
3
3

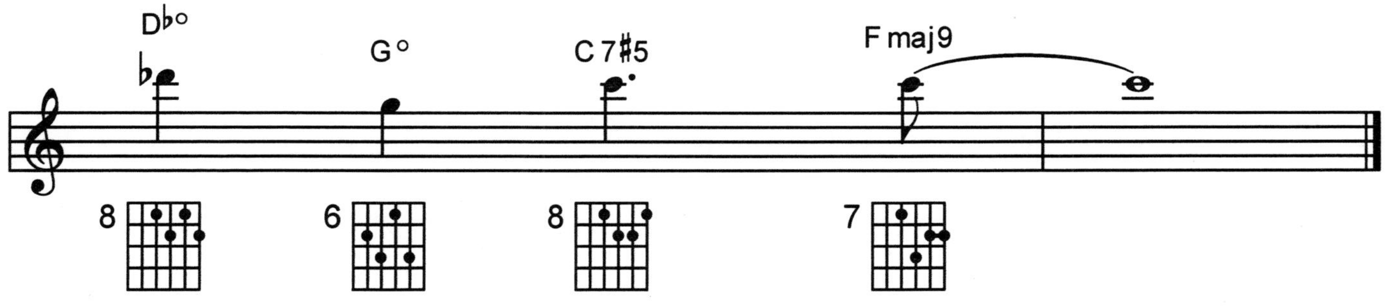

Dbo
Go
C 7#5
F maj9
8
6
8
7

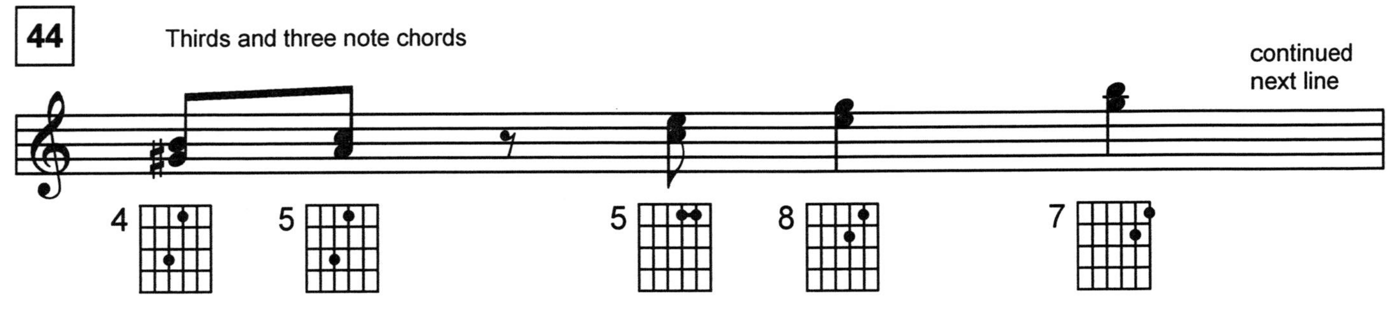

44
Thirds and three note chords
continued
next line
4   5   5   8   7

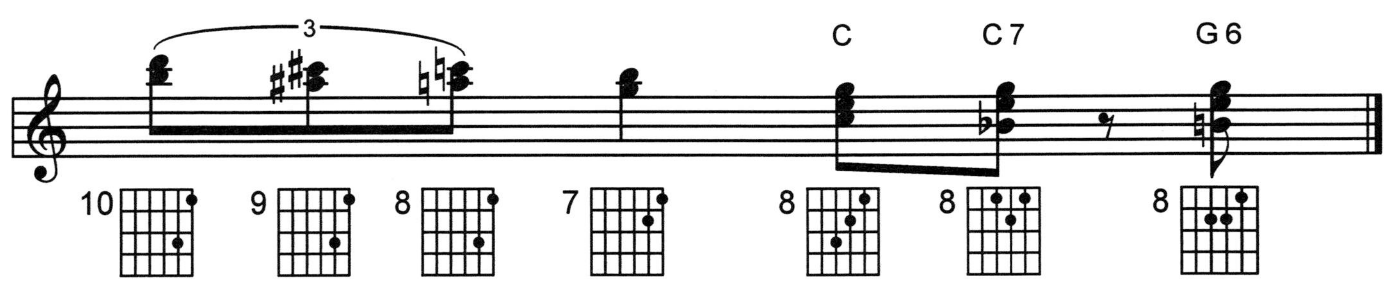

3
C   C 7   G 6
10   9   8   7   8   8   8

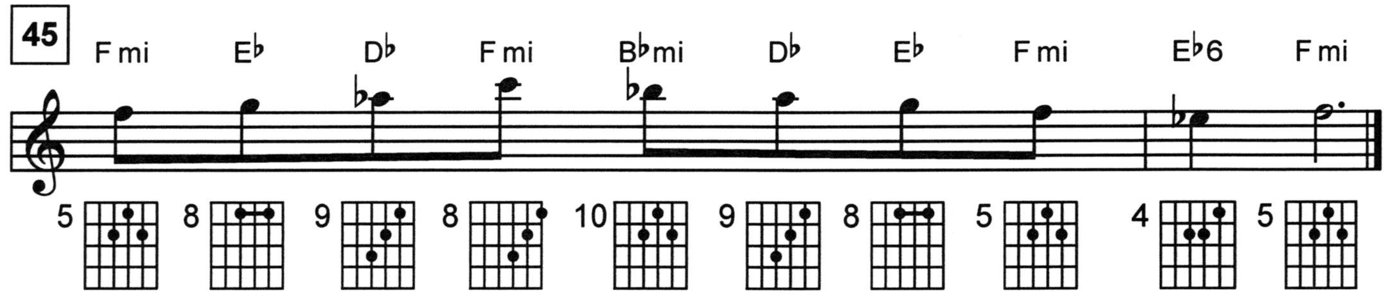

45
F mi   E♭   D♭   F mi   B♭mi   D♭   E♭   F mi   E♭6   F mi
5   8   9   8   10   9   8   5   4   5

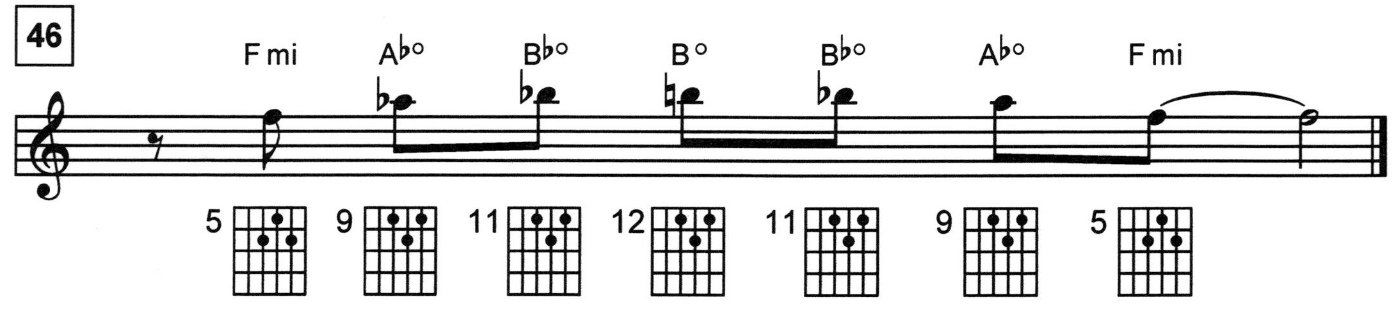

46
F mi   A♭o   B♭o   B o   B♭o   A♭o   F mi
5   9   11   12   11   9   5

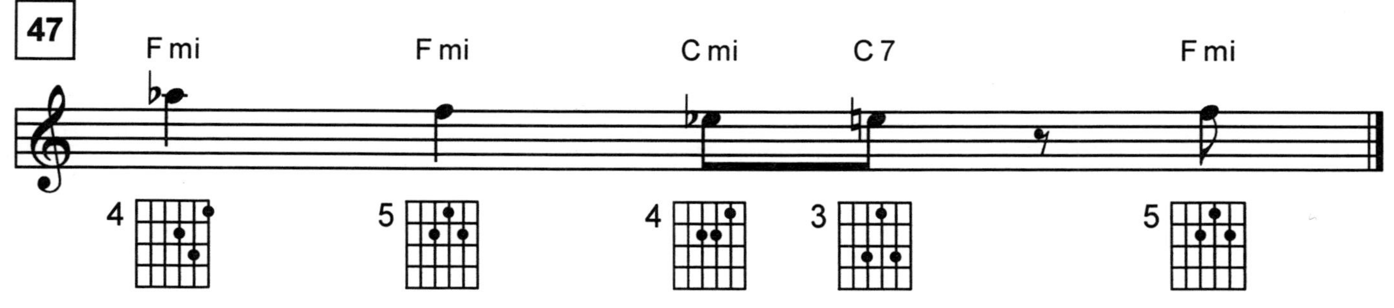

47
F mi
F mi
C mi
C 7
F mi
4
5
4
3
5

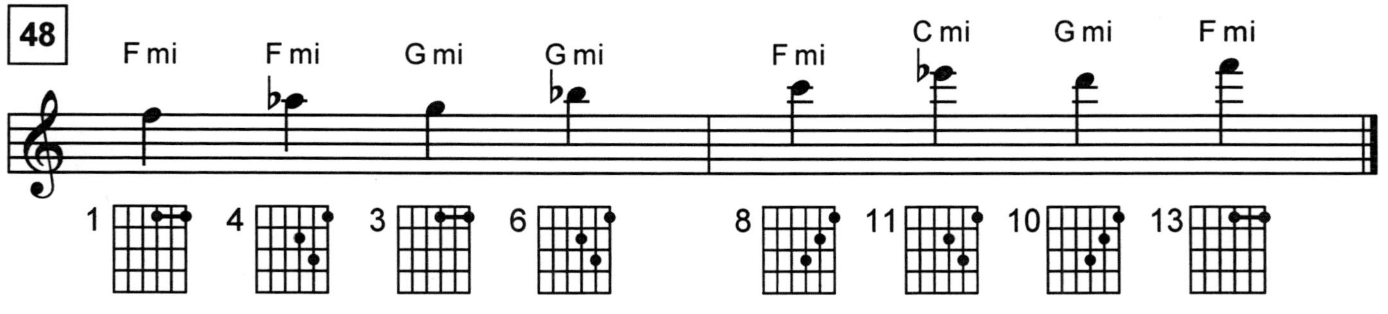

48
F mi
F mi
G mi
G mi
F mi
C mi
G mi
F mi
1
4
3
6
8
11
10
13

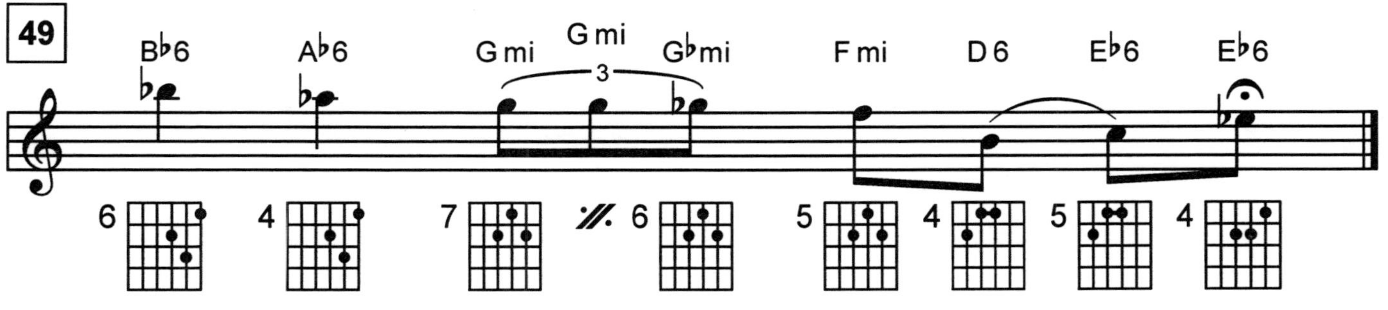

49
Bb6
Ab6
G mi
G mi
Gb mi
F mi
D 6
Eb6
Eb6
3
6
4
7
6
5
4
5
4

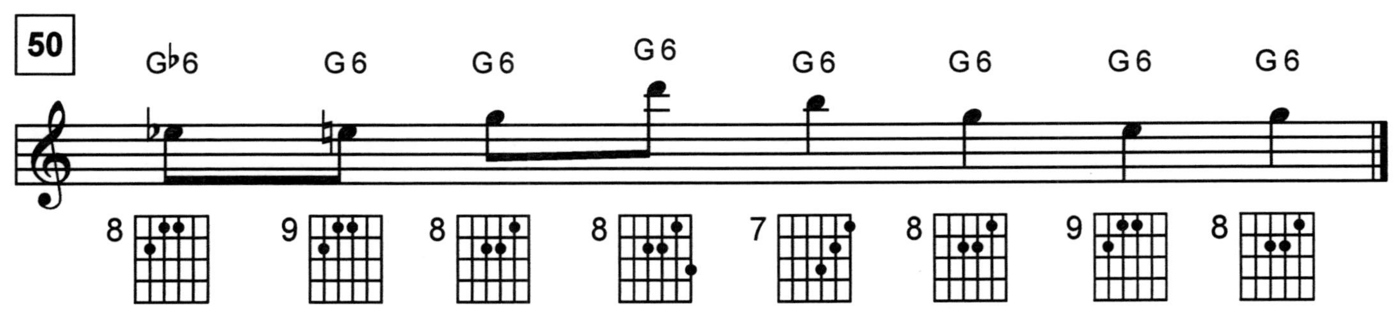

50
Gb6
G 6
G 6
G 6
G 6
G 6
G 6
G 6
8
9
8
8
7
8
9
8

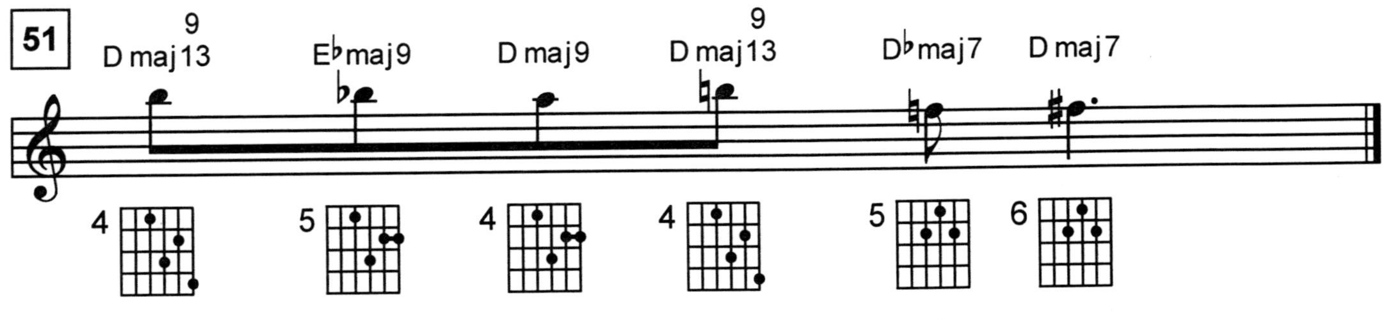

51
D maj13 9
E♭maj9
D maj9
D maj13 9
D♭maj7
D maj7
4
5
4
4
5
6

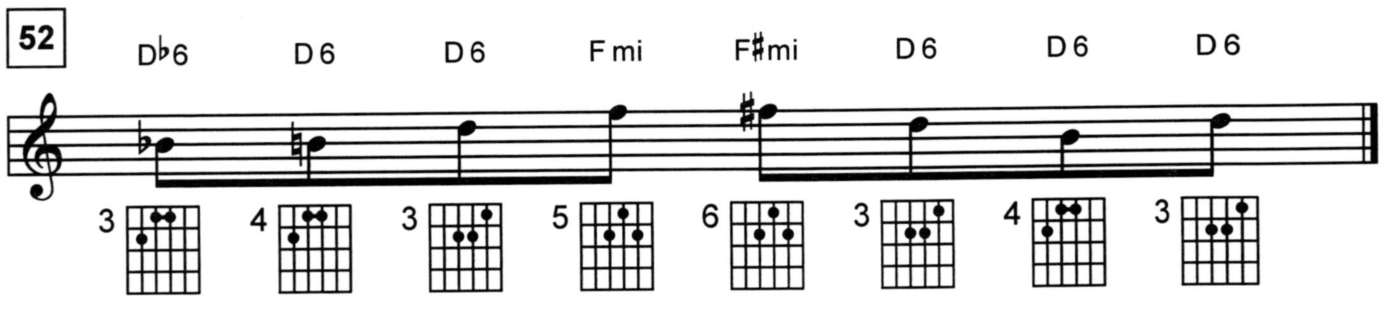

52
D♭6
D 6
D 6
F mi
F#mi
D 6
D 6
D 6
3
4
3
5
6
3
4
3

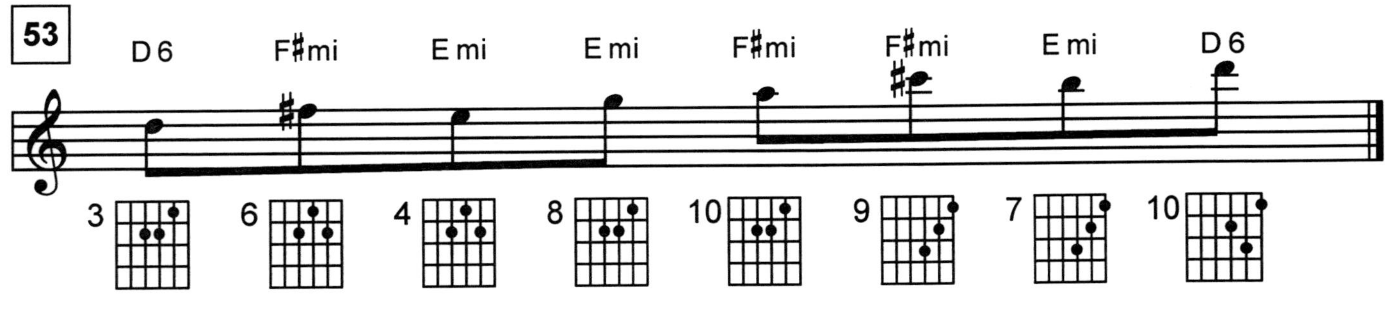

53
D 6
F#mi
E mi
E mi
F#mi
F#mi
E mi
D 6
3
6
4
8
10
9
7
10

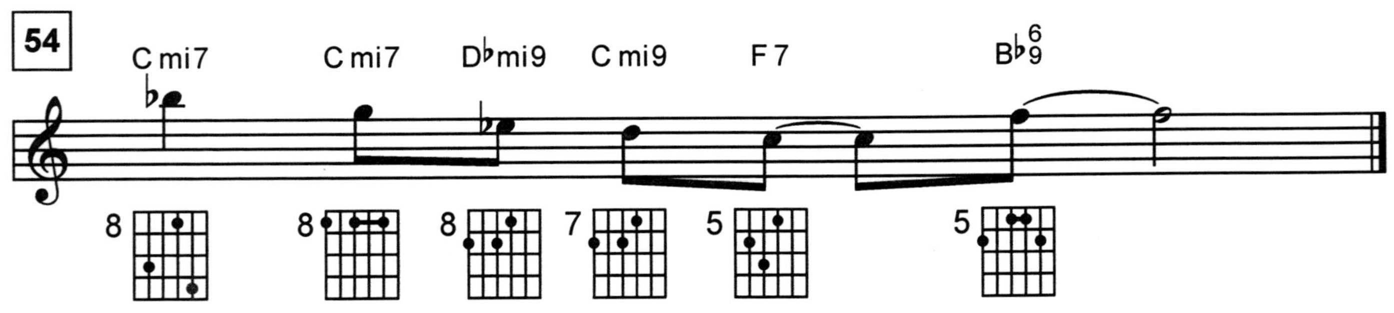

54
C mi7
C mi7
D♭mi9
C mi9
F 7
B♭9 6
8
8
8
7
5
5

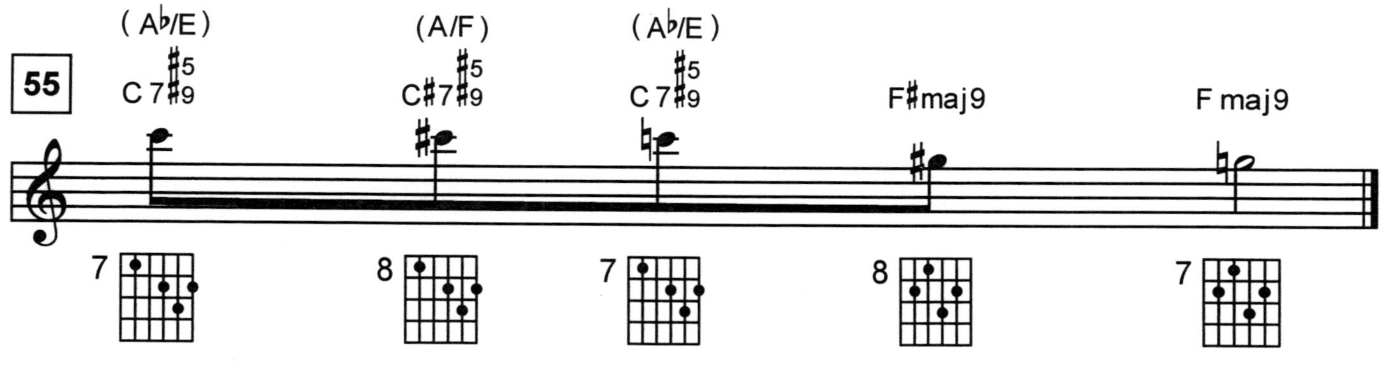
55
(A♭/E)   (A/F)   (A♭/E)
C 7#9#5   C# 7#9#5   C 7#9#5   F#maj9   F maj9
7   8   7   8   7

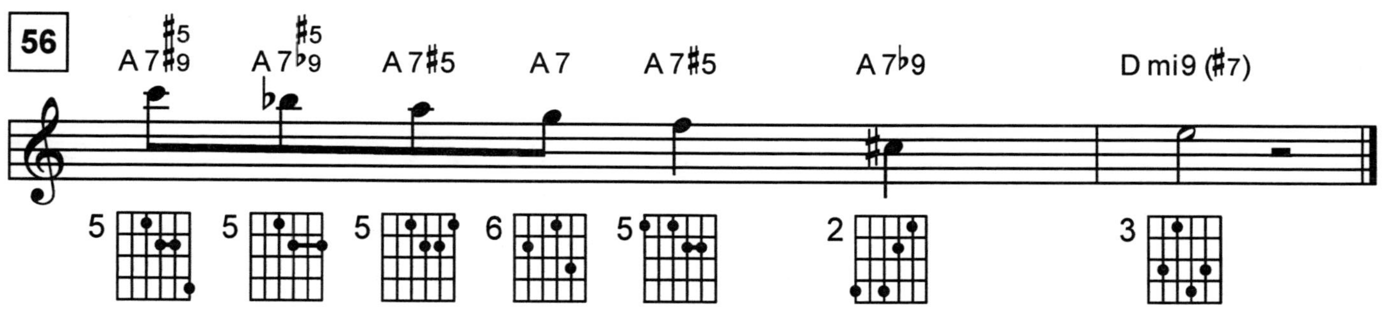
56
A 7#9#5   A 7♭9#5   A 7#5   A 7   A 7#5   A 7♭9   D mi9 (#7)
5   5   5   6   5   2   3

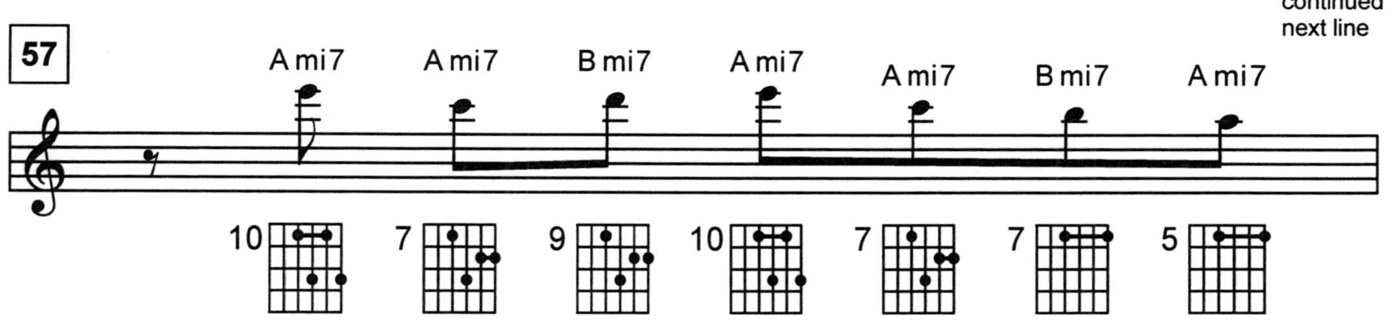
continued
next line
57
A mi7   A mi7   B mi7   A mi7   A mi7   B mi7   A mi7
10   7   9   10   7   7   5

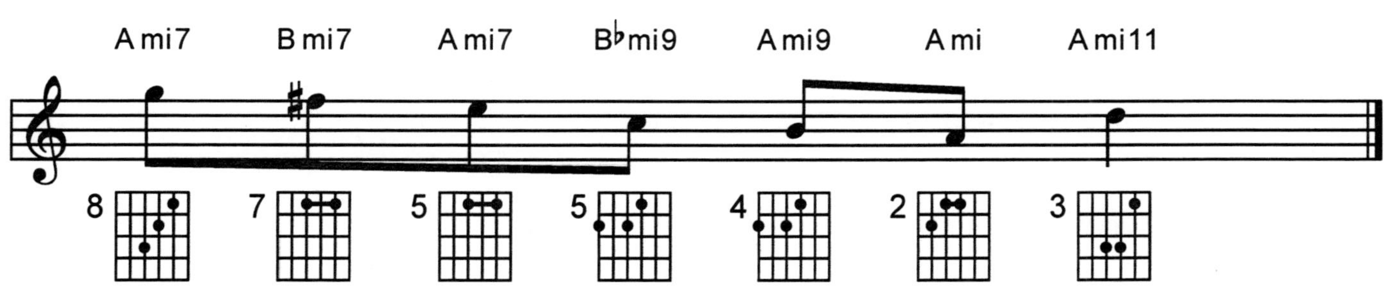
A mi7   B mi7   A mi7   B♭mi9   A mi9   A mi   A mi11
8   7   5   5   4   2   3

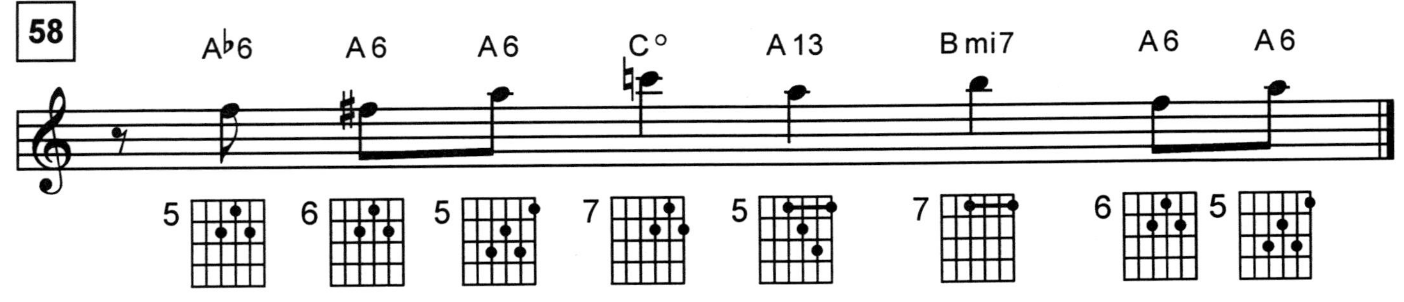

58
A♭6   A6   A6   C°   A13   Bmi7   A6   A6
5   6   5   7   5   7   6   5

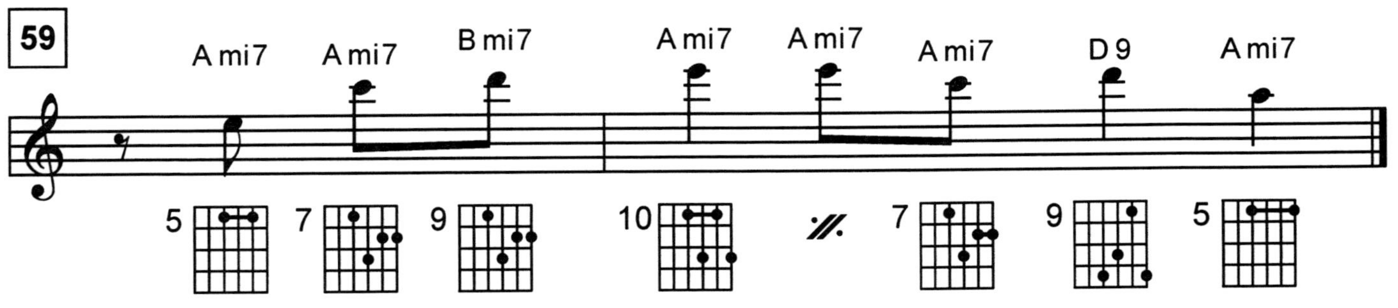

59
Ami7   Ami7   Bmi7   Ami7   Ami7   Ami7   D9   Ami7
5   7   9   10   ://.   7   9   5

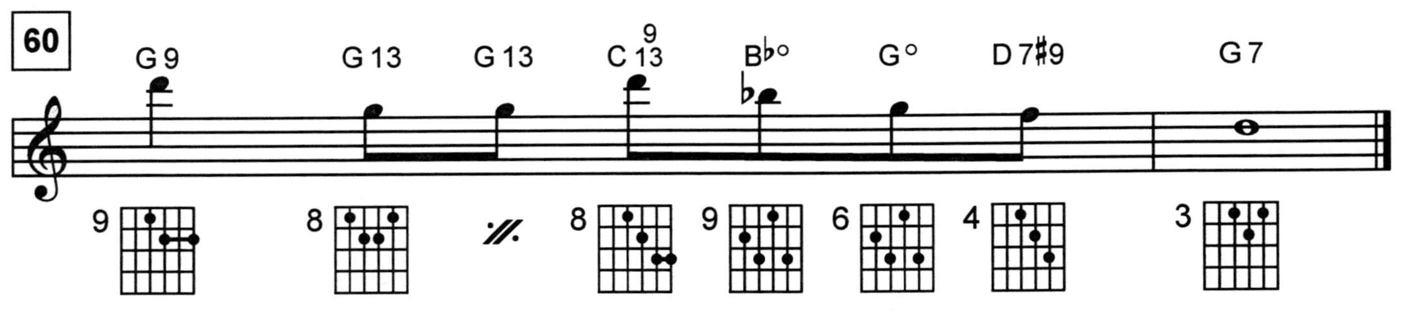

60
G9   G13   G13   C13⁹   B♭°   G°   D7#9   G7
9   8   ://.   8   9   6   4   3

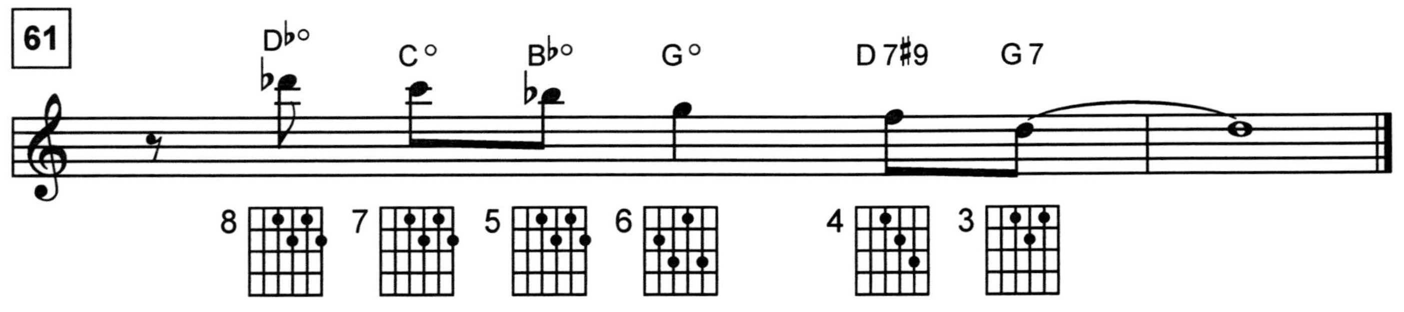

61
D♭°   C°   B♭°   G°   D7#9   G7
8   7   5   6   4   3

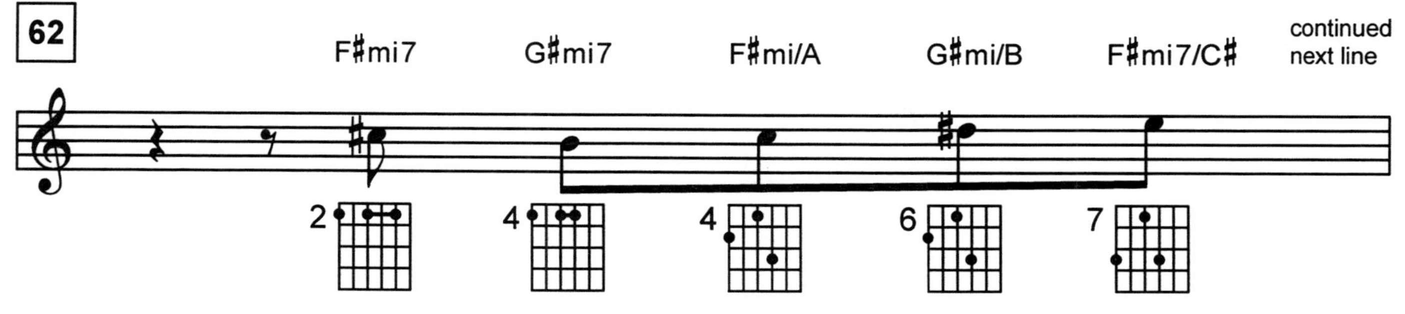
62
continued next line
F#mi7
G#mi7
F#mi/A
G#mi/B
F#mi7/C#
2
4
4
6
7

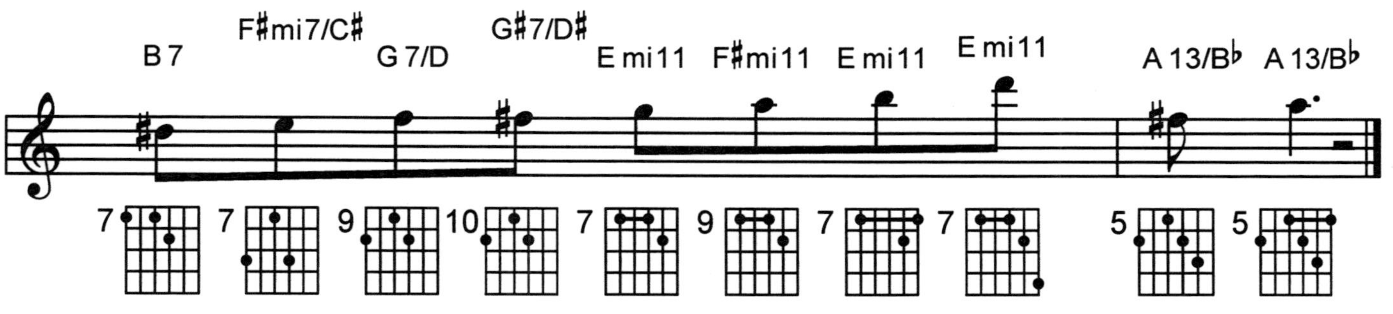
B 7
F#mi7/C#
G 7/D
G#7/D#
E mi11
F#mi11
E mi11
E mi11
A 13/Bb
A 13/Bb
7
7
9
10
7
9
7
7
5
5

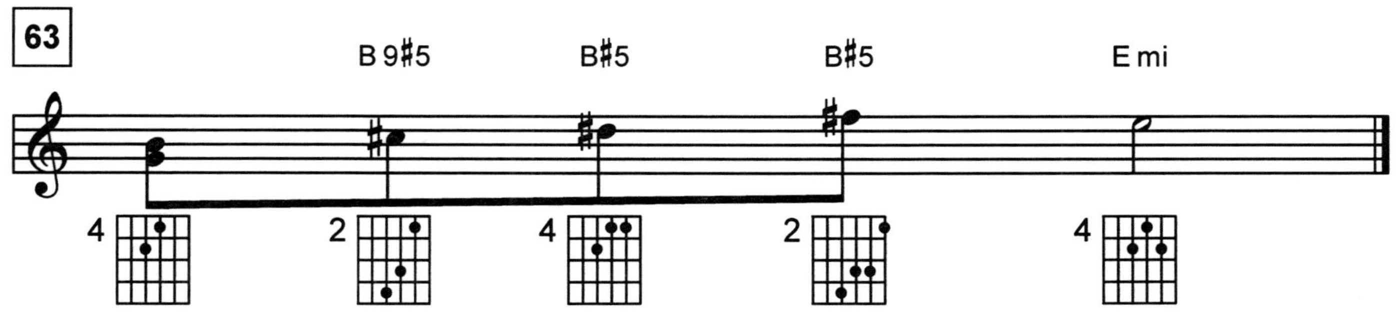
63
B 9#5
B#5
B#5
E mi
4
2
4
2
4

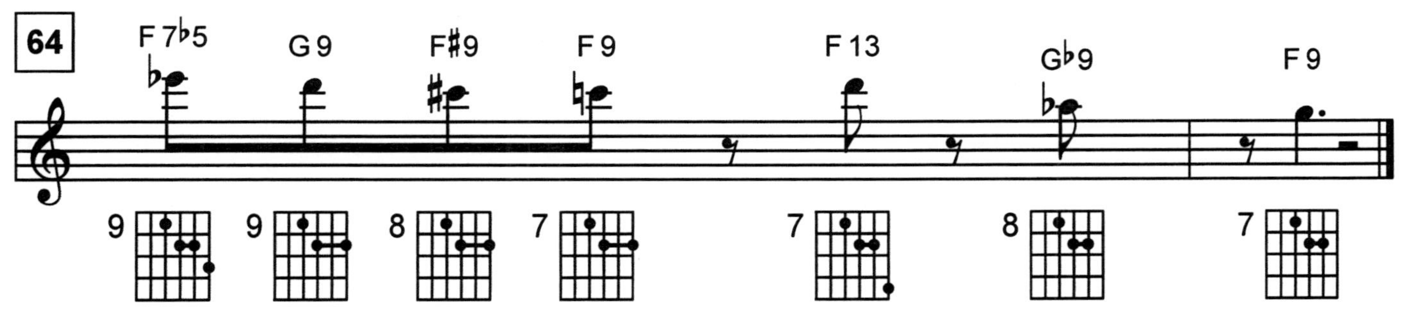
64
F 7b5
G 9
F#9
F 9
F 13
Gb9
F 9
9
9
8
7
7
8
7

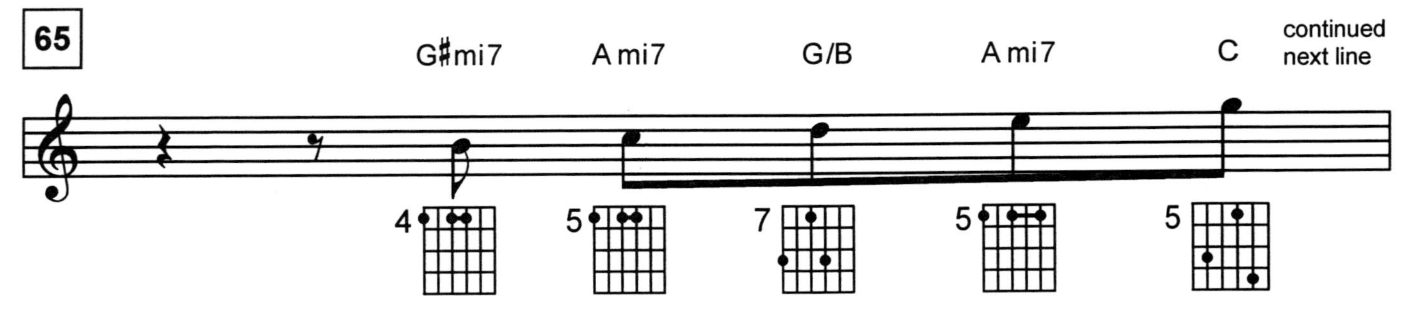

65
continued next line
G#mi7   Ami7   G/B   Ami7   C
4   5   7   5   5

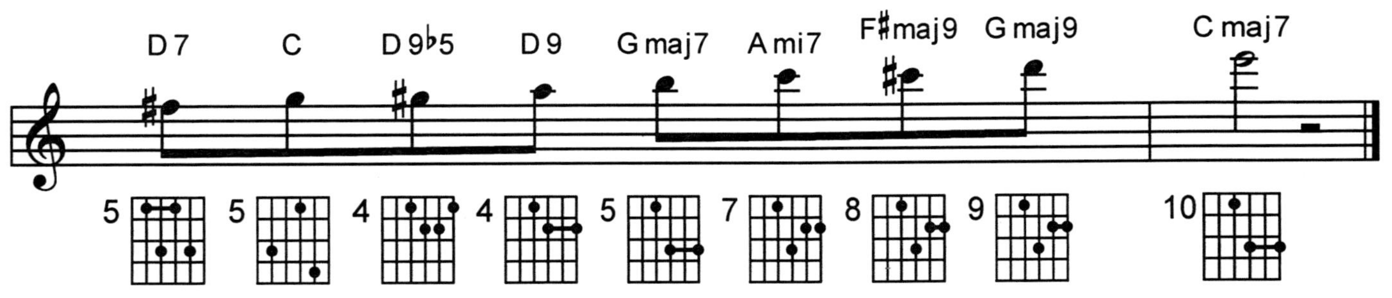

D7   C   D9b5   D9   Gmaj7   Ami7   F#maj9   Gmaj9   Cmaj7
5   5   4   4   5   7   8   9   10

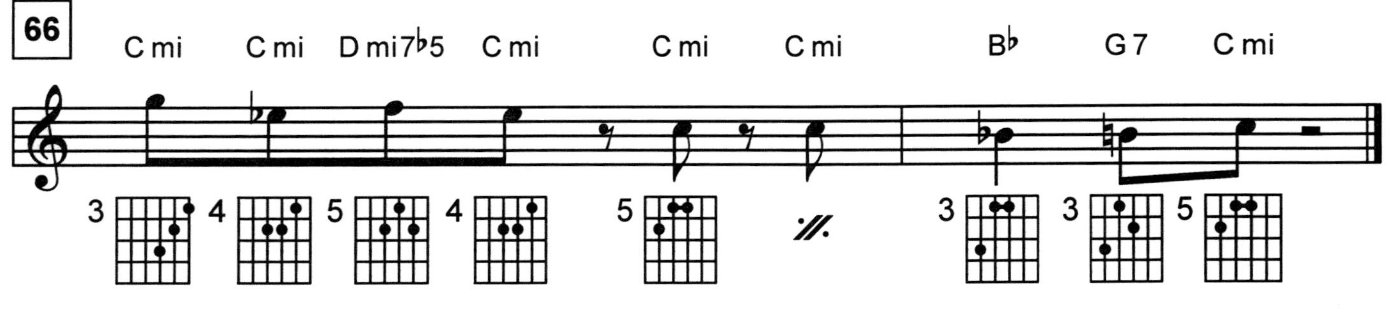

66
Cmi   Cmi   Dmi7b5   Cmi   Cmi   Cmi   Bb   G7   Cmi
3   4   5   4   5   ://.   3   3   5

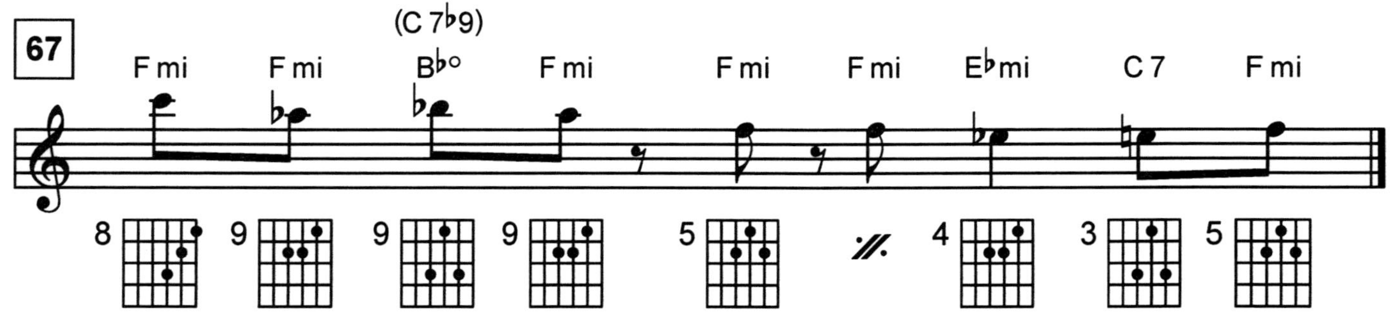

67
(C7b9)
Fmi   Fmi   Bbo   Fmi   Fmi   Fmi   Ebmi   C7   Fmi
8   9   9   9   5   ://.   4   3   5

A starter sequence for an F blues, I progressing to IV:

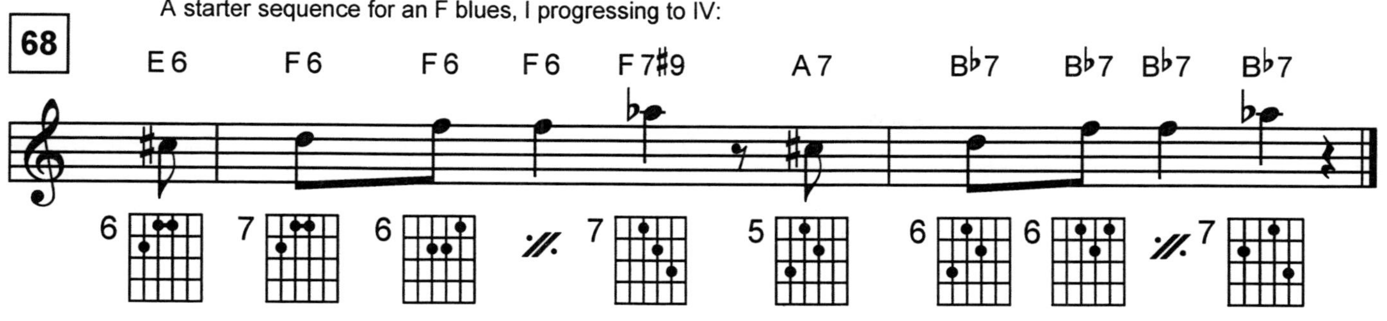

68
E 6   F 6   F 6   F 6   F 7#9   A 7   Bb7   Bb7 Bb7 Bb7
6   7   6   ⅞.   7   5   6   6   ⅞.   7

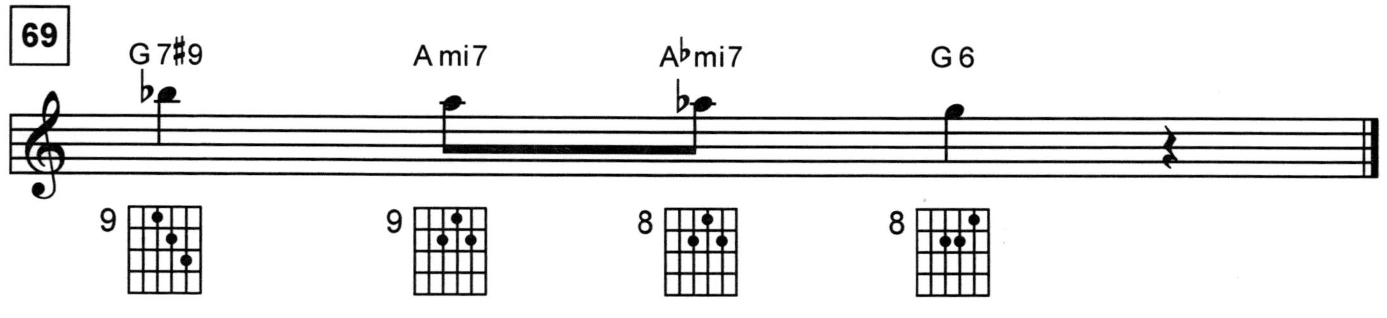

69
G 7#9   A mi7   Ab mi7   G 6
9   9   8   8

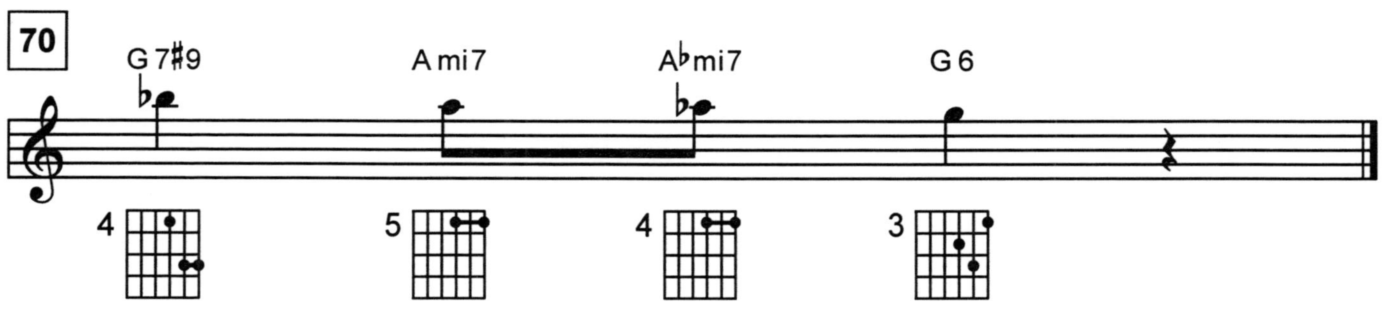

70
G 7#9   A mi7   Ab mi7   G 6
4   5   4   3

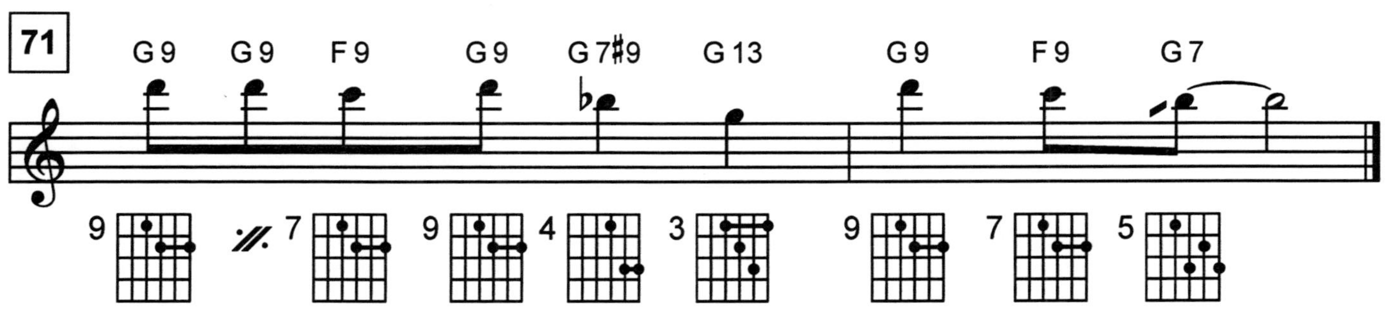

71
G 9   G 9   F 9   G 9   G 7#9   G 13   G 9   F 9   G 7
9   ⅞.   7   9   4   3   9   7   5

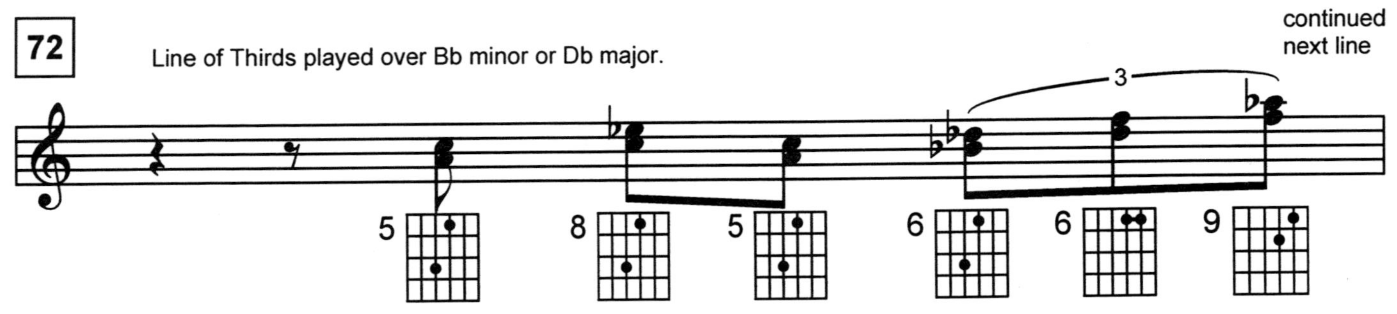

72
continued
next line
Line of Thirds played over Bb minor or Db major.
3
5 8 5 6 6 9

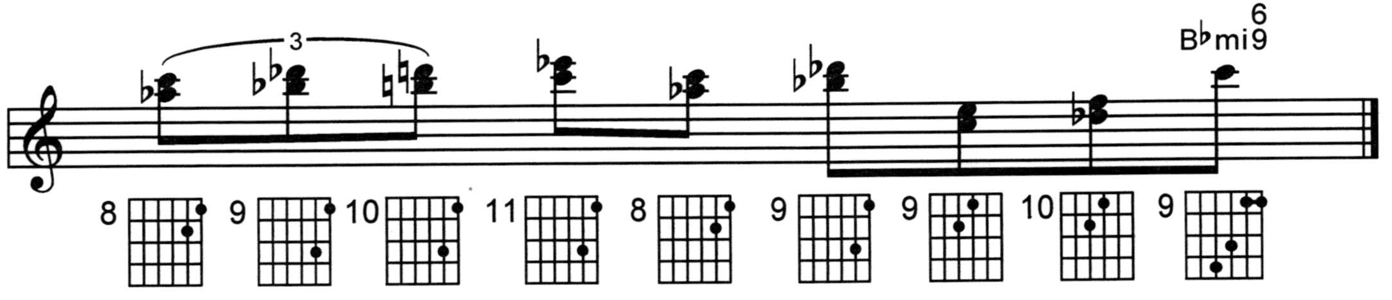

3
6
B♭mi9
8 9 10 11 8 9 9 10 9

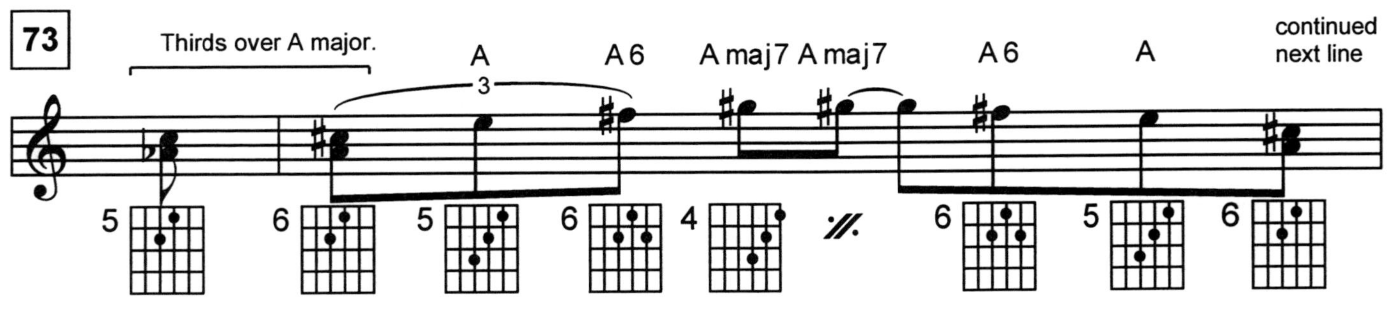

73
continued
next line
Thirds over A major.
A   A 6   A maj7 A maj7   A 6   A
3
5 6 5 6 4 6 5 6

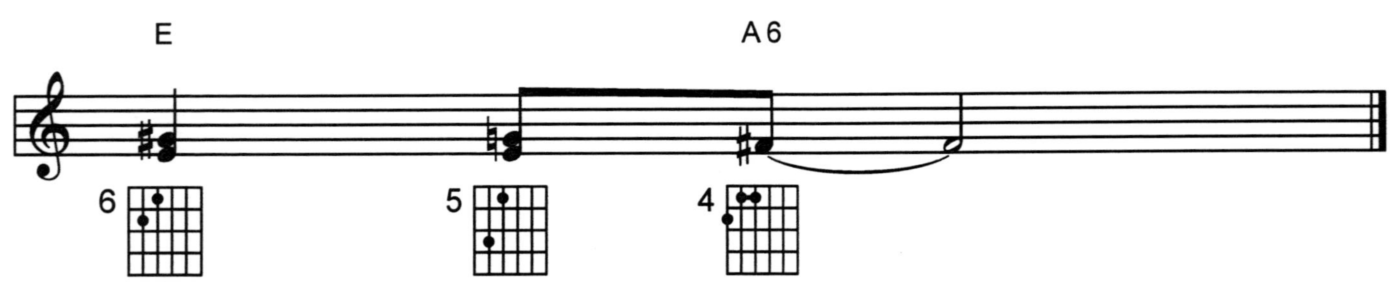

E
A 6
6 5 4

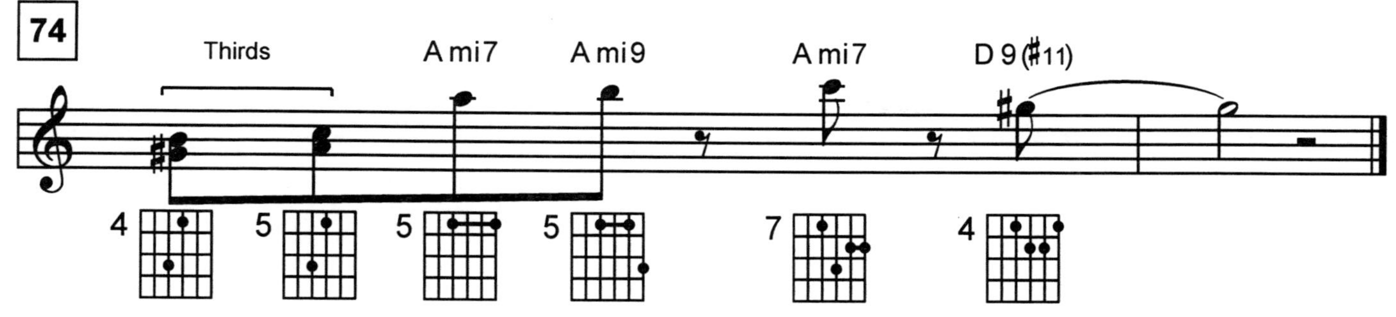
74
Thirds
A mi7
A mi9
A mi7
D 9 (#11)
4 5 5 5 7 4

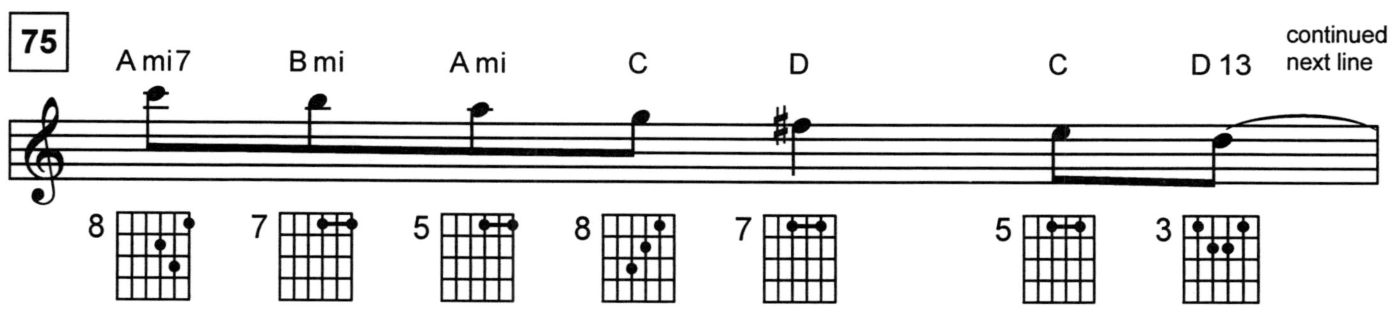
75
A mi7
B mi
A mi
C
D
C
D 13
continued
next line
8 7 5 8 7 5 3

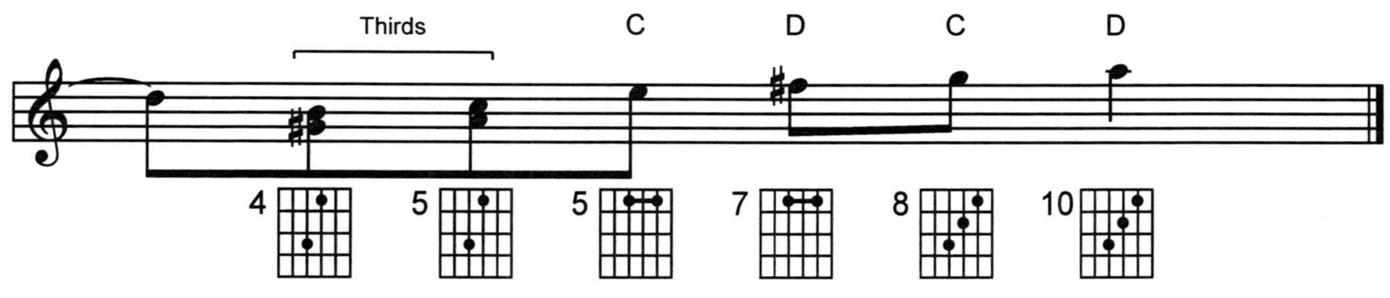
Thirds
C
D
C
D
4 5 5 7 8 10

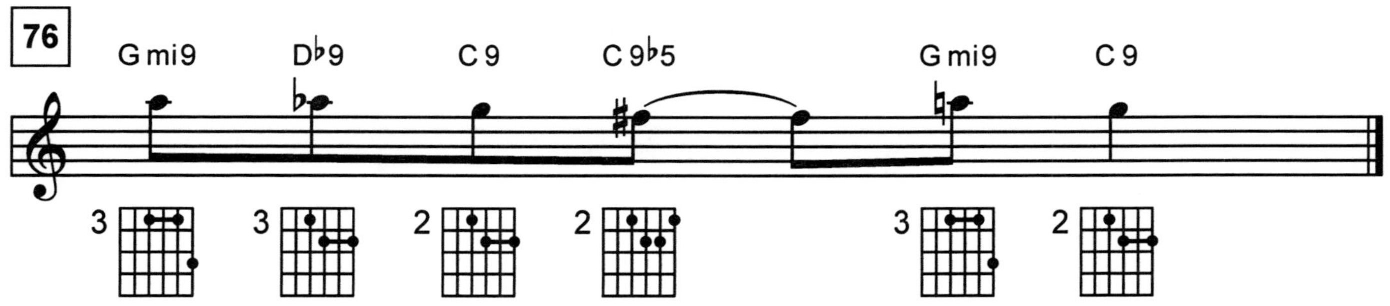
76
G mi9
Db9
C 9
C 9b5
G mi9
C 9
3 3 2 2 3 2

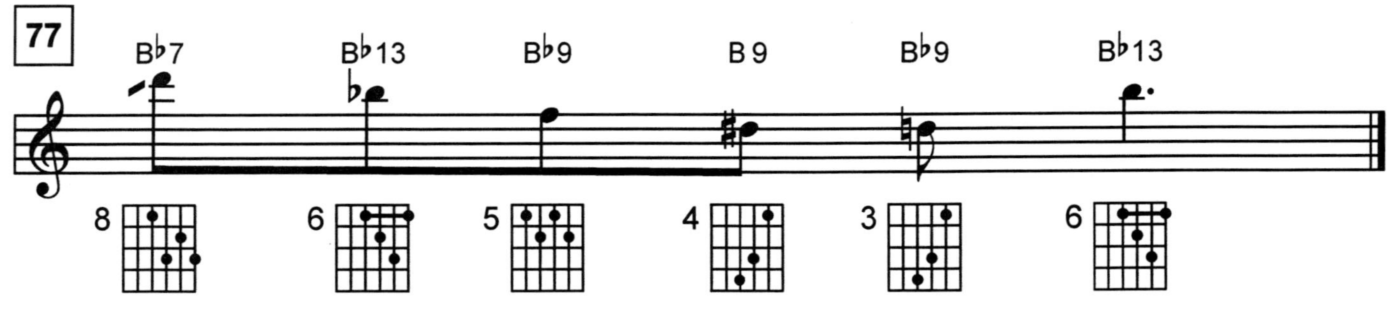

77
Bb7   Bb13   Bb9   B9   Bb9   Bb13
8   6   5   4   3   6

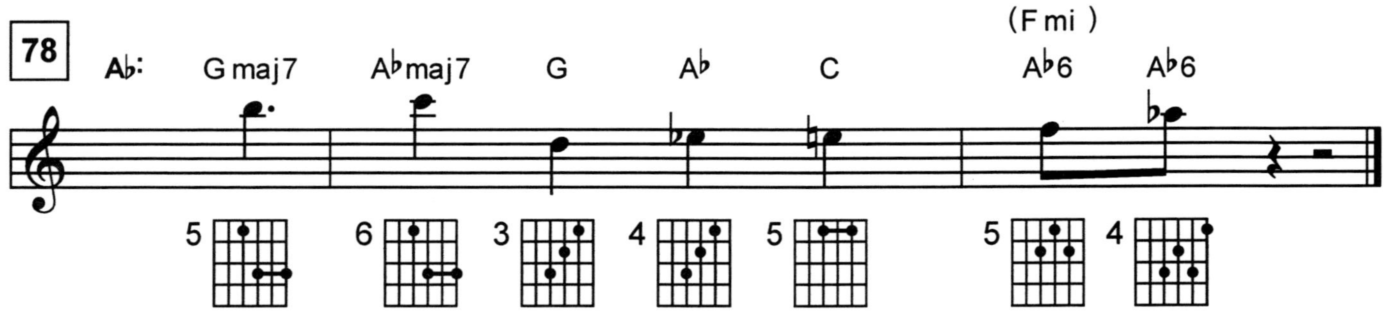

78
Ab: Gmaj7   Abmaj7   G   Ab   C   (Fmi)   Ab6   Ab6
5   6   3   4   5   5   4

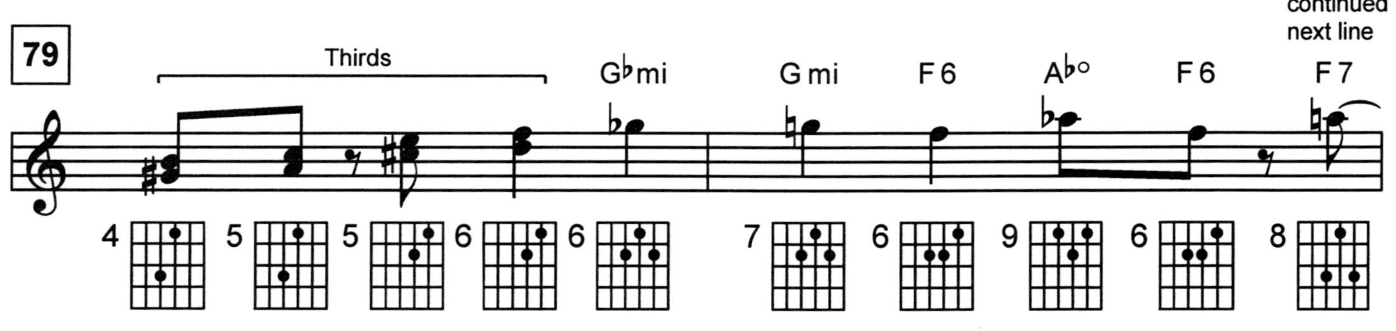

79
Thirds   Gbmi   Gmi   F6   Abo   F6   F7
continued next line
4   5   5   6   6   7   6   9   6   8

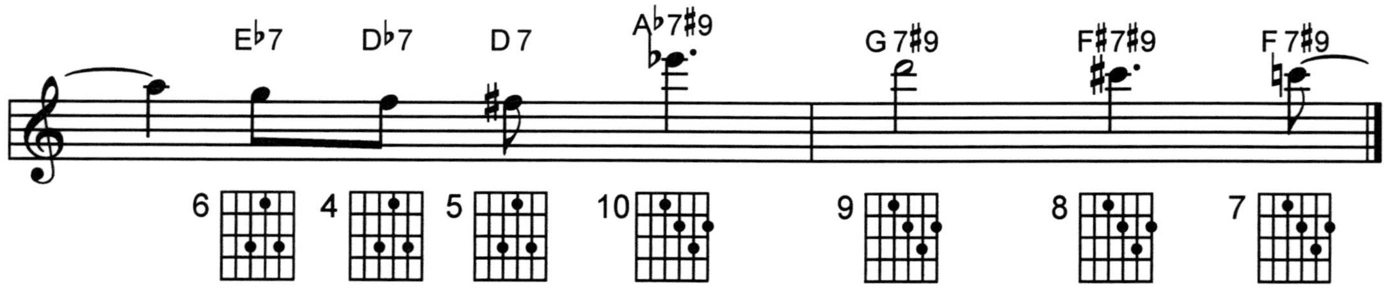

Eb7   Db7   D7   Ab7#9   G7#9   F#7#9   F7#9
6   4   5   10   9   8   7

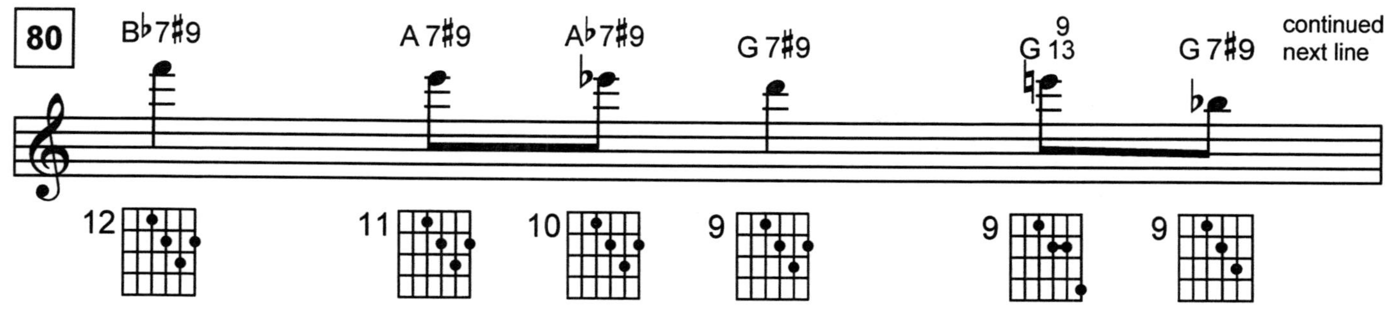

80
B♭7♯9   A7♯9   A♭7♯9   G7♯9   G13 9   G7♯9   continued next line
12   11   10   9   9   9

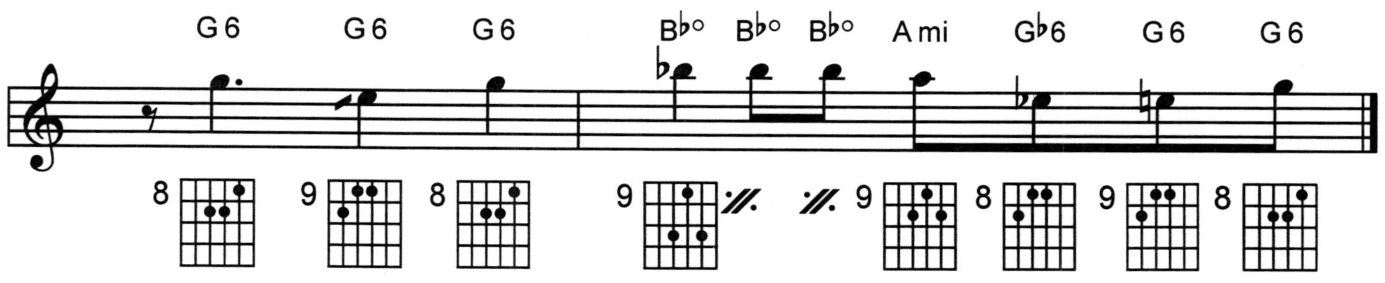

G6   G6   G6   B♭o   B♭o   B♭o   Ami   G♭6   G6   G6
8   9   8   9   ℅.   ℅.   9   8   9   8

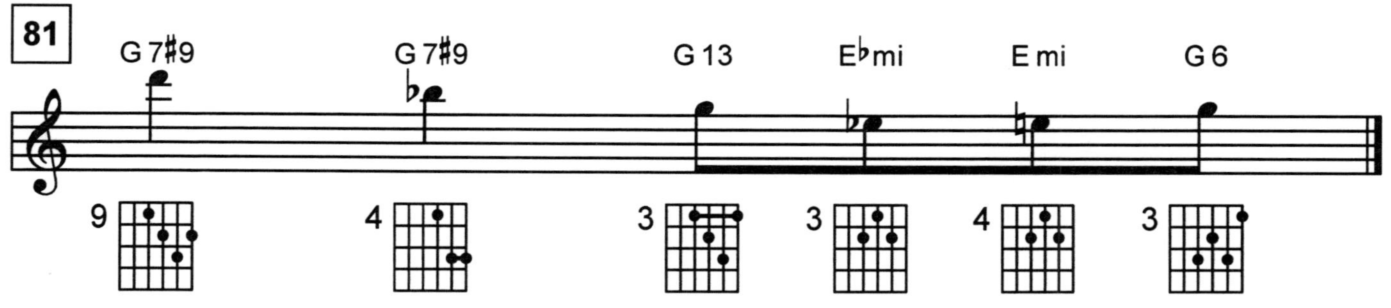

81
G7♯9   G7♯9   G13   E♭mi   Emi   G6
9   4   3   3   4   3

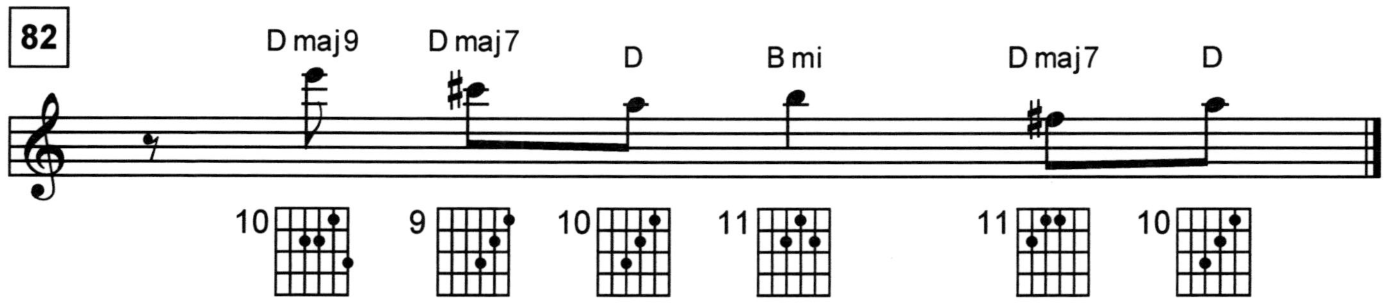

82
Dmaj9   Dmaj7   D   Bmi   Dmaj7   D
10   9   10   11   11   10

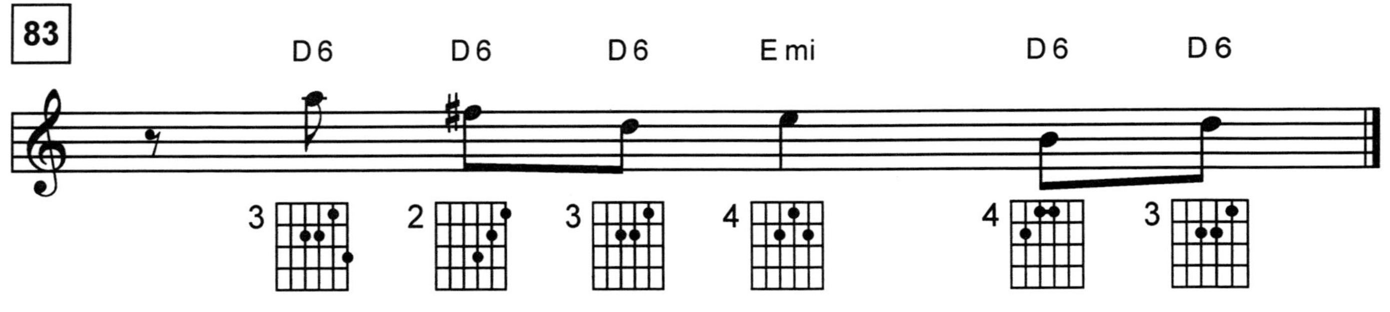

83
D 6   D 6   D 6   E mi   D 6   D 6
3 2 3 4 4 3

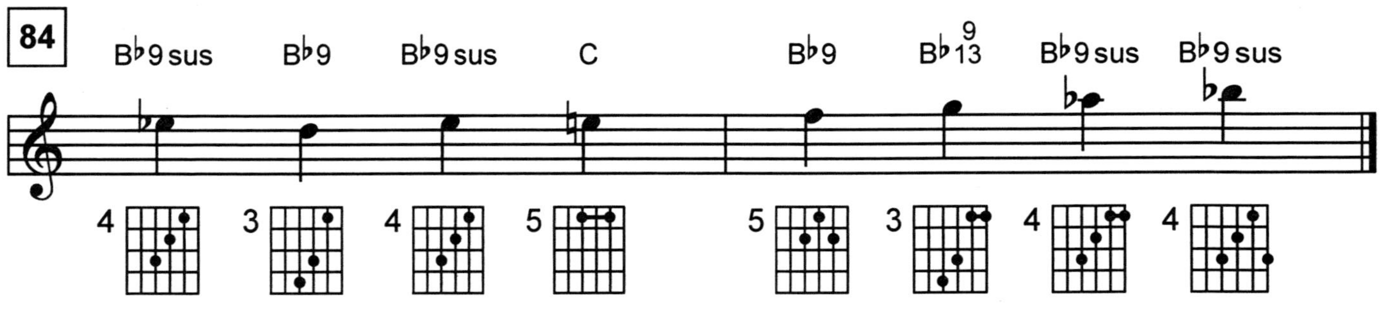

84
B♭9 sus   B♭9   B♭9 sus   C   B♭9   B♭13⁹   B♭9 sus   B♭9 sus
4 3 4 5 5 3 4 4

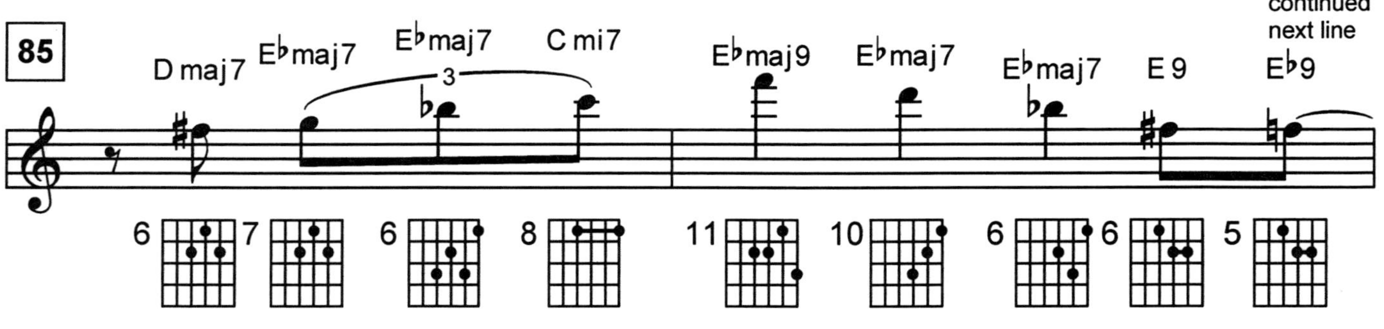

continued
next line
85
D maj7   E♭maj7   E♭maj7   C mi7   E♭maj9   E♭maj7   E♭maj7   E 9   E♭9
3
6 7 6 8 11 10 6 6 5

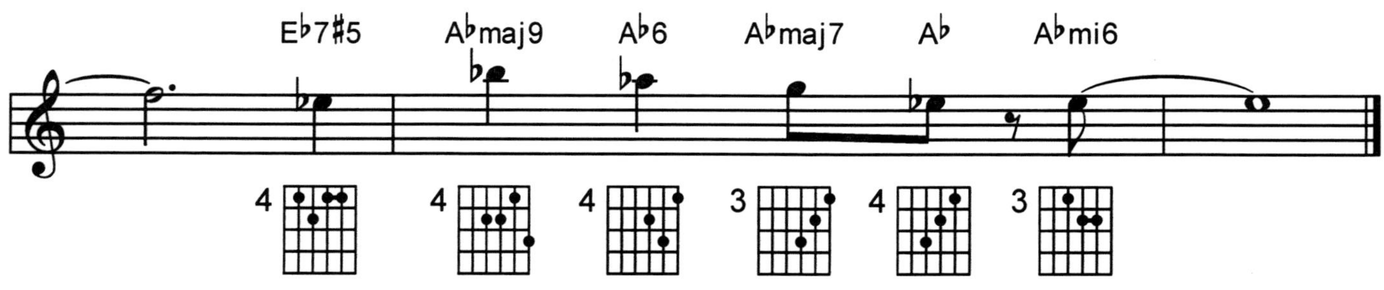

E♭7♯5   A♭maj9   A♭6   A♭maj7   A♭   A♭mi6
4 4 4 3 4 3

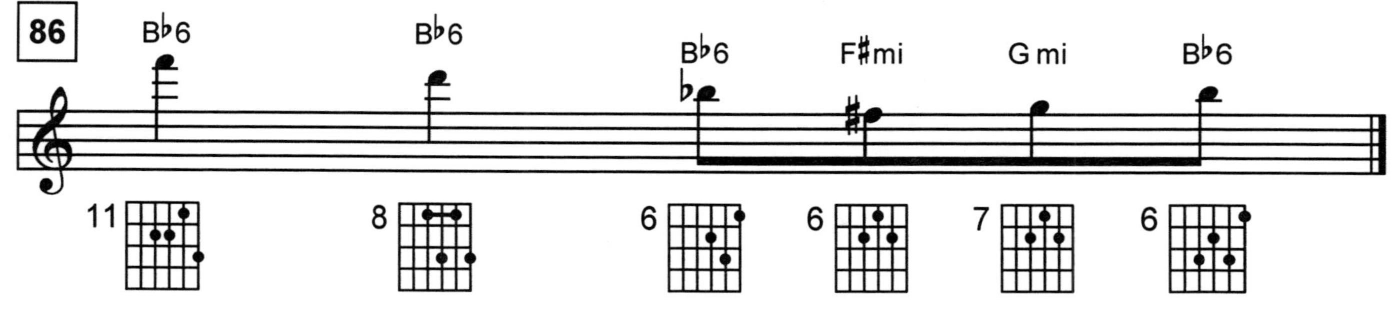

86
B♭6
B♭6
B♭6
F♯mi
G mi
B♭6
11
8
6
6
7
6

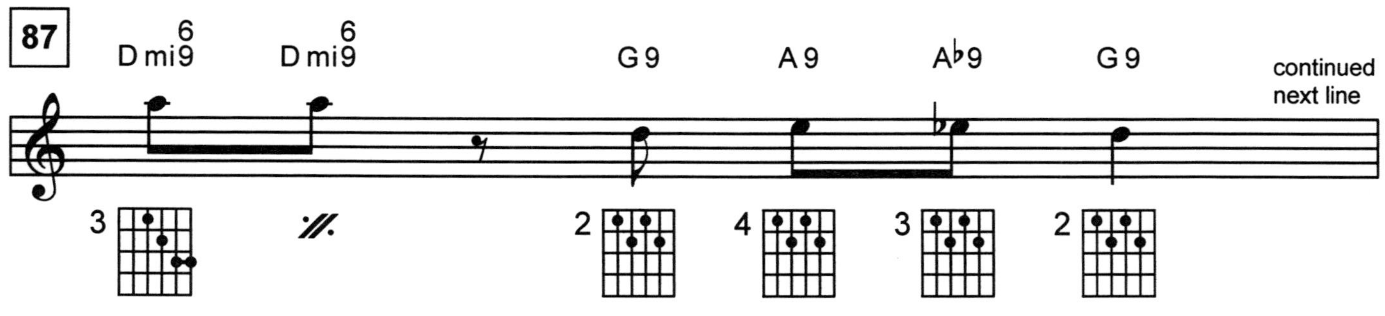

87
D mi9
6
D mi9
6
G 9
A 9
A♭9
G 9
continued
next line
3
2
4
3
2

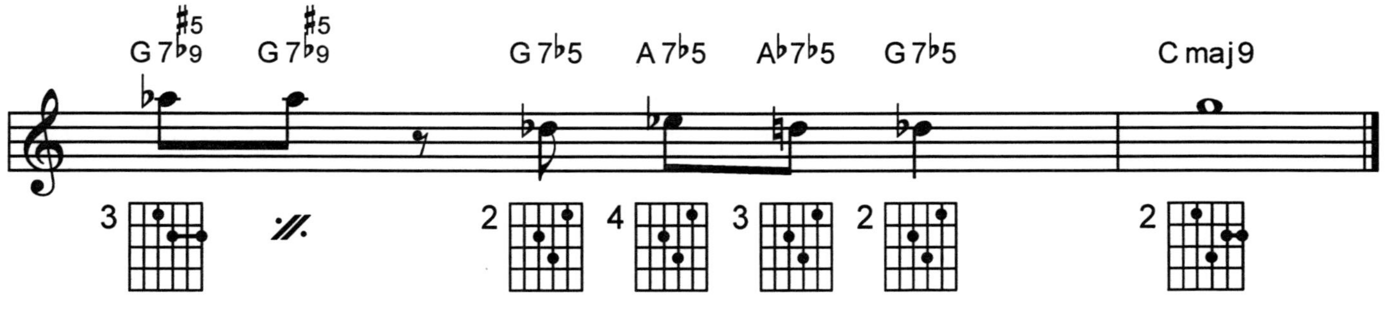

G 7♭9
♯5
G 7♭9
♯5
G 7♭5
A 7♭5
A♭7♭5
G 7♭5
C maj9
3
2
4
3
2
2

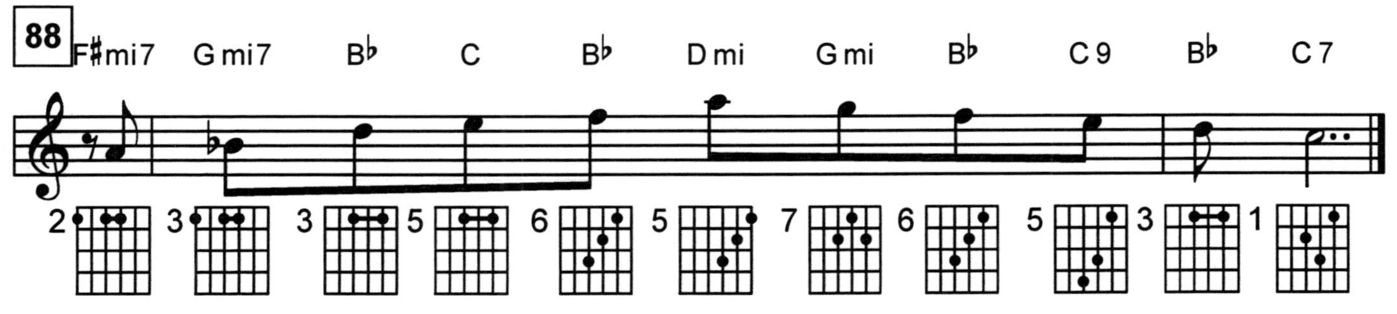

88
F♯mi7
G mi7
B♭
C
B♭
D mi
G mi
B♭
C 9
B♭
C 7
2
3
3
5
6
5
7
6
5
3
1

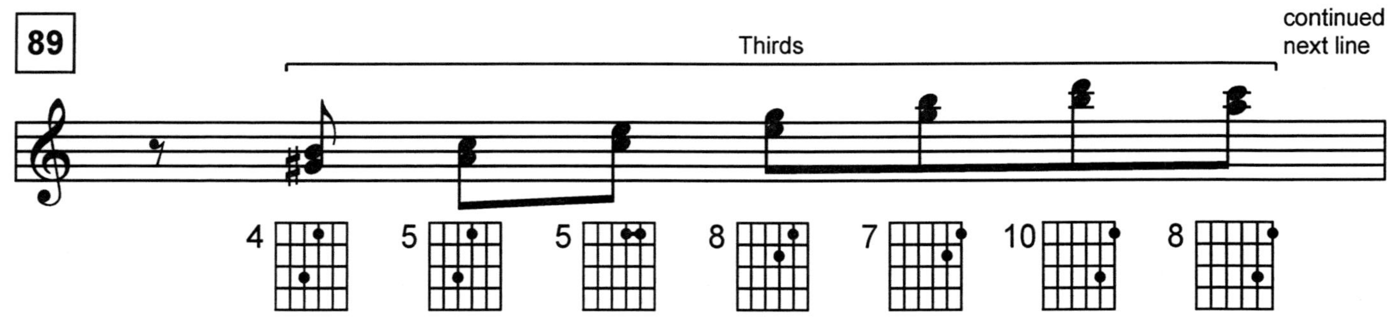

89
Thirds
continued
next line
4 5 5 8 7 10 8

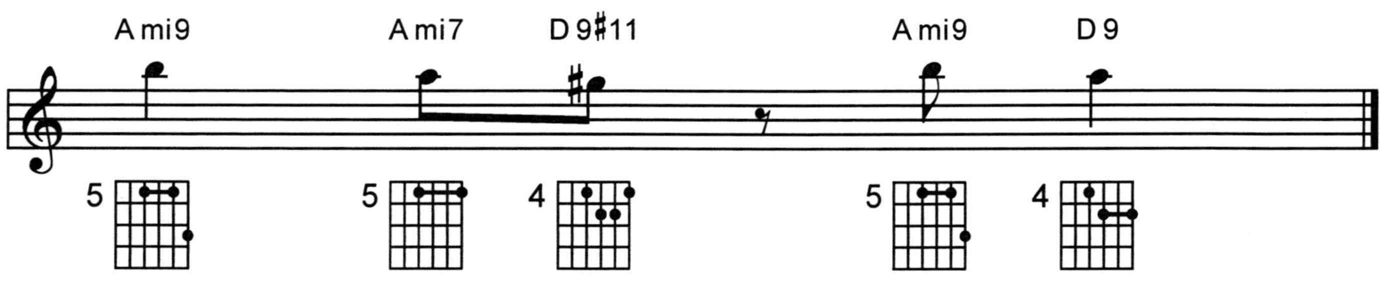

A mi9   A mi7   D 9#11   A mi9   D 9
5   5   4   5   4

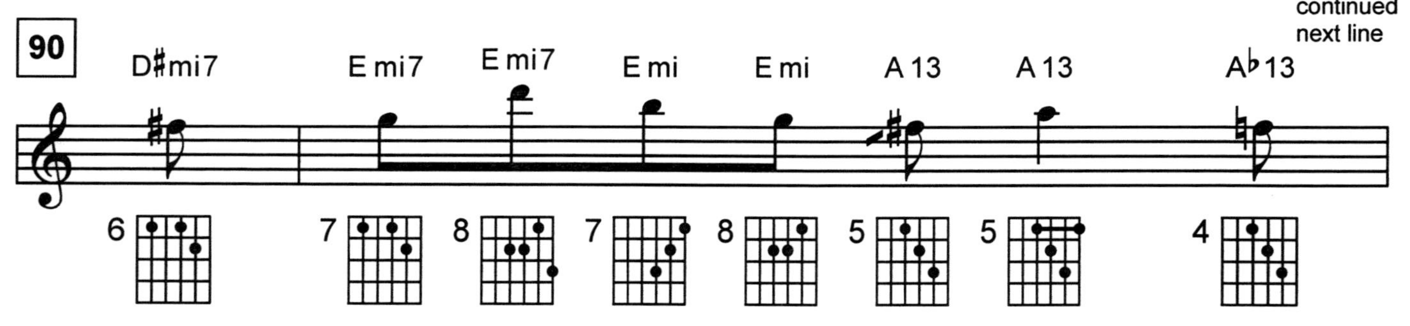

90
continued
next line
D#mi7   E mi7   E mi7   E mi   E mi   A 13   A 13   Ab13
6   7   8   7   8   5   5   4

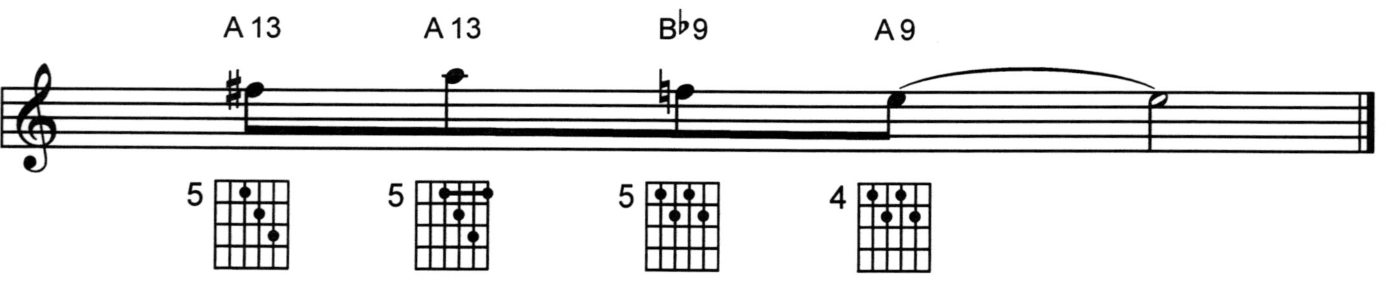

A 13   A 13   Bb9   A 9
5   5   5   4

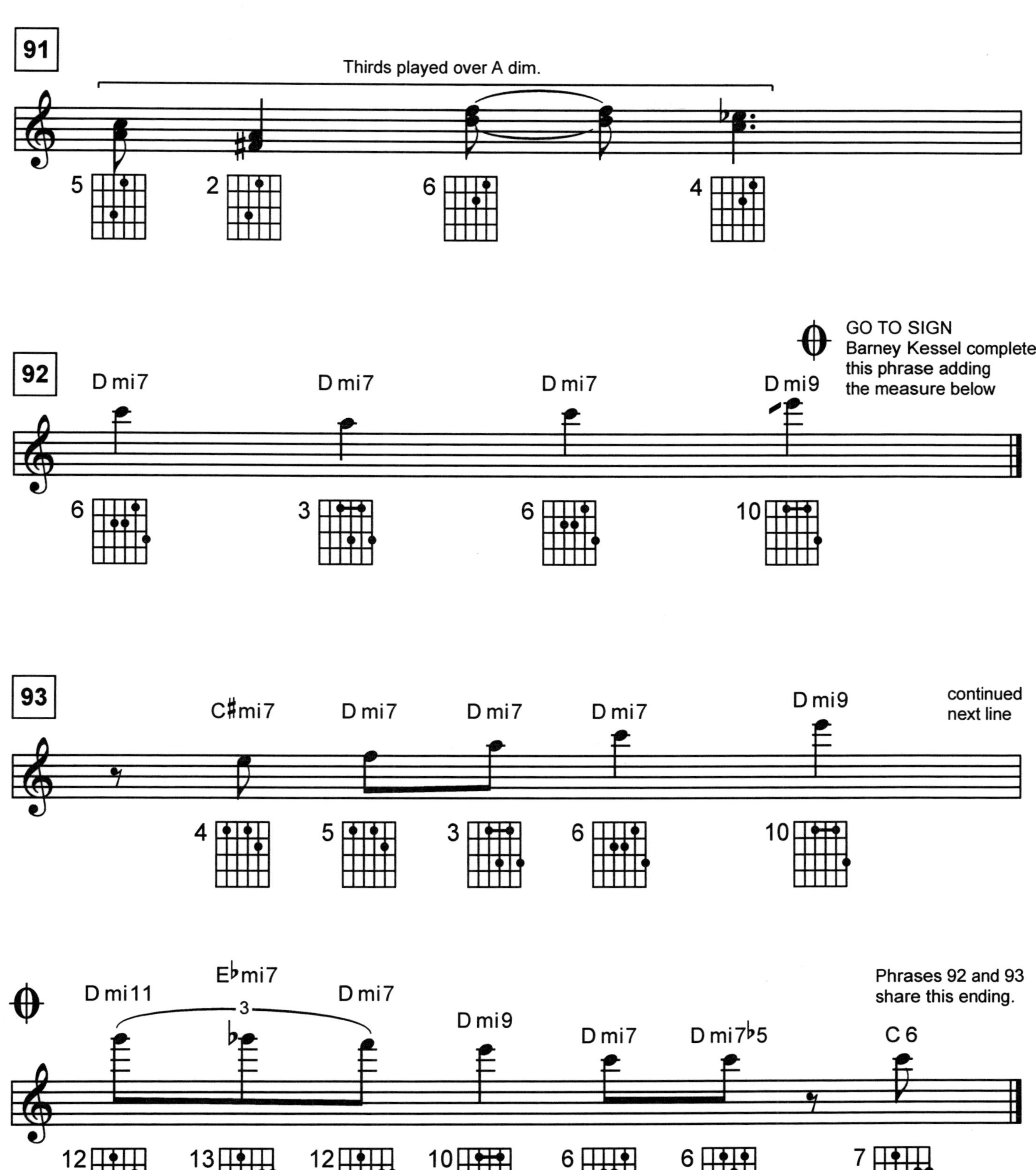

91
Thirds played over A dim.
5   2   6   4
92
D mi7   D mi7   D mi7   D mi9
GO TO SIGN
Barney Kessel completes
this phrase adding
the measure below
6   3   6   10
93
C#mi7   D mi7   D mi7   D mi7   D mi9
continued
next line
4   5   3   6   10
D mi11   E♭mi7   D mi7
3
Phrases 92 and 93
share this ending.
D mi9   D mi7   D mi7♭5   C 6
12   13   12   10   6   6   7

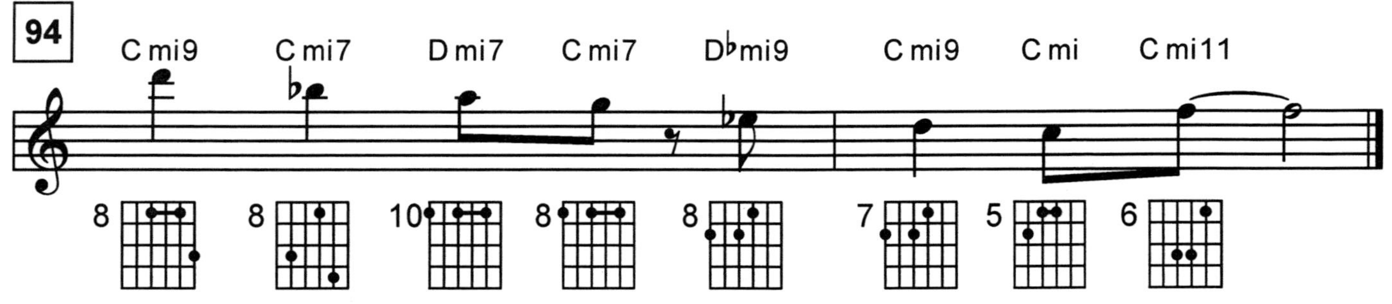
94
C mi9   C mi7   D mi7   C mi7   D♭mi9   C mi9   C mi   C mi11
8   8   10   8   8   7   5   6

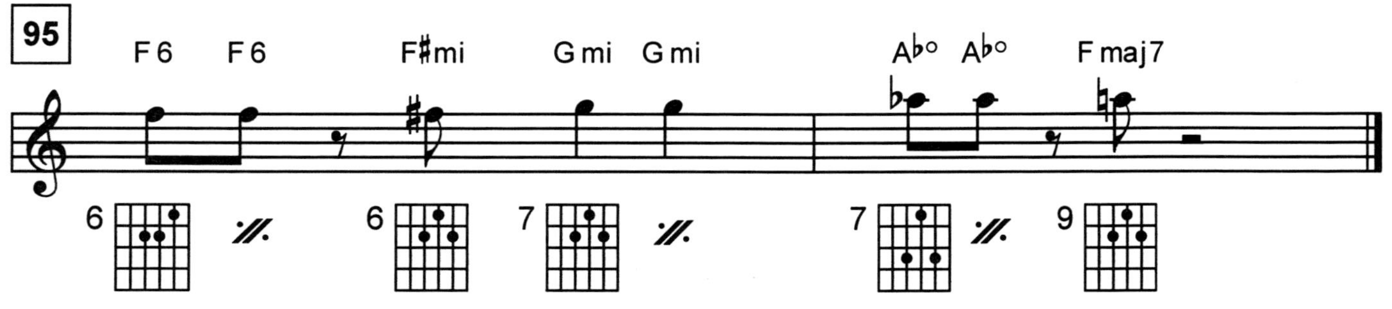
95
F 6   F 6   F#mi   G mi   G mi   A♭o   A♭o   F maj7
6   6   7   7   9

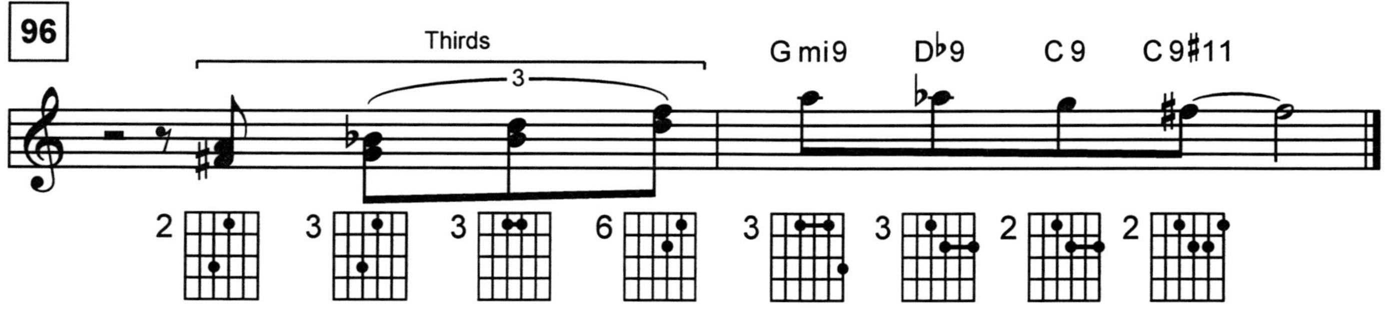
96
Thirds
3
G mi9   D♭9   C 9   C 9#11
2   3   3   6   3   3   2   2

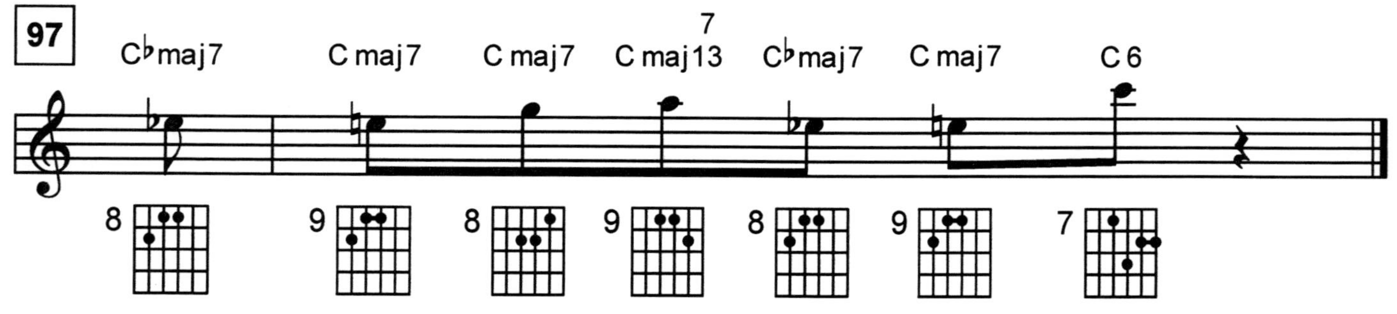
97
C♭maj7   C maj7   C maj7   C maj13   C♭maj7   C maj7   C 6
7
8   9   8   9   8   9   7

Bb Major Pentatonic

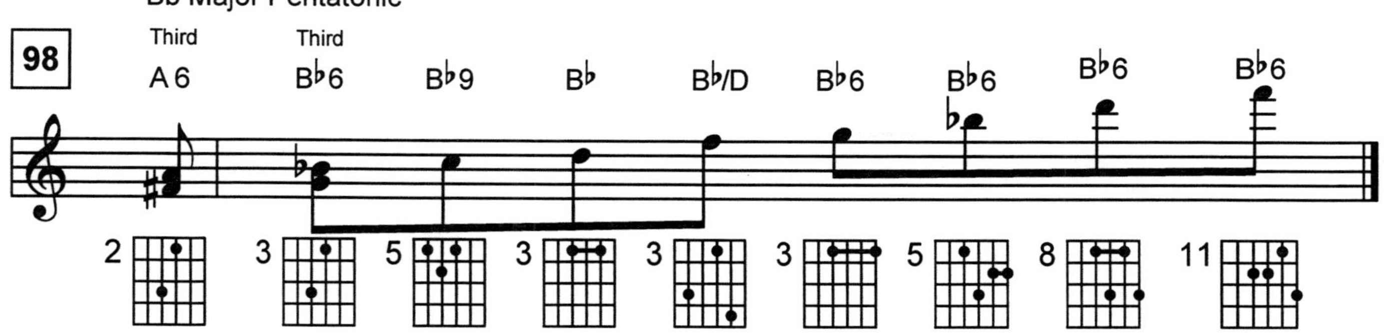

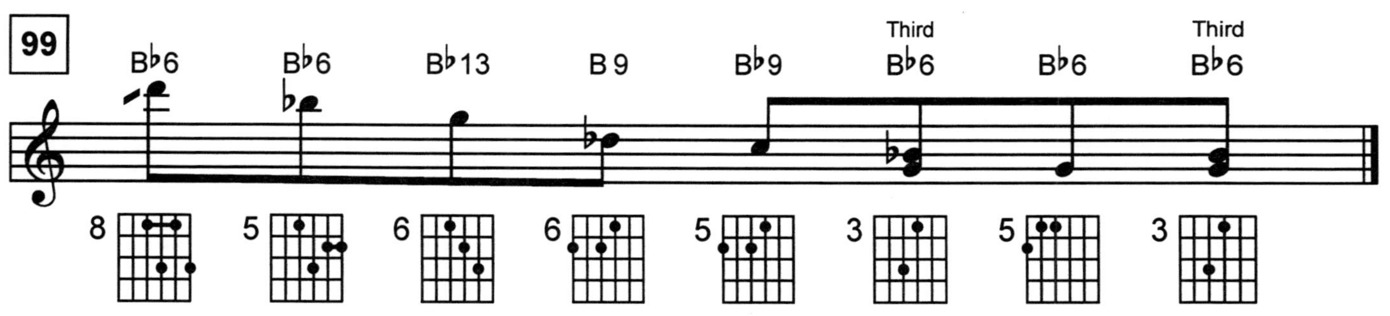

Bb Minor Pentatonic

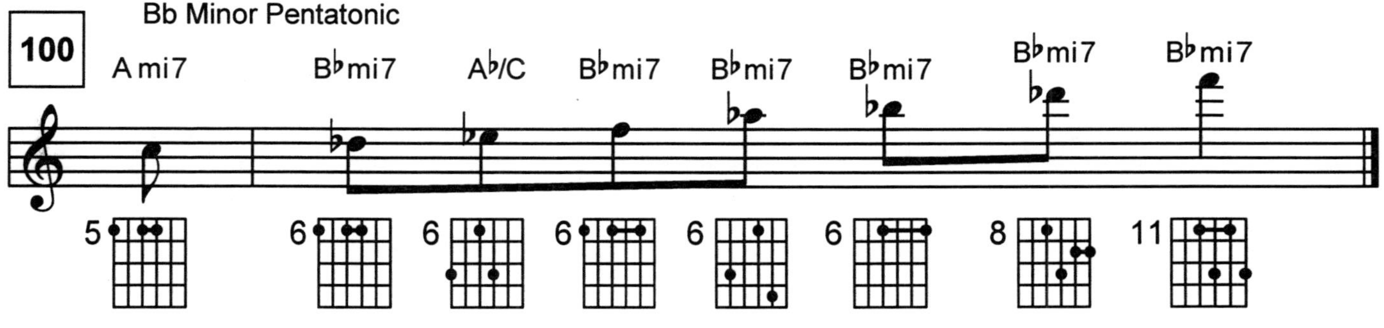

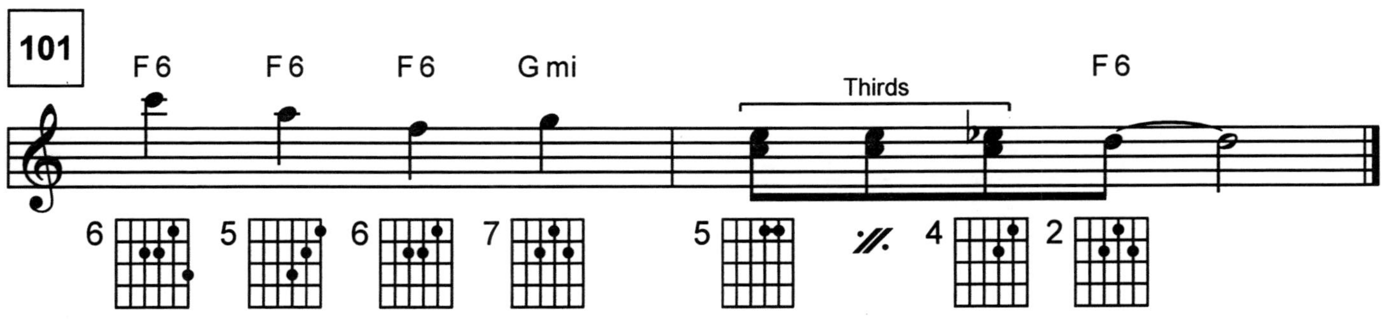

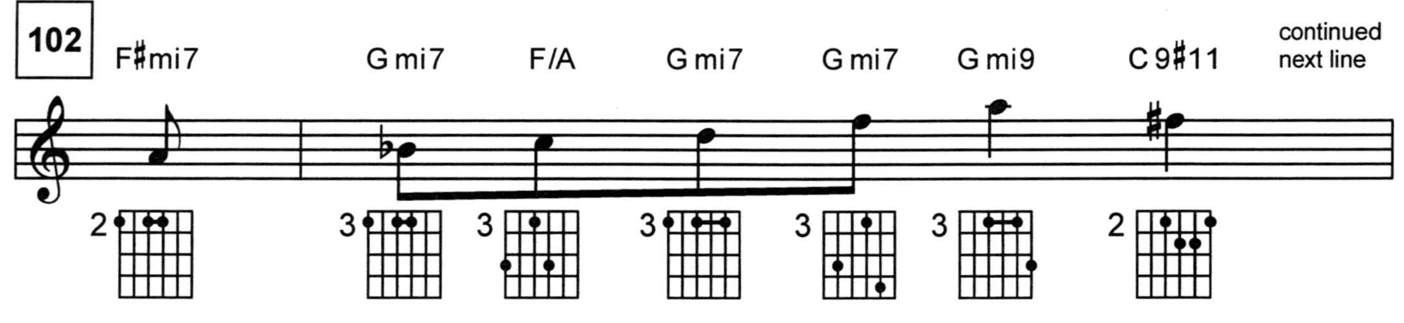

102
F#mi7   G mi7   F/A   G mi7   G mi7   G mi9   C 9#11
continued next line
2   3   3   3   3   3   2

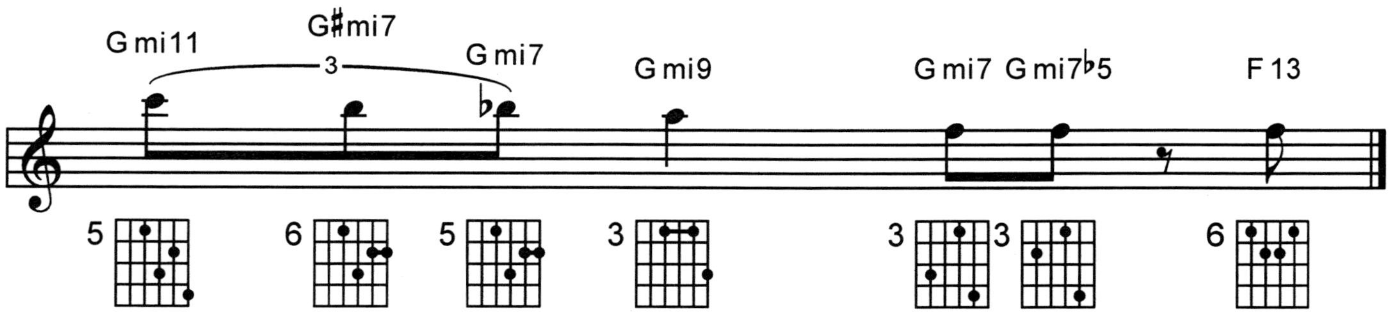

G mi11   G#mi7   G mi7   3   G mi9   G mi7 G mi7b5   F 13
5   6   5   3   3 3   6

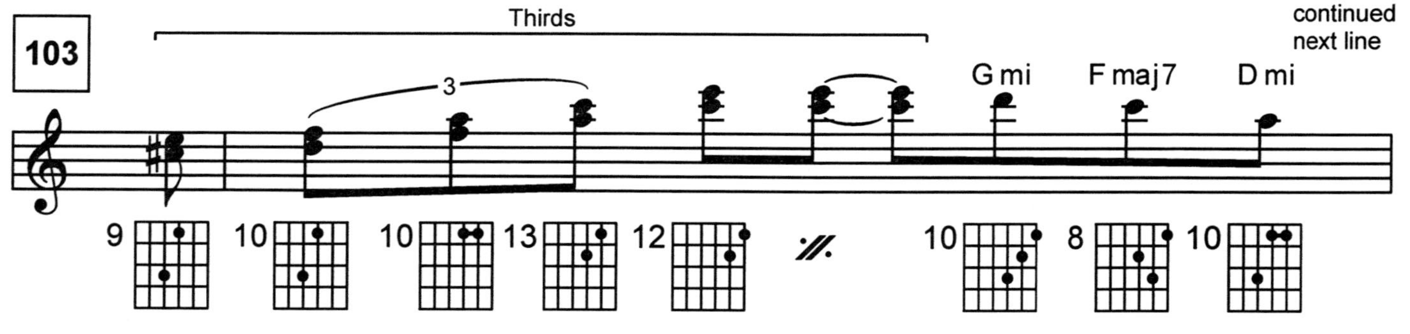

103
Thirds
3
G mi   F maj7   D mi
continued next line
9   10   10 13   12   %.   10   8   10

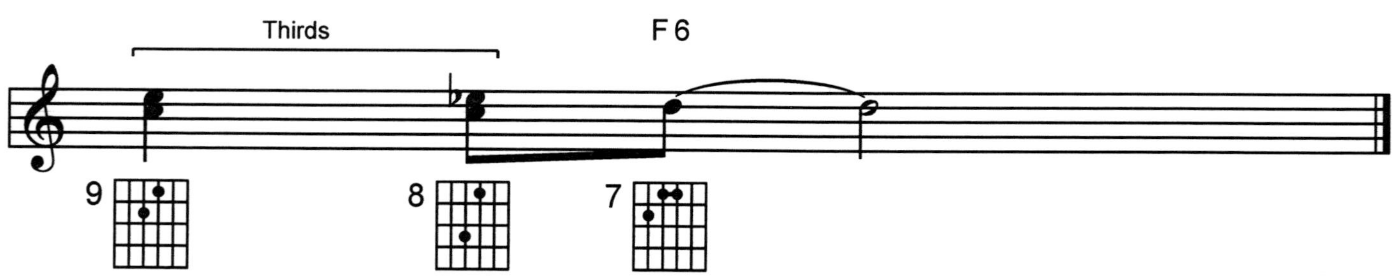

Thirds   F 6
9   8   7

Diminished Scale. Practice starting the scale on string set 5432 and moving to string set 4321.

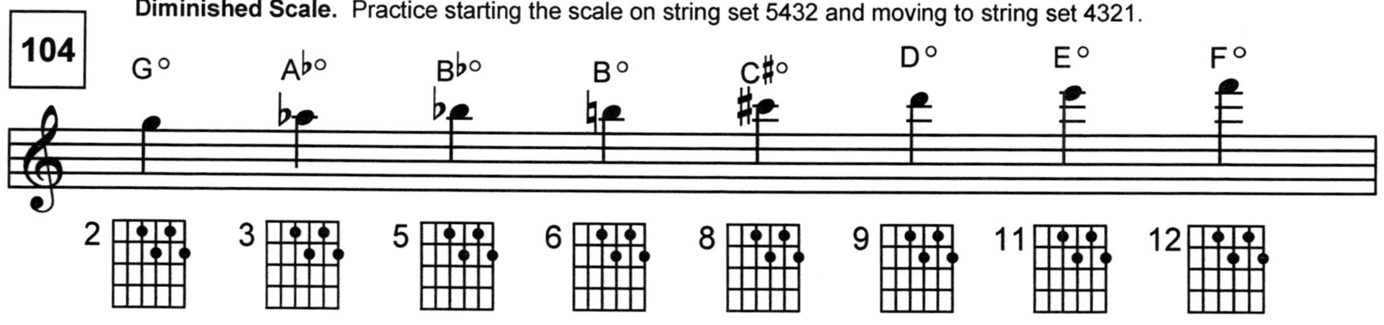
104
G° A♭° B♭° B° C#° D° E° F°
2 3 5 6 8 9 11 12

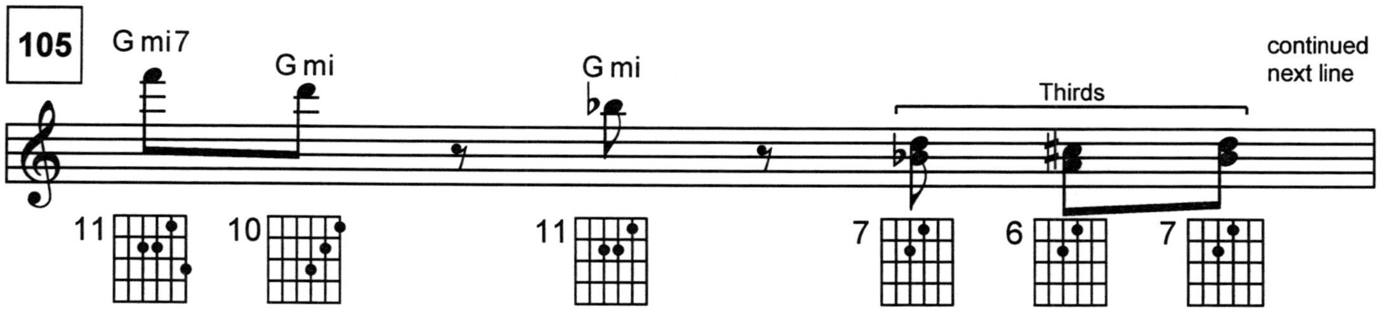
105
G mi7 G mi G mi Thirds continued next line
11 10 11 7 6 7

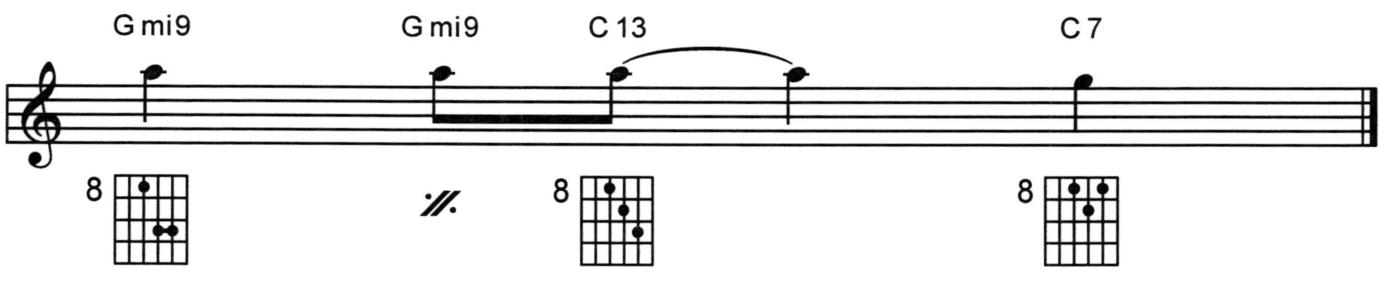
G mi9 G mi9 C 13 C 7
8 8 8

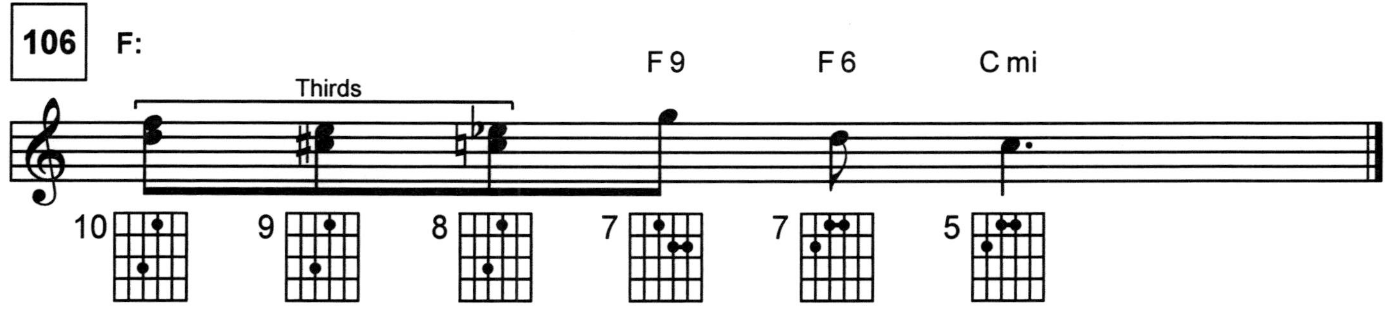
106 F: Thirds F 9 F 6 C mi
10 9 8 7 7 5

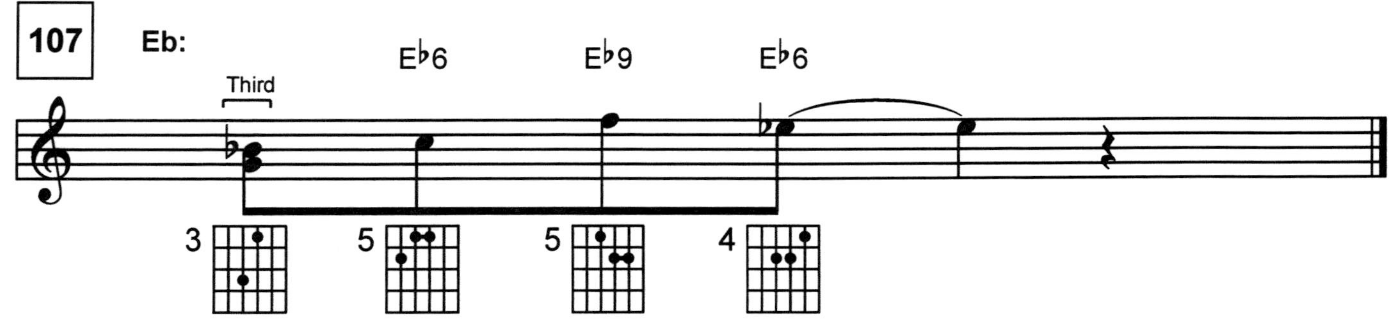

107
Eb:
Third
Eb6   Eb9   Eb6
3   5   5   4

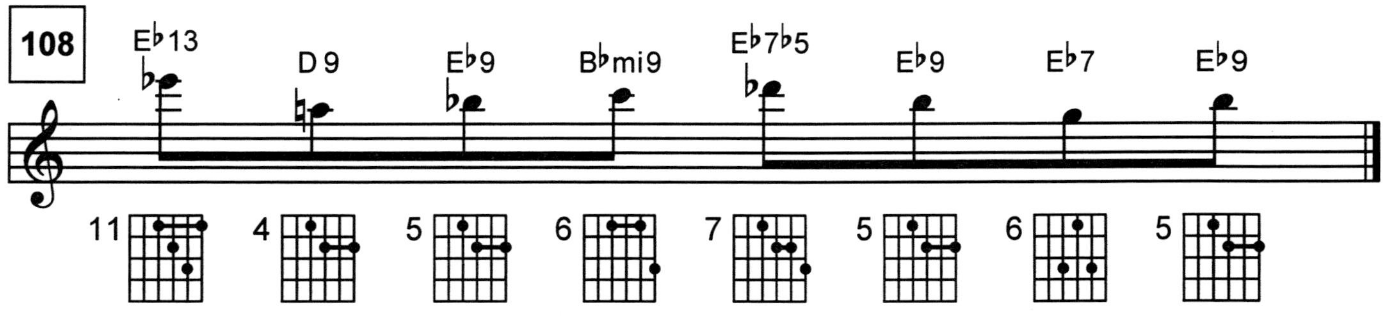

108
Eb13   D9   Eb9   Bbmi9   Eb7b5   Eb9   Eb7   Eb9
11   4   5   6   7   5   6   5

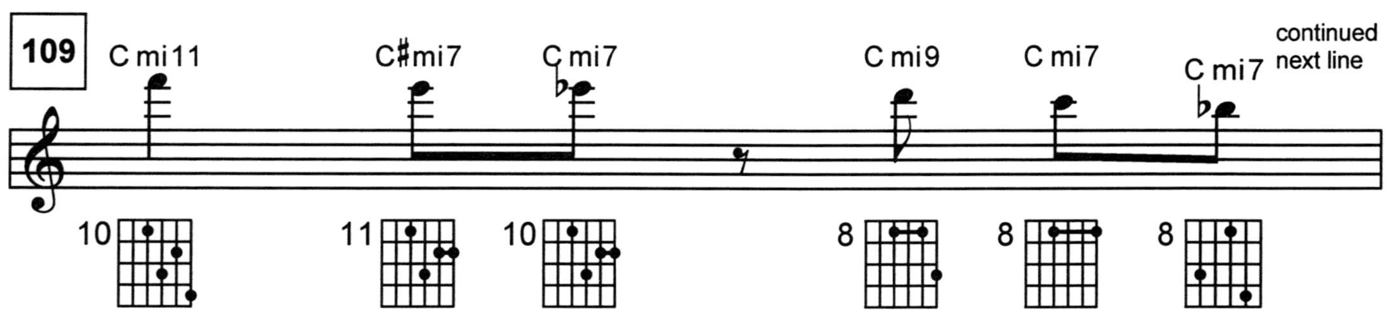

109
Cmi11   C#mi7   Cmi7   Cmi9   Cmi7   Cmi7   continued next line
10   11   10   8   8   8

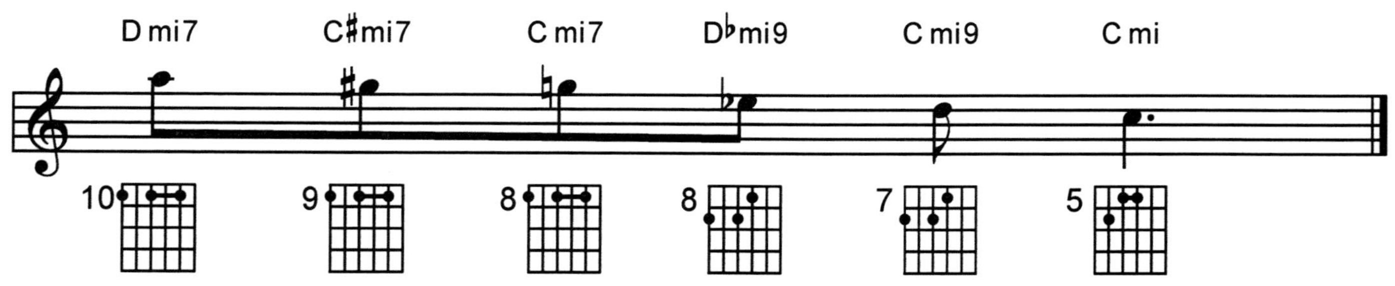

Dmi7   C#mi7   Cmi7   Dbmi9   Cmi9   Cmi
10   9   8   8   7   5

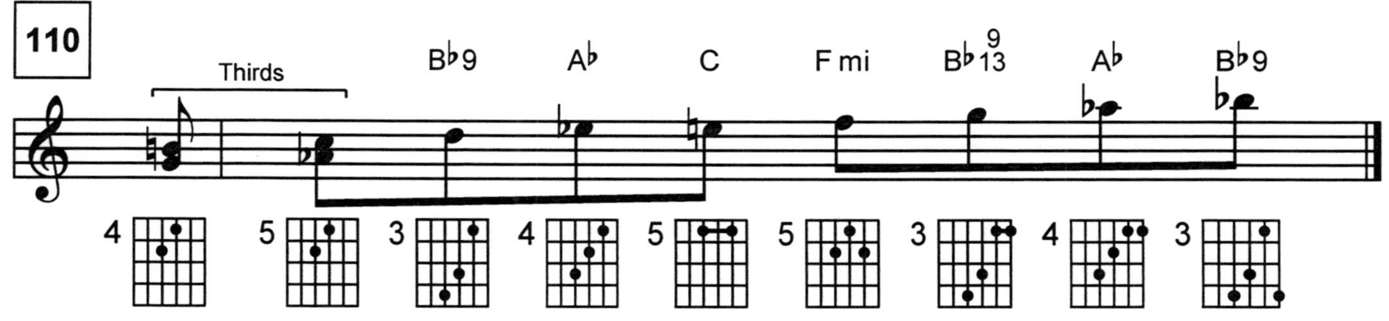

110
Thirds
B♭9   A♭   C   F mi   B♭13⁹   A♭   B♭9
4   5   3   4   5   5   3   4   3

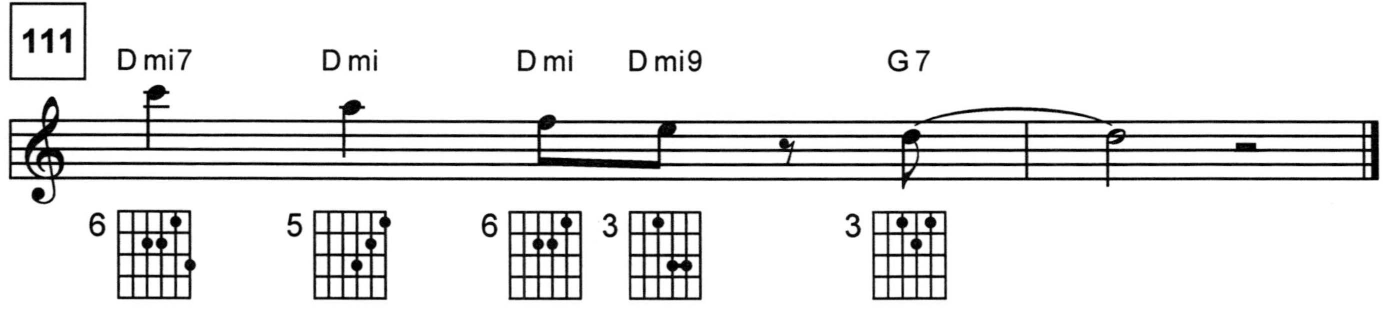

111
D mi7   D mi   D mi   D mi9   G 7
6   5   6   3   3

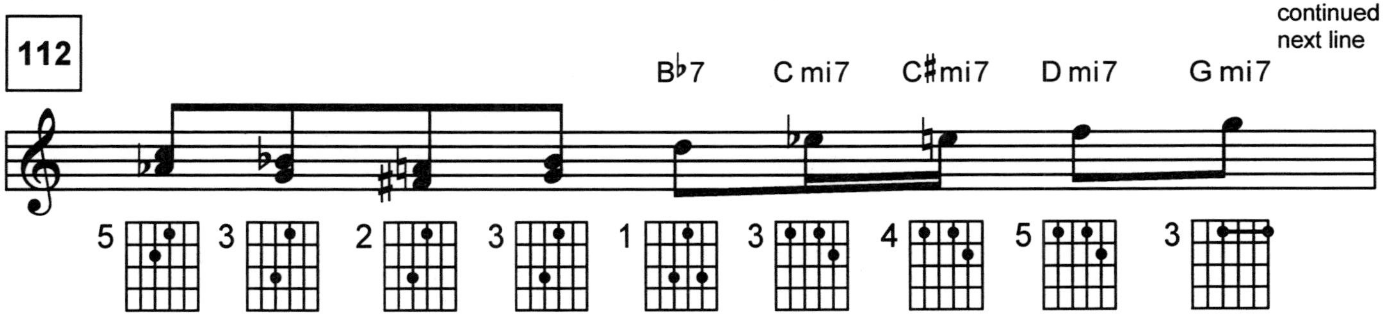

continued
next line
112
B♭7   C mi7   C#mi7   D mi7   G mi7
5   3   2   3   1   3   4   5   3

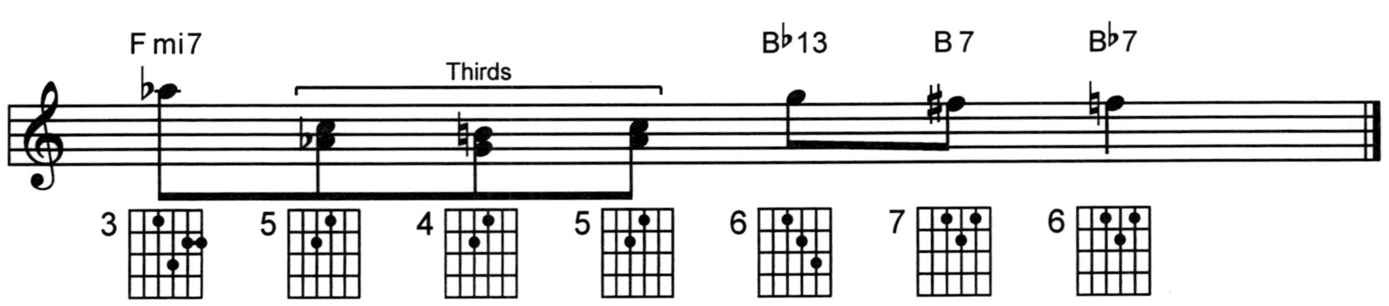

F mi7   Thirds   B♭13   B 7   B♭7
3   5   4   5   6   7   6

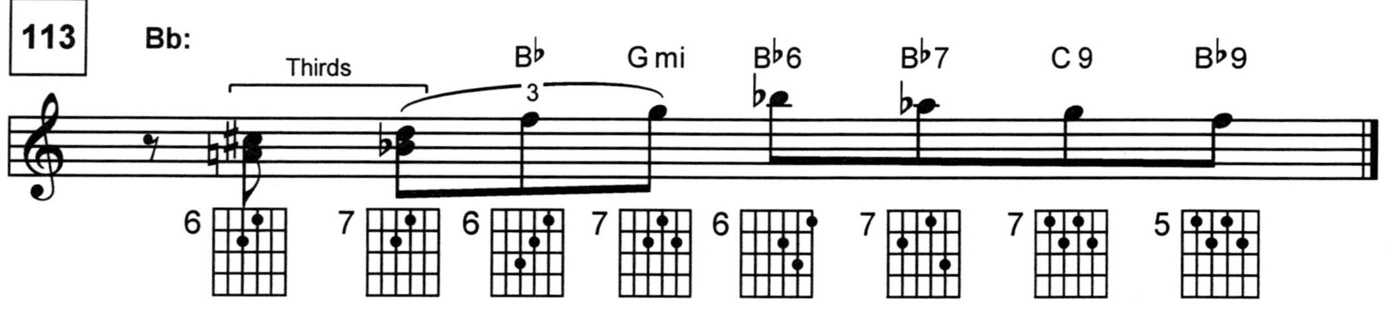

113
Bb:
Thirds
Bb
G mi
Bb6
Bb7
C 9
Bb9
6 7 6 7 6 7 7 5

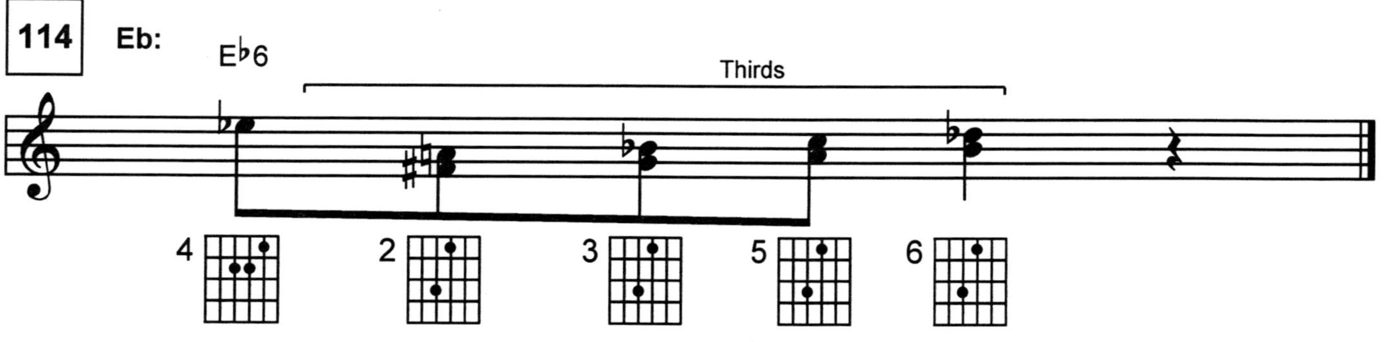

114
Eb:
Eb6
Thirds
4 2 3 5 6

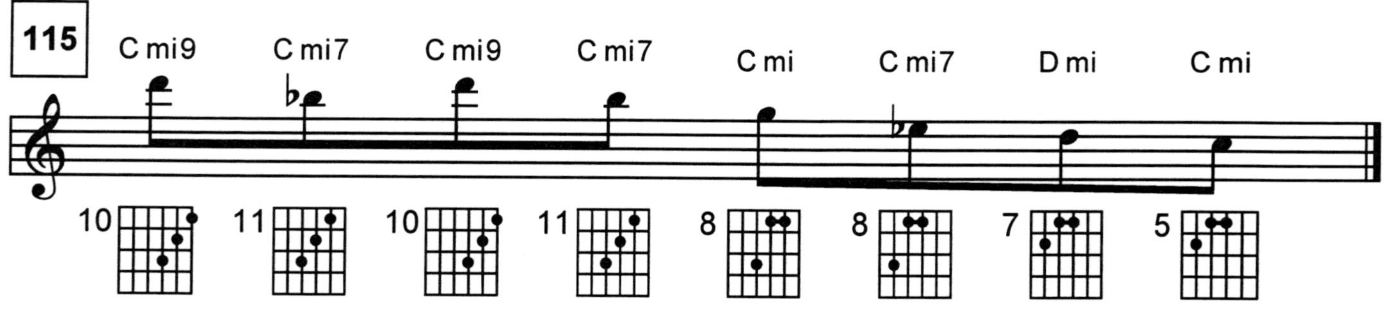

115
C mi9
C mi7
C mi9
C mi7
C mi
C mi7
D mi
C mi
10 11 10 11 8 8 7 5

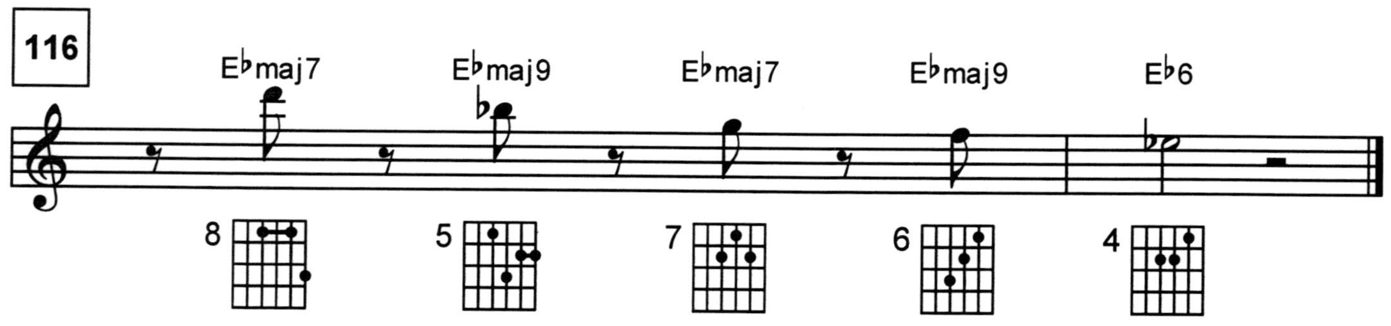

116
Ebmaj7
Ebmaj9
Ebmaj7
Ebmaj9
Eb6
8 5 7 6 4

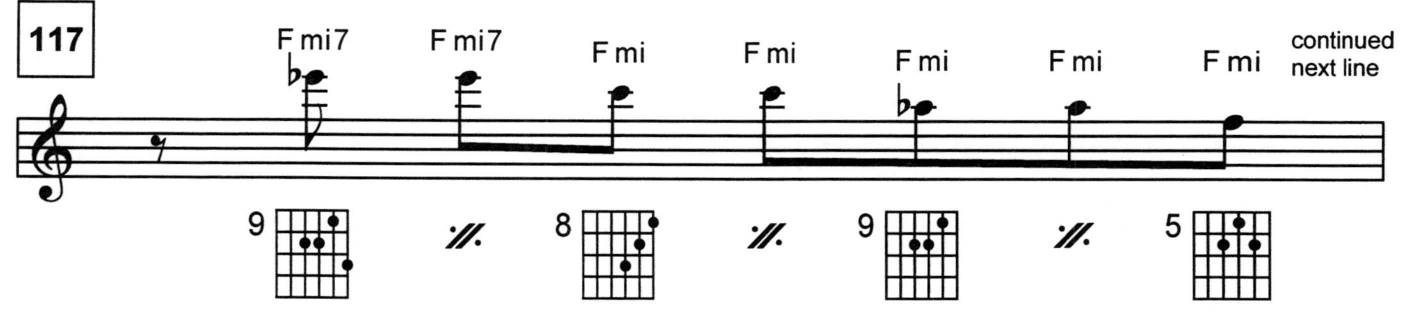
117
continued
next line
F mi7   F mi7   F mi   F mi   F mi   F mi   F mi
9   8   9   5

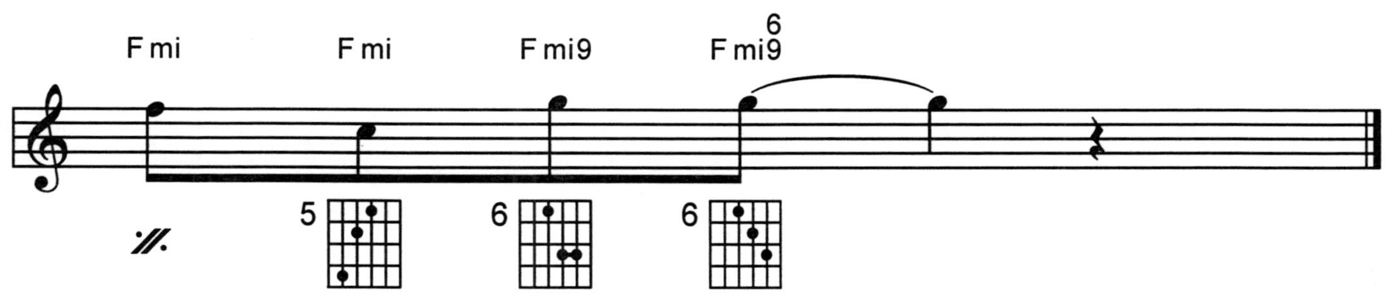
F mi   F mi   F mi9   F mi9 6
5   6   6

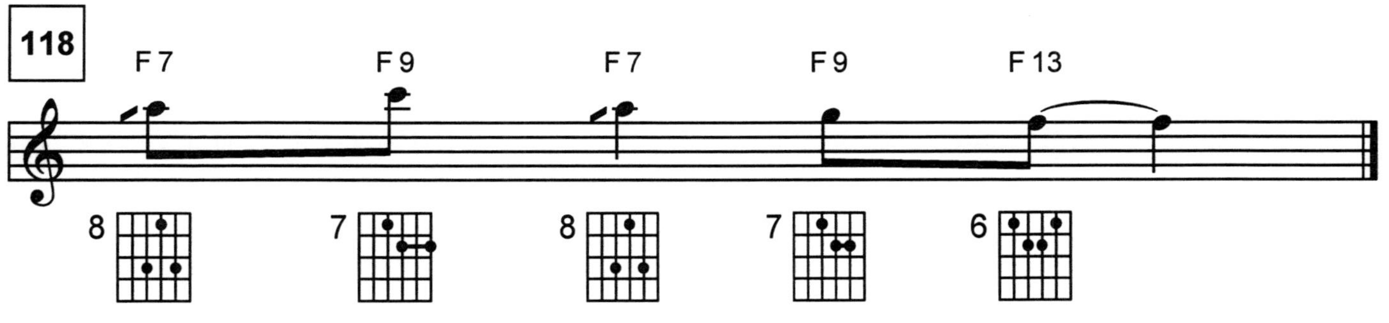
118
F 7   F 9   F 7   F 9   F 13
8   7   8   7   6

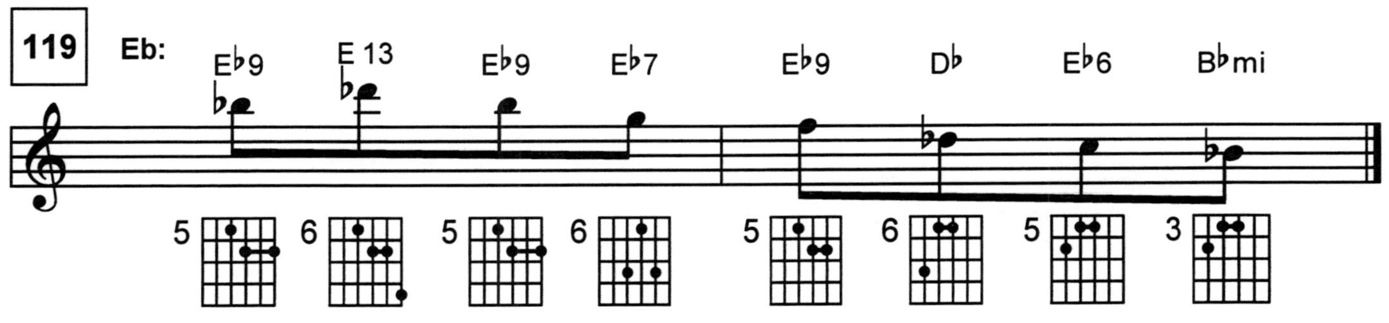
119   Eb:
Eb9   E 13   Eb9   Eb7   Eb9   Db   Eb6   Bbmi
5   6   5   6   5   6   5   3

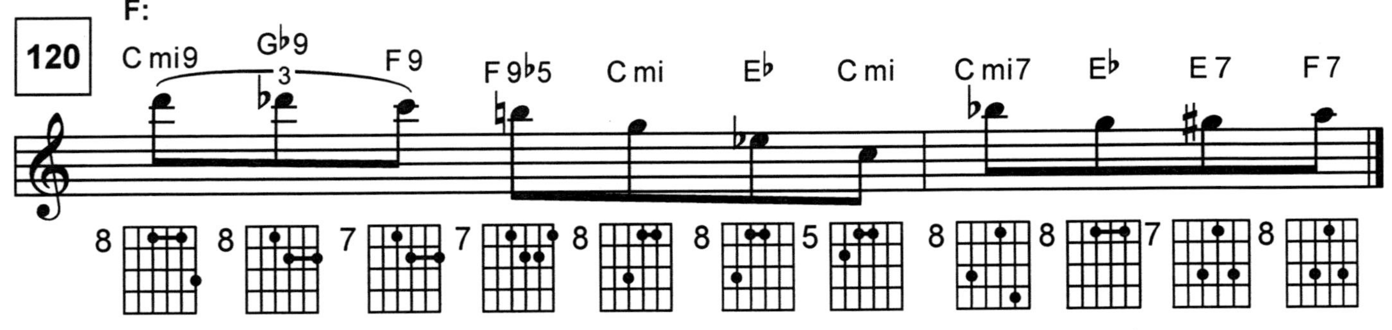
120
F:
C mi9   G♭9   F 9   F 9♭5   C mi   E♭   C mi   C mi7   E♭   E 7   F 7
3
8 8 7 7 8 8 5 8 8 7 8

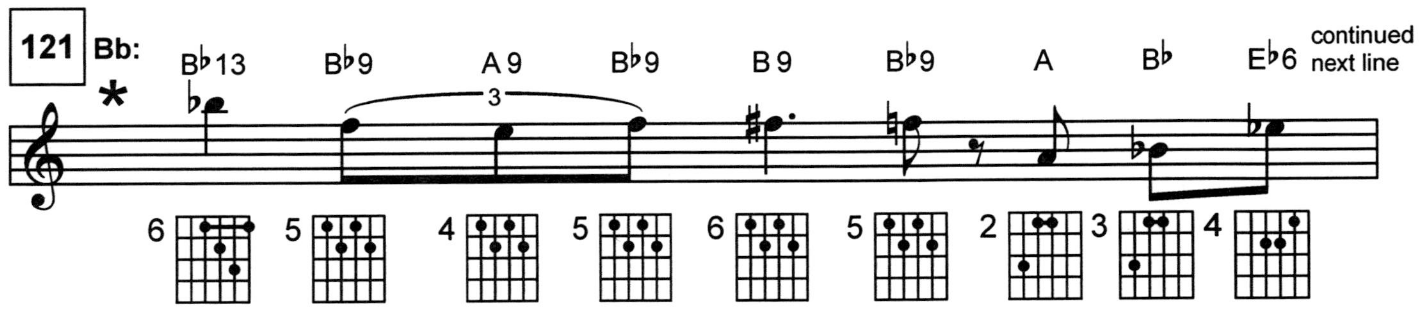
121
Bb:
*
B♭13   B♭9   A 9   B♭9   B 9   B♭9   A   B♭   E♭6   continued next line
3
6 5 4 5 6 5 2 3 4

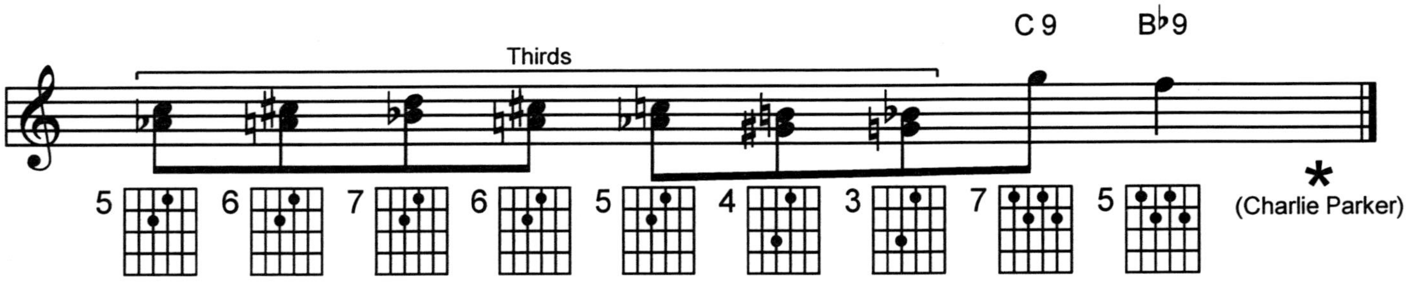
Thirds
C 9   B♭9
5 6 7 6 5 4 3 7 5
*
(Charlie Parker)

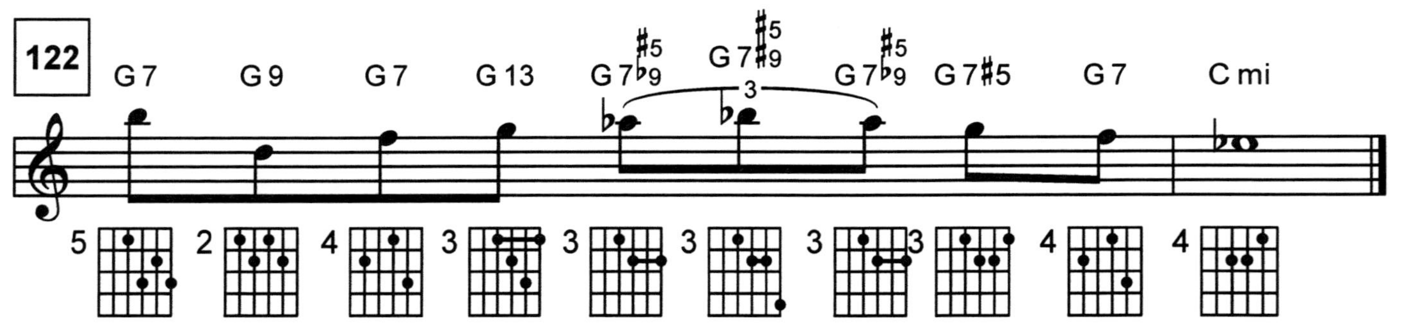
122
G 7   G 9   G 7   G 13   G 7♭9   G 7#9   G 7♭9   G 7#5   G 7   C mi
#5   #5   #5
3
5 2 4 3 3 3 3 3 4 4

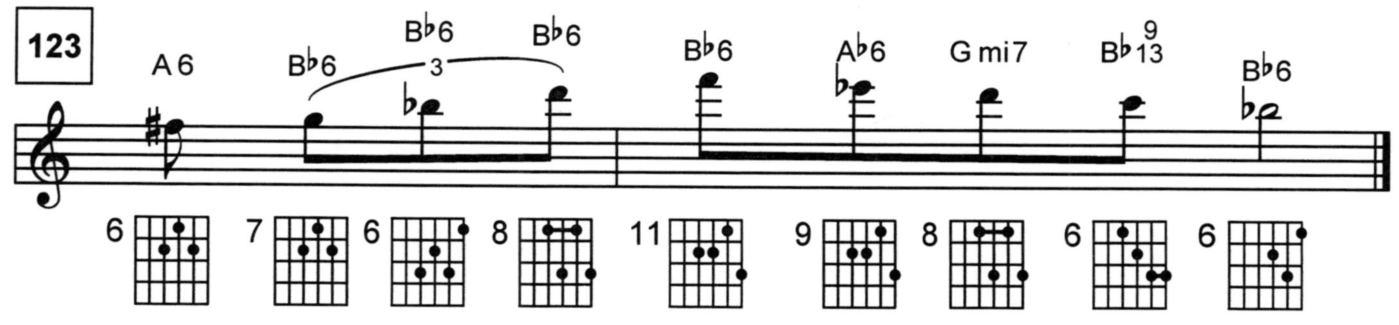

123
A 6
B♭6
B♭6
B♭6
B♭6
A♭6
G mi7
B♭13 9
B♭6
6 7 6 8 11 9 8 6 6

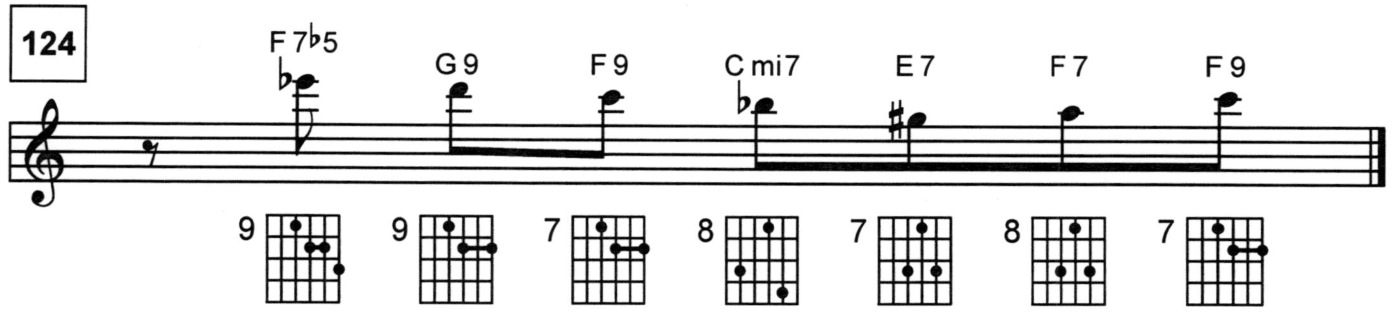

124
F 7♭5
G 9
F 9
C mi7
E 7
F 7
F 9
9 9 7 8 7 8 7

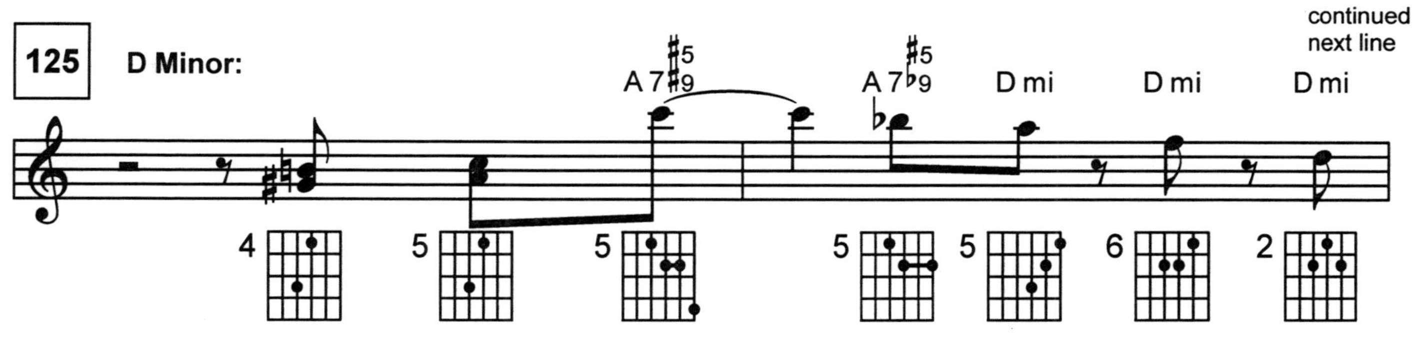

125
D Minor:
A 7♯5♯9
A 7♭9♯5
D mi
D mi
D mi
continued next line
4 5 5 5 5 6 2

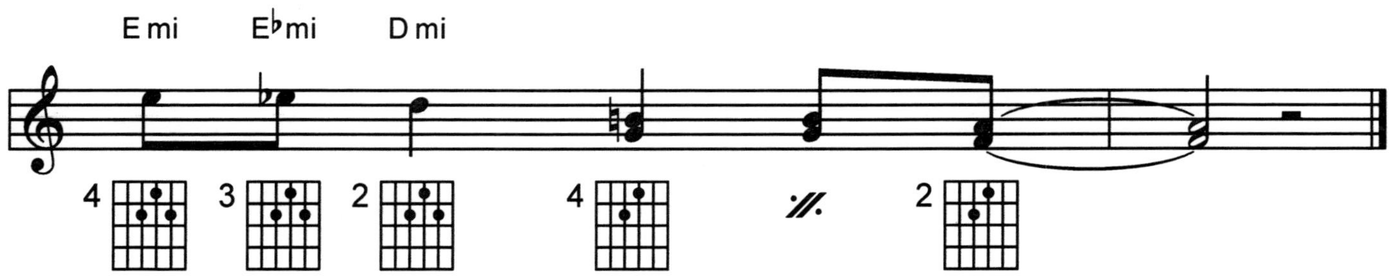

E mi
E♭ mi
D mi
4 3 2 4 ⁒. 2

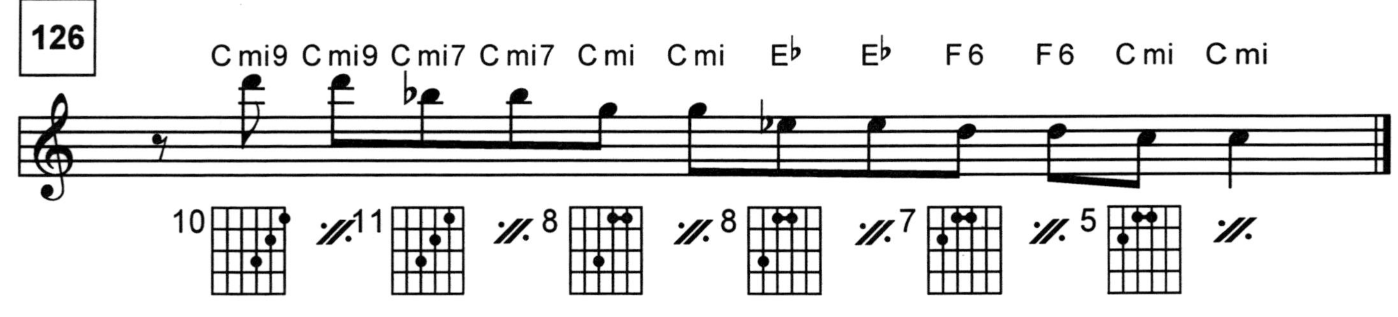

126
C mi9 C mi9 C mi7 C mi7 C mi   C mi   Eb   Eb   F 6   F 6   C mi   C mi
10   11   8   8   7   5

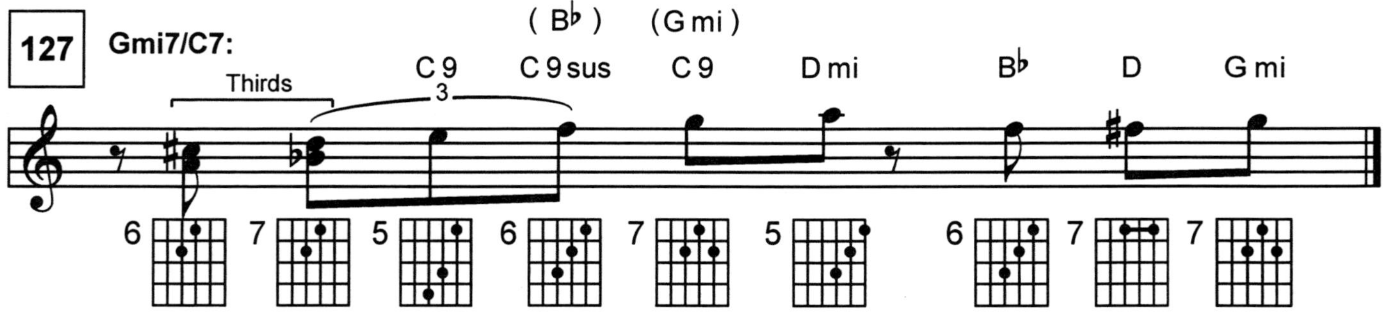

127
Gmi7/C7:
Thirds
(Bb)   (G mi)
C 9   C 9 sus   C 9   D mi   Bb   D   G mi
3
6   7   5   6   7   5   6   7   7

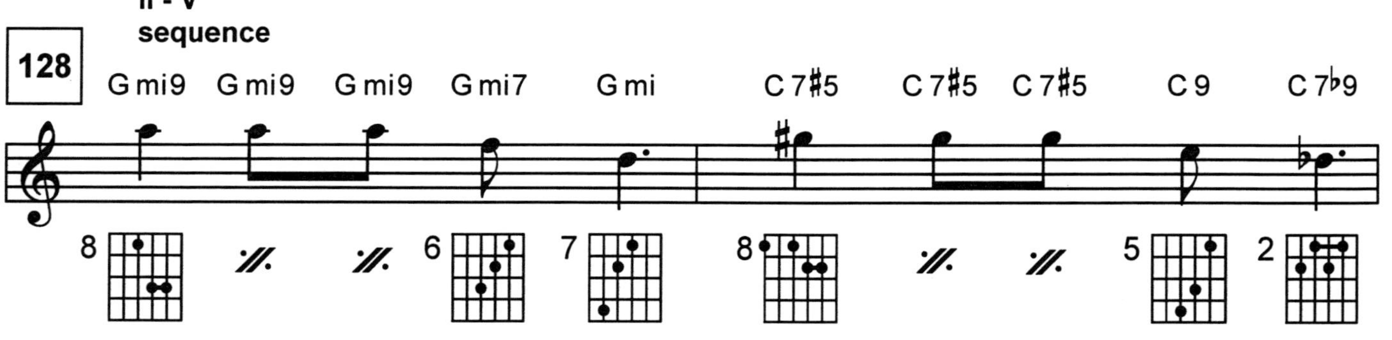

ii - V
sequence
128
G mi9   G mi9   G mi9   G mi7   G mi   C 7#5   C 7#5   C 7#5   C 9   C 7b9
8   6   7   8   5   2

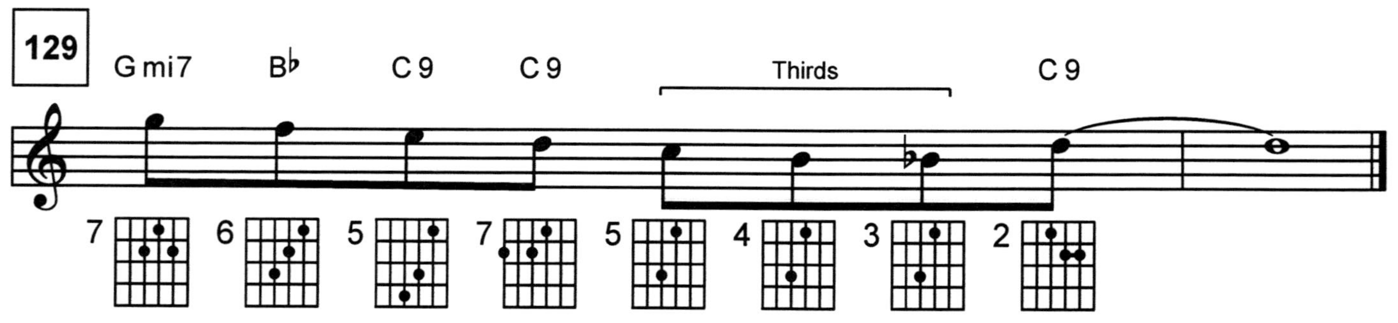

129
G mi7   Bb   C 9   C 9   Thirds   C 9
7   6   5   7   5   4   3   2

On the following pages you will find entire solos and parts of solos that demonstrate masterful execution of the chordal bebop style. These excerpts have been transcribed from Barney Kessel and Wes Montgomery recordings and are my interpretations of this improvised material. In some places, these works have been edited to make them more 'playable', and occasionally educated guesses have been made as to what voicings were employed. Nevertheless, they accurately portray the style and the content of what each artist was trying to convey.

Highlights....

Barney's solo material on **Autumn Leaves** has the effect of a big band shout chorus throughout. It is just a stellar example of short chordal riffs, thirds, use of three and four note chords, and occasionally some single-string activity. This is classic Barney at his best. He recorded this tune many times over his career, and vestiges of this solo are often repeated in his other solos, almost lick for lick. Barney was never ashamed to admit that he worked out parts of his 'improvisations' ahead of time.

You're the One for Me is a solo that is worth learning from the record in its entirety. It is a model of solo development that starts in single lines and escalates in excitement to the shout -chorus type chordal lines. Melodic connecting between keys, even while improvising in chord lines, was never a problem for Barney, and this solo has some good examples of that. As with all of the excerpts, this one has some good fragments that should be isolated and moved to different keys for practice.

The Look of Love excerpt shows: (1) Barney's penchant for using a limited number of three and four note 'pet' voicings, especially major and minor triads, and (2) the marvelous lines that can be created with a limited number of chord shapes! A uniquely Barney-esque feature is his unexpected use of 'borrowed' major triads, used as passing chords: In the first line of page two of this solo, there is a D major triad used as a passing chord moving to Bb major. (See also page 5 of the Autumn Leaves material [line 3]: a Db major triad [tritone sub of G7] is followed by C minor). Within this solo, as in all his solos, Barney tends to rely heavily on triadic shapes, very melodic riff phrases, and a generous amount of reliance on the melody with heavy syncopation. *Here, we are reminded that early serious jazz players improvised from the melody!*

Wes' solo material on **West Coast Blues** shows a striking similarity in use of voicings, to those found in Barney's performances. The four-note inversions on the top string set are favorites of Wes.   Changing keys in mid chordal line is no worry for Wes as he drifts between Gb major and Bb major. Some of Wes' historically favored devices are shown in these excerpts: repeated riffs, sequences (riff repeated at a lower pitch level), diminished passing chords, and constant structure augmented chords. Wes often ends his solo statements in quarter notes almost as if the quarter notes bring a certain resolution, a slowing down, and a return to tranquility. Even in triple meter Wes' ease of execution shines out.

In **Missile Blues**, Wes relies heavily on the use of the passing diminished chord to convey both the blues scale and the diminished scale. These invariably resolve back to tonic G function chords (G6, Gmaj7, etc). Note several ii-V 'slips' on pages 2 through 4 of this solo.

The **Delilah Take 3** and **Delilah Take 4** solos are presented here in their entirety. Seeing two 'takes' reveals something about Wes' approach on this tune. The solos further confirm Wes' preference for chord inversions (especially Gmi and Cmi inversions on this tune) with use of the diminished chord often sprinkled in-between. As seen in "Missile Blues", diminished chords again provide the substance for execution of the blues scale and diminished scale, and these occur in almost the same places on both Delilah versions. We can conclude that such scale patterns are part of Wes' regular arsenal (the pet phrases we referred to earlier) and were worked out and internalized long ago. The diminished chord often provides Wes with a vehicle for the filling-in of longer eighth-note lines (see Delilah Take 3, page 2, line 3; and Delilah Take 4, page 5, line 1). Each solo is one chorus in length (A-A-B-A form) and on Take 4 Wes elects to shift to octaves to execute the bridge (8 bars) but then returns to chords for the completion of his solo. Exhibiting a strong organizational and compositional sense, Wes' use of single-notes, octaves, and chords, almost always follow the different sections of a tune. This is a contrasting approach to that of Barney Kessel or Cal Collins, who interspersed whichever technique occurred to them at the moment.

Suggestions....

Practice the solos slowly and repetitively. Good technique, creating a good tone, and keeping time should be in the spotlight. A relaxed right hand technique (whether holding a pick or using the thumb) is vital to getting a good tone as well as preventing injury. Sing the melody line in order to fully hear what you are about to harmonize.

Isolate shorter phrases within the solos that you would like to incorporate into your personal vocabulary. Before playing through the solos, it is advised that you first read the *conclusion* at the end of this book, which may change your focus in what to watch for in the solos.

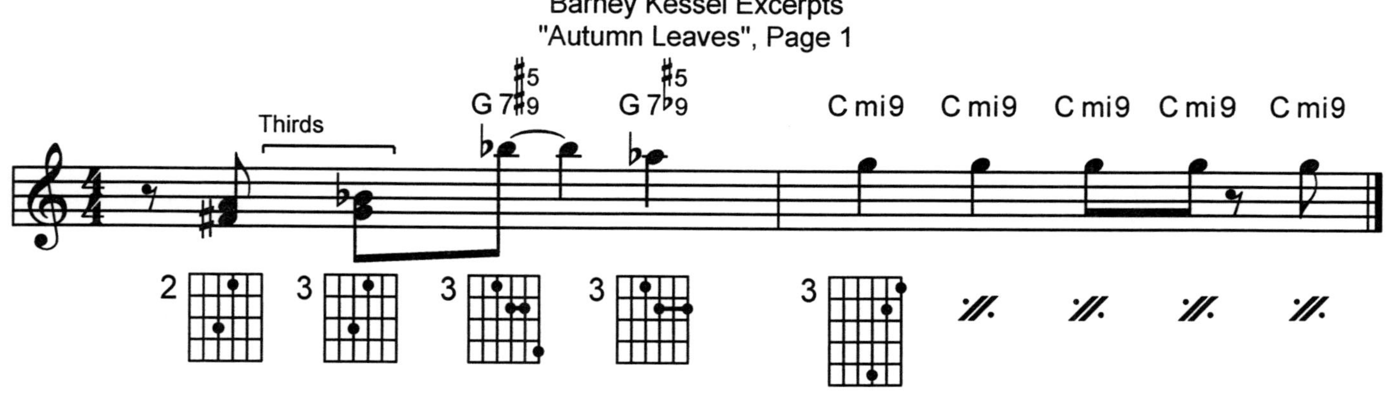
Thirds
G 7#9 #5
G 7b9 #5
C mi9   C mi9   C mi9   C mi9   C mi9

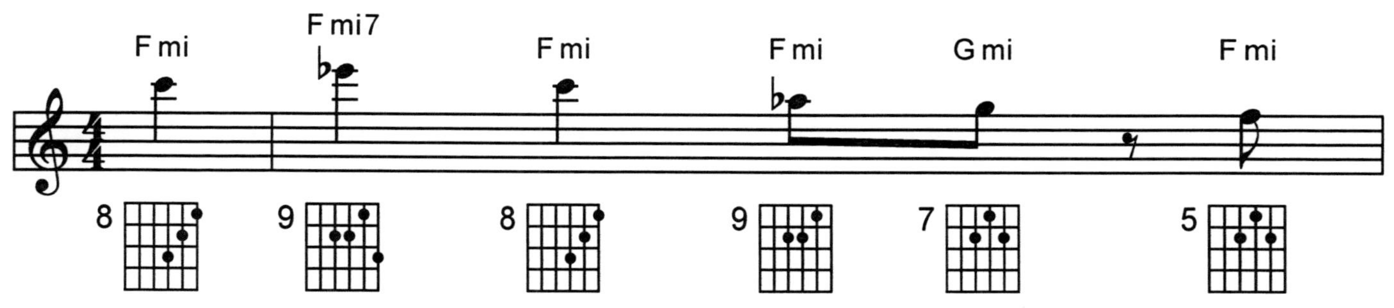
F mi
F mi7
F mi
F mi
G mi
F mi

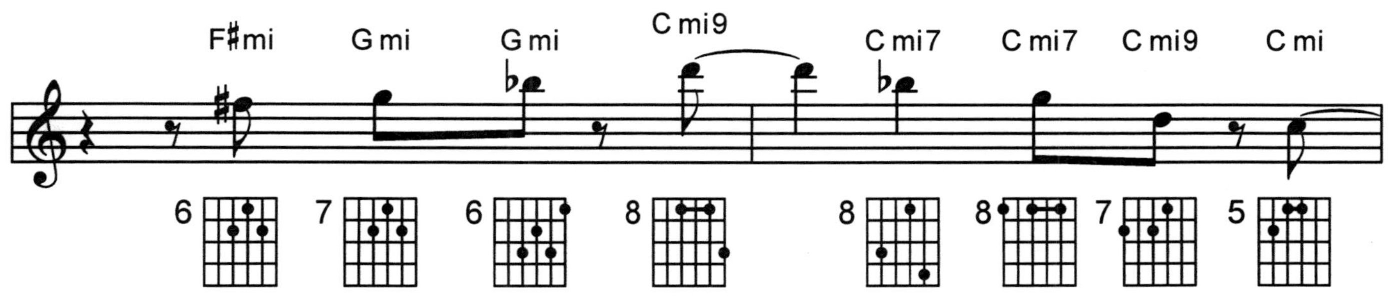
F#mi   G mi   G mi   C mi9   C mi7   C mi7   C mi9   C mi

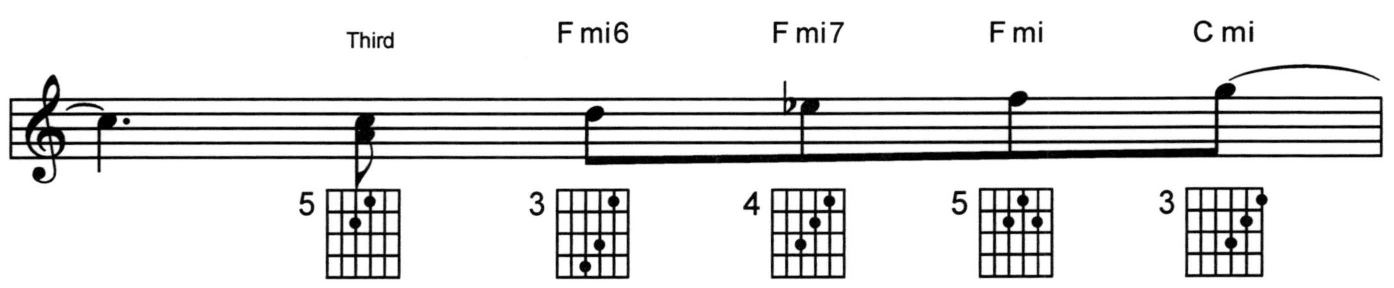
Third   F mi6   F mi7   F mi   C mi

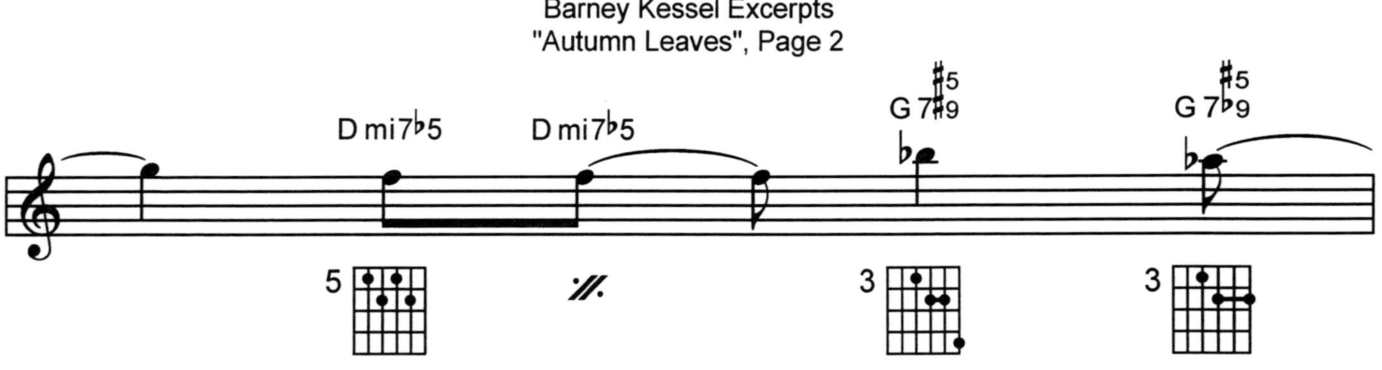
D mi7♭5
D mi7♭5
G 7♯9 #5
G 7♭9 #5
5
3
3

Single String
3

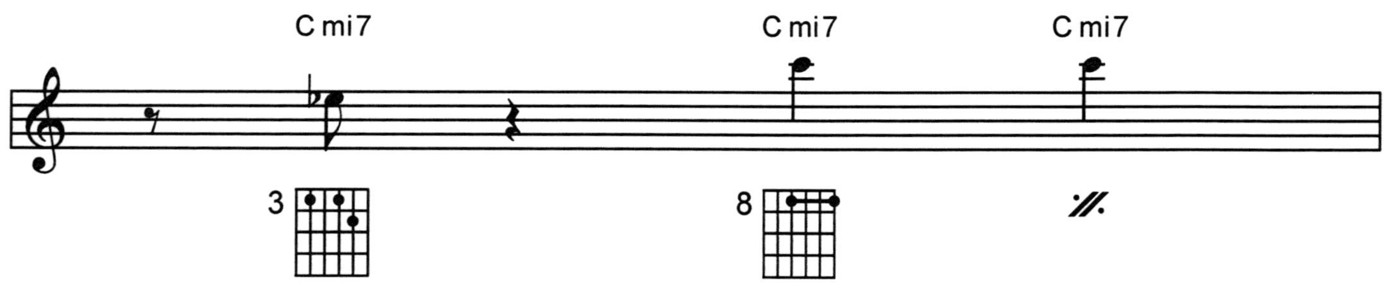
C mi7
C mi7
C mi7
3
8

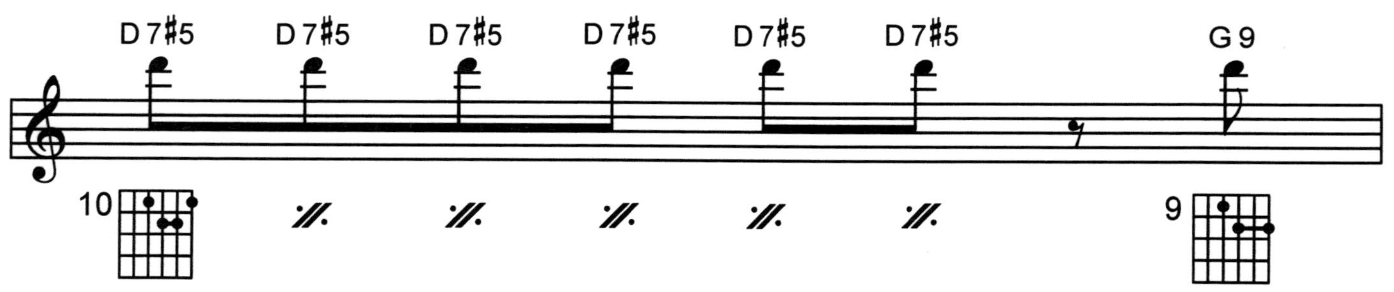
D 7♯5
D 7♯5
D 7♯5
D 7♯5
D 7♯5
D 7♯5
G 9
10
9

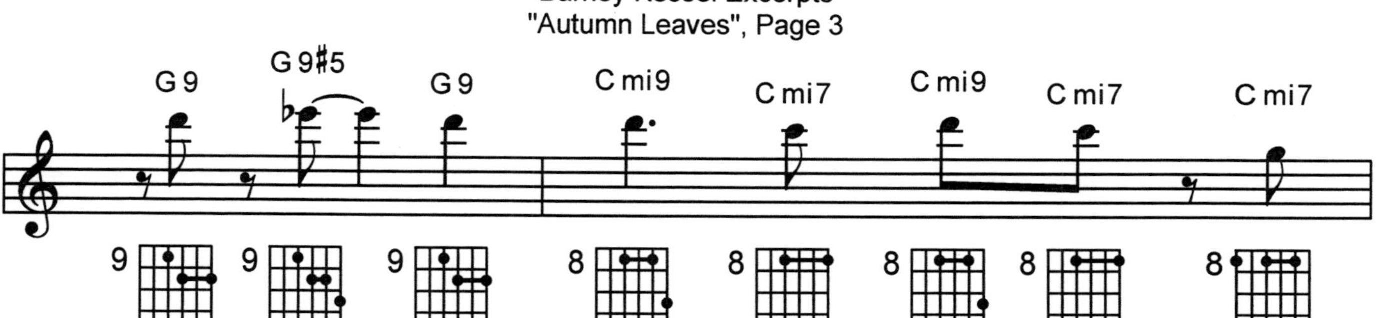
G 9
G 9#5
G 9
C mi9
C mi7
C mi9
C mi7
C mi7
9
9
9
8
8
8
8
8

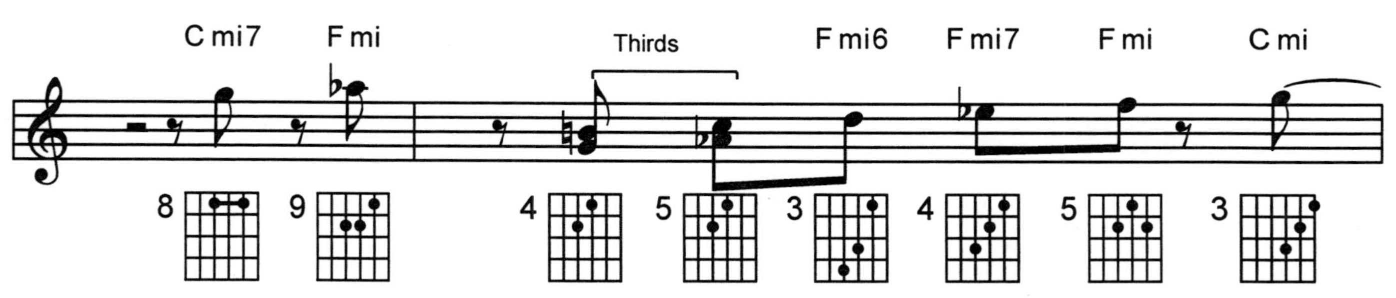
C mi7
F mi
Thirds
F mi6
F mi7
F mi
C mi
8
9
4
5
3
4
5
3

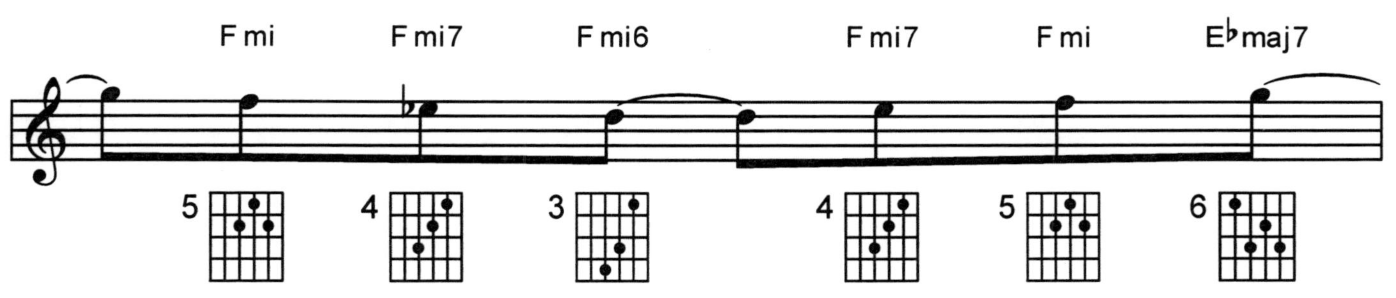
F mi
F mi7
F mi6
F mi7
F mi
E♭maj7
5
4
3
4
5
6

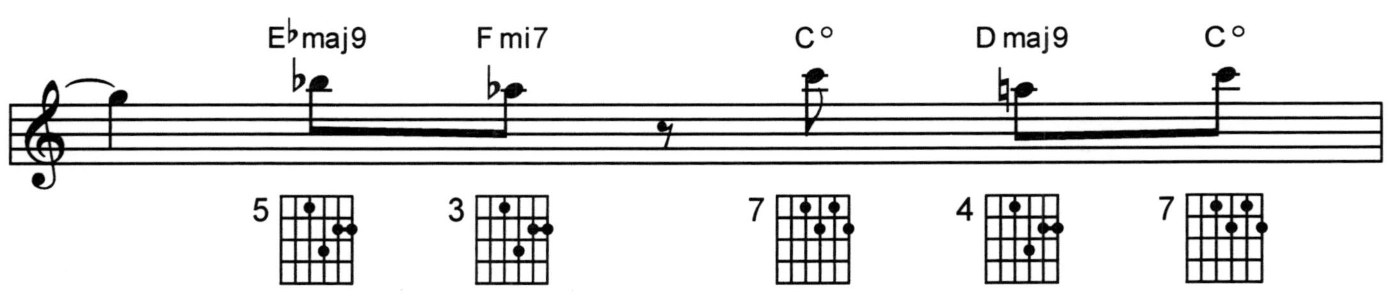
E♭maj9
F mi7
C °
D maj9
C °
5
3
7
4
7

Barney Kessel Excerpt
"Autumn Leaves", Page 4
Repeated Shout Chorus

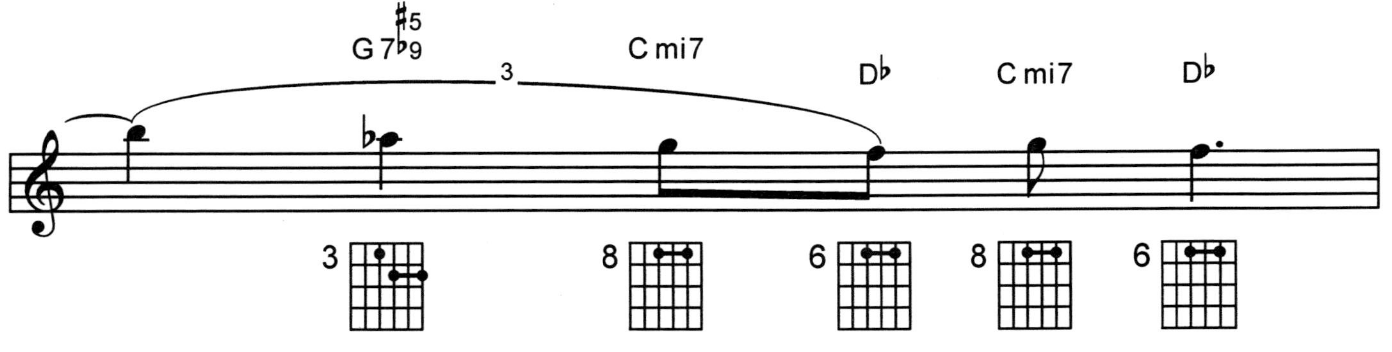

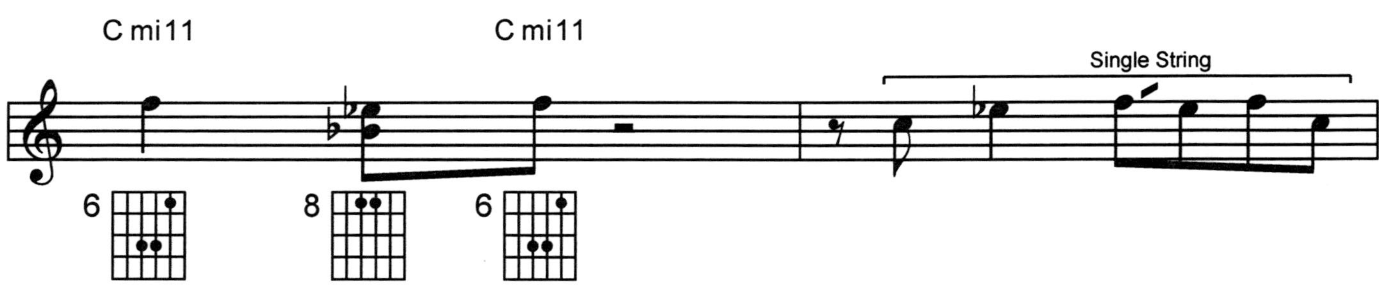

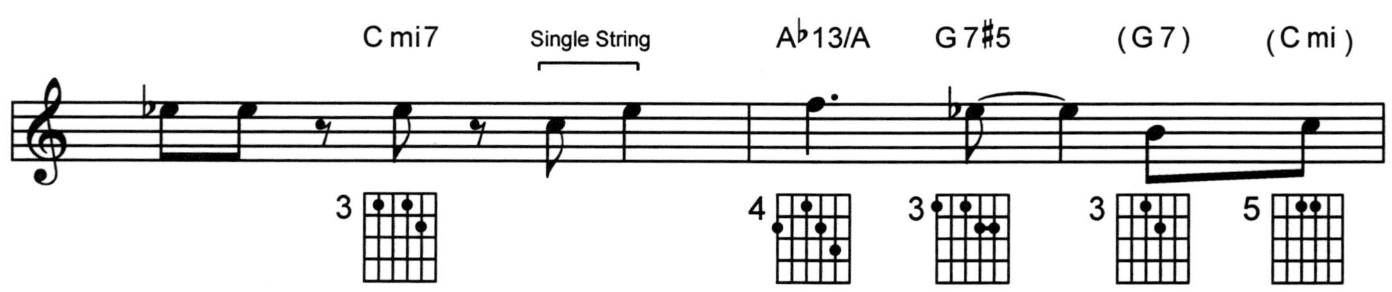

Barney Kessel Excerpt
"Autumn Leaves", Page 5
Repeated Shout Chorus

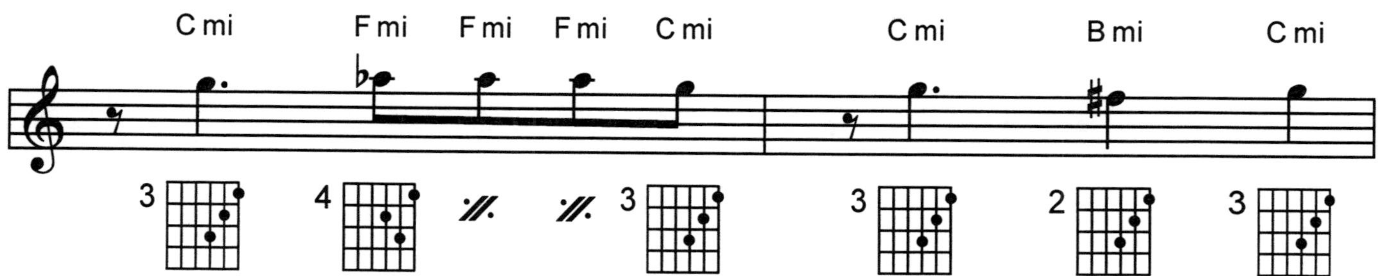

Repeated Shout Chorus

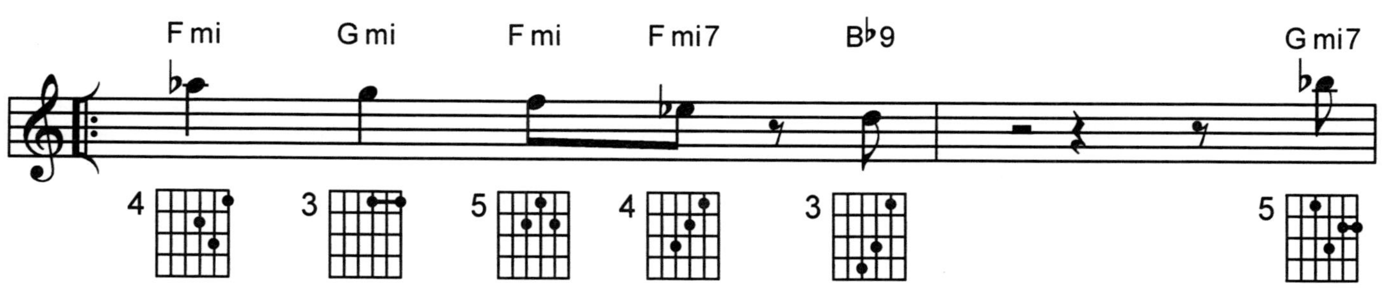

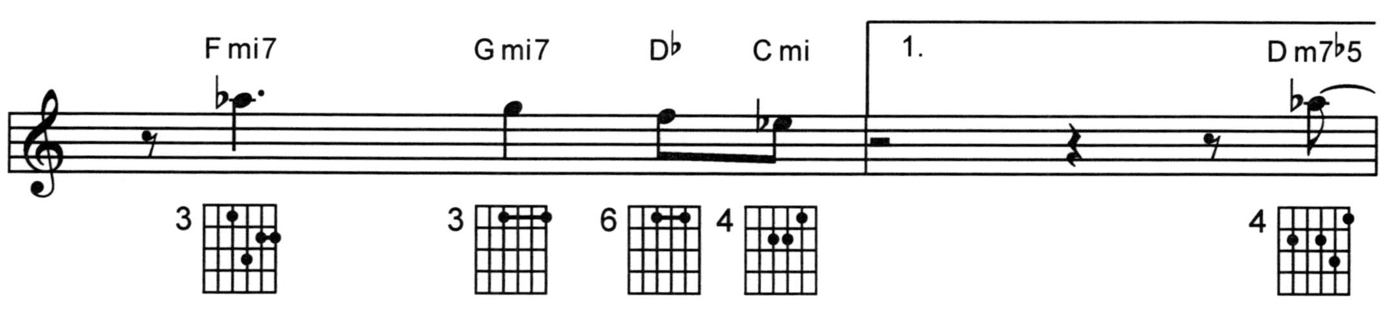

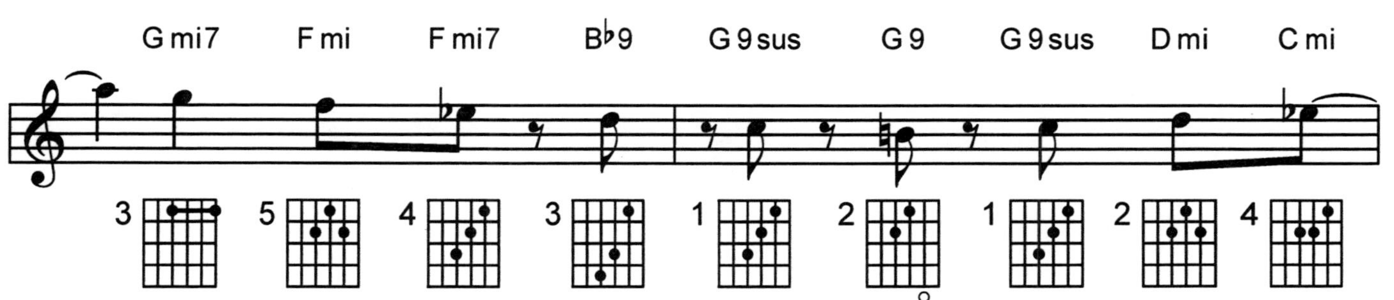

Barney Kessel Excerpt
"Autumn Leaves", Page 6
Repeated Shout Chorus

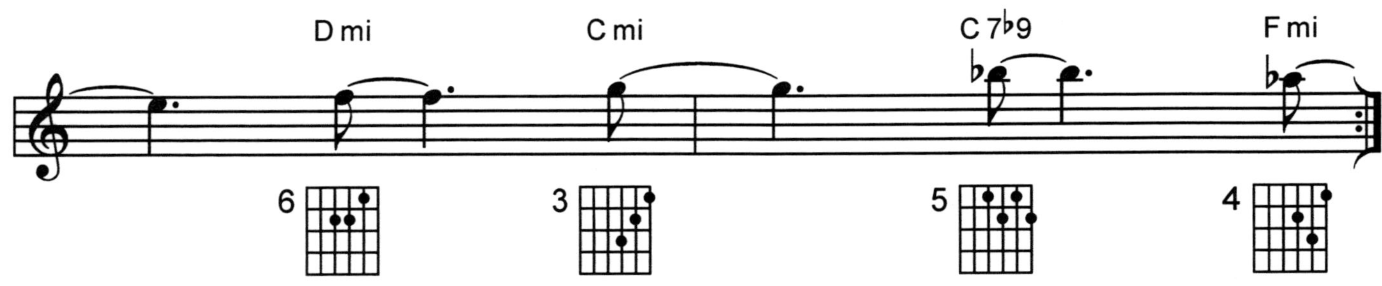

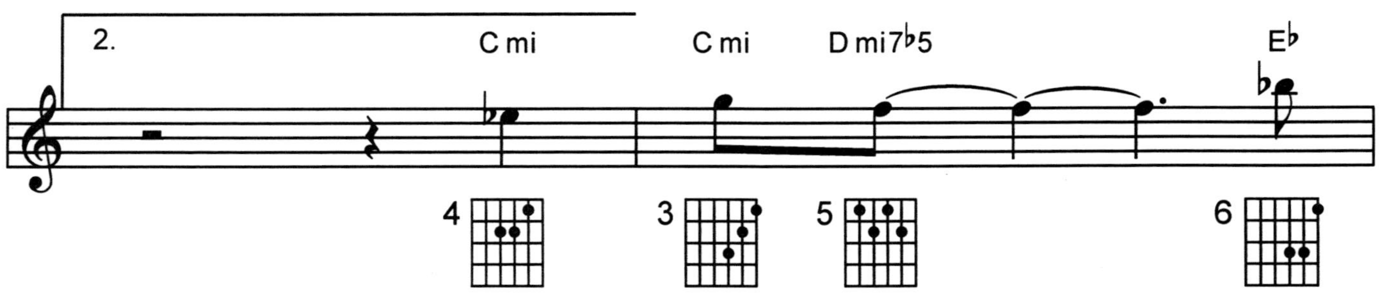

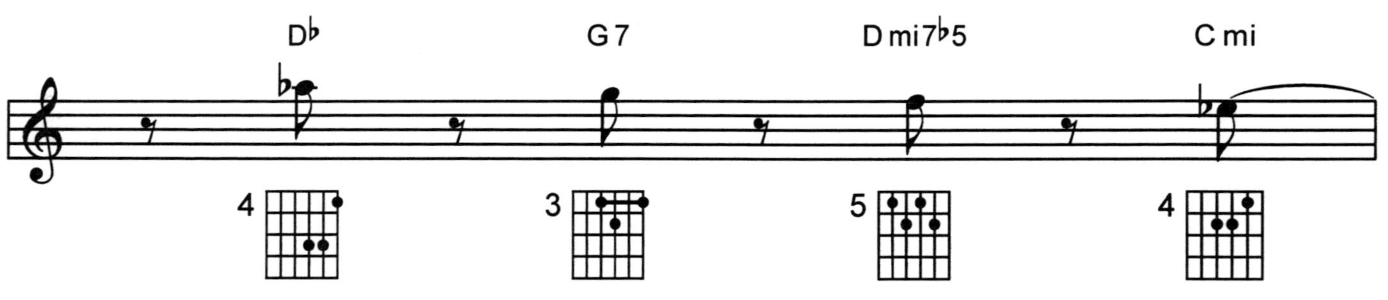

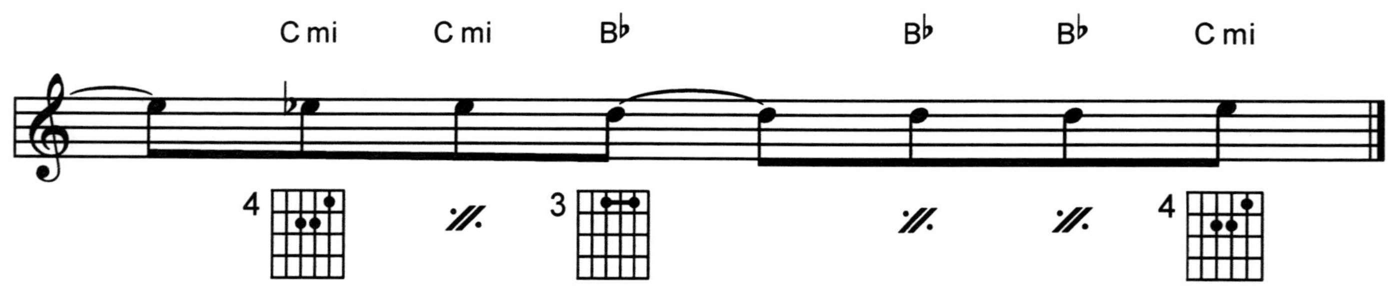

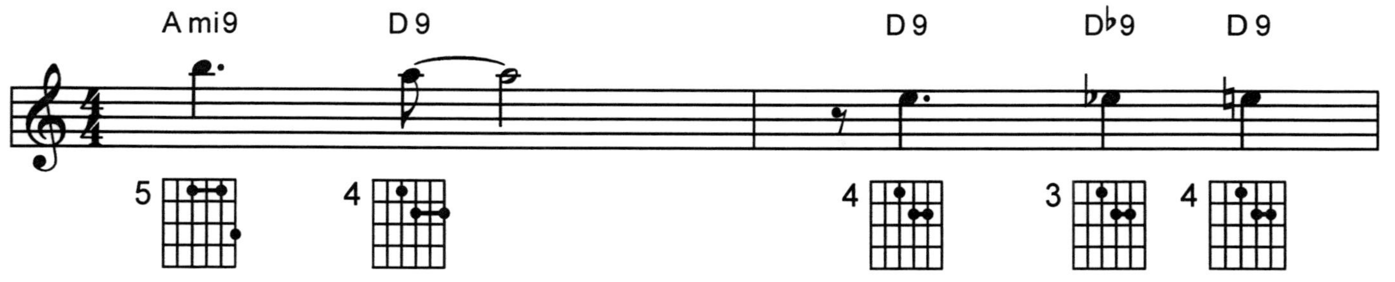
A mi9
D 9
D 9
D♭9
D 9
5
4
4
3
4

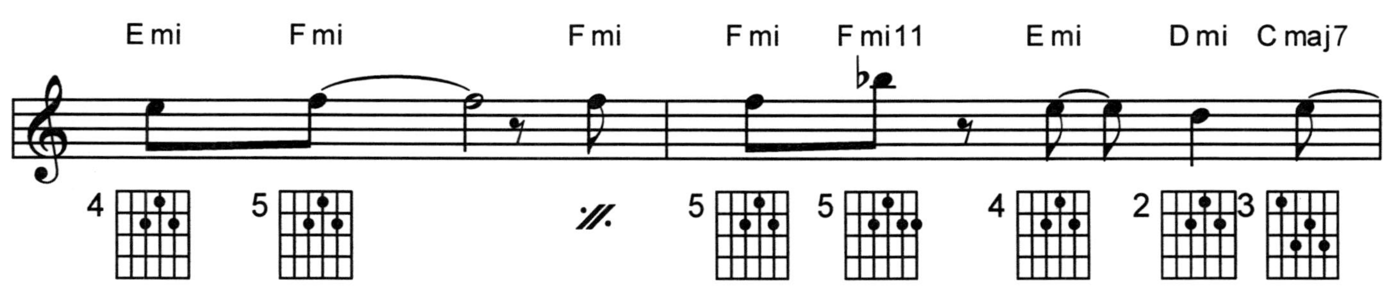
E mi
F mi
F mi
F mi
F mi11
E mi
D mi
C maj7
4
5
5
5
4
2
3

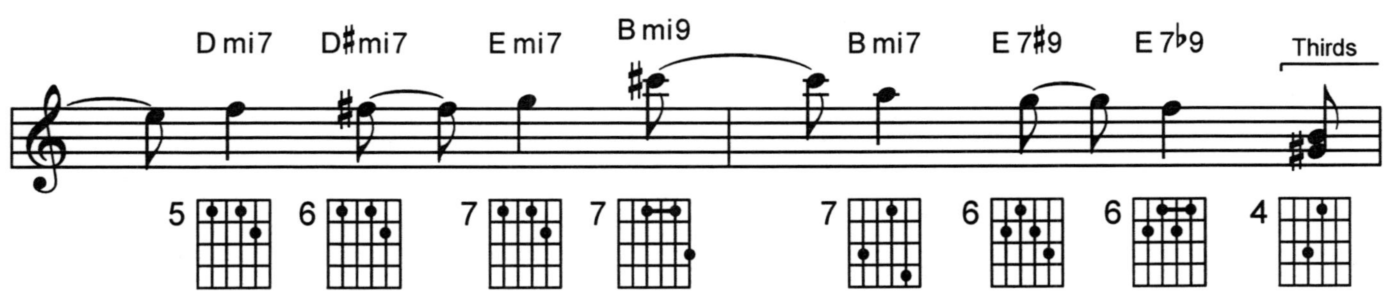
D mi7
D#mi7
E mi7
B mi9
B mi7
E 7#9
E 7♭9
Thirds
5
6
7
7
7
6
6
4

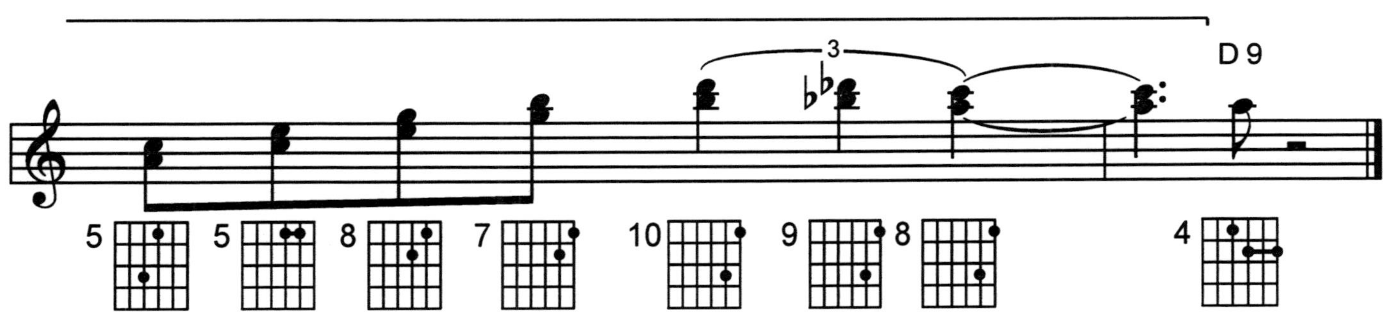
3
D 9
5
5
8
7
10
9
8
4

Barney Kessel Solo Excerpt
"You're The One For Me", Page 2

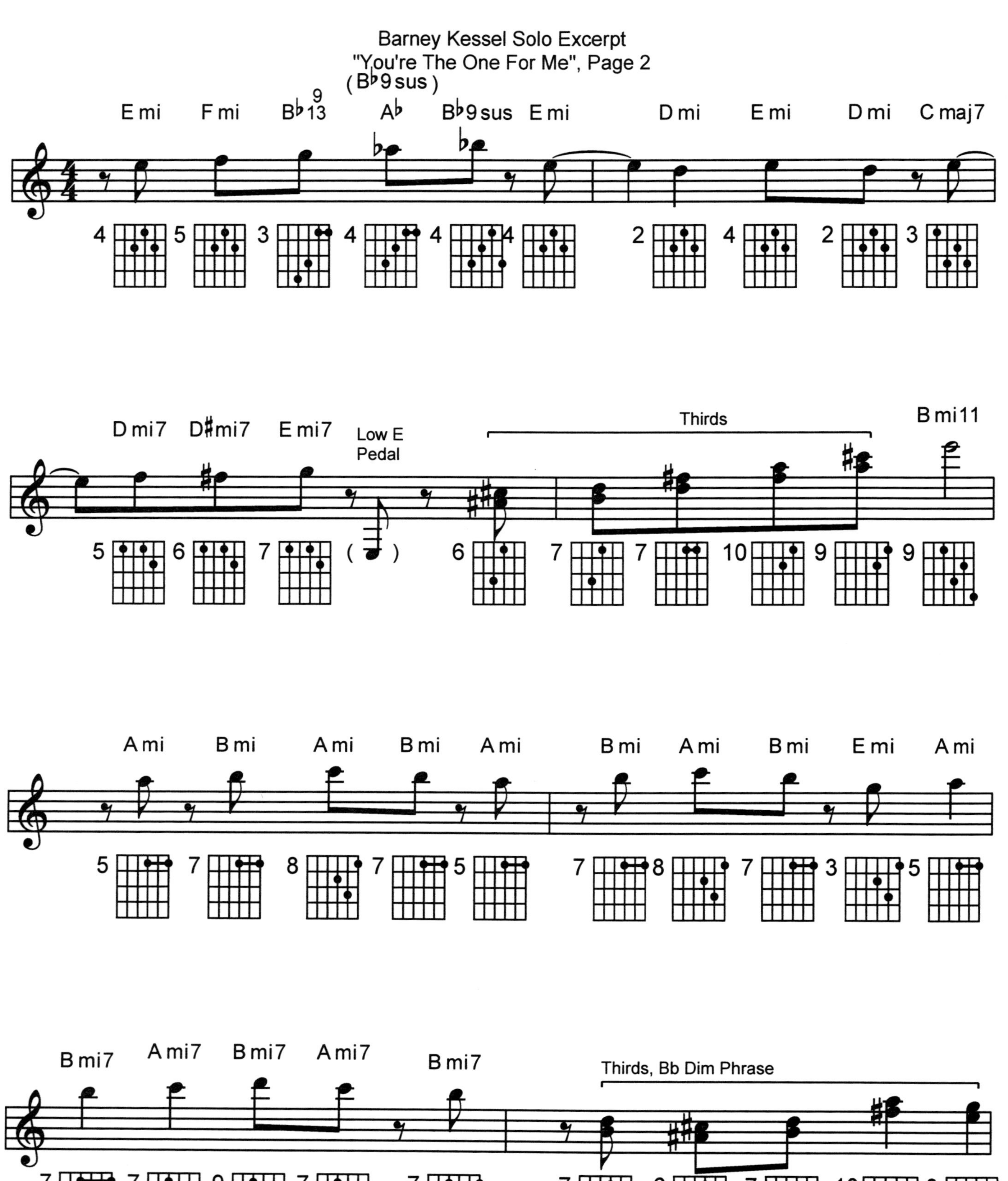

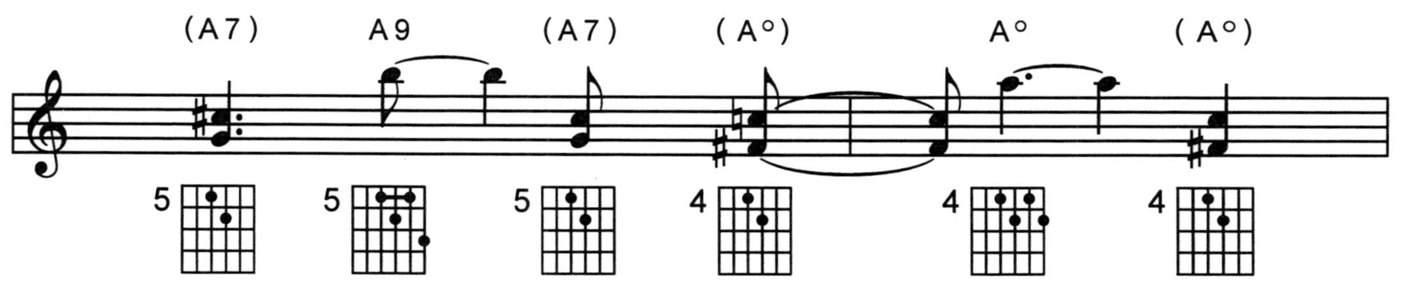
(A7)   A9   (A7)   (A°)   A°   (A°)
5   5   5   4   4   4

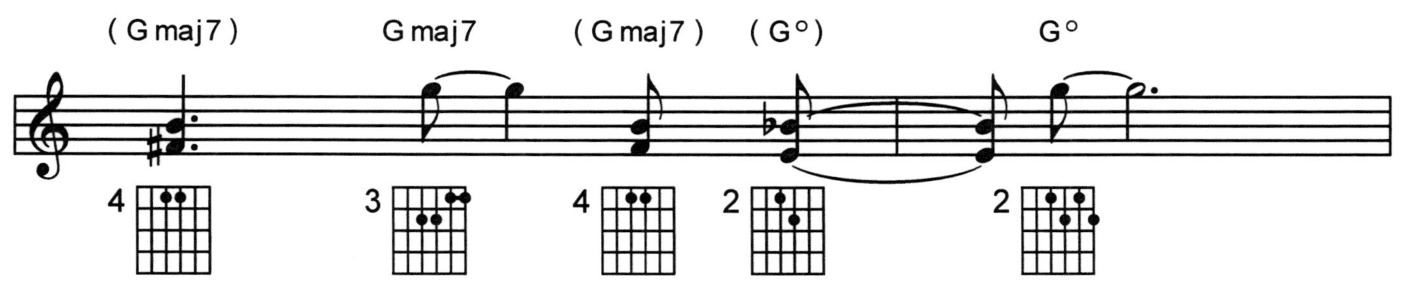
(Gmaj7)   Gmaj7   (Gmaj7)   (G°)   G°
4   3   4   2   2

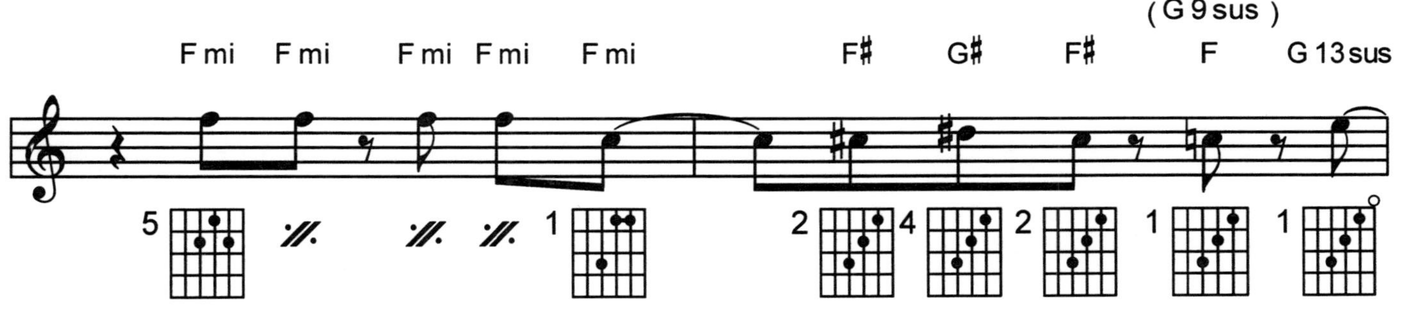
Fmi   Fmi   Fmi Fmi   Fmi   F#   G#   F#   F   (G9sus)   G13sus
5   //.   //.   //.   1   2   4   2   1   1

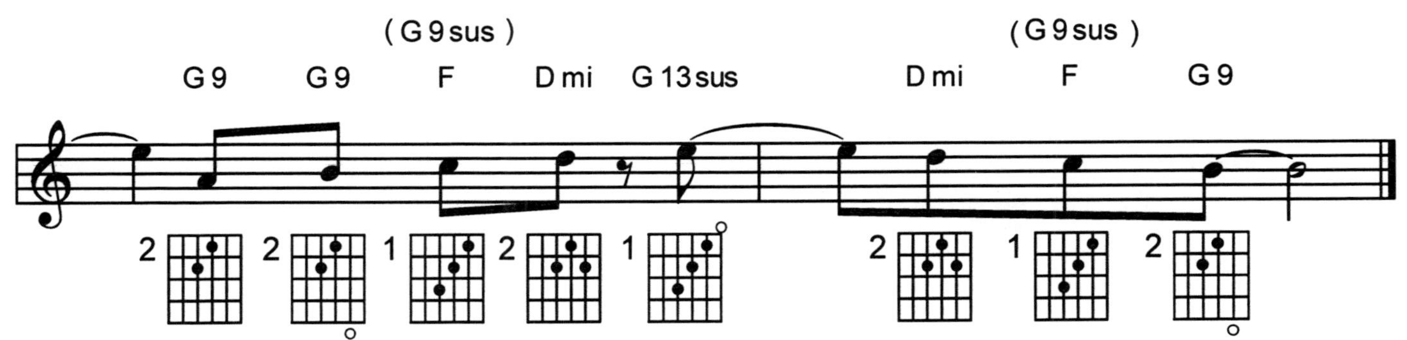
(G9sus)
G9   G9   F   Dmi   G13sus   (G9sus)   Dmi   F   G9
2   2   1   2   1   2   1   2

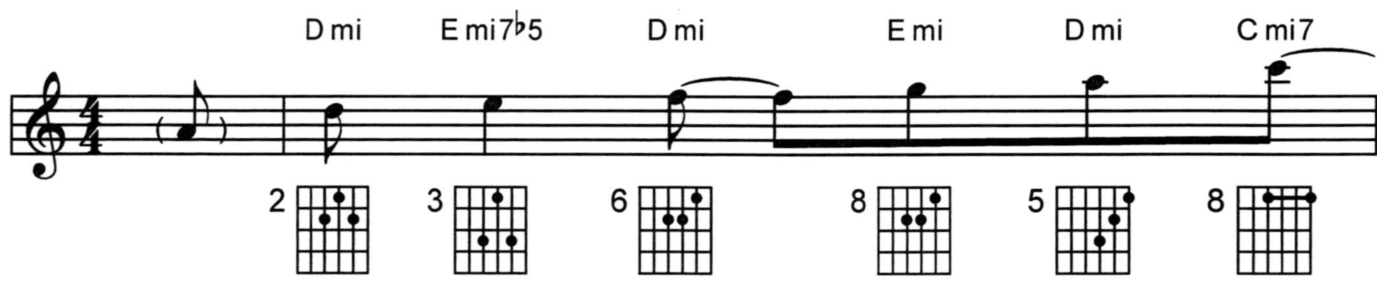
D mi
E mi7♭5
D mi
E mi
D mi
C mi7
2
3
6
8
5
8

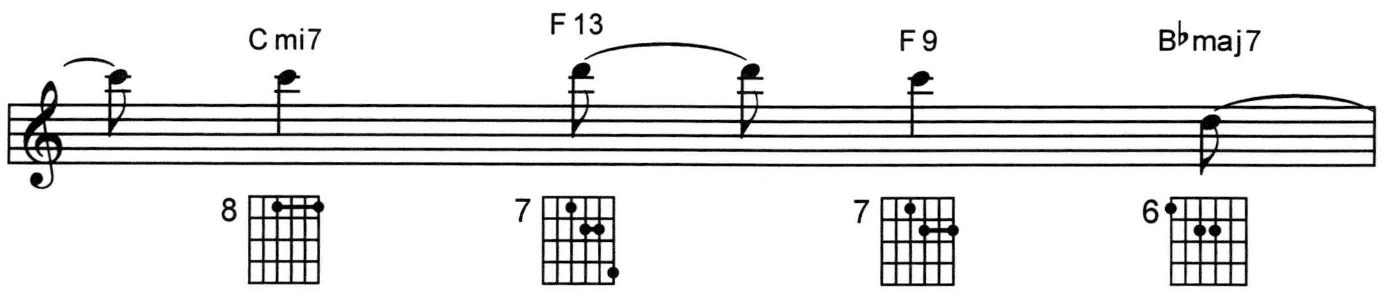
C mi7
F 13
F 9
B♭maj7
8
7
7
6

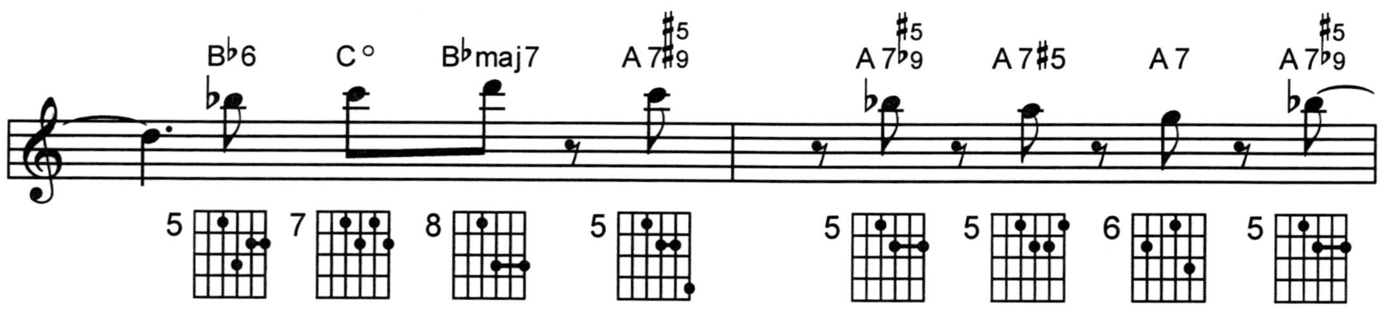
B♭6
C°
B♭maj7
A 7#9
#5
A 7♭9
#5
A 7#5
A 7
A 7♭9
#5
5
7
8
5
5
5
6
5

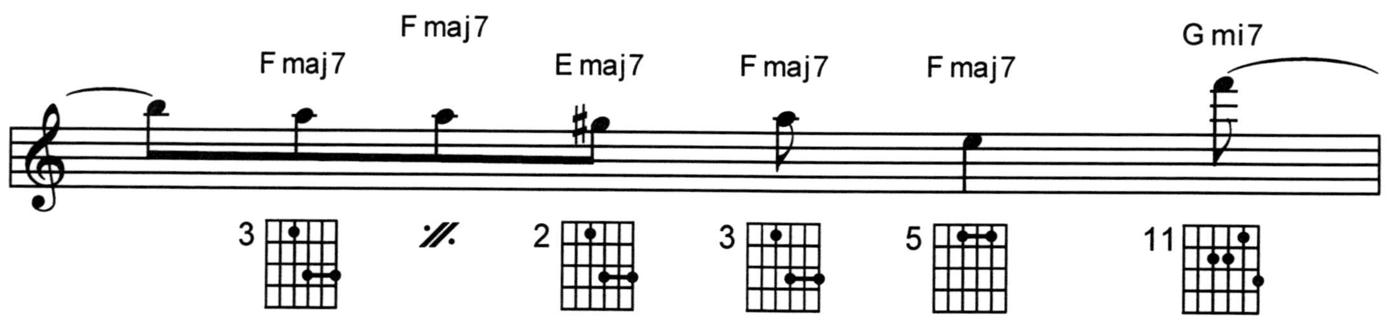
F maj7
F maj7
E maj7
F maj7
F maj7
G mi7
3
2
3
5
11

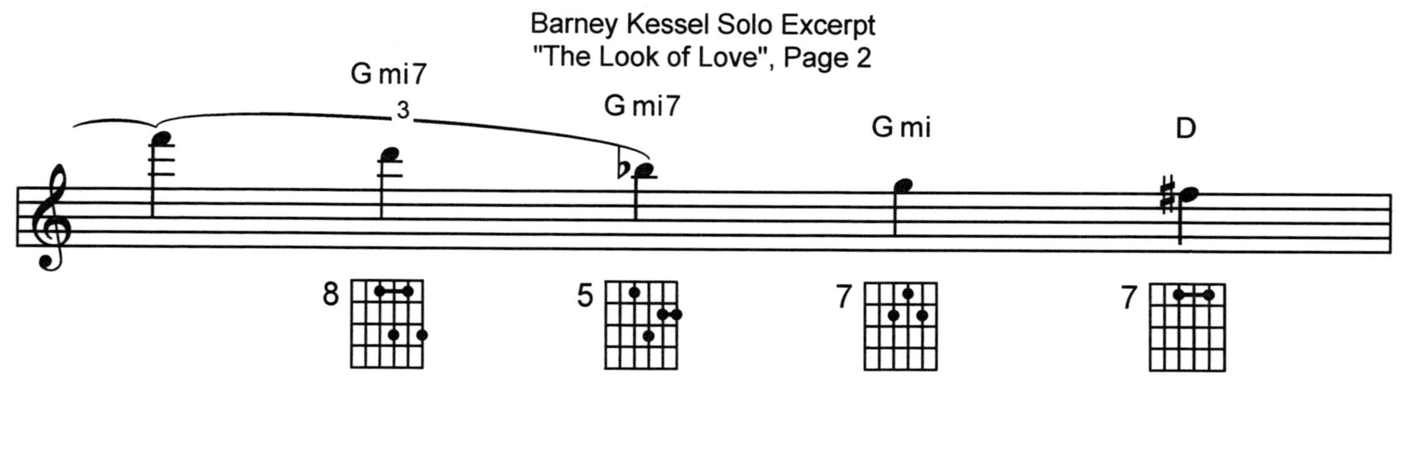

Barney Kessel Solo Excerpt
"The Look of Love", Page 2
G mi7
G mi7
G mi
D
3
8
5
7
7

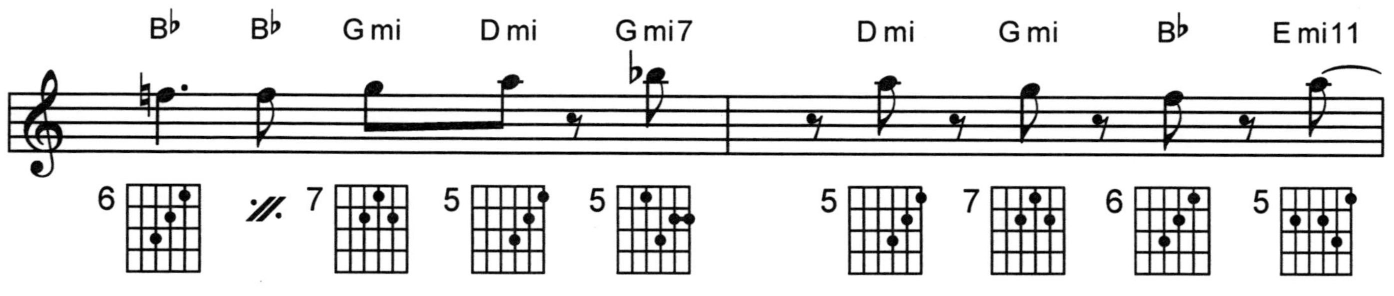

B♭
B♭
G mi
D mi
G mi7
D mi
G mi
B♭
E mi11
6
7
5
5
5
7
6
5

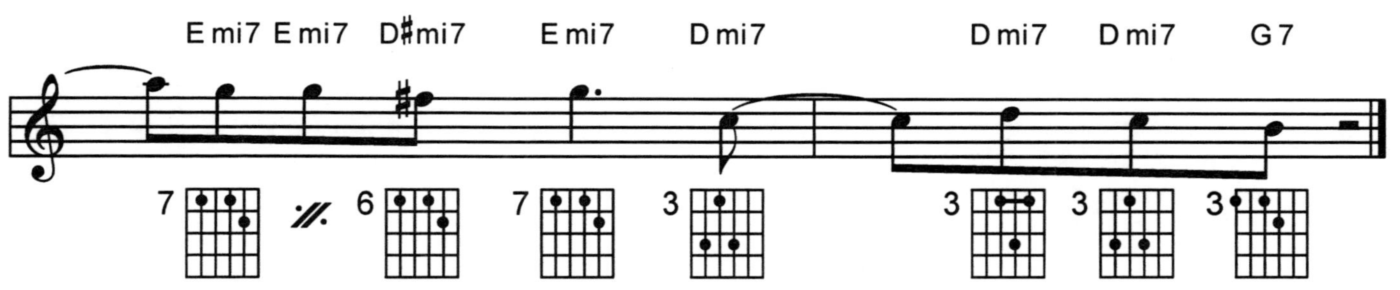

E mi7 E mi7 D♯mi7
E mi7
D mi7
D mi7
D mi7
G 7
7
6
7
3
3
3
3

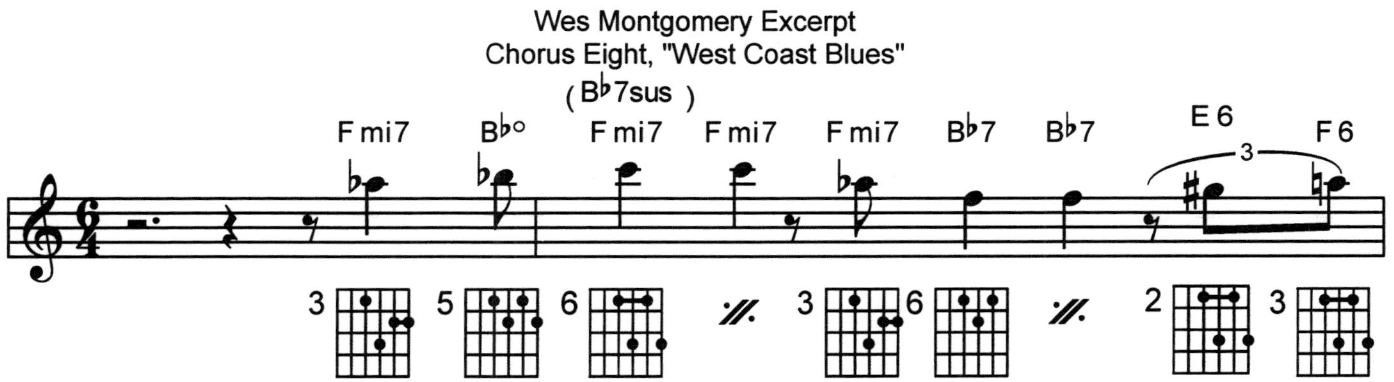

Wes Montgomery Excerpt
Chorus Eight, "West Coast Blues"
(B♭7sus)
F mi7
B♭o
F mi7
F mi7
F mi7
B♭7
B♭7
E 6
F 6
3
3
5
6
3
6
2
3

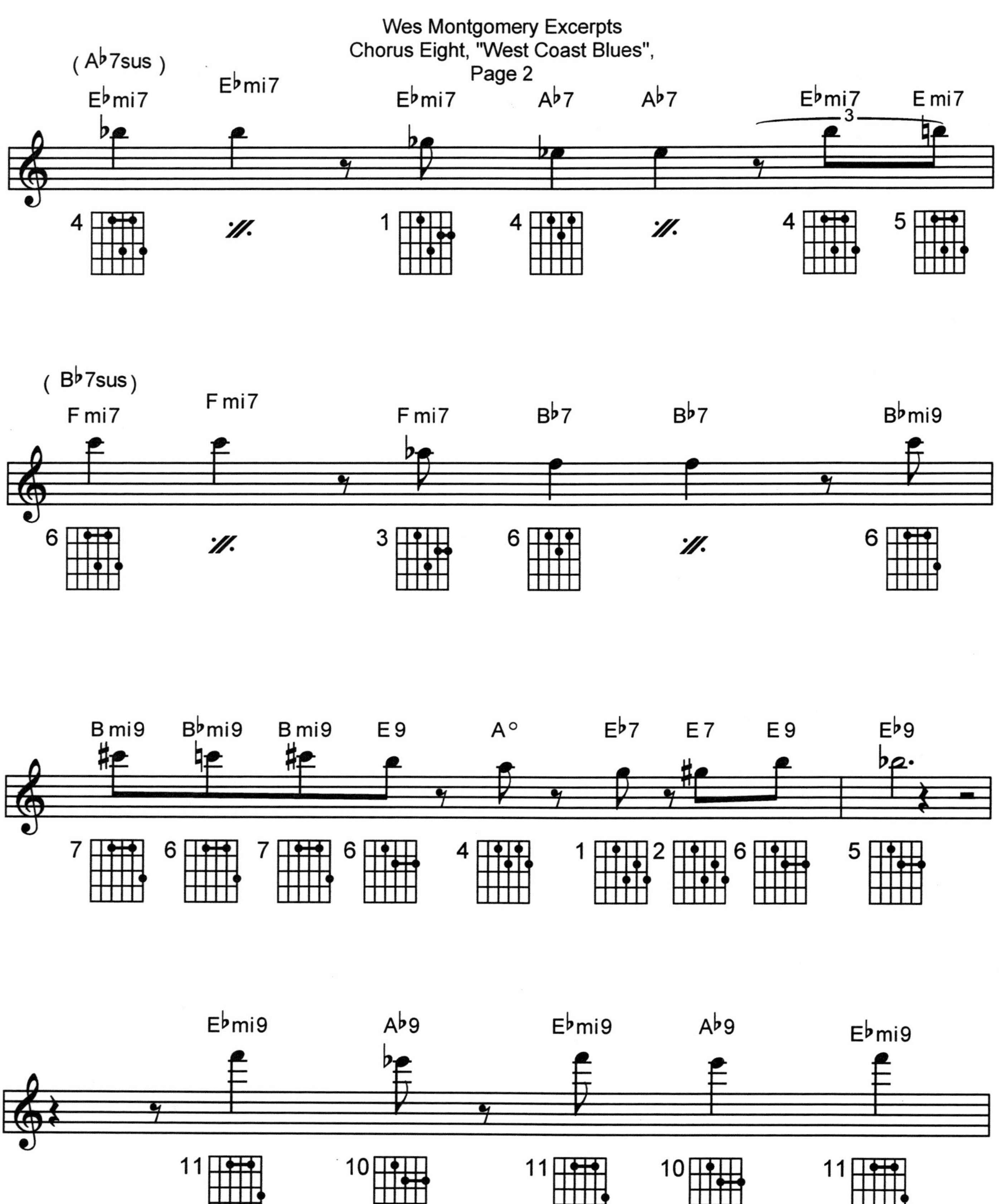
(A♭7sus)
E♭mi7
E♭mi7
E♭mi7
A♭7
A♭7
E♭mi7
E mi7
4
1
4
4
5
(B♭7sus)
F mi7
F mi7
F mi7
B♭7
B♭7
B♭mi9
6
3
6
6
B mi9
B♭mi9
B mi9
E 9
A°
E♭7
E 7
E 9
E♭9
7
6
7
6
4
1
2
6
5
E♭mi9
A♭9
E♭mi9
A♭9
E♭mi9
11
10
11
10
11

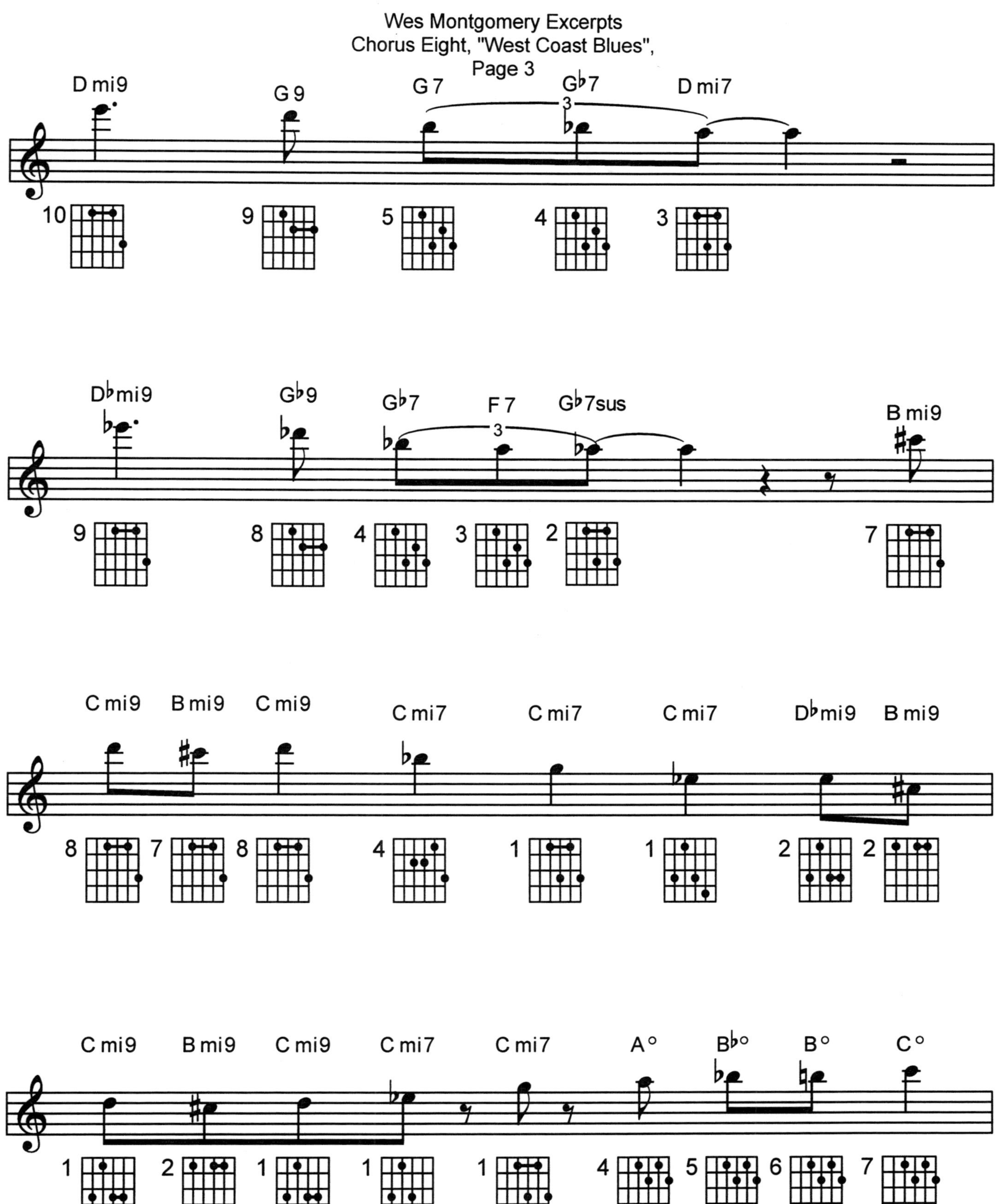

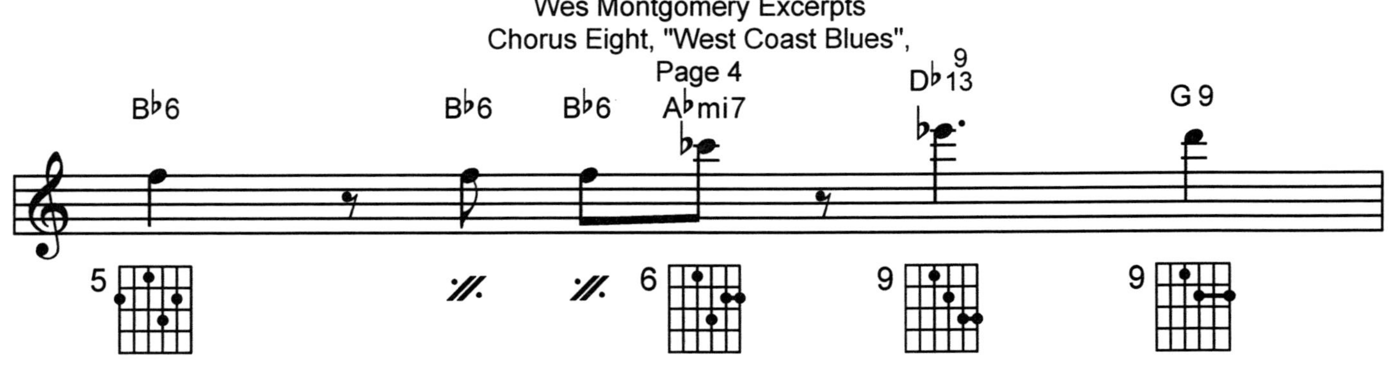

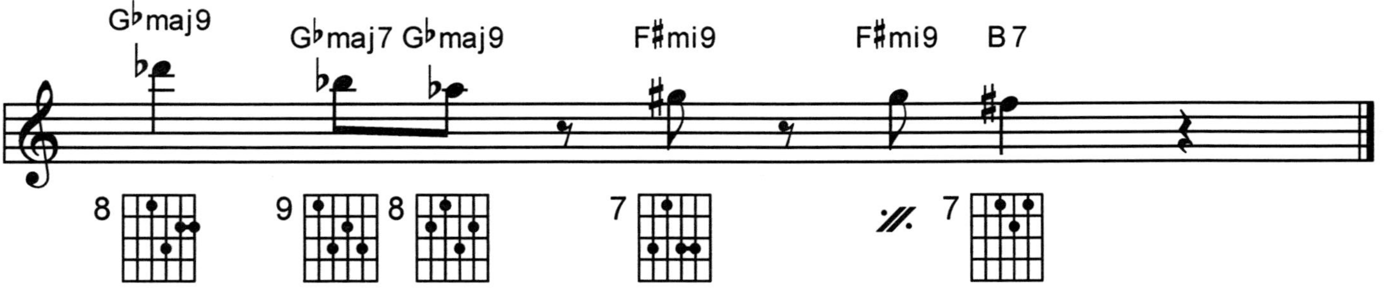

Constant Structure Augmented Chords

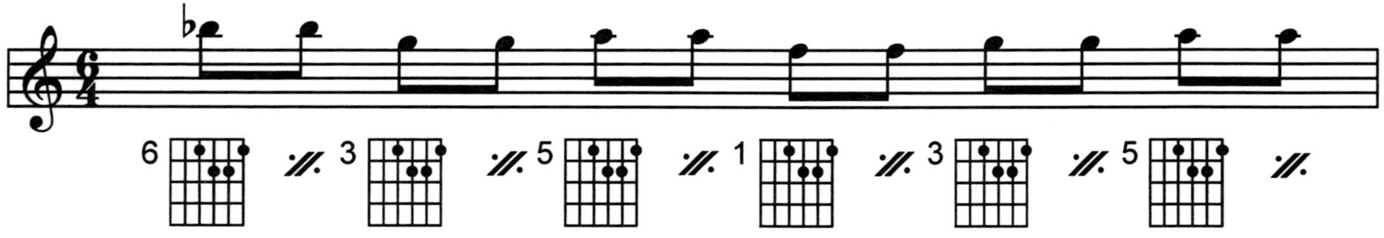

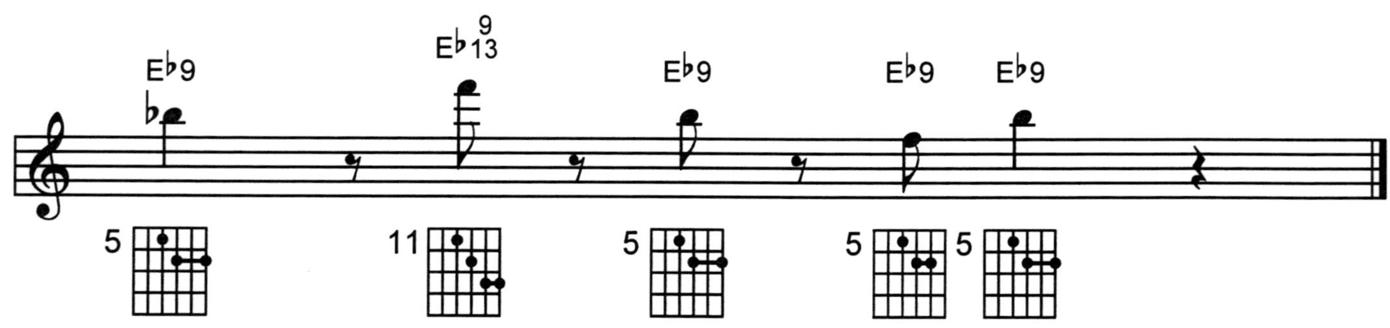

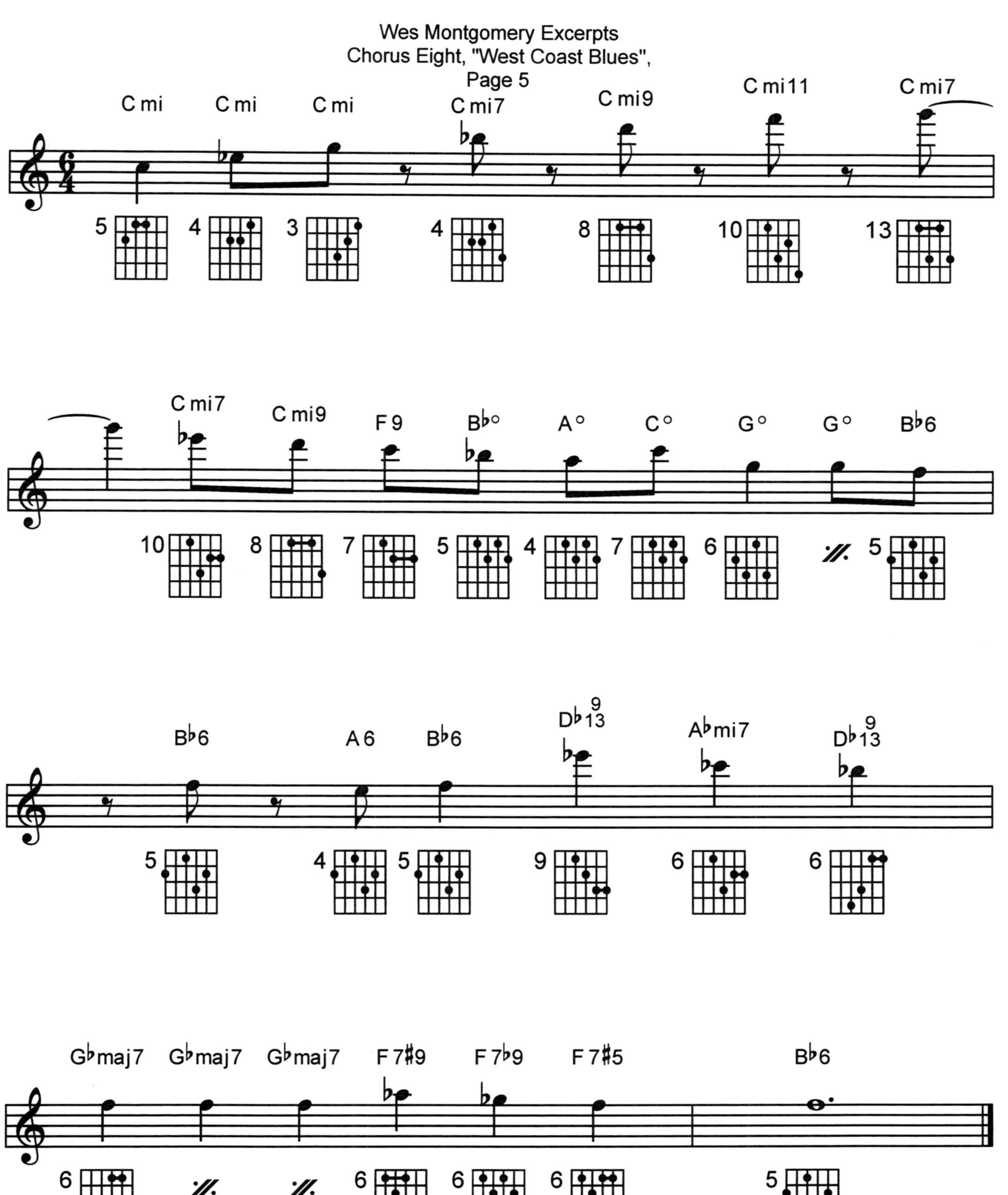

Wes Montgomery Excerpts
Chorus Eight, "West Coast Blues",
Page 5

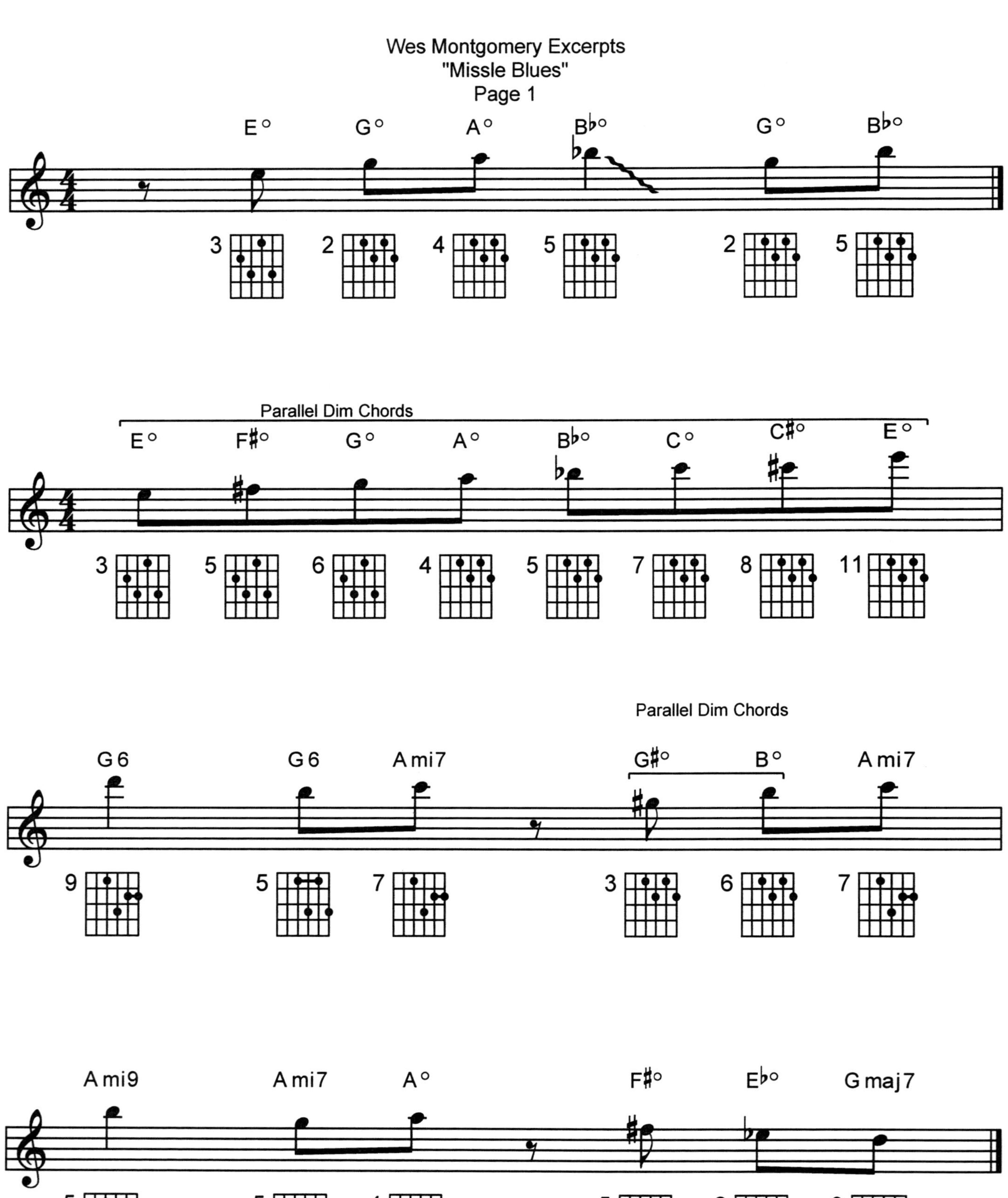

Wes Montgomery Excerpts
"Missle Blues"
Page 1
E° G° A° B♭° G° B♭°
Parallel Dim Chords
E° F#° G° A° B♭° C° C#° E°
Parallel Dim Chords
G 6 G 6 A mi7 G#° B° A mi7
A mi9 A mi7 A° F#° E♭° G maj7

Parallel Dim Chords

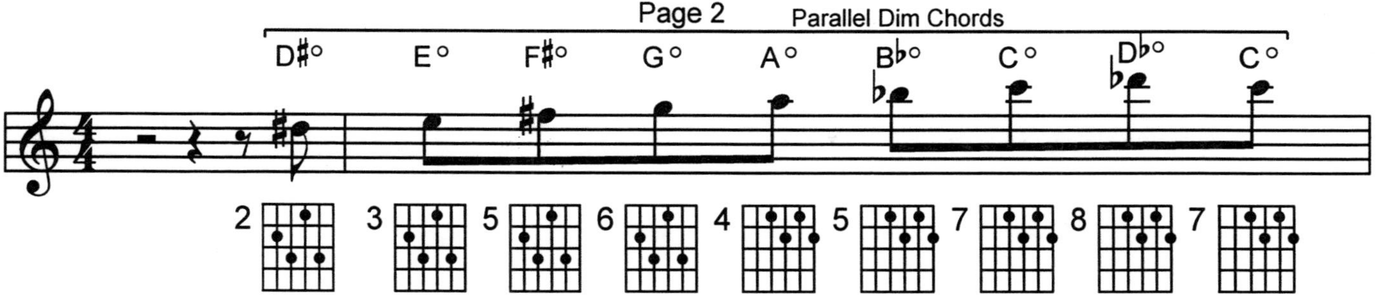

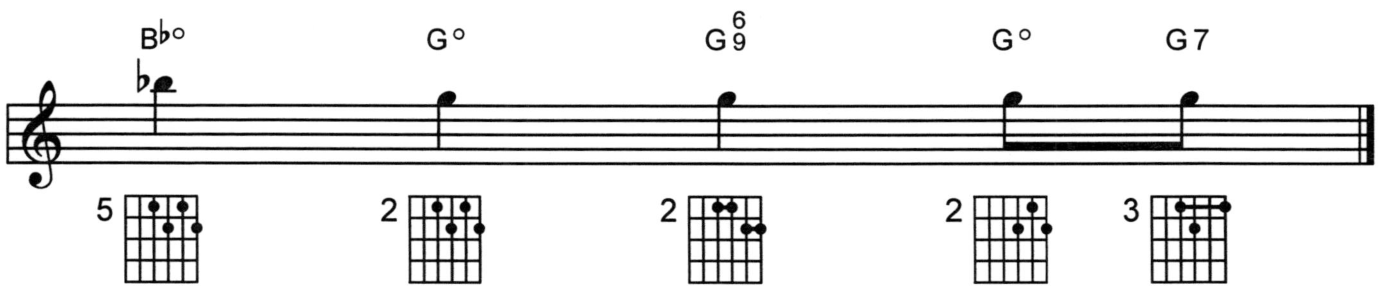

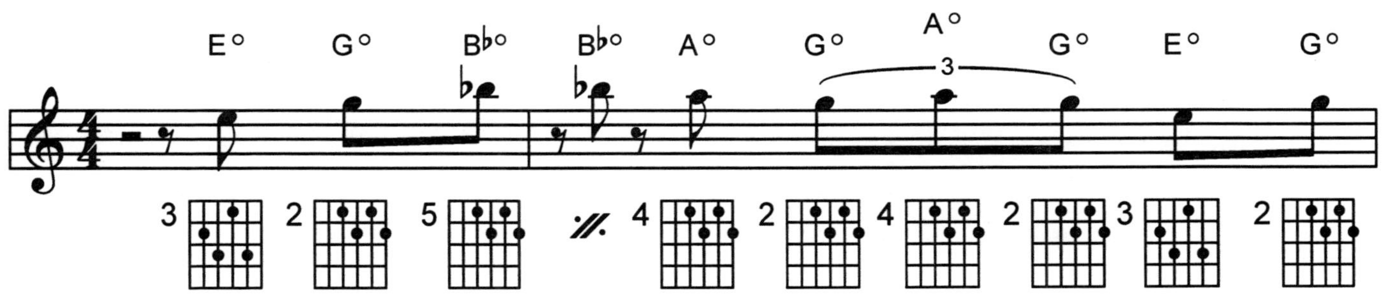

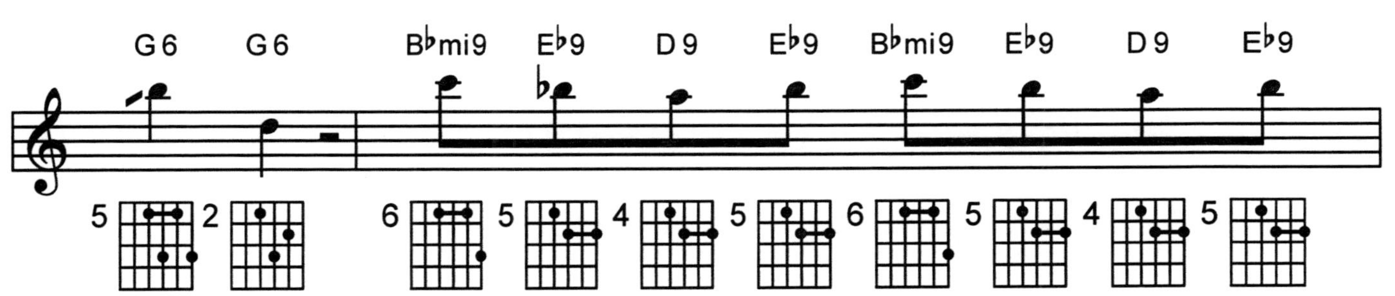

Wes Montgomery Excerpts
"Missle Blues"
Page 3

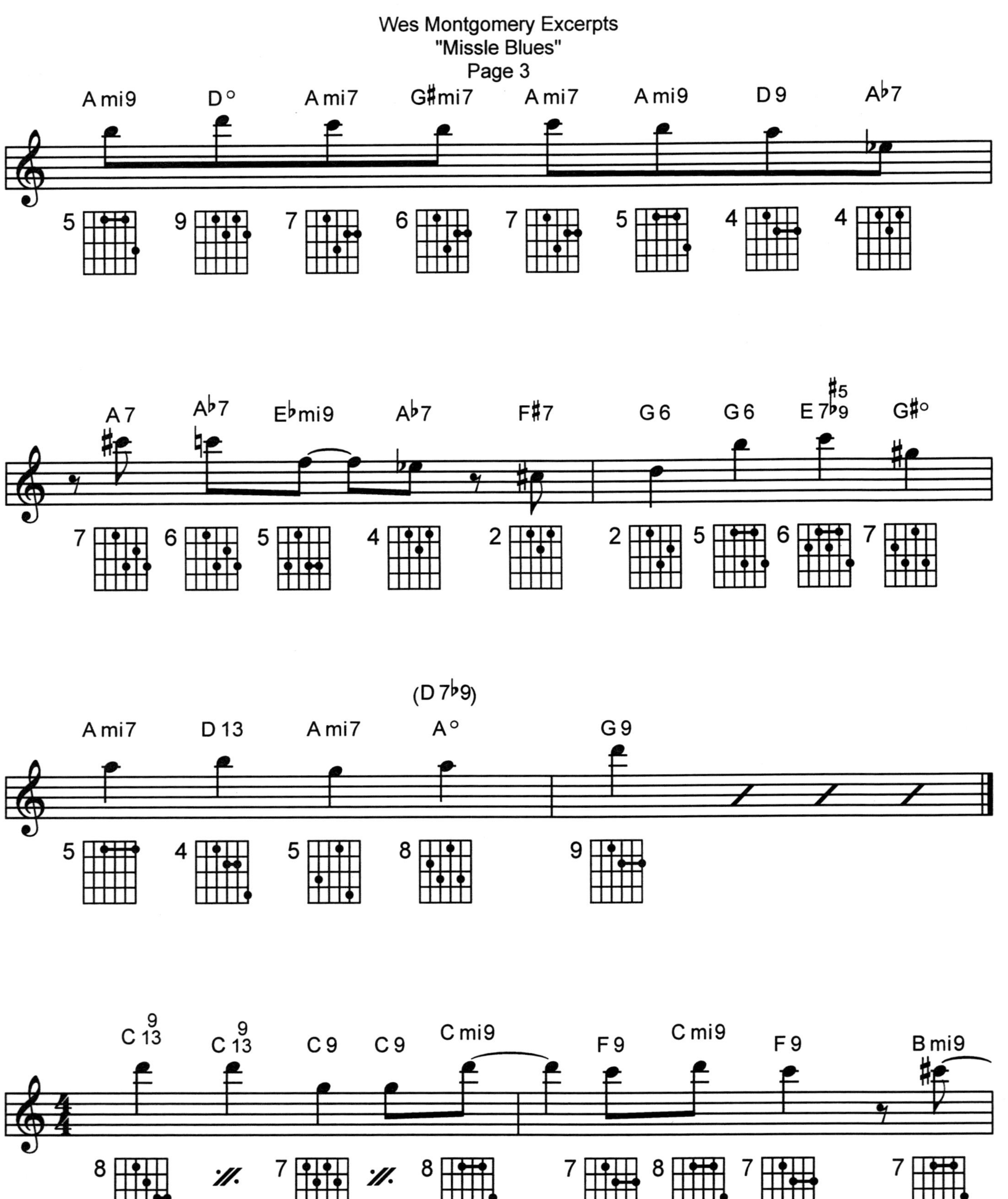

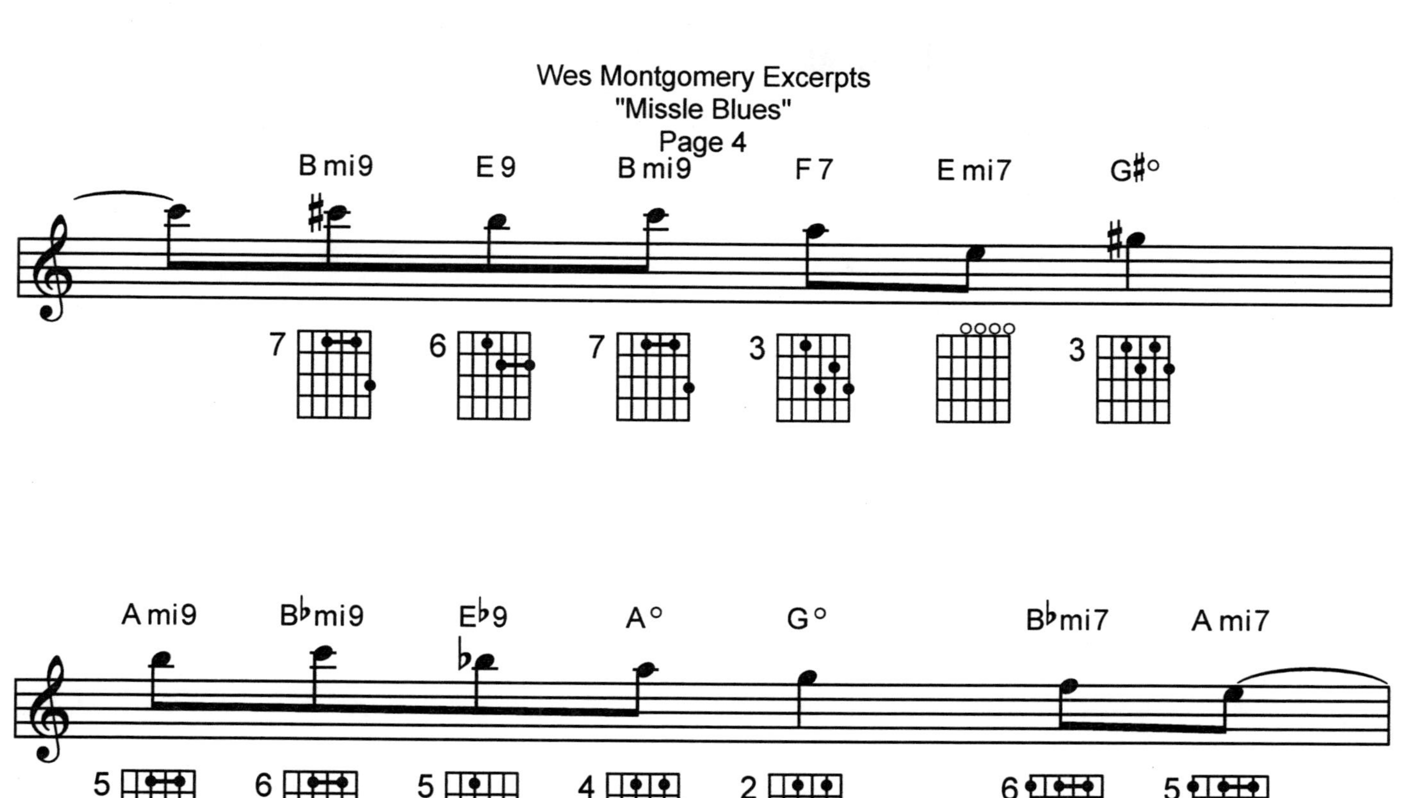
B mi9
E 9
B mi9
F 7
E mi7
G#o
7
6
7
3
3
A mi9
Bb mi9
Eb 9
Ao
Go
Bb mi7
A mi7
5
6
5
4
2
6
5

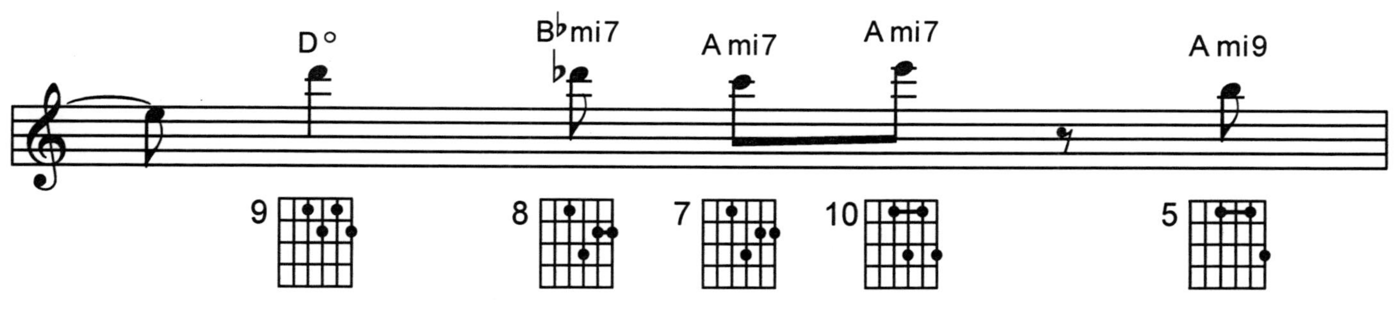
Do
Bb mi7
A mi7
A mi7
A mi9
9
8
7
10
5

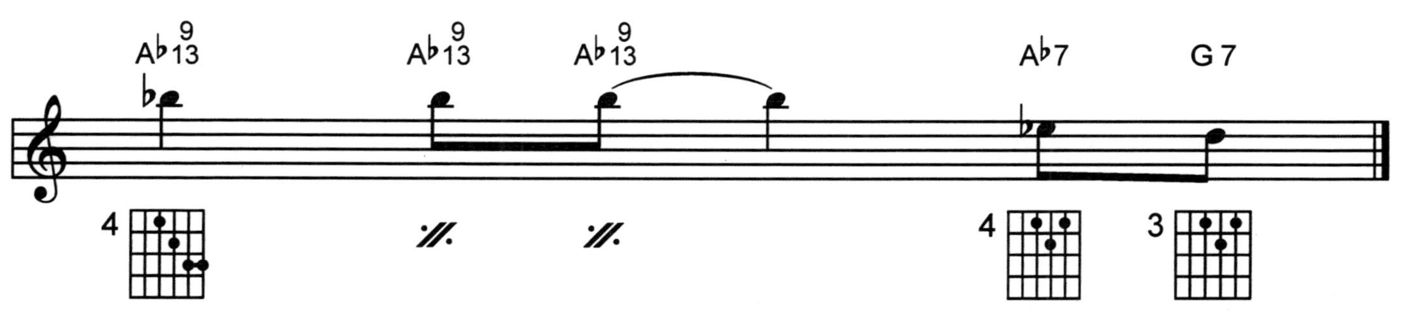
Ab 13 9
Ab 13 9
Ab 13 9
Ab 7
G 7
4
%.
%.
4
3

Wes Montgomery Excerpts
"Delilah Take 3"
Page 1

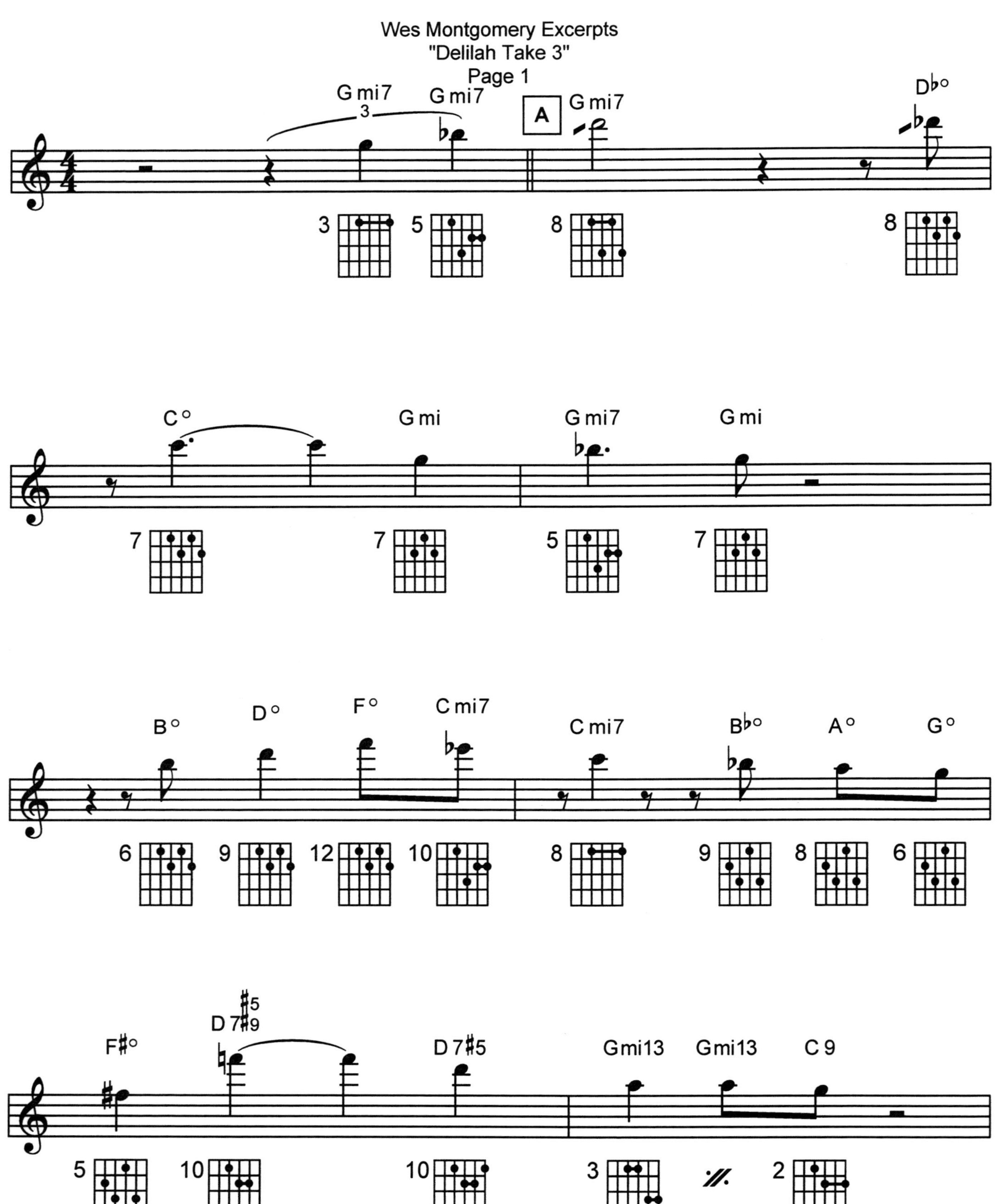

Wes Montgomery Excerpts
"Delilah Take 3"
Page 2

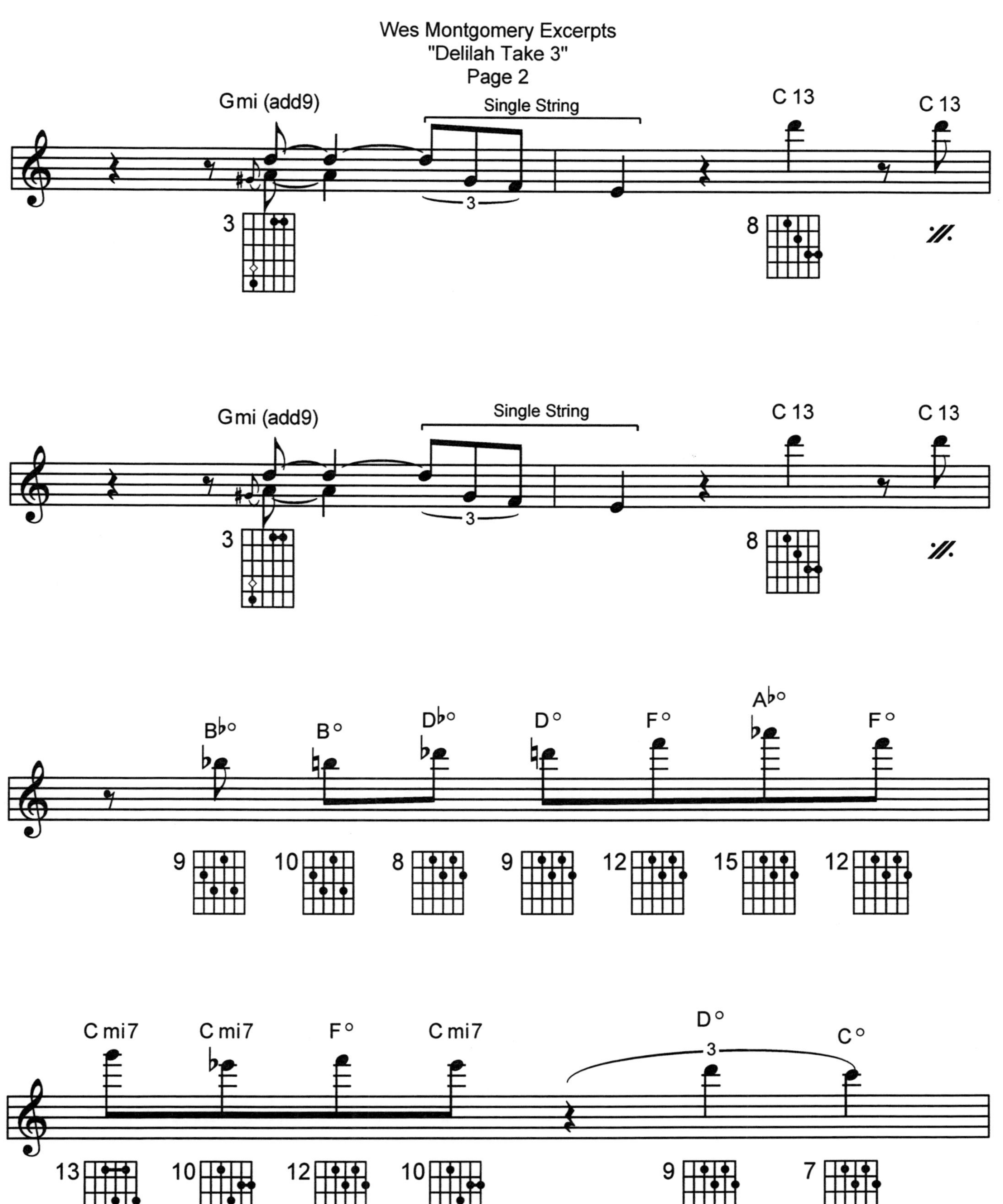

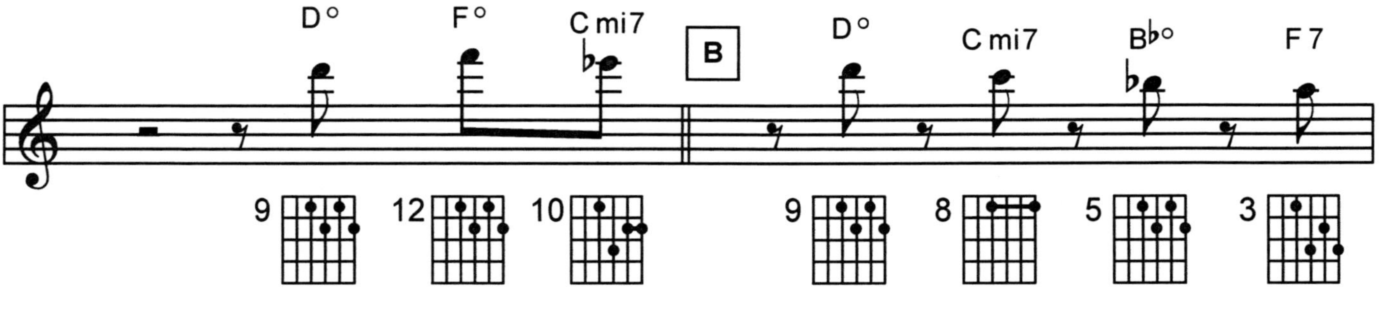

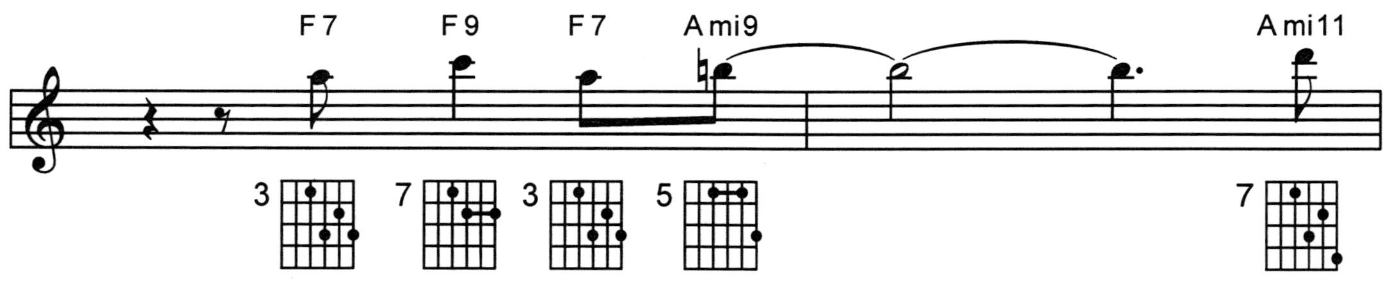

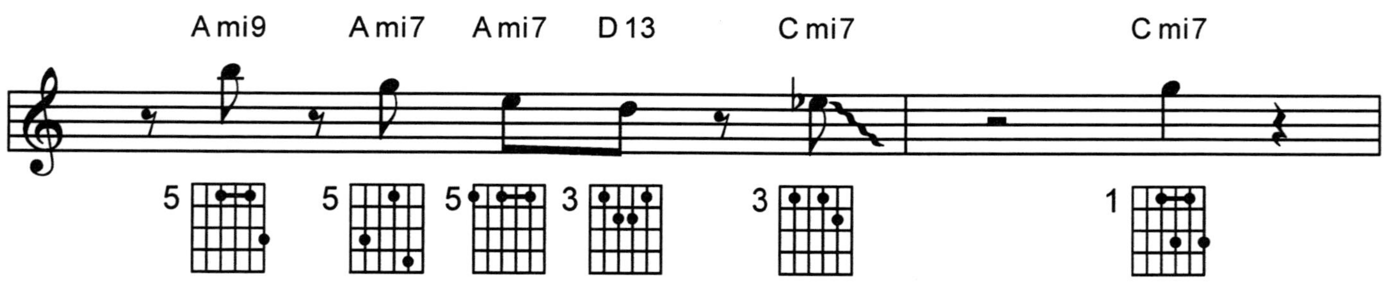

A mi9 A mi7 A mi7 D 13 C mi7 C mi7
5 5 5 3 3 1

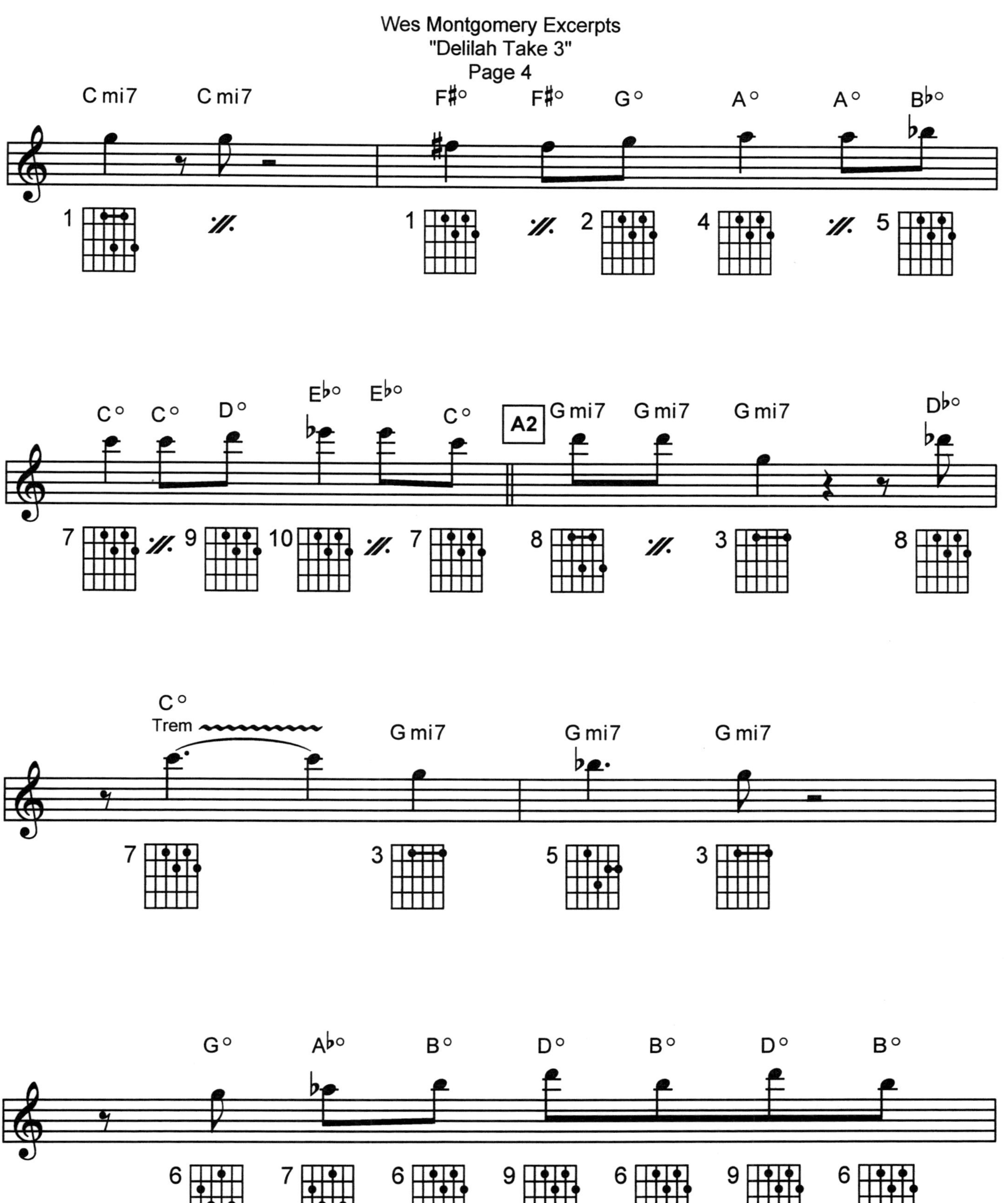
C mi7
C mi7
F#°
F#°
G°
A°
A°
Bb°
1
1
2
4
5
C°
C°
D°
Eb°
Eb°
C°
A2
G mi7
G mi7
G mi7
Db°
7
9
10
7
8
3
8
C°
Trem
G mi7
G mi7
G mi7
7
3
5
3
G°
Ab°
B°
D°
B°
D°
B°
6
7
6
9
6
9
6

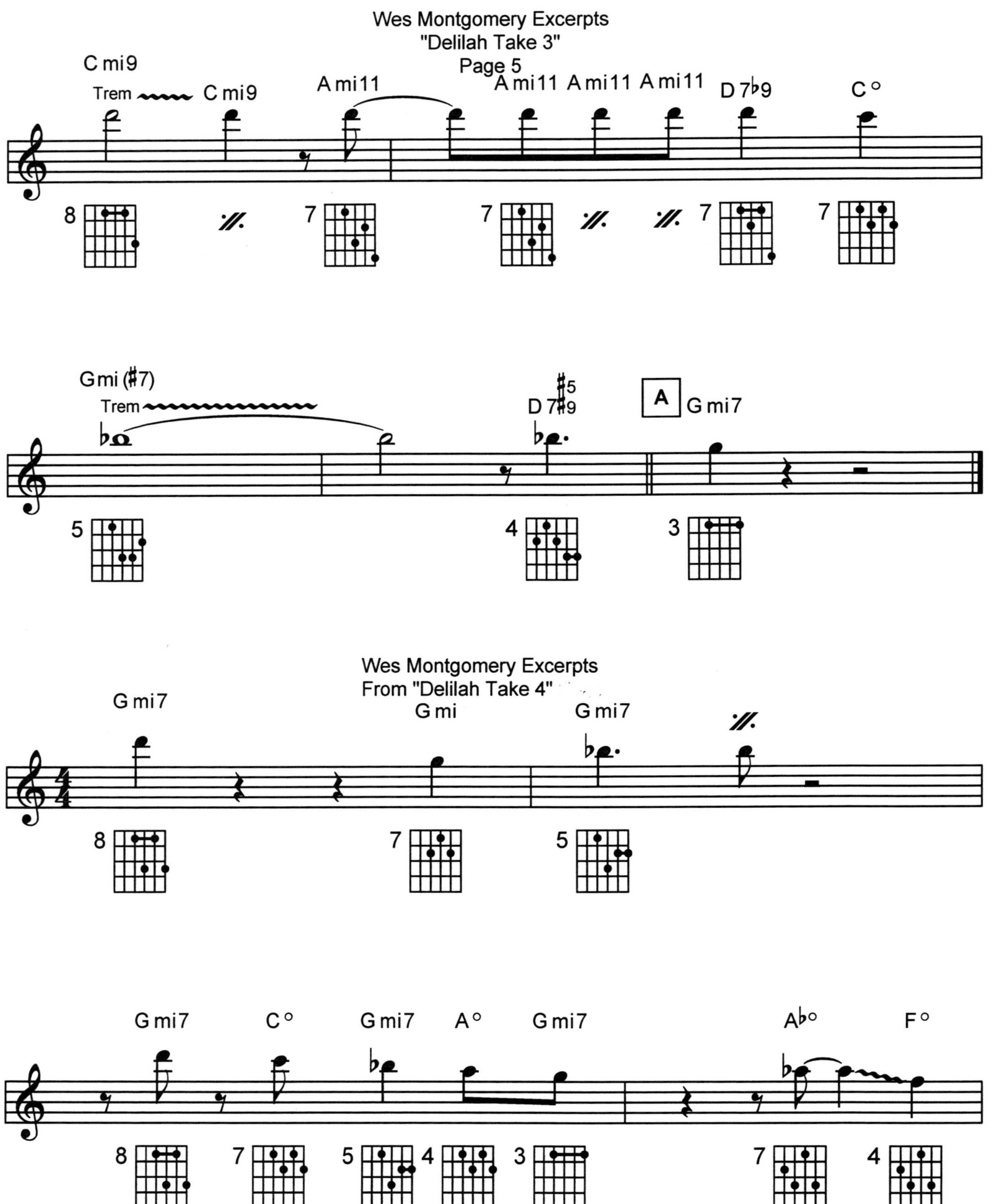

Wes Montgomery Excerpts
"Delilah Take 3"
Page 5
C mi9
Trem C mi9
A mi11
A mi11 A mi11 A mi11
D 7b9
C o
8 7 7 7
G mi (#7)
Trem
D 7#9 #5
A G mi7
5 4 3
Wes Montgomery Excerpts
From "Delilah Take 4"
G mi7
G mi
G mi7
8 7 5
G mi7 C o G mi7 A o G mi7
Ab o F o
8 7 5 4 3 7 4

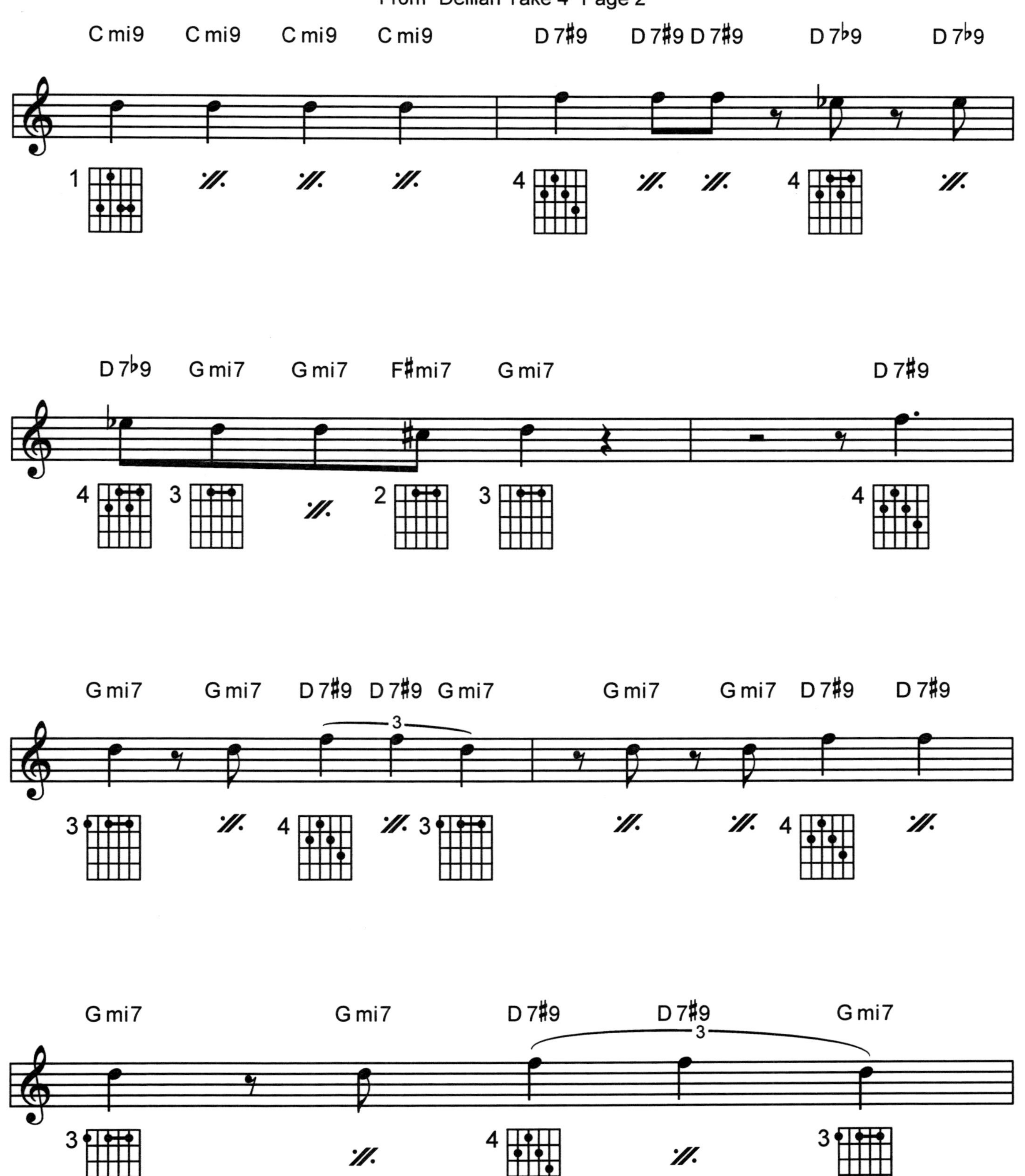

Wes Montgomery Excerpts
From "Delilah Take 4" Page 2
C mi9   C mi9   C mi9   C mi9   D 7#9   D 7#9 D 7#9   D 7♭9   D 7♭9
D 7♭9   G mi7   G mi7   F#mi7   G mi7   D 7#9
G mi7   G mi7   D 7#9 D 7#9 G mi7   G mi7   G mi7 D 7#9   D 7#9
G mi7   G mi7   D 7#9   D 7#9   G mi7

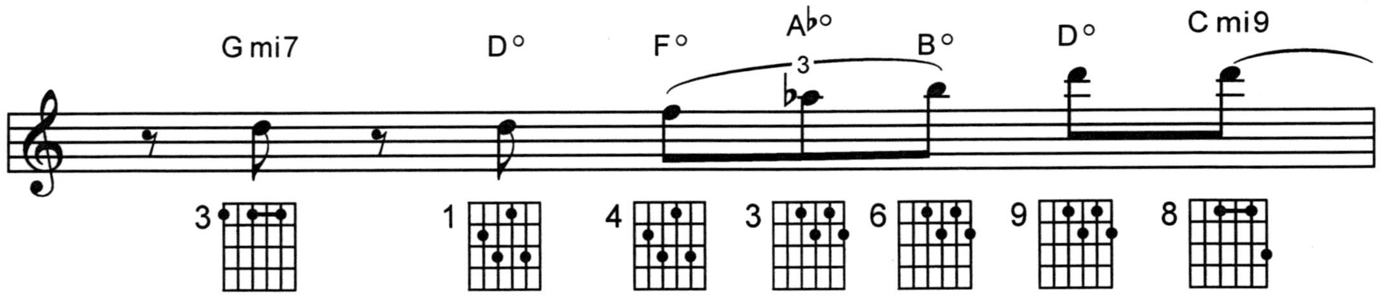
G mi7
D °
F °
A♭°
B °
D °
C mi9
3
1
4
3
6
9
8

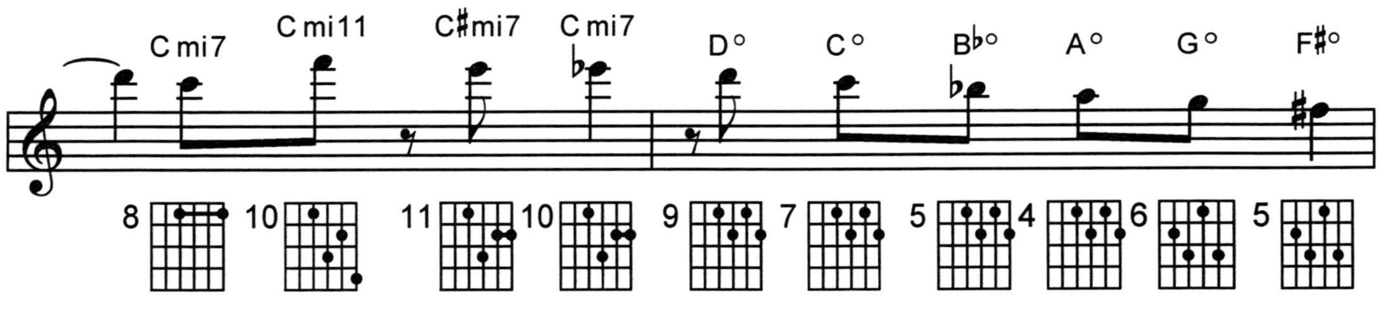
C mi7
C mi11
C#mi7
C mi7
D °
C °
B♭°
A °
G °
F#°
8
10
11
10
9
7
5
4
6
5

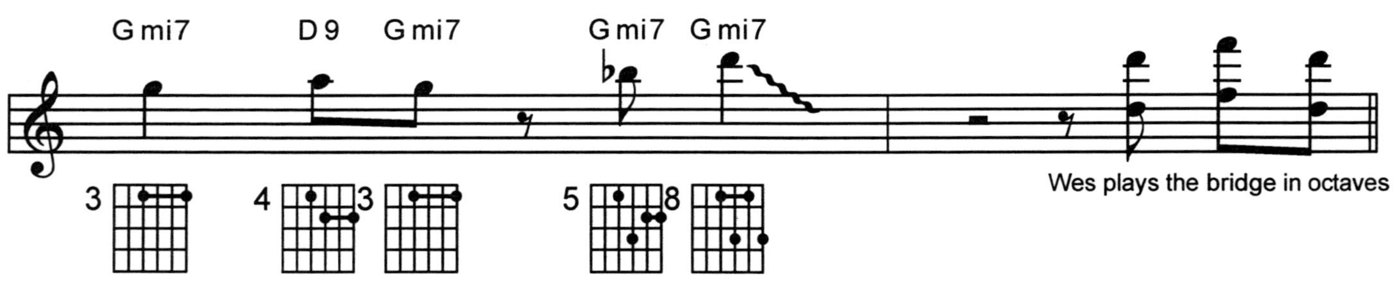
G mi7
D 9
G mi7
G mi7
G mi7
Wes plays the bridge in octaves
3
4
3
5
8

B
(C mi7)

(A m7♭5)
(D 7♯9)

(C mi7)

(A mi11)
(D 7alt)

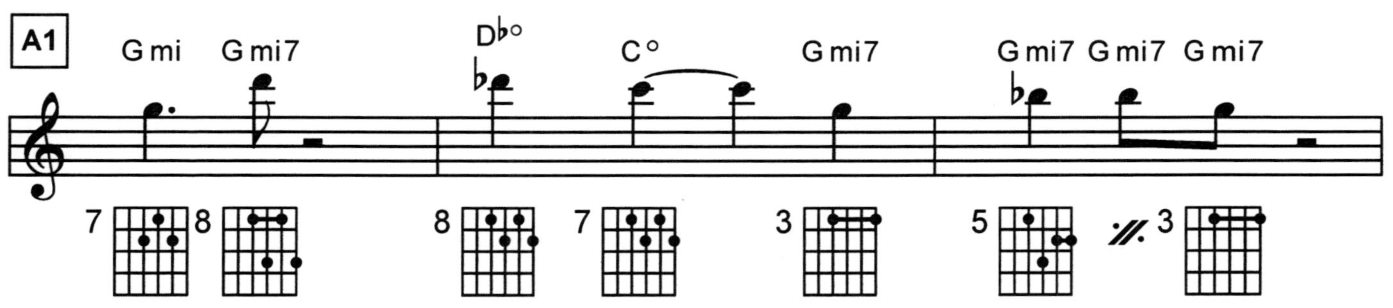
A1
G mi   G mi7
D♭°
C°
G mi7
G mi7 G mi7 G mi7
7   8
8   7
3
5   ∥. 3

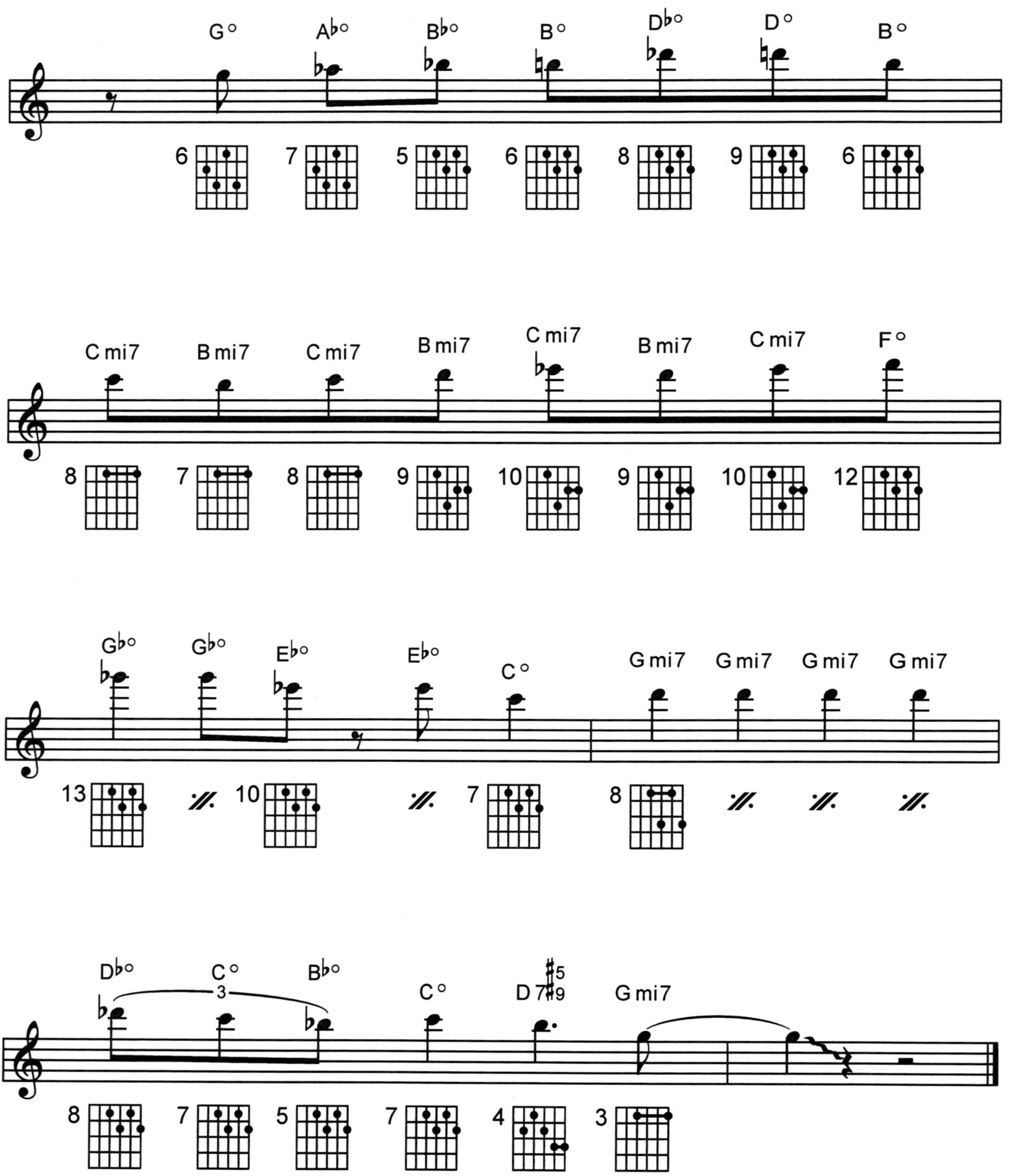
G° A♭° B♭° B° D♭° D° B°
C mi7 B mi7 C mi7 B mi7 C mi7 B mi7 C mi7 F°
G♭° G♭° E♭° E♭° C° G mi7 G mi7 G mi7 G mi7
D♭° C° B♭° C° D7♯9 G mi7

CONCLUSION

What can we conclude from what we see in the solo excerpts - and from listening to their recordings - about how the masters arrived at a chordal bebop linear approach?

- They all have pet phrases and pet chord scales/patterns *that were worked out ahead of time*, and these could be altered to fit varied situations. Such phrases had been internalized and then performed without labor. (Kenny Werner reminds us that those techniques, which are known so well that they flow and are not thought about, are the ones which can be used for greatest expressivity).
- They have a limited set of chords that they rely on over and over again, without fail.
- They have a preferred time and place for using the chordal passages (almost always later in the solo). Invariably, the chordal lines are used to create greater excitement.
- There is the same tension/release process present in chord work that would be used in single-line bebop improvisation: tonic function chords alternate with V function chords/phrases.
- Chordal lines can create greater drama in the solo (especially when riff playing and shout-chorus ideas are employed). This naturally occurs later in the solo, if one follows the traditional ideas about solo development.
- Beautiful lines of considerable depth can be created with really simple triads and 4-note chords. The degree to which an idea has a strong melodic content will determine the success or failure of that chordal line. *Ultimately, the melody is what is most important.*
- Syncopation that is used by these masters is rooted in traditional bebop and big band style.
- *Know the melody.* Knowledge of - and internalization of - the original melody is paramount. Especially in Barney's solos, the original melody is never too far away, and we can hear it being referred to and improvised on.
- These players almost always use devices to set up the next chord change. For example, when the piece is driving to the IV chord (Delilah, Missile Blues), ideas that function as V/IV are employed. For example, in every "A" section of both Delilah solos, Wes precedes movement to the iv chord (C minor) with diminished chords that function as G7b9. Thus, the movement becomes tonic (G minor) to V/iv (G7b9) to iv (C minor).
- They internalized a vocabulary from listening to records and working things out on the instrument...there were no books like this available at that time! They became fluid using this vocabulary and were able to adapt it at will.
- It takes, for most people, a long period of time to work through this chordal approach and also to then internalize it. Key to the process is commitment, patience, determination, love of the music, access to like-minded players, and a desire to express oneself on a different artistic plane. *Good Luck!*

CHORDED SOLOS

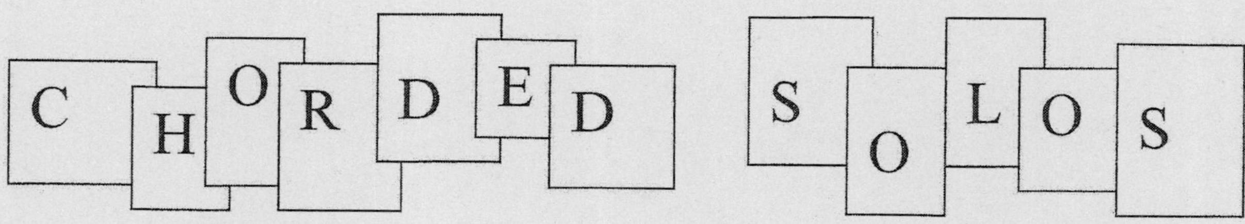

WORKBOOK

Volume 3: HOW TO PLAY CHORDAL BEBOP LINES, FOR GUITAR

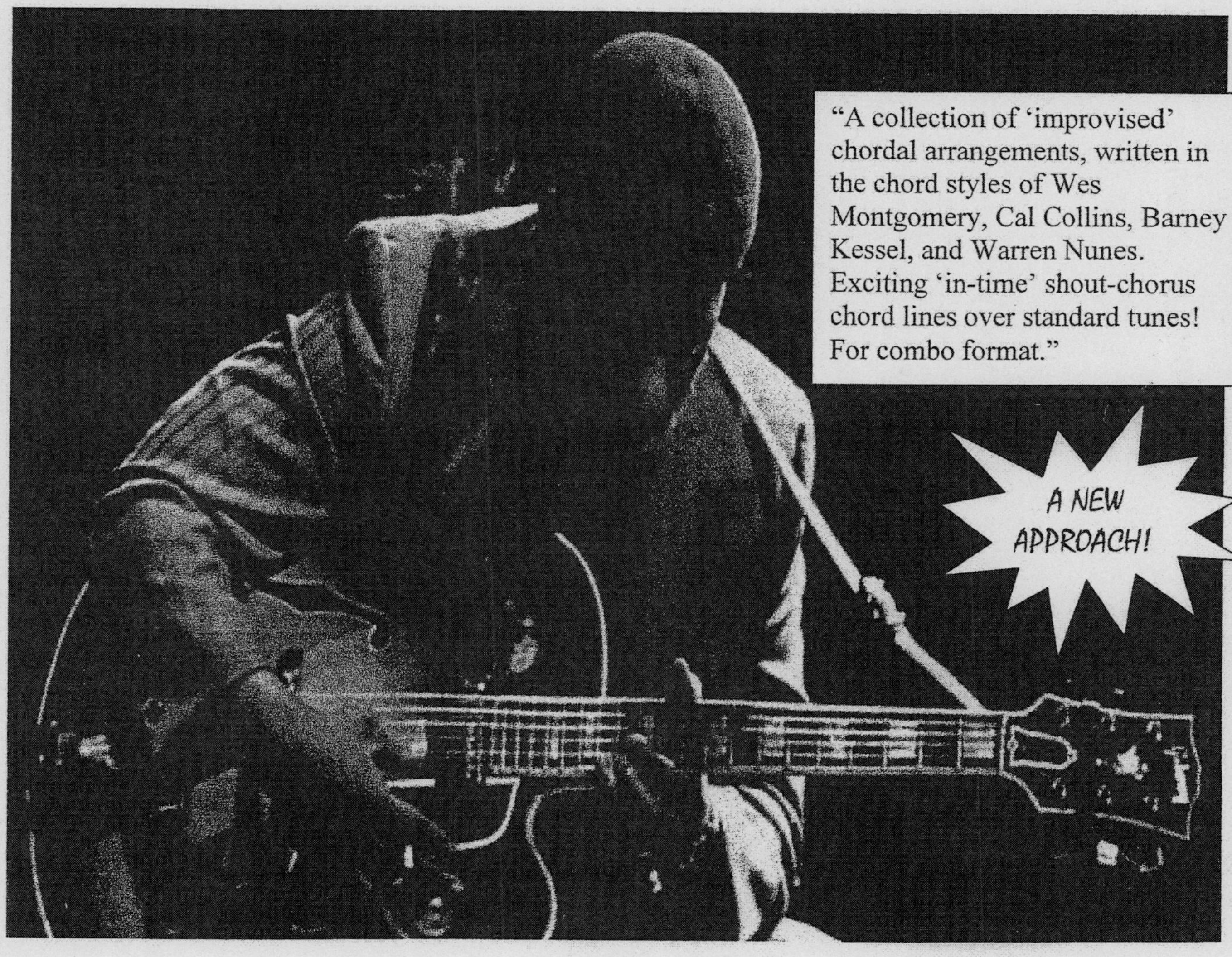

JIM BASTIAN

COASTAL PUBLISHING

NEW 2011 REVISED EDITION

How To Play

CHORDAL BEBOP LINES

For Guitar

VOLUME III

CHORDED SOLOS WORKBOOK

Jim Bastian

Layout by John Alexander

SpeakPeace Press

Educational Resources Division

All rights reserved. No part of this book may be reproduced or copied in any manner whatsoever without written permission.

Copyright 2017 by
SpeakPeace Press and Jim Bastian
Original Copyright Registration 2008; Library of Congress,
U.S. Copyright Office, Washington, D.C.

Printed in the United States of America

Table of Contents

Introduction 2

The Days of Wine and Roses

     Chord progression 4

     Solo 5

Confirmation

     Chord progression 8

     Solo 9

Dexter's Textures (G Blues)

     Chord progression 12

     Solo 13

Ceora

     Chord Progression 16

     Solo 17

Conclusion 20

Introduction

The <u>Chorded Solos Workbook</u> (Volume 3 of the Chordal Bebop Lines for Guitar series) is a collection of prearranged 'improvisations', written in chordal fashion for guitar. Meant to be played 'in time' in a combo setting, these are examples of the types of improvised 'shout choruses' that can be used within ones improvised solos. Over time, players can learn to improvise in this style, once they learn to apply the types of chorded phrases, lines, scales, patterns, and licks that are found in Volumes 1 and 2 of this series.

Rehearsed Improvisations

Johnny Smith and Barney Kessel – two founding fathers in jazz guitar technique – have both asserted their preference for working out solos and parts of solos ahead of time, and then using those in performance situations. Johnny Smith has admitted that many of his great recordings have a high number of rehearsed, prearranged solos. Likewise, if you listen to any of the numerous recordings of *Autumn Leaves* performed by Barney Kessel, you will hear quite a few phrases played almost note for note in each version. These are in a sense prearranged, rehearsed improvisations. Likewise, some of Barney's recordings of chord solos are nearly identical at each hearing. This book can serve as a point of departure for the working out of your own pre-arranged solos. Writing out solos (both single line and chorded), in the harmonic and melodic language of your choosing, is a way to move towards a unique style in jazz.

Use of Chord Lines Within a Solo

A typical Wes Montgomery improvised solo often escalates in interest from single lines, to octaves, to chords. The arrangements in this book are written in the harmonic language of that chord style. Each of the solos – all of which occupy one or more complete choruses – might be thought of as 'shout chorus' improvisations that could come in the latter part of the solo. Many of the chords chosen in these four arrangements were the favored voicings of Wes and Barney, as well as Cal Collins and Warren Nunes. The melodic style employed is also reminiscent of those artists. It should be pointed out that Wes, when he moved into the chordal style, usually stayed there for an entire chorus. This workbook is written in that approach. In contrast to that style, Cal Collins and Barney Kessel would often go back and forth between chordal phrases and single line phrases. Ultimately, it will be up to the student to decide how he/she will employ the chordal vocabulary that is put forth in the volumes 1, 2, and 3 of Chordal Bebop Lines, for Guitar.

Methodology

This collection of arrangements uses many of the chordal bebop phrases that appear in Volumes 1 and 2, and the solos are written as examples of how chordal patterns can be linked together over active chord progressions. Volumes 1 and 2 present an extensive vocabulary of chordal patterns, and when integrated, the types of solos herein become possible.

Full integration has taken place when the patterns can be melodically woven together over changing tonal centers, and in a manner that puts forth a strong melodic composition. It is an advanced technique, especially when one tries to do it "on the spot".

Connecting Tonal Centers Over the Song Form

The chord progressions from standard tunes have been chosen for this project, and a 'fake sheet' of the basic chord progression precedes each solo. It is important to compare the basic chord changes of each tune to the written solos, as a means of understanding how the chordal phrases are employed, and to see how they connect changing tonal centers. For example, consider an underlying harmony that simply reads "G7". In the written solos, a number of devices might be used to create an interesting line. The melodic guide tones found within the chord (and in the chord's extensions – 9, 11, 13) become melodic targets, so progressions often resolve to these notes. But within the G7 'phrase', other types of chords might be used (other than simply inversions of G7). These might include chromatic slips (such as A7 to Ab7 to G7, or Ebmi7 to Ab7 to G7). "Borrowed chords" might be used: D7 #9 to G7, as well as chords from close families (such as creating a ii-V out of the G7 chord: Dmi7 to G7). The latter suggests that any inversion of Dmi7 can be used over the G7 harmony. All the while, we are interested in the highest sounding note of the chords you choose, since this is what will create your melody. Although the melody is most often the highest sounding voice, occasionally it might be an inner moving voice that becomes the obvious melody (bars 21 and 22 of the *Ceora* solo illustrate an inner moving melodic voice and create a sequence over the Db and Dmi chords).

Tips for Practice

- Sing the melodic lines before beginning, using your guitar to 'check' yourself as you go. This will increase your awareness of the melody you are harmonizing.
- As in the development of any technique, the work should be practiced slowly and repetitively.
- Any chorded phrase can be isolated and practiced in different keys.
- The student can self-record a bass line and then, in play-a-long fashion, perform the solos with the bass accompaniment. This allows the underlying harmony to be fully heard against the chord lines. (This approach is better than buying the recordings of a rhythm section, since you become responsible for creating the accompaniment and will therefore more fully understand it).
- Use the fake sheet progressions to write out your own chorded solos.
- Keep a practice journal/workbook which contains melodic phrases that you have harmonized into chord lines. (Books which contain transcribed solos of name artists are great resources for finding melodic lines to harmonize – I like the Charlie Parker OmniBook for this process!)
- Practice with the goal in mind, not simply of memorizing these solos, but of advancing your own vocabulary of chordal bebop lines. Such a vocabulary can then be employed over any tune or chord progression. Volumes 1, 2, and 3 can be used simultaneously toward the reaching of that goal.

Song Form Chord Changes on
"The Days of Wine and Roses"

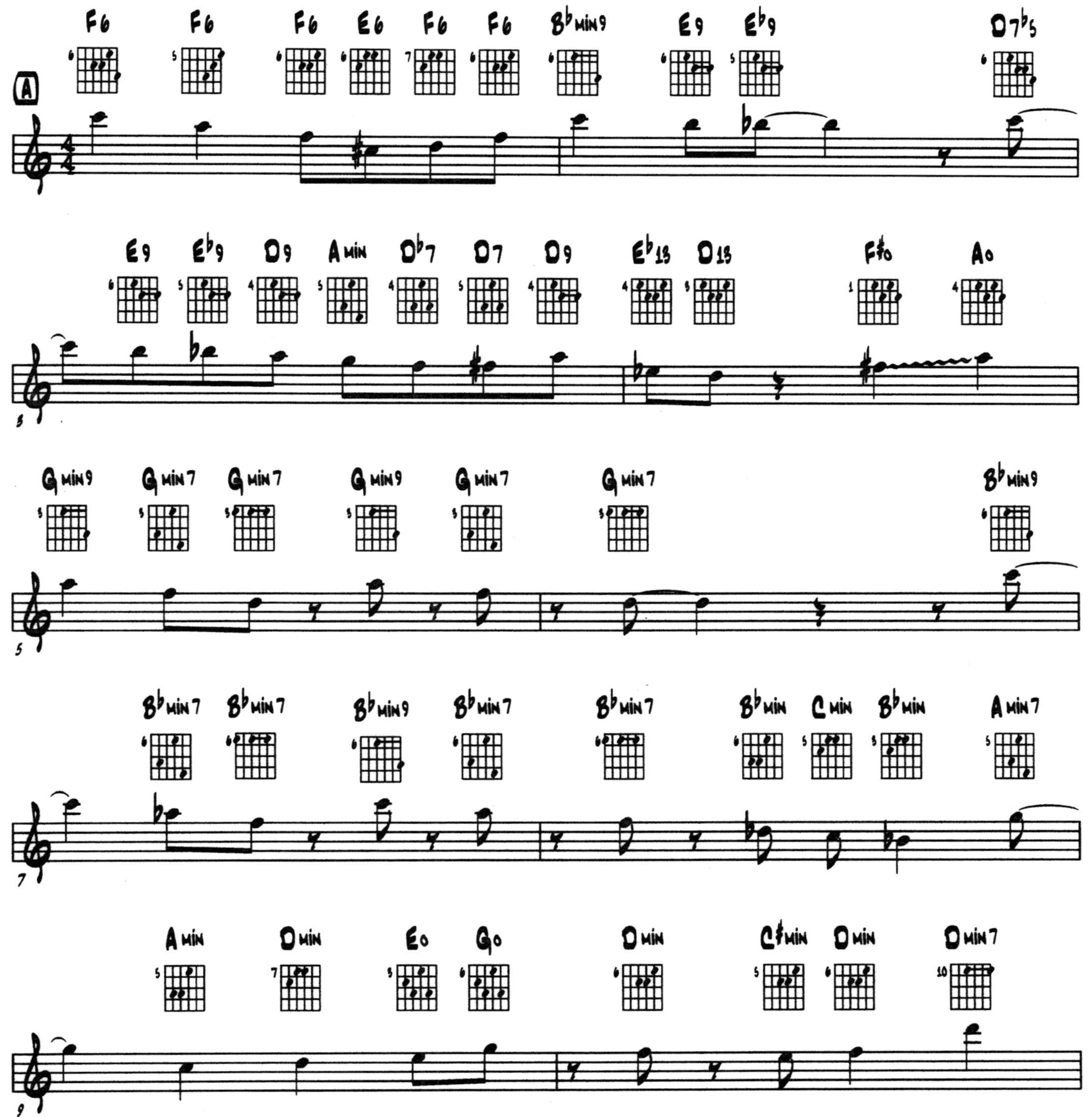
♩ = 92
Chord Solo Over The Changes On The Song
"Days of Wine and Roses"
SLOW SWING
A
F6 F6 F6 E6 F6 F6 Bbmin9 E9 Eb9 D7b5
E9 Eb9 D9 Amin Db7 D7 D9 Eb13 D13 F#o Ao
Gmin9 Gmin7 Gmin7 Gmin9 Gmin7 Gmin7 Bbmin9
Bbmin7 Bbmin7 Bbmin9 Bbmin7 Bbmin7 Bbmin Cmin Bbmin Amin7
Amin Dmin Eo Go Dmin C#min Dmin Dmin7

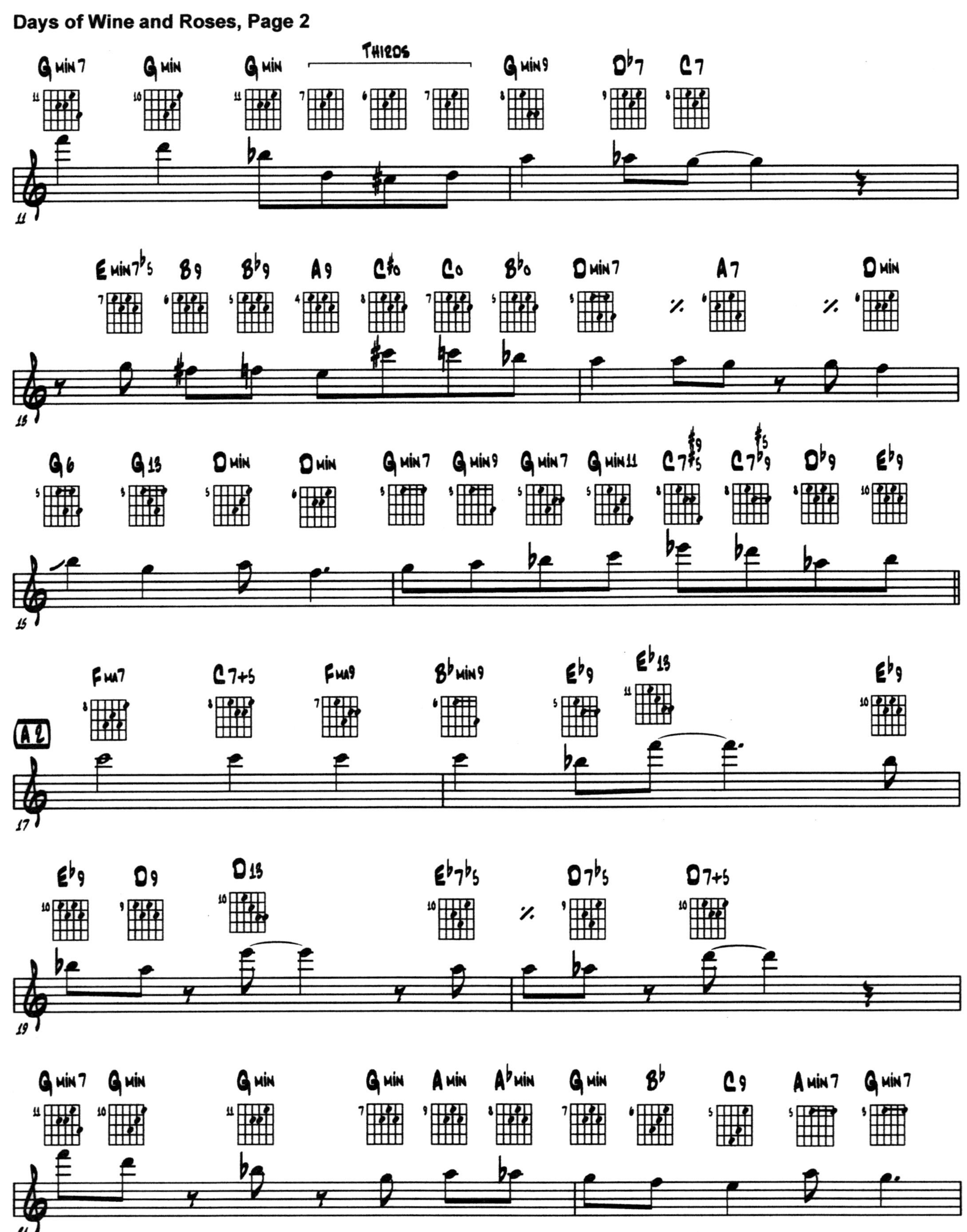

6

Bb min7
Bb min11
Bb min9
Bb min7
Bb min7
Bb min9
Bb min7
Bb min7
C min7
B min7
Bb min7
A min7
A min7
D min7
D min
D min
E min
D min
B min11 b5
B min7 b5
F9
Bo
Bb 9 13
Bb 9
Bb 9 b5
Do
A min7
A min7
E min7
D min7
THIRDS
Bb
G min9
Gb ma9
F ma9
G min9
G min7
G min7
G min7
C 7 b9
F ma7

"Confirmation"

Chord Solo Over The Changes On The Song
"Confirmation"

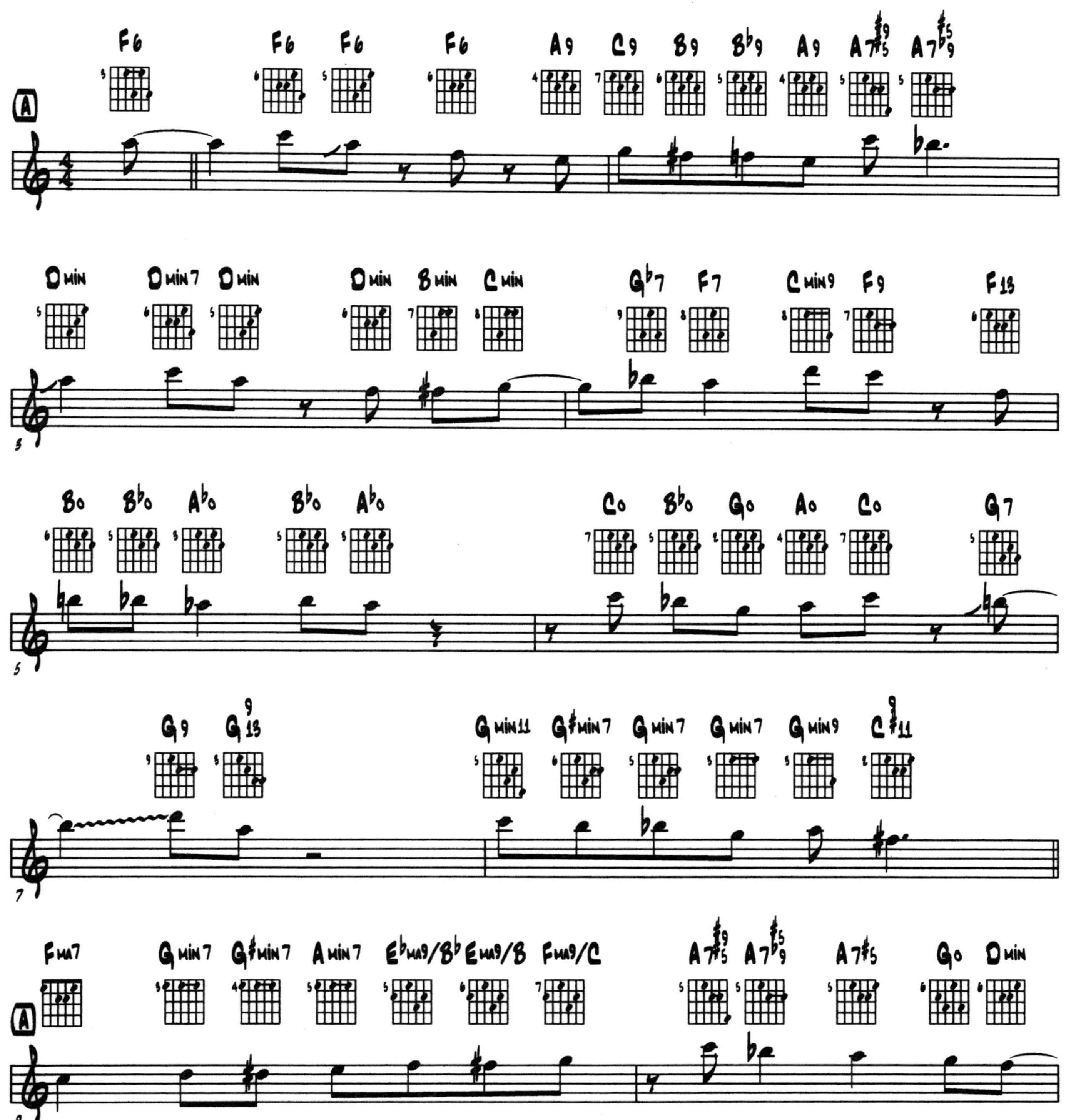

9

G13 Cmin F13 A7
Bb7 A7 Bb7 Bb9/13 Bb13 Amin G#min Amin Eb9 Eb9 D9
Gmin9 Gmin11 Gmin7 Gmin9 Bb Bo F13 Bmin9
Cmin9 Cmin7 Cmin Cmin7 Cmin9 Cmin7 Cmin7b5 BbMA9
BbMA7 Bb BbMA7 Bb BbMA7 Bb6/9 BbMA7
Dmin Ebmin Ebmin Ebmin7 Ebmin Ab7 Ab13 Ab7 Ab9 DbMA7

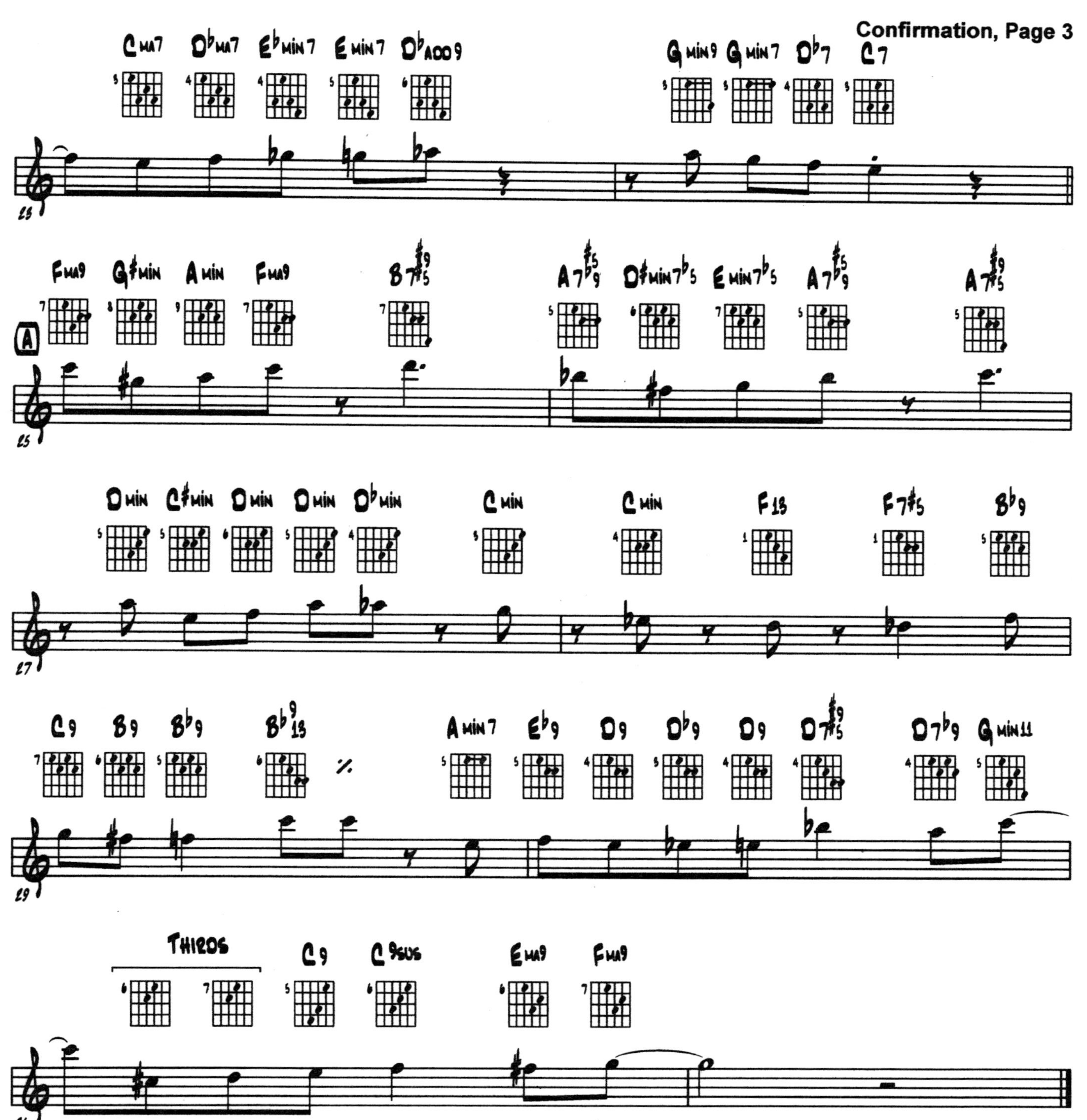
CMA7 DbMA7 EbMIN7 EMIN7 DbADD9
GMIN9 GMIN7 Db7 C7
FMA9 G#MIN AMIN FMA9 B7#9/#5 A7#5/b9 D#MIN7b5 EMIN7b5 A7#5/b9 A7#9/#5
DMIN C#MIN DMIN DMIN DbMIN CMIN CMIN F13 F7#5 Bb9
C9 B9 Bb9 Bb9/13 AMIN7 Eb9 D9 Db9 D9 D7#9/#5 D7b9 GMIN11
THIRDS C9 C9SUS EMA9 FMA9

"Dexter's Textures" (Blues in G)

Dexter's Textures (G Blues)

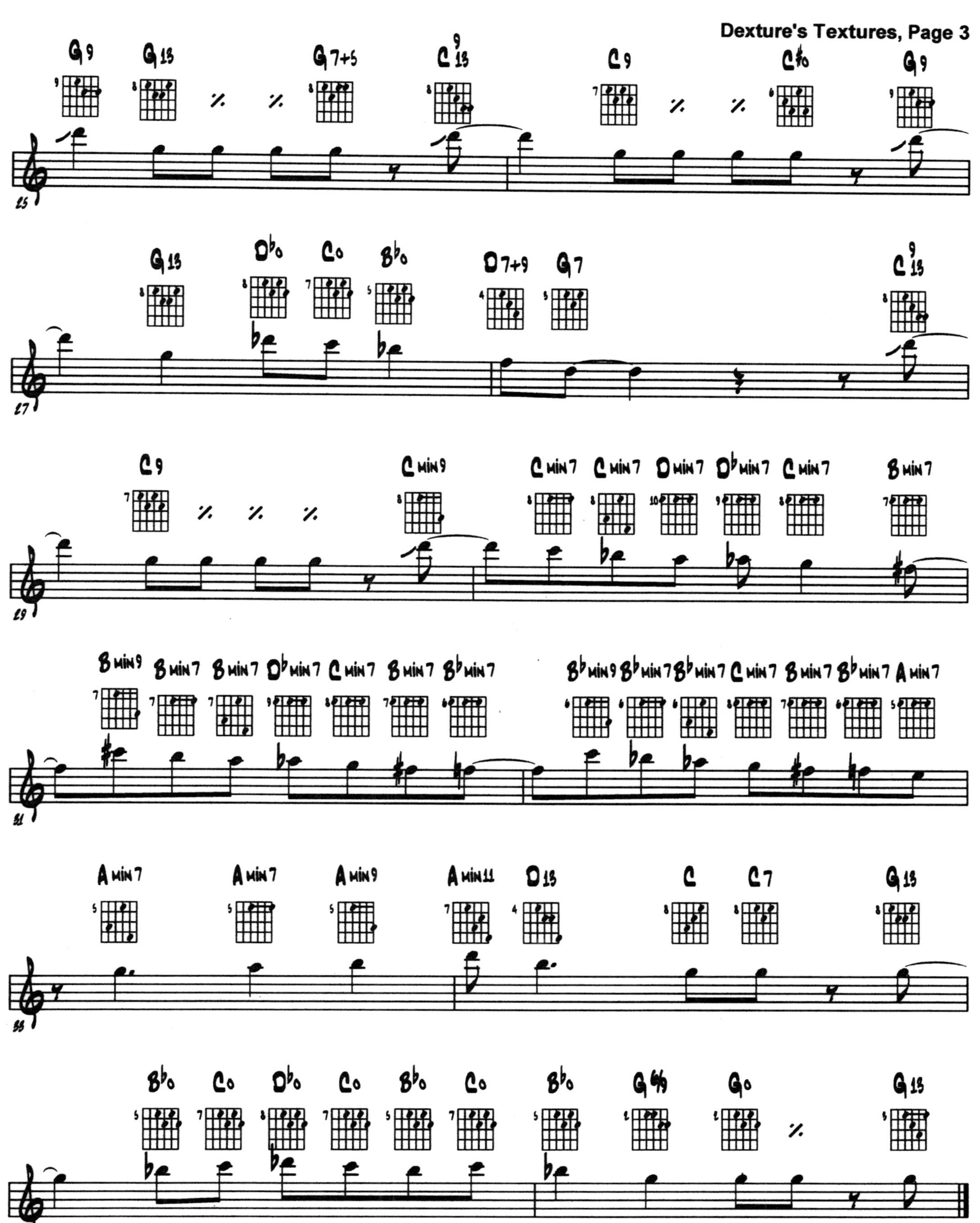

Song Form Chord Changes on
"Ceora"

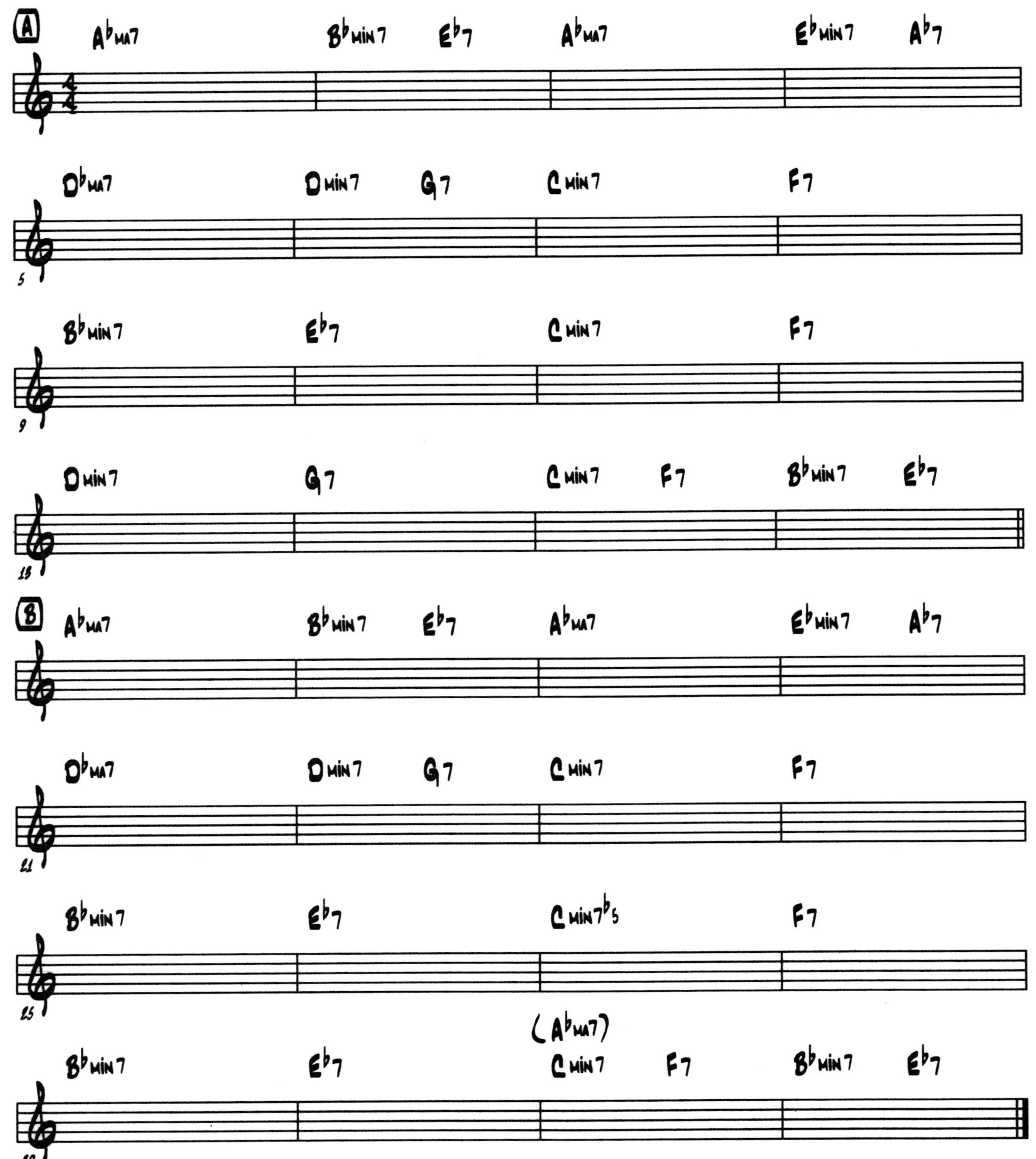

Chord Solo Over The Changes On The Song
"Ceora"
♩ = 88
BOSSA

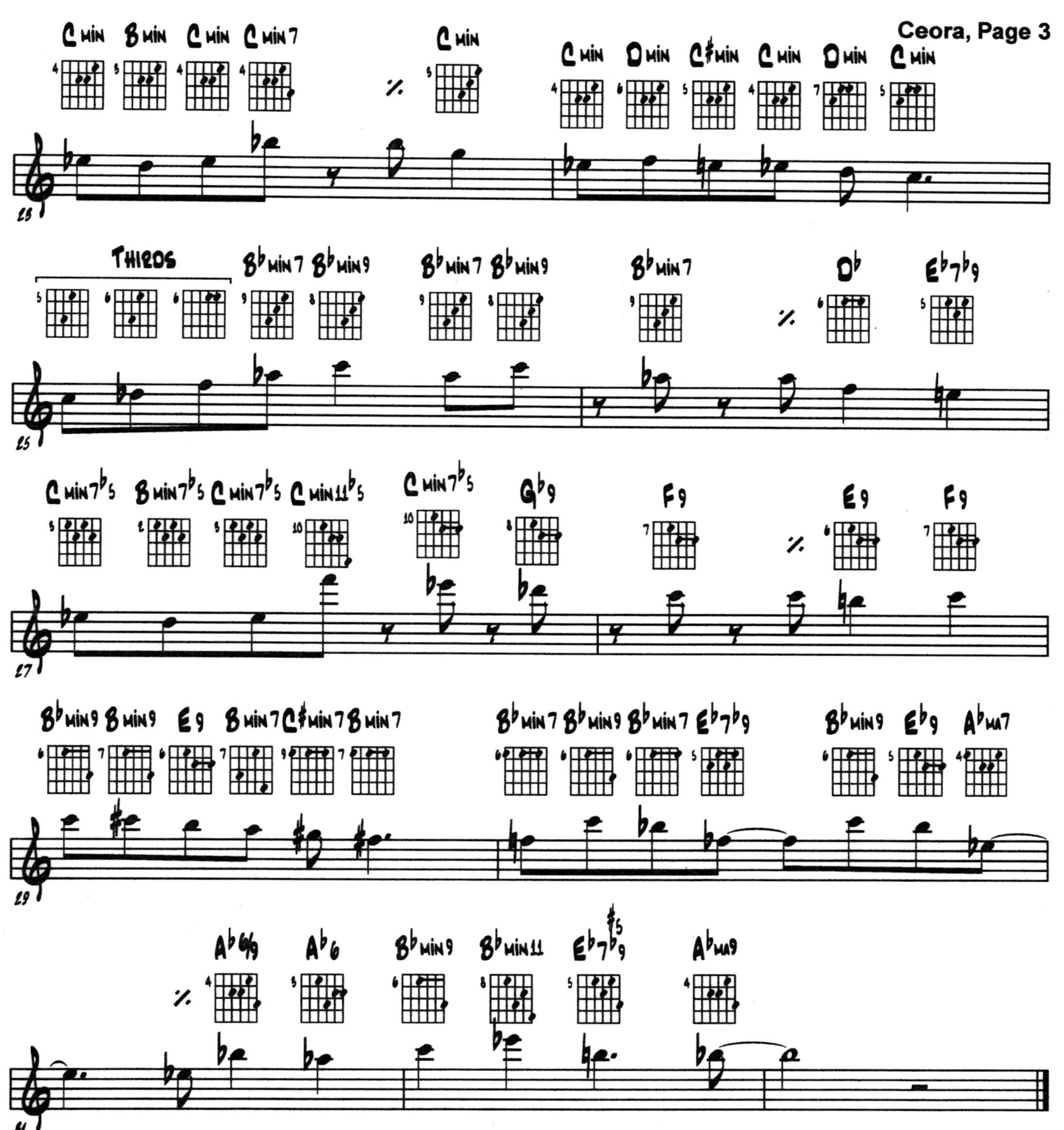
THIRDS

- The masters of this style all had their own pet phrases and pet chord scales/patterns *that were worked out ahead of time*, and these could be altered to fit varied situations. The goal is to internalize such patterns and thus perform them without labor. (Kenny Werner reminds us that those techniques, which are known so well that they flow and are not thought about, are the ones, which can be used for greatest expressivity).
- The masters each had a limited set of chords that they relied on over and over again, without fail.
- They had a preferred time and place for using the chordal passages (almost always later in the solo). Invariably, the chordal lines are used to create greater excitement.
- There is the same tension/release process present in chord work that would be used in single-line bebop melody: tonic function chords alternate with V function chords/phrases.
- Chordal lines can create greater drama in the solo (especially when riff playing and shout-chorus ideas are employed). This naturally occurs later in the solo, if one follows the traditional ideas about solo development.
- Beautiful lines of considerable depth can be created with really simple triads and 4-note chords. The degree to which an idea has a <u>strong melodic content</u> will determine the success or failure of that chordal line. *<u>Ultimately, the melody is what is most important.</u>*
- Syncopation that is used by the masters is rooted in traditional bebop and big band style.
- Knowledge of - and internalization of - the original melody is paramount. For many of the masters, the original melody is never too far away, and we can hear it being referred to and improvised on.
- The masters almost always use devices to set up, and anticipate, the next chord change. (For example, a I chord becomes V/IV, when going to a IV chord). A feeling of movement is thus created.
- The masters internalized a vocabulary from listening to records and working things out on the instrument. They became fluid using this vocabulary and were able to adapt it at will.
- It takes, for most people, a long period of time to develop a chordal vocabulary and also to then internalize it. Key to the process is commitment, patience, determination, love of the music, access to like-minded players, and a desire to express oneself on a different artistic plane. *Good Luck!*